MW01006433

Michel Foucault, acknowledged as the preeminent philosopher of France in the seventies and eighties, continues to have enormous impact throughout the world in many disciplines.

Arnold I. Davidson is the Robert O. Anderson Distinguished Service Professor at the University of Chicago and Professor of the History of Political Philosophy at the University of Pisa. He is the coeditor of the volume *Michel Foucault: Philosophie.*

Translator Graham Burchell has written essays on Michel Foucault and was an editor of *The Foucault Effect.*

*Also in this series*

SOCIETY MUST BE DEFENDED
ABNORMAL
HERMENEUTICS OF THE SUBJECT
PSYCHIATRIC POWER
SECURITY, TERRITORY, POPULATION

*Forthcoming in this series*

THE WILL TO KNOW
PENAL THEORIES AND INSTITUTIONS
THE PUNITIVE SOCIETY
ON THE GOVERNMENT OF THE LIVING
SUBJECTIVITY AND TRUTH
THE GOVERNMENT OF SELF AND OTHERS
THE COURAGE OF TRUTH

# Michel Foucault

# *The Birth of Biopolitics*

## Lectures at the Collège de France, 1978–1979

Edited by Michel Senellart
General Editors: François Ewald and Alessandro Fontana

English Series Editor: Arnold I. Davidson

*Translated by Graham Burchell*

Picador

palgrave macmillan
New York

www.picadorusa.com



For information on Picador Reading Group Guides, please contact Picador. E-mail: readinggroupguides@picadorusa.com

ISBN 978-0-312-20341-2

First published in France as *Naissance de la Biopolitique: Cours au Collège de France, 1978–1979* by Éditions du Seuil/Gallimard

First published in the United States by Palgrave Macmillan

20 19 18 17 16 15

# CONTENTS

# Foreword

MICHEL FOUCAULT TAUGHT AT the Collège de France from January 1971 until his death in June 1984 (with the exception of 1977 when he took a sabbatical year). The title of his chair was "The History of Systems of Thought."

On the proposal of Jules Vuillemin, the chair was created on 30 November 1969 by the general assembly of the professors of the Collège de France and replaced that of "The History of Philosophical Thought" held by Jean Hyppolite until his death. The same assembly elected Michel Foucault to the new chair on 12 April 1970.[1] He was 43 years old.

Michel Foucault's inaugural lecture was delivered on 2 December 1970.[2] Teaching at the Collège de France is governed by particular rules. Professors must provide 26 hours of teaching a year (with the possibility of a maximum of half this total being given in the form of seminars[3]). Each year they must present their original research and this obliges them to change the content of their teaching for each course. Courses and seminars are completely open; no enrolment or qualification is required and the professors do not award any qualifications.[4] In the terminology of the Collège de France, the professors do not have students but only auditors.

Michel Foucault's courses were held every Wednesday from January to March. The huge audience made up of students, teachers, researchers and the curious, including many who came from outside France, required two amphitheaters of the Collège de France. Foucault often complained about the distance between himself and his "public" and of how few exchanges the course made possible.[5] He would have liked a seminar in which real collective work could take place and made a number of attempts to bring this about. In the final years he devoted a long period to answering his auditors' questions at the end of each course.

This is how Gérard Petitjean, a journalist from *Le Nouvel Observateur*, described the atmosphere at Foucault's lectures in 1975:

> When Foucault enters the amphitheater, brisk and dynamic like someone who plunges into the water, he steps over bodies to reach his chair, pushes away the cassette recorders so he can put down his papers, removes his jacket, lights a lamp and sets off at full speed. His voice is strong and effective, amplified by loudspeakers that are the only concession to modernism in a hall that is barely lit by light spread from stucco bowls. The hall has three hundred places and there are five hundred people packed together, filling the smallest free space ... There is no oratorical effect. It is clear and terribly effective. There is absolutely no concession to improvisation. Foucault has twelve hours each year to explain in a public course the direction taken by his research in the year just ended. So everything is concentrated and he fills the margins like correspondents who have too much to say for the space available to them. At 19.15 Foucault stops. The students rush towards his desk; not to speak to him, but to stop their cassette recorders. There are no questions. In the pushing and shoving Foucault is alone. Foucault remarks: "It should be possible to discuss what I have put forward. Sometimes, when it has not been a good lecture, it would need very little, just one question, to put everything straight. However, this question never comes. The group effect in France makes any genuine discussion impossible. And as there is no feedback, the course is theatricalized. My relationship with the people there is like that of an actor or an acrobat. And when I have finished speaking, a sensation of total solitude ... "[6]

Foucault approached his teaching as a researcher: explorations for a future book as well as the opening up of fields of problematization were formulated as an invitation to possible future researchers. This is why the courses at the Collège de France do not duplicate the published books. They are not sketches for the books even though both books and courses share certain themes. They have their own status. They arise from a specific discursive regime within the set of Foucault's "philosophical activities." In particular they set out the programme for a genealogy of knowledge/power relations, which are the terms in which he thinks of his work from the beginning of the 1970s, as opposed to the program of an archeology of discursive formations that previously orientated his work.[7]

The courses also performed a role in contemporary reality. Those who followed his courses were not only held in thrall by the narrative that unfolded week by week and seduced by the rigorous exposition, they also found a perspective on contemporary reality. Michel Foucault's art consisted in using history to cut diagonally through contemporary reality. He could speak of Nietzsche or Aristotle, of expert psychiatric opinion or the Christian pastoral, but those who attended his lectures always took from what he said a perspective on the present and contemporary events. Foucault's specific strength in his courses was the subtle interplay between learned erudition, personal commitment, and work on the event.

With their development and refinement in the 1970s, Foucault's desk was quickly invaded by cassette recorders. The courses—and some seminars—have thus been preserved.

This edition is based on the words delivered in public by Foucault. It gives a transcription of these words that is as literal as possible.[8] We would have liked to present it as such. However, the transition from an oral to a written presentation calls for editorial intervention: at the very least it requires the introduction of punctuation and division into paragraphs. Our principle has been always to remain as close as possible to the course actually delivered.

Summaries and repetitions have been removed whenever it seemed to be absolutely necessary. Interrupted sentences have been restored and faulty constructions corrected. Suspension points indicate that the recording is inaudible. When a sentence is obscure there is a conjectural integration or an addition between square brackets. An asterisk directing the reader to the bottom of the page indicates a significant divergence between the notes used by Foucault and the words actually uttered. Quotations have been checked and references to the texts used are indicated. The critical apparatus is limited to the elucidation of obscure points, the explanation of some allusions and the clarification of critical points. To make the lectures easier to read, each lecture is preceded by a brief summary that indicates its principal articulations.

The text of the course is followed by the summary published by the *Annuaire du Collège de France*. Foucault usually wrote these in June, some time after the end of the course. It was an opportunity for him to pick out retrospectively the intention and objectives of the course. It constitutes the best introduction to the course.

Each volume ends with a "context" for which the course editors are responsible. It seeks to provide the reader with elements of the biographical, ideological, and political context, situating the course within the published work and providing indications concerning its place within the corpus used in order to facilitate understanding and to avoid misinterpretations that might arise from a neglect of the circumstances in which each course was developed and delivered.

*The Birth of Biopolitics*, the course delivered in 1979, is edited by Michel Senellart.

A new aspect of Michel Foucault's "œuvre" is published with this edition of the Collège de France courses.

Strictly speaking it is not a matter of unpublished work, since this edition reproduces words uttered publicly by Foucault, excluding the often highly developed written material he used to support his lectures. Daniel Defert possesses Michel Foucault's notes and he is to be warmly thanked for allowing the editors to consult them.

This edition of the Collège de France courses was authorized by Michel Foucault's heirs who wanted to be able to satisfy the strong demand for their publication, in France as elsewhere, and to do this under indisputably responsible conditions. The editors have tried to be equal to the degree of confidence placed in them.

FRANÇOIS EWALD AND ALESSANDRO FONTANA

1. Michel Foucault concluded a short document drawn up in support of his candidacy with these words: "We should undertake the history of systems of thought." "Titres et travaux," in *Dits et Écrits, 1954-1988*, four volumes, eds. Daniel Defert and François Ewald (Paris: Gallimard, 1994) vol. 1, p. 846; English translation by Robert Hurley, "Candidacy Presentation: Collège de France" in *The Essential Works of Michel Foucault, 1954-1984, vol. 1: Ethics: Subjectivity and Truth*, ed. Paul Rabinow (New York: The New Press, 1997) p. 9.
2. It was published by Gallimard in May 1971 with the title *L'Ordre du discours*, Paris, 1971. English translation by Rupert Swyer, "The Order of Discourse," appendix to M. Foucault, *The Archeology of Knowledge* (New York: Pantheon, 1972).
3. This was Foucault's practice until the start of the 1980s.
4. Within the framework of the Collège de France.
5. In 1976, in the vain hope of reducing the size of the audience, Michel Foucault changed the time of his course from 17.45 to 9.00. See the beginning of the first lecture (7 January 1976) of *"Il faut défendre la société". Cours au Collège de France, 1976* (Paris: Gallimard/Seuil, 1997); English translation by David Macey, *"Society Must be Defended." Lectures at the Collège de France 1975-1976* (New York: Picador, 2003).
6. Gérard Petitjean, "Les Grands Prêtres de l'université française," *Le Nouvel Observateur*, 7 April 1975.
7. See especially, "Nietzsche, la généalogie, l'histoire," in *Dits et Écrits*, vol. 2, p. 137. English translation by Donald F. Brouchard and Sherry Simon, "Nietzsche, Genealogy, History" in *The Essential Works of Michel Foucault 1954-1984, vol. 2: Aesthetics, Method, and Epistemology*, ed. James Faubion (New York: The New Press, 1998) pp. 369-392.
8. We have made use of the recordings made by Gilbert Burlet and Jacques Lagrange in particular. These are deposited in the Collège de France and the Institut Mémoires de l'Édition Contemporaine.

# one

## 10 January 1979

*Questions of method. ~ Suppose universals do not exist. ~ Summary of the previous year's lectures: the limited objective of the government of* raison d'État *(external politics) and unlimited objective of the police state (internal politics). ~ Law as principle of the external limitation of* raison d'État. *~ Perspective of this year's lectures: political economy as principle of the internal limitation of governmental reason. ~ What is at stake in this research: the coupling of a set of practices and a regime of truth and the effects of its inscription in reality. ~ What is liberalism?*

[YOU KNOW] FREUD'S QUOTATION: "*Acheronta movebo.*"[1] Well, I would like to take the theme for this year's lectures from another, less well-known quotation from someone who, generally speaking at least, is also less well-known, the English Statesman Walpole,[2] who, with reference to his way of governing, said: "*Quieta non movere,*"[3] "Let sleeping dogs lie."* In a sense, this is the opposite of Freud. In fact, this year I would like to continue with what I began to talk about last year, that is to say, to retrace the history of what could be called the art of government. You recall the strict sense in which I understood "art of government," since in using the word "to govern" I left out the thousand and one different modalities and possible ways that exist for guiding men,

* Foucault gives the French translation of the Latin phrase as: "À ce qui reste tranquille il ne faut pas toucher" (or "Do not disturb what is at rest or settled")

directing their conduct, constraining their actions and reactions, and so on. Thus I left to one side all that is usually understood, and that for a long time was understood, as the government of children, of families, of a household, of souls, of communities, and so forth. I only considered, and again this year will only consider the government of men insofar as it appears as the exercise of political sovereignty.

So, "government" in the strict sense, but also "art," "art of government" in the strict sense, since by "art of government" I did not mean the way in which governors really governed. I have not studied and do not want to study the development of real governmental practice by determining the particular situations it deals with, the problems raised, the tactics chosen, the instruments employed, forged, or remodeled, and so forth. I wanted to study the art of governing, that is to say, the reasoned way of governing best and, at the same time, reflection on the best possible way of governing. That is to say, I have tried to grasp the level of reflection in the practice of government and on the practice of government. In a sense, I wanted to study government's consciousness of itself, if you like, although I don't like the term "self-awareness (*conscience de soi*)" and will not use it, because I would rather say that I have tried, and would like to try again this year to grasp the way in which this practice that consists in governing was conceptualized both within and outside government, and anyway as close as possible to governmental practice. I would like to try to determine the way in which the domain of the practice of government, with its different objects, general rules, and overall objectives, was established so as to govern in the best possible way. In short, we could call this the study of the rationalization of governmental practice in the exercise of political sovereignty.

This immediately entails a choice of method that one day I will finally try to come back to at greater length, but I would like to point out straightaway that choosing to talk about or to start from governmental practice is obviously and explicitly a way of not taking as a primary, original, and already given object, notions such as the sovereign, sovereignty, the people, subjects, the state, and civil society, that is to say, all those universals employed by sociological analysis, historical analysis, and political philosophy in order to account for real governmental practice. For my part, I would like to do exactly the opposite and, starting from this practice as it is given, but at the same time as it reflects on itself and is rationalized, show how certain things—state and society, sovereign and subjects, etcetera—were actually able to be formed, and the status of which should obviously be questioned. In other words, instead of deducing concrete phenomena from universals, or instead of starting with universals as an obligatory grid of intelligibility for certain concrete practices, I would like to start with these concrete practices and, as it were, pass these universals through the grid of these practices. This is not what could be called a historicist reduction, for that would consist precisely in starting from these universals as given and then seeing how history inflects them, or alters them, or finally invalidates them. Historicism starts from the universal and, as it were, puts it through the grinder of history. My problem is exactly the opposite. I start from the theoretical and methodological decision that consists in saying: Let's suppose that universals do not exist. And then I put the question to history and historians: How can you write history if you do not accept a priori the existence of things like the state, society, the sovereign, and subjects? It was the same question in the case of madness. My question was not: Does madness exist? My reasoning, my method, was not to examine whether history gives me or refers me to something like madness, and then to conclude, no, it does not, therefore madness does not exist. This was not the argument, the method in fact. The method consisted in saying: Let's suppose that madness does not exist. If we suppose that it does not exist, then what can history make of these different events and practices which are apparently organized around something that is supposed to be madness?[4] So what I would like to deploy here is exactly the opposite of historicism: not, then, questioning universals by using history as a critical method, but starting from the decision that universals do not exist, asking what kind of history we can do. I will come back to this at greater length later.[5]

You recall that last year I tried to study one of those important episodes in the history of government. Roughly, this episode was that of the organization of what was called at the time *raison d'État*, in an infinitely stronger, stricter, more rigorous, and also fuller sense than was later given to this notion.[6] I tried to locate the emergence of a particular type of rationality in governmental practice, a type of rationality that would enable the way of governing to be modeled on something called the state which, in relation to this governmental practice, to this calculation of governmental practice, plays the role both of a given—since one only governs a state that is already there, one only governs within the framework of a state—but also, at the same time, as an objective to be constructed. The state is at once that which exists, but which does not yet exist enough. *Raison d'État* is precisely a practice, or rather the rationalization of a practice, which places itself between a state presented as given and a state presented as having to be constructed and built. The art of government must therefore fix its rules and rationalize its way of doing things by taking as its objective the bringing into being of what the state should be. What government has to do must be identified with what the state should be. Governmental *ratio* is what will enable a given state to arrive at its maximum being in a considered, reasoned, and calculated way. What is it to govern? To govern according to the principle of *raison d'État* is to arrange things so that the state becomes sturdy and permanent, so that it becomes wealthy, and so that it becomes strong in the face of everything that may destroy it.

A few words on what I tried to say last year, by way of a summary of last year's lectures. I would like to emphasize two or three points. First, you recall that the characteristic feature of this new governmental rationality of *raison d'État*, which was broadly formed during the sixteenth century, was that it defined the state and separated it out as both a specific and an autonomous, or relatively autonomous, reality. That is to say, government of the state must obviously respect a number of principles and rules which are above or dominate the state and are external to it. The government of the state must respect divine, moral, and natural laws as laws which are not homogeneous with or intrinsic to the state. But while respecting these laws, government has to do something other than ensure the salvation of its subjects in the hereafter, whereas in the Middle Ages the sovereign was commonly defined as someone who must help his subjects gain their salvation in the next world. Henceforth, government of the state no longer has to concern itself with the salvation of its subjects in the hereafter, at least not directly. It no longer has to extend its paternal benevolence over its subjects or establish father-child relationships with them, whereas in the Middle Ages the sovereign's paternal role was always very emphatic and marked. In other words, the state is not a household, a church, or an empire. The state is a specific and discontinuous reality. The state exists only for itself and in relation to itself, whatever obedience it may owe to other systems like nature or God. The state only exists through and for itself, and it only exists in the plural. That is to say, there is nothing like an imperial structure which it has to merge with or submit to at a more or less distant point on the historical horizon and which would in some way represent God's theophany in the world, leading men to a finally united humanity on the threshold of the end of the world. So there is no integration of the state in the Empire. The state only exists as states, in the plural.

Specificity and plurality of the state. I tried to show you how this specific plurality of the state was embodied in a number of precise ways of governing with their correlative institutions. First, on the economic side, was mercantilism, that is to say, a form of government. Mercantilism is not an economic doctrine; it is something much more than and very different from an economic doctrine. It is a particular organization of production and commercial circuits according to the principle that: first, the state must enrich itself through monetary accumulation; second, it must strengthen itself by increasing population; and third, it must exist and maintain itself in a state of permanent competition with foreign powers. The second way for government according to *raison d'État* to organize and embody itself in a practice is internal management, that is to say, what at the time was called police, or the unlimited regulation of the country according to the model of a tight-knit urban organization. Finally, third, is the development of a permanent army along with a permanent diplomacy: the organization, if you like, of a permanent military-diplomatic apparatus with the objective of keeping the plurality of states free from imperial absorption in such a way that an equilibrium can be established between them without the production of imperial types of unification across Europe.

So, we have mercantilism with the police state and European balance: all of this was the concrete body of this new art of government organized in terms of the principle of *raison d'État*. These are three interdependent ways of governing in accordance with a rationality whose principle and domain of application is the state. I tried to show you through this that the state is far from being a kind of natural-historical given which develops through its own dynamism like a "cold monster"[7] whose seed having been sown at a given moment has gradually eaten away at history. The state is not a cold monster; it is the correlative of a particular way of governing. The problem is how this way of governing develops, what its history is, how it expands, how it contracts, how it is extended to a particular domain, and how it invents, forms, and develops new practices. This is the problem, and not making [the state]* a puppet show policeman overpowering the different figures of history.

Several comments on this subject. First of all, I think there is a distinctive feature of this art of government organized in terms of *raison d'État* which is important for understanding what comes after. This is that in its foreign policy, let's say in its relations with other states, the state, or rather government according to *raison d'État*, has a limited objective in comparison with the ultimate horizon, the project and desire of most sovereigns and governments in the Middle Ages to occupy the imperial position with regard to other states so that one will have a decisive role both in history and in the theophany. *Raison d'État*, on the other hand, accepts that every state has its interests and consequently has to defend these interests, and to defend them absolutely, but the state's objective must not be that of returning to the unifying position of a total and global empire at the end of time. It must not dream that one day it will be the empire of the last day. Each state must limit its objectives, ensure its independence, and ensure that its forces are such that it will never be in an inferior position with respect to the set of other countries, or to its neighbors, or to the strongest of all the other countries (there are different theories of European balance at this time, but that's not important here). In any case, this external self-limitation is the distinctive feature of *raison d'État* as it manifests itself in the formation of the military-diplomatic apparatuses of the seventeenth century. From the Treaty of Westphalia to the Seven Years War, or to the revolutionary wars that introduce a completely different dimension, military-diplomatic policy is organized by reference to the principle of the state's self-limitation, to the principle of the necessary and sufficient competition between different states.

---

* An evident slip. Foucault says: history

On the other hand, what is entailed by what we will now call internal policy, by the police state? Well, it entails precisely an objective or set of objectives that could be described as unlimited, since for those who govern in the police state it is not only a matter of taking into account and taking charge of the activity of groups and orders, that is to say, of different types of individuals with their particular status, but also of taking charge of activity at the most detailed, individual level. All the great seventeenth and eighteenth century treatises of police that collate and try to systematize the different regulations are in agreement on this and say explicitly: The object of police is almost infinite. That is to say, when it is a question of an independent power facing other powers, government according to *raison d'État* has limited objectives. But there is no limit to the objectives of government when it is a question of managing a public power that has to regulate the behavior of subjects. Competition between states is precisely the hinge connecting these limited and unlimited objectives, because it is precisely so as to be able to enter into competition with other states, that is to say, maintain an always uneven, competitive equilibrium with other states, that government [has to regulate the life of] its subjects, to regulate their economic activity, their production, the price [at which] they sell goods and the price at which they buy them, and so on [ ... ]. The correlative of this limitation of the international objective of government according to *raison d'État*, of this limitation in international relations, is the absence of a limit in the exercise of government in the police state.

The second remark I would like to make about the functioning of *raison d'État* in the seventeenth century and at the start of the eighteenth century is that while there is no limit to the internal objectives of government according to *raison d'État*, or of the police state, this does not mean that there are no compensating mechanisms, or rather a number of positions that form the basis for trying to establish a boundary or frontier to the unlimited objective prescribed to the police state by *raison d'État*. There were, of course, a number of ways in which theology was called upon to fix limits to *raison d'État*, but what I would like to emphasize is another principle of limitation at this time, and this is law.

In actual fact, something curious took place. What fundamentally was the basis for the growth of royal power in the Middle Ages? It was, of course, the army. The growth of royal power was also based on judicial institutions. It was as the keystone of a state of justice, of a system of justice, doubled by a military system, that the king gradually reduced the complex interplay of feudal powers. Throughout the Middle Ages, judicial practice was a multiplier of royal power. Now when this new governmental rationality develops in the sixteenth century, and especially from the start of the seventeenth century, law provides the basis for anyone who wants to limit in one way or another this indefinite extension of *raison d'État* that is becoming embodied in a police state. Legal theory and judicial institutions no longer serve as the multiplier, but rather as the subtractor of royal power. Thus, from the sixteenth century and throughout the seventeenth century we see the development of a series of problems, polemics, and battles around, for example, fundamental laws of the realm that jurists argue, against *raison d'État*, cannot be called into question by governmental practice or *raison d'État*. These fundamental laws exist, as it were, before the state, since they are constitutive of the state, and so, some jurists say, the king, however absolute his power, must not tamper with them. The law constituted by these fundamental laws thus appeared to be outside *raison d'État* and a principle of its limitation.

There is also the theory of natural law and the assertion of imprescriptible natural rights that a sovereign may not transgress under any circumstances. Then there is the theory of the contract that individuals enter into in order to constitute a sovereign and which contains clauses to which he must abide, since it is precisely on completion of this contract, and of the clauses formulated in it, that the sovereign becomes sovereign. In England, more than in France, there is the theory of an agreement established between sovereign and subjects in order to constitute a state and on completion of which the sovereign is committed to doing some things and not others. There is also a whole part of this historical-juridical reflection, which I spoke about two or three years ago, I no longer remember when exactly,[8] in which there was the historical claim that for a long time royal power was far from having been an absolute government, that the reason that reigned and was established between the sovereign and his subjects was not at all *raison d'État*, but was rather a sort of transaction between, for example, the nobility and the military leader whom they had charged with the functions of military chief during, and maybe for a short while after, a period of war. The king would be the outcome of this kind of situation of original law, later abusing this situation in order to overturn these historically original laws that must now be rediscovered.

Anyway, these discussions of law, their liveliness, and what's more the development of all the problems and theories of what could be called public law, the reappearance of the themes of natural law, original law, the contract, and so forth, which were formulated in the Middle Ages in a completely different context, are all in a way the other side and consequence, and the reaction against, this new way of governing on the basis of *raison d'État*. In fact, law and the judicial institutions intrinsic to the development of royal power now become, as it were, external and excessive in relation to government exercised according to *raison d'État*. It is not surprising that all these problems of law are always formulated, in the first place at least, by those opposed to the new system of *raison d'État*. In France, for example, it is members of the *parlements*, protestants, and the nobility who take up the historical-juridical aspect. In England it is the bourgeoisie against the absolute monarchy of the Stuarts, and religious dissidents from the start of the seventeenth century. In short, the opposition always makes a legal objection to *raison d'État* and consequently uses juridical reflection, legal rules, and legal authority against it. In a word, let's say that in the seventeenth and eighteenth centuries public law is oppositional,* although it is true that some theorists favorable towards royal power took up the problem and tried to integrate questions of law, legal questioning, within *raison d'État* and its justification. Anyway, I think we should keep it in mind that even if it is true that *raison d'État* formulated and manifested as the police state, embodied in the police state, has unlimited objectives, it is also the case that in the sixteenth and seventeenth centuries there are constant attempts to limit *raison d'État*, and the principle or reason of this limitation is found in juridical reason. But you can see that it is an external limitation. Moreover, the jurists are fully aware that their question of law is extrinsic to *raison d'État* insofar as this is precisely that which exceeds the legal domain.

---

* The manuscript clarifies, p. 10: "(except in the German states, which had to be legally founded against the Empire)."

External legal limits to the state, to *raison d'État*, means first of all that the limits one tries to impose on *raison d'État* are those that come from God, or those which were laid down once and for all at the origin, or those which were formulated in the distant past of history. Saying that they are extrinsic to *raison d'État* also means that they function in a purely restrictive, dramatic way, since basically the law will only object to *raison d'État* when the latter crosses these legal limits, at which point the law will be able to define the government as illegitimate, to argue against its encroachments, and if necessary to release subjects from their duty of obedience.

Broadly speaking, this is how I tried to describe this way of governing called *raison d'État*. I would now like to place myself around the middle of the eighteenth century—with the qualification that I will talk about in a moment—when Walpole said: "*quieta non movere*" ("let sleeping dogs lie"). I think it is around this time that we are forced to note an important transformation that in a general way will be a characteristic feature of what could be called modern governmental reason. In what does this transformation consist? Well, in a word, it consists in establishing a principle of limitation that will no longer be extrinsic to the art of government, as was law in the seventeenth century, [but] intrinsic to it: an internal regulation of governmental rationality. What is this internal regulation in abstract and general terms? How can it be understood before any precise and concrete historical form? What can an internal limitation of governmental rationality be?

In the first place, it will be a de facto regulation, a de facto limitation. That is to say, it will not be a legal limitation, although at some point the law will have to transcribe it in the form of rules which must not be infringed. At any rate, to say that it is a de facto limitation means that if the government happens to push aside this limitation and go beyond the bounds laid down for it, it will not thereby be illegitimate, it will not have abandoned its own essence as it were, and it will not be deprived of its basic rights. To say that there is a de facto limitation of governmental practice means that a government that ignores this limitation will not be an illegitimate, usurping government, but simply a clumsy, inadequate government that does not do the proper thing.

Second, intrinsic limitation of the art of government means that, while being a de facto limitation, it is nonetheless general. That is to say, it is not simply a question of sorts of recommendations of prudence which point out that in a particular circumstance it would be better not to do something, that in this or that circumstance it would be better to refrain from intervention. No. Internal regulation means that there really is a limitation that is general while being de facto, that is to say, that, whatever happens, follows a relatively uniform line in terms of principles valid at all times and in all circumstances. The problem is precisely one of defining this general and de facto limit that government will have to impose on itself.

Third, internal limitation means that in looking for the principle of this limitation, because we need to know what this generality depends on, we will not seek it in the natural rights prescribed by God to all men, for example, or in revealed Scripture, or even in the wills of subjects who at a given moment agree to enter into society. No, the principle of this limitation is not to be sought in what is external to government, but in what is internal to governmental practice, that is to say, in the objectives of government. And this limitation will then appear as one of the means, and maybe the fundamental means, of attaining precisely these objectives. To attain these objectives it may be necessary to limit governmental action. Governmental reason does not have to respect these limits because they are limits laid down once and for all somewhere outside, before, or around the state. Not at all. Governmental reason will have to respect these limits inasmuch as it can calculate them on its own account in terms of its objectives and [the] best means of achieving them.

Fourth, this de facto, general limitation, which is effectuated in terms of governmental practice itself, will establish, of course, a division between what must be done and what it is advisable not to do. It will mark out the limit of a governmental action, but this will not be drawn in the subjects, the individuals-subjects directed by government. That is to say, one will not try to determine a division within subjects between one part that is subject to governmental action, and another that is definitively, once and for all, reserved for freedom. In other words, this governmental reason does not divide subjects between an absolutely reserved dimension of freedom and another dimension of submission which is either consented to or imposed. In fact, the division is not made within individuals, men, or subjects, but in the very domain of governmental practice, or rather within governmental practice itself, between the operations that can be carried out and those that cannot, between what to do and the means to use on the one hand, and what not to do on the other. The problem, therefore, is not: Where are the basic rights, and how do they separate the domain of fundamental freedom from the domain of possible governmentality? The dividing line is established between two sets of things that Bentham listed in one of his most important texts (to which I will try to return):[9] the division between the *agenda* and the *non-agenda*, between what to do and what not to do.

Fifth, this limitation is therefore a de facto, general limitation, a limitation in terms of the objectives of government that does not divide the subjects but the things to be done, and it is not those who govern who, in complete sovereignty and full reason, will decide on this internal limitation.* Inasmuch as the government of men is a practice which is not imposed by those who govern on those who are governed, but a practice that fixes the definition and respective positions of the governed and governors facing each other and in relation to each other, "internal regulation" means that this limitation is not exactly imposed by either one side or the other, or at any rate not globally, definitively, and totally, but by, I would say, transaction, in the very broad sense of the word, that is to say, "action between," that is to say, by a series of conflicts, agreements, discussions, and reciprocal concessions: all episodes whose effect is finally to establish a de facto, general, rational division between what is to be done and what is not to be done in the practice of governing.

In a word, the principle of right—whether historically or theoretically defined doesn't matter here—previously confronted the sovereign and what he could do with a certain limit: You will not step over this line, you will not infringe this right, and you will not violate this basic freedom. At this time the principle of right balanced *raison d'État* with an external principle. Let's say that now we enter—you can see it quite clearly—an age of critical governmental reason. You can see that this critical governmental reason, or internal criticism of governmental reason, no longer revolves around the question of right and the question of the sovereign's usurpation or legitimacy. It will no longer have that kind of penal appearance that public law still had in the sixteenth and seventeenth

---

* M.F.: will decide themselves on what is to be done and what is not to be done.

centuries when it said: If the sovereign breaks this law, then he must be punished by a sanction of illegitimacy. The whole question of critical governmental reason will turn on how not to govern too much.[10] The objection is no longer to the abuse of sovereignty but to excessive government. And it is by reference to excessive government, or at any rate to the delimitation of what would be excessive for a government, that it will be possible to gauge the rationality of governmental practice.

Before giving this abstract description, I said that this fundamental transformation in the relations between law and governmental practice, this emergence of an internal limitation of governmental reason could be located roughly around the middle of the eighteenth century. What permitted its emergence? How did it come about? Obviously, we should take into account an entire, comprehensive transformation (I will come back to this, at least partially, afterwards), but today I would just like to indicate the intellectual instrument, the form of calculation and rationality that made possible the self-limitation of governmental reason as a de facto, general self-regulation which is intrinsic to the operations of government and can be the object of indefinite transactions. Well, once again, the intellectual instrument, the type of calculation or form of rationality that made possible the self-limitation of governmental reason was not the law. What is it, starting from the middle of the eighteenth century? Obviously, it is political economy.

The very ambiguities of the term "political economy," and of its meaning at this time, indicate what was basically at issue in all this, since you know that between 1750 and 1810-1820 the expression "political economy" oscillates between two semantic poles. Sometimes this expression aims at a particular strict and limited analysis of the production and circulation of wealth. But, in a broader and more practical sense, "political economy" also refers to any method of government that can procure the nation's prosperity. And finally, political economy—the term employed by Rousseau in his famous article in the *Encyclopedia*[11]—is a sort of general reflection on the organization, distribution, and limitation of powers in a society. I think that fundamentally it was political economy that made it possible to ensure the self-limitation of governmental reason.

Why and how did political economy make this possible? Here again—I will go into a bit more detail later—I would just like to indicate some points which I think are indispensable for understanding the set of things I want to talk about this year. First, unlike sixteenth and seventeenth century juridical thought, political economy was not developed outside *raison d'État*. It was not developed against *raison d'État* and in order to limit it, at least not in the first place. Rather, it was formed within the very framework of the objectives set for the art of government by *raison d'État*, for what objectives did political economy set itself? Well, it set itself the objective of the state's enrichment. Its objective was the simultaneous, correlative, and suitably adjusted growth of population on the one hand, and means of subsistence on the other. Political economy offered to ensure suitable, adjusted, and always favorable competition between states. It proposed precisely the maintenance of an equilibrium between states such that competition can take place. That is to say, it took up exactly the objectives of *raison d'État* and the police state that mercantilism and the European balance had tried to realize. So, to start with, political economy lodges itself within the governmental reason of the sixteenth and seventeenth centuries and to that extent is not in the kind of external position occupied by juridical thought.

Second, political economy does not put itself forward as an external objection to *raison d'État* and its political autonomy since—and this will be an historically important point—the first political consequence of the first economic reflection to exist in the history of European thought is precisely a consequence which goes completely against what the jurists were after and concludes that total despotism is necessary. The first political economy was, of course, that of the physiocrats, and you know that from the very start of their economic analysis the physiocrats—I will come back to this—concluded that political power must be a power without external limitation, without external counterbalance, and without any bounds other than those arising from itself, and this is what they called despotism.[12] Despotism is an economic government, but an economic government which is not hemmed in and whose boundaries are not drawn by anything but an economy which it has itself defined and which it completely controls. It is a matter of absolute despotism and so you can see that in that respect political economy does not reverse the tendency marked out by *raison d'État*, at least not at first or at that level, and political economy can appear to be in a direct line of descent from a *raison d'État* that gave the monarch total and absolute power.

Third, on what does political economy reflect, what does it analyze? It is not something like prior rights inscribed in human nature or in the history of a given society. Political economy reflects on governmental practices themselves, and it does not question them to determine whether or not they are legitimate in terms of right. It considers them in terms of their effects rather than their origins, not by asking, for example, what authorizes a sovereign to raise taxes, but by asking, quite simply: What will happen if, at a given moment, we raise a tax on a particular category of persons or a particular category of goods? What matters is not whether or not this is legitimate in terms of law, but what its effects are and whether they are negative. It is then that the tax in question will be said to be illegitimate or, at any rate, to have no raison d'être. The economic question is always to be posed within the field of governmental practice, not in terms of what may found it by right, but in terms of its effects: What are the real effects of the exercise of governmentality? Not: What original rights can found this governmentality? This is the third reason why political economy, in its reflection and its new rationality, was able to find a place, if you like, within the governmental practice and reason established in the previous epoch.

The fourth reason is that, in responding to this type of question, political economy revealed the existence of phenomena, processes, and regularities that necessarily occur as a result of intelligible mechanisms. These intelligible and necessary mechanisms may, of course, be impeded by the practices of some forms of governmentality. They may be impeded, jammed, or obscured, but they cannot be avoided and it will not be possible to suspend them totally and definitively. In any case, they will force a reappraisal of governmental practice. In other words, political economy does not discover natural rights that exist prior to the exercise of governmentality; it discovers a certain naturalness specific to the practice of government itself. The objects of governmental action have a specific nature. There is a nature specific to this governmental action itself and this is what political economy will study. The notion* of nature will thus be transformed with the appearance of political economy. For political economy, nature is not an original and reserved region on which the exercise of power should not impinge, on pain of being illegitimate.

* Foucault adds: natural and

Nature is something that runs under, through, and in the exercise of governmentality. It is, if you like, its indispensable hypodermis. It is the other face of something whose visible face, visible for the governors, is their own action. Their action has an underside, or rather, it has another face, and this other face of governmentality, its specific necessity, is precisely what political economy studies. It is not background, but a permanent correlative. Thus, the *économistes* explain, the movement of population to where wages are highest, for example, is a law of nature; it is a law of nature that customs duty protecting the high price of the means of subsistence will inevitably entail something like dearth.

Finally, the last point explaining how and why political economy was able to appear as the first form of this new self-limiting governmental *ratio* is that if there is a nature specific to the objects and operations of governmentality, then the consequence of this is that governmental practice can only do what it has to do by respecting this nature. If it were to disrupt this nature, if it were not to take it into account or go against laws determined by this naturalness specific to the objects it deals with, it would immediately suffer negative consequences. In other words, there will be either success or failure; success or failure, rather than legitimacy or illegitimacy, now become the criteria of governmental action. So, success replaces [legitimacy].* We touch here on the whole problem of utilitarian philosophy, which we will have to talk about. You can see how utilitarian philosophy will be able to plug directly into these new problems of governmentality. This is not important for the moment; we will come back to it.

Success or failure, then, will replace the division between legitimacy and illegitimacy—but there is more. What makes a government, despite its objectives, disrupt the naturalness specific to the objects it deals with and the operations it carries out? What will lead it to violate this nature despite the success it seeks? Violence, excess, and abuse? Maybe, but ultimately these are not merely or fundamentally a matter of the wickedness of the prince. What is at issue, what explains this, is precisely that when a government violates these laws of nature, it quite simply ignores them. It ignores them because it is unaware of their existence, mechanisms,

---

* M.F.: failure

and effects. In other words, governments can be mistaken. And the greatest evil of government, what makes it a bad government, is not that the prince is wicked, but that he is ignorant. In short, through political economy there is the simultaneous entry into the art of government of, first, the possibility of self-limitation, that is, of governmental action limiting itself by reference to the nature of what it does and of that on which it is brought to bear, [and second, the question of truth].* The possibility of limitation and the question of truth are both introduced into governmental reason through political economy.

You will tell me that this is certainly not the first time that the question of truth and the question of the self-limitation of governmental practice are raised. After all, what was traditionally understood by the prince's wisdom? The prince's wisdom told him: I know God's laws too well, I know human weakness too well, and I know my own limits too well not to restrain my power and fail to respect my subject's right. But we can see that the relationship between the principle of truth and the principle of self-limitation in the prince's wisdom is completely different from their relationship in the emerging governmental practice that is anxious to know the natural consequences of its actions in the objects it deals with and manipulates. The prudent counselors who previously fixed limits of wisdom to the prince's presumption no longer have anything to do with these new economic experts whose task is to tell the government what in truth the natural mechanisms are of what it is manipulating.

So, with political economy we enter an age whose principle could be this: A government is never sufficiently aware that it always risks governing too much, or, a government never knows too well how to govern just enough. The principle of maximum/minimum replaces the notion of equitable equilibrium, of "equitable justice" that previously organized the prince's wisdom. With this question of self-limitation by the principle of truth, I think political economy introduced a formidable wedge into the unlimited presumption of the police state. This is evidently a crucial moment since it establishes, in its most important features, not

---

* Unfinished sentence. Manuscript p. 20: "In short, through political economy there is the simultaneous entry into the art of government of the possibility of self-limitation and the question of truth."

of course the reign of truth in politics, but a particular regime of truth which is a characteristic feature of what could be called the age of politics and the basic apparatus of which is in fact still the same today. When I say regime of truth I do not mean that at this moment politics or the art of government finally becomes rational. I do not mean that at this moment a sort of epistemological threshold is reached on the basis of which the art of government could become scientific. I mean that the moment I am presently trying to indicate is marked by the articulation of a particular type of discourse and a set of practices, a discourse that, on the one hand, constitutes these practices as a set bound together by an intelligible connection and, on the other hand, legislates and can legislate on these practices in terms of true and false.

In concrete terms this means the following. Basically, from the sixteenth and seventeenth centuries, and even before, until the middle of the eighteenth century, there was a whole set of practices of tax levies, customs charges, manufacture regulations, regulations of grain prices, the protection and codification of market practices, and so on. But what were these practices, and how were they thought about? Well, all of this was conceived of as the exercise of sovereign rights, of feudal rights, as the maintenance of customs, as effective procedures of enrichment for the Treasury, or as techniques for preventing urban revolt due to the discontent of this or that group of subjects. In short, all of these practices were certainly reflected on, but on the basis of different events and principles of rationalization. From the middle of the eighteenth century it becomes possible to establish a reasoned, reflected coherence between these different practices going from customs charges to tax levies, to the regulation of the market and production, and so on; a coherence established by intelligible mechanisms which link together these different practices and their effects, and which consequently allows one to judge all these practices as good or bad, not in terms of a law or moral principle, but in terms of propositions subject to the division between true and false. Thus, in this way a whole section of governmental activity enters into a new regime of truth with the fundamental effect of reconfiguring all the questions formerly posed by the art of governing. At one time these amounted to the question: Am I governing in proper conformity to moral, natural, or divine laws? Then, in the sixteenth and seventeenth centuries, with *raison d'État*, it was: Am I governing with sufficient intensity, depth, and attention to detail so as to bring the state to the point fixed by what it should be, to bring it to its maximum strength? And now the problem will be: Am I governing at the border between the too much and too little, between the maximum and minimum fixed for me by the nature of things—I mean, by the necessities intrinsic to the operations of government? The emergence of this regime of truth as the principle of the self-limitation of government is the object I would like to deal with this year.

The question here is the same as the question I addressed with regard to madness, disease, delinquency, and sexuality. In all of these cases, it was not a question of showing how these objects were for a long time hidden before finally being discovered, nor of showing how all these objects are only wicked illusions or ideological products to be dispelled in the [light]* of reason finally having reached its zenith. It was a matter of showing by what conjunctions a whole set of practices—from the moment they become coordinated with a regime of truth—was able to make what does not exist (madness, disease, delinquency, sexuality, etcetera), nonetheless become something, something however that continues not to exist. That is to say, what I would like to show is not how an error—when I say that which does not exist becomes something, this does not mean showing how it was possible for an error to be constructed—or how an illusion could be born, but how a particular regime of truth, and therefore not an error, makes something that does not exist able to become something. It is not an illusion since it is precisely a set of practices, real practices, which established it and thus imperiously marks it out in reality.

The point of all these investigations concerning madness, disease, delinquency, sexuality, and what I am talking about now, is to show how the coupling of a set of practices and a regime of truth form an apparatus (*dispositif*) of knowledge-power that effectively marks out in reality that which does not exist and legitimately submits it to the division between true and false.

---

* A clear slip. M.F.: mist

In the things I am presently concerned with, the moment when that which does not exist is inscribed in reality, and when that which does not exist comes under a legitimate regime of the true and false, marks the birth of this dissymmetrical bipolarity of politics and the economy. Politics and the economy are not things that exist, or errors, or illusions, or ideologies. They are things that do not exist and yet which are inscribed in reality and fall under a regime of truth dividing the true and the false.

This moment, whose main components I have tried to indicate, is situated between Walpole, whom I have talked about, and another text. Walpole said: "*quieta non movere*" ("let sleeping dogs lie"). This is no doubt a counsel of prudence, and we are still in the realm of the wisdom of the prince, that is to say: When the people are peaceful, when they are not agitating and there is no discontent or revolt, stay calm. So, wisdom of the prince. I think he said this around the 1740s. In 1751 an anonymous article appeared in the *Journal économique*. It was in fact written by the marquis d'Argenson,[13] who, had just given up his official activities. Recalling what the merchant Le Gendre said to Colbert—when Colbert asked him: "What can I do for you?" Le Gendre replied: "What can you do for us? Leave us alone (*Laissez-nous faire*)"[14]—in this text to which I will come back,[15] d'Argenson says that what he would like to do is comment on this principle of "*laissez-nous faire*,"[16] because, he shows, in economic matters this really is the essential principle which all governments must respect and follow.[17] At this moment he has laid down clearly the principle of the self-limitation of governmental reason. But what does "the self-limitation of governmental reason" mean? What is this new type of rationality in the art of government, this new type of calculation that consists in saying and telling government: I accept, wish, plan, and calculate that all this should be left alone? I think that this is broadly what is called "liberalism."*

---

* In inverted commas in the manuscript. Foucault does not read the last pages of the manuscript (pp. 25-32). Elements of this conclusion are taken up and developed in the next lecture.

"The word ['liberalism'] should be understood very broadly.
1. Acceptance of the principle that somewhere there must be a limitation of government and that this is not just an external right.
2. Liberalism is also a practice: where exactly is the principle of the limitation of government to be found and how are the effects of this limitation to be calculated?

I thought I could do a course on biopolitics this year. I will try to show how the central core of all the problems that I am presently trying to identify is what is called population. Consequently, this is the basis on which something like biopolitics could be formed. But it seems to me that the analysis of biopolitics can only get under way when we

---

3. In a narrower sense, liberalism is the solution that consists in the maximum limitation of the forms and domains of government action.
4. Finally, liberalism is the organization of specific methods of transaction for defining the limitation of government practices:
—constitution, parliament
—opinion, the press
—commissions, inquiries

[p. 27] One of the forms of modern governmentality. A characteristic feature is the fact that instead of coming up against limits formalized by jurisdictions, it [gives?] itself intrinsic limits formulated in terms of veridiction.

a. Of course, there are not two systems, one after the other, or in insuperable conflict with each other. Heterogeneity does not mean contradiction, but tensions, frictions, mutual incompatibilities, successful or failed adjustments, unstable mixtures, and so on. It also means a constantly resumed because never completed task of establishing either a coincidence or at least a common regime. This task is that of giving a legal form to the self-limitation that knowledge (*le savoir*) prescribes to government.

[p. 28] From the eighteenth [century] to the present, this task will take two forms:
—Either, questioning governmental reason, and the necessity of its limitation, in order to identify, through what must be left free, what rights can be recognized and given status within governmental practice. Thus, questioning the objectives, ways, and means of an enlightened and so self-limited government can give rise to the right to property, to possible means of subsistence, to work, etcetera.
—Or, questioning the basic rights, asserting them all and at once. And, on this basis, only allowing a government to be formed on condition that its self-regulation reproduces all of them. Method [crossed out: revolutionary] of governmental subordination.

[p. 29] Liberal practice adopts the method of the necessary and sufficient juridical remainder. Revolutionary procedure adopts the method of exhaustive governmental conditions.

b. Second comment: this self-limitation of governmental reason characteristic of 'liberalism' has a strange relationship with the regime of *raison d'État*.—The latter opens up an unlimited domain of intervention to governmental practice, but on the other hand, through the principle of a competitive balance between states, it gives itself limited international objectives.
—The self-limitation of governmental practice by liberal reason is accompanied by the break-up of these international objectives and the appearance of unlimited objectives with imperialism.

[p. 30] *Raison d'État* was correlative with the disappearance of the imperial principle and its replacement by competitive equilibrium between states. Liberal reason is correlative with activation of the imperial principle, not in the form of the Empire, but in the form of imperialism, and this in connection with the principle of the free competition between individuals and enterprises.
Chiasmus between limited and unlimited objectives with regard to the domain of internal intervention and the field of international action.

c. Third comment: liberal reason is established as self-limitation of government on the basis of a 'naturalness' of the objects and practices specific to government. What is this naturalness?

have understood the general regime of this governmental reason I have talked about, this general regime that we can call the question of truth, of economic truth in the first place, within governmental reason. Consequently, it seems to me that it is only when we understand what is at stake in this regime of liberalism opposed to *raison d'État*—or rather, fundamentally modifying [it] without, perhaps, questioning its bases—only when we know what this governmental regime called liberalism was, will we be able to grasp what biopolitics is.

So, forgive me, for some weeks—I cannot say in advance how many—I will talk about liberalism. In this way, it may become a bit clearer what is at stake in this—for, after all, what interest is there in talking about liberalism, the physiocrats, d'Argenson, Adam Smith, Bentham, and the English utilitarians, if not because the problem of liberalism arises for us in our immediate and concrete actuality? What does it mean when we speak of liberalism when we apply a liberal politics to ourselves, today, and what relationship may there be between this and those questions of right that we call freedoms or liberties? What is going on in all this, in today's debate in which Helmut Schmidt's[18] economic principles bizarrely echo the voice of dissidents in the East, in this problem of liberty, of liberalism? Fine, it is a problem of our times. So, if you like, after having situated the historical point of origin of all this by bringing out what, according to me, is the new governmental reason from the eighteenth century, I will jump ahead and talk about contemporary German liberalism since, however paradoxical it may seem, liberty in the second half of the twentieth century, well let's say more accurately, liberalism, is a word that comes to us from Germany.

---

—Naturalness of wealth? Yes, but only as increasing or diminishing, stagnant or [p. 31] circulating means of payment. But goods rather insofar as they produced, are useful and utilized, insofar as they are exchanged between economic partners.
—It is also the naturalness of individuals. Not, however, as obedient or intractable subjects, but insofar as they are themselves linked to this economic naturalness, insofar as their longevity, health, and ways of conducting themselves have complex and tangled relationships with these economic processes.
With the emergence of political economy, with the introduction of the restrictive principle in governmental practice itself, an important substitution, or doubling rather, is carried out, since the subjects of right on which political sovereignty is exercised appear as a *population* that a government must manage.

[p. 32] This is the point of departure for the organizational line of a 'biopolitics.' But who does not see that this is only part of something much larger, which [is] this new governmental reason? Studying liberalism as the general framework of biopolitics."

1. Quotation from Virgil, *Aeneid*, VIII, 312, placed as an epigraph of the *Tramdeutung* (Leipzig: Deutike, 1911); English translation by James Strachey, *The Interpretation of Dreams* in *The Standard Edition of the Complete Psychological Works of Sigmund Freud* (London: The Hogarth Press and the Institute of Pscyho-analysis, 1958) vol. IV (First Part) p. ix, and repeated in the text (vol. V, Second Part, p. 608, fn. 1): "*Flectere si nequeo Superos, Acheronta movebo*" where it is translated as: "If I cannot bend the Higher Powers, I will move the Infernal Regions" [or more colloquially, "I will raise hell"; G.B.]. The phrase was quoted by Foucault, without explicit reference to Freud, in *La Volonté de savoir* (Paris: Gallimard, 1976) p. 103; English translation by Robert Hurley as *The History of Sexuality, Vol. One: An Introduction* (New York: Pantheon, 1978; Harmondsworth: Penguin, 1984) p. 79: "In reality, this question so often repeated nowadays, is but the recent form of a considerable affirmation and a secular prescription: there is where the truth is; go see if you can uncover it. *Acheronta movebo:* an age-old decision." Before Freud, this quotation was already much appreciated by Bismarck, who used it several times in his *Pensées et Souvenirs*. See C. Schmitt, *Theorie des Partisanen* (Berlin: Duncker and Humblot, 1963); French translation by M.L. Steinhauser, *Théorie du partisan* (Paris: Calmann-Lévy, 1972) p. 253.
2. Robert Walpole, 1st Earl of Orford (1676-1745), Whig leader who, as first Lord of the Treasury and Chancellor of the Exchequer from 1720 to 1742, was effectively Britain's first Prime Minister; he governed pragmatically, using Parliamentary corruption, with the aim of preserving political peace.
3. See Foucault's clarification on p. 20: "I think he said it around the 1740s." The formula is known for being Walpole's motto, as evidenced by various writings of his son Horace; see, for example, *Letters*, VIII (London and New York: Lawrence and Bullen; G.P. Putnam's Sons, 1903) p. 121. See L. Stephen, *History of English Thought in the Eighteenth Century* (London: Smith and Elder, 1902; reprint. Bristol: Thoemmes Antiquarian Books, 1991) vol. 2, p. 168. The phrase comes from Sallust, *De Conjuration Catilinae*, 21, 1: "Postquam accepere ea homines, quibus mala abunde monia erant, sed neque res neque spes bona ulla, tametsi illis *quieta movere* magna merces videbatur ( ... )"; French translation by F. Richard, *Conjuration de Catilina* (Paris: Garnier-Flammarion, 1968) p. 43; English translation by A.W. Pollard, *The Catiline of Sallust* (London: Macmillan, 1928), p. 19: "These words were listened to by men who had every evil in abundances, but no good fortune, nor any hope of it. Great, however, as the wages of revolution appeared to them ... "; and by J.C. Rolfe, "The War with Catiline" in *Sallust* (London and Cambridge Mass.: William Heinemann/Harvard University Press, The Loeb Classical Library, 1947) p. 39: "When these words fell upon the ears of men who had misfortune of every kind in excess, but neither means nor any honourable hope, although disorder alone seemed to them an ample reward ... " It illustrates the rule of precedent in English Common Law, according to which, in judicial matters one must keep to what has been decided and not modify what exists ("stare decisis" and "quieta non movere"). It is also cited by F. Hayek, *The Constitution of Liberty* (London: Routledge and Kegan Paul, (1960) 1976) p. 410: "Though *quieta non movere* may at times be a wise maxim for the Statesman, it cannot satisfy the political philosopher."
4. See Paul Veyne, "Foucault révolutionne l'histoire" (1978), in Paul Veyne, *Comment on écrit l'histoire* (Paris: Le Seuil, "Points Histoire," 1979) pp. 227-230; English translation by Catherine Porter, "Foucault Revolutionizes History" in Arnold I. Davidson, ed., *Foucault and his Interlocutors* (Chicago and London: University of Chicago Press, 1997) pp. 167-170, on methodological nominalism with regard to the phrase "madness does not exist." In view of the fact that Veyne's text dates from 1978, it would seem that Foucault is here pursuing his dialogue with the author of *Le Pain et le Cirque*, to which he paid tribute in the previous year's lectures (see *Sécurité, Territoire, Population. Cours au Collège de France, 1977-1978*, ed. Michel Senellart (Paris: Gallimard-Le Seuil, 2004); English translation by Graham Burchell, *Security, Territory, Population. Lectures at the Collège de France, 1977-1978*, English series ed. Arnold I. Davidson (London and New York: Palgrave Macmillan, 2007), lecture of 8 March 1978, p. 239. See also Foucault's comments on the same theme in the lecture of 8 February 1978, p. 118. The criticism of universals is also reaffirmed in the article "Foucault" which appeared in 1984 in the *Dictionnaire des philosophes* of

Denis Huismans, under the pseudonym Maurice Florens. See, M. Foucault, "Foucault" in *Dits et Écrits, 1954-1988*, four volumes, eds. D. Defert and F. Ewald, with the collaboration of J. Lagrance (Paris: Gallimard, 1994) vol. 4, p. 634; English translation by Robert Hurley, in *Essential Works of Foucault 1954-1984, volume 2: Aesthetics, Method, and Epistemology*, ed. James D. Faubion, trans. Robert Hurley and others (New York: The New Press, 1998) p. 461: the first choice of method entailed by "the question of the relations between the subject and truth" was "a systematic skepticism toward all anthropological universals."

5. Foucault does not return to this question in the following lectures.
6. See *Sécurité, Territoire, Population*; *Security, Territory, Population*, lectures of 8, 15, and 22 March 1978.
7. See ibid. lecture of 1 February 1978; (Eng.) ibid. p. 109 and note 39.
8. See, *"Il faut défendre la société." Cours au Collège de France, 1975-1976*, eds. M. Bertani and A. Fontana (Paris: Gallimard-Le Seuil, 1997); English translation by David Macey, *"Society Must be Defended." Lectures at the Collège de France, 1975-1976*, English series ed. Arnold I. Davidson (New York: Picador, 2003).
9. Jeremy Bentham (1748-1832), *Method and Leading Features of an Institute of Political Economy (including finance) considered not only as a science but as an art* (1800-1804), in *Jeremy Bentham's Economic Writings*, ed. W. Stark (London: George Allen and Unwin, 1954) vol. 3, pp. 305-380. It is at the end of the first part, "The Science," in the section on "Genesis of the Matter of Wealth," that Bentham introduces the famous distinction between *sponte acta*, *agenda* and *non-agenda*, which structures the three chapters ("Wealth," "Population," and "Finance") of the following part, "The Art." The *sponte acta* are economic activities spontaneously developed by members of a community without any governmental intervention. The *agenda* and *non-agenda* designate the economic activities of government according to whether or not they increase happiness (the maximization of pleasure and minimization of pain), which is the aim of all political action. The division of the domains between these three classes varies according to time and place, the extension of the *sponta acta* being relative to a country's level of economic development. Foucault makes another brief reference to Bentham's list of the *agenda* in the lecture of 7 March 1979 (see below p. 195), but strictly speaking he does not speak again of the text cited (except, perhaps, indirectly at the end of the lecture of 24 January (below p. 67), with regard to the panopticon as a general formula of liberal government).
10. The formula "do not govern too much (*pas trop gouverner*)" is from the marquis d'Argenson (see below, note 16). See also, B. Franklin, *Principles of Trade* (London: Brotherton and Sewell, 1774, 2nd edition) p. 34: "It is said, by a very solid Writer of the same Nation, that he is well advanced in the Science of Politics, who knows the full Force of that Maxim *Pas trop gouverner*: Not to govern too strictly." [In same section, pp. 33-34 there is following: "When Colbert assembled some wise old Merchants of France; and desired their Advice and Opinion, how he could best serve and promote Commerce; their answer, after Consultation, was, in three Words only, *Laissez nous faire*. Let us alone."]
11. This article was printed for the first time in volume 5 of the *Encyclopédie* pp. 337-349, which appeared in November 1755. See Jean-Jacques Rousseau, "Économie politique," in *Œuvres complètes* (Paris: Gallimard, 1964) vol. III, pp. 241-278; English translation by G.D.H. Cole, *A Discourse on Political Economy*, in *The Social Contract and Discourses* (London: J.M. Dent, 1993). On this text, see *Sécurité, Territoire, Population*; *Security, Territory, Population*, lecture of 1 February 1978, p. 95 and note 21.
12. See P.P.F.J.H. Le Mercier de La Rivière, *L'Ordre naturel et essentiel des sociétés politiques* (published without the author's name, London: Jean Nourse, and Paris: Desaint, 1767) ch. 24: "Du despotisme legal." The text was republished twice in the twentieth century: (i) Paris: P. Geuthner, "Collection des économistes et des réformateurs sociaux de la France," 1910, and (ii) Paris: Fayard, "Corpus des œuvres de philosophie en langue française," 2000.
13. René-Louis de Voyer, marquis d'Argenson (1694-1757), Secretary of State for Foreign Affairs 1744 to 1747, the author of *Mémoires et Journal*, published and annotated by the Marquis d'Argenson, Paris, 1858 (a first, very incomplete edition appeared in 1835 in the Baudouin collection of "Mémoires sur la Révolution française") and of *Considérations sur le gouvernement ancien et présent de la France* (Amsterdam: Rey, 1764). With the abbot de Saint-Pierre, he was one of the assiduous members of the Club de l'Entresol, opened in 1720 on

the initiative of the abbot Alary and closed in 1731 by cardinal Fleury. "Laissez faire" was already a recurring expression in the sketch of a memorandum on free trade, dated 31 July 1742 (*Journal et Mémoire*, ed. J.B. Rathery [Paris: Renouard, 1862] vol. IV: "Memorandum to be written to consider the arguments for and against and to decide whether France should allow the free entry and exit into the kingdom of all national and foreign goods").

14. L.-P. Abeille, *Lettre d'un négociant sur la nature du commerce des grains* (Marseille: 8 October 1763); republished in *Premiers opuscules sur le commerce des grains: 1763-1764*, introduction and analytical table b E. Depitre (Paris: P. Geuthner, 1911) p. 103: "I cannot end this letter better except by applying particularly to the corn trade what a merchant of Rouen said to M. Colbert on commerce in general: *Laissez-nous faire*."
15. Foucault does not refer to this text again.
16. D'Argenson, "Lettre à l'auteur du *Journal économique* au sujet de la *Dissertation sur le commerce* de M. le Marquis Belloni," *Journal économique*, April 1751, pp. 107-117; republished in G. Klotz, ed., *Politique et Économie au temps des Lumières* (Publications de l'Université de Saint-Étienne, 1995) pp. 41-44: "It is told that M. Colbert gathered several delegates of commerce at his home in order to ask them what he could do for commerce; the most reasonable and least flatterer of them told him simply: *Laissez-nous faire*. Have we ever sufficiently considered the great meaning of these words? This is only an attempt at commentary" (p. 42). The name of Le Gendre is first mentioned in the eighteenth century in Turgot's *L'Éloge de Gournay*, written in 1759 ("We know Le Gendre's words to Colbert: *laissez-nous faire*") in *Œuvres de Turgot*, ed. E. Daire (Paris: Guillaumin, 1844) vol. 1, p. 288; Turgot, *Formation et Distribution des richesses* (Paris: Garnier-Flammarion) pp. 150-151. D'Argenson is also the author of the maxim "do not govern too much (*pas trop gouverner*)." See G. Weulersse, *Le Mouvement physiocratique en France, de 1756 à 1770*, in two volumes (Paris: Félix Alcan, 1910) vol. 1, pp. 17-18, which quotes this extract from the tribute that appeared in the *Éphémérides du citoyen*, July, 1768, p. 156: "He composed a book with the excellent object and title: *do not govern too much*." D'Argenson claims to have written a treatise entitled *Pour gouverner mieux, il faudrait gouverner moins* (*Mémoires et Journal*, vol. V, p. 362; quoted by A. Oncken, *Die Maxime "Laissez faire et laissez passer"* (Bern: K.J. Wyss, 1886) p. 58.
17. D'Argenson, "Lettre à l'auteur du *Journal économique*" p. 44: "Yes, regular and enlightened freedom will always do more for a nation's commerce than the most intelligent domination." He defends the same position with regard to the grain trade in another article in the *Journal économique*, May 1754, pp. 64-79: "Arguments en faveur de la liberté du commerce des grains," republished in G. Klotz, ed., *Politique et Économie*, pp. 45-54.
18. Helmut Schmidt (born 1918): deputy for the SPD in the Bundestag in 1953, he became Chancellor in May 1974 after the retirement of Willy Brandt. Losing his majority, he gave way to Helmut Kohl in 1982.

two

# 17 JANUARY 1979

*Liberalism and the implementation of a new art of government in the eighteenth century. ~ Specific features of the liberal art of government (I): (1) The constitution of the market as site of the formation of truth and not just as domain of jurisdiction. ~ Questions of method. The stakes of research undertaken around madness, the penal order, and sexuality: sketch of a history of "regimes of veridiction." ~ The nature of a political critique of knowledge (*savoir*). ~ (2) The problem of limiting the exercise of power by public authorities. Two types of solution: French juridical radicalism and English utilitarianism. ~ The question of "utility" and limiting the exercise of power by public authorities. ~ Comment on the status of heterogeneity in history: strategic against dialectical logic. ~ The notion of "interest" as operator (*opérateur*) of the new art of government.*

I WOULD LIKE TO refine a little the theses or hypotheses that I put forward last week with regard to what I think is a new art of government that began to be formulated, reflected upon, and outlined around the middle of the eighteenth century. I think an essential characteristic of this new art of government is the organization of numerous and complex internal mechanisms whose function—and this is what distinguishes them from *raison d'État*—is not so much to ensure the growth of the state's forces, wealth, and strength, to ensure its unlimited growth, as to limit the exercise of government power internally.

This art of government is certainly new in its mechanisms, its effects, and its principle. But it is so only up to a point, because we should not imagine that this art of government is the suppression, obliteration, abolition, or, if you prefer, the *Aufhebung* of the *raison d'État* I tried to talk about last week. In fact, we should not forget that this new art of government, or this art of the least possible government, this art of governing between a maximum and a minimum, and rather minimum than maximum, should be seen as a sort of intensification or internal refinement of *raison d'État*; it is a principle for maintaining it, developing it more fully, and perfecting it. It is not something other than *raison d'État*, an element external to and in contradiction with *raison d'État*, but rather its point of inflection in the curve of its development. If you like, to use a not very satisfactory expression, I would say that it is the reason of the least state within and as organizing principle of *raison d'État* itself, or again: it is the reason of least government as the principle organizing *raison d'État* itself. There is someone, unfortunately I've not been able to find his name in my papers, but when I do I will tell you, but certainly from the end of the eighteenth century, who spoke about "frugal government."[1] Well, I think that actually at this moment we are entering what could be called the epoch of frugal government, which is, of course, not without a number of paradoxes, since during this period of frugal government, which was inaugurated in the eighteenth century and is no doubt still not behind us, we see both the intensive and extensive development of governmental practice, along with the negative effects, with the resistances and revolts which we know are directed precisely against the invasive intrusions of a government which nevertheless claims to be and is supposed to be frugal. Let's say—and this will be why we can say that we are living in the age of frugal government—that this extensive and intensive development of a government that is nevertheless supposed to be frugal has been constantly accompanied, outside and within government, by the question of the too much and the too little. Stretching things and giving a caricature of them, I would say that whatever the extension and intensive development of government there may be in fact, the question of frugality has been at the very heart of the reflection which has revolved around government.* The question of frugality has, if not replaced, at least overtaken and to an extent forced back and somewhat marginalized a different question which preoccupied political reflection in the sixteenth and seventeenth centuries, and even up to the start of the eighteenth century, which was the problem of the constitution. Certainly, all the questions concerning monarchy, aristocracy, and democracy do not disappear. But just as they were the fundamental questions, I was going to say the royal questions, in the seventeenth and eighteenth centuries, so starting from the end of the eighteenth century, throughout the nineteenth century, and obviously more than ever today, the fundamental problem is not the constitution of states, but without a doubt the question of the frugality of government. [The] question of the frugality of government is indeed the question of liberalism. I would now like to take up two or three of the points I mentioned last week in order to clarify and refine them.

Last week I tried to show you that this idea, this theme, or this regulative principle rather, of frugal government was formed on the basis of what could be called or what I roughly designated as the connecting up of *raison d'État* and its calculation with a particular regime of truth that finds its theoretical expression and formulation in political economy. I tried to suggest that the appearance of political economy and the problem of least government were linked. But I think we should try to be a bit clearer about the nature of this connection. When I say connecting up of political economy with *raison d'État*, does this mean that political economy put forward a particular model of government? Does it mean that statesmen were initiated into political economy or that they began to listen to the economists? Did the economic model become the organizing principle of governmental practice? Clearly this is not what I wanted to say. What I meant, what I tried to designate, was something of a rather different nature and situated at a different level. The principle of this connection between the practice of government and a regime of truth that I tried to identify would be this: [ ... ] there was something in the regime of government, in the governmental practice of the sixteenth and seventeenth centuries, and already of the Middle Ages also, that was

* Foucault adds: and which it has posed.

one of the privileged objects of governmental intervention and regulation, that was the privileged object of government vigilance and intervention. And it is not economic theory but this place itself that from the eighteenth century became a site and a mechanism of the formation of truth. And [instead of] continuing to saturate this site of the formation of truth with an unlimited regulatory governmentality, it is recognized—and this is where the shift takes place—that it must be left to function with the least possible interventions precisely so that it can both formulate its truth and propose it to governmental practice as rule and norm. This site of truth is not in the heads of economists, of course, but is the market.

Let's put it more clearly. The market, in the very general sense of the word, as it operated in the Middle Ages, and in the sixteenth and seventeenth centuries, was, in a word, essentially a site of justice. In what sense was it a site of justice? In several senses. In the first place it was, of course, invested with extremely prolific and strict regulations: it was regulated with regard to the objects brought to market, their type of manufacture, their origin, the duties to be paid, the procedures of sale, and, of course, the prices fixed. So, the market was a site invested with regulations. It was also a site of justice in the sense that the sale price fixed in the market was seen, both by theorists and in practice, as a just price, or at any rate a price that should be the just price,[2] that is to say a price that was to have a certain relationship with work performed, with the needs of the merchants, and, of course, with the consumers' needs and possibilities. The market was a site of justice to such an extent that it had to be a privileged site of distributive justice, since as you know, for at least some basic products, like food products, the rules of the market operated to ensure that, if not all, then at least some of the poorest could buy things as well as those who were more well-off. So in this sense the market was a site of distributive justice. Finally, what was it that essentially had to be ensured in the market, by the market, or rather by the regulations of the market, and which makes it a site of justice? Was it the truth of prices, as we would say now? Not at all. What had to be ensured was the absence of fraud. In other words, it was the protection of the buyer. The aim of the regulation of the market was, on the one hand, a distribution of goods that was as just as possible, and then, on the other hand, the absence of theft and crime. In other words, the market was basically seen at this time as a risk, maybe for the merchant, but certainly for the buyer. The buyer had to be protected against the danger of bad goods and the fraud of the person selling them. It was necessary then to ensure the absence of fraud with regard to the nature of the objects, their quality, and so forth. This system—regulation, the just price, the sanction of fraud—thus meant that the market was essentially, and really functioned as, a site of justice, a place where what had to appear in exchange and be formulated in the price was justice. Let's say that the market was a site of jurisdiction.

Now this is where the change takes place for a number of reasons that I will mention shortly. In the middle of the eighteenth century the market no longer appeared as, or rather no longer had to be a site of jurisdiction. On the one hand, the market appeared as something that obeyed and had to obey "natural,"* that is to say, spontaneous mechanisms. Even if it is not possible to grasp these mechanisms in their complexity, their spontaneity is such that attempts to modify them will only impair and distort them. On the other hand—and this is the second sense in which the market becomes a site of truth—not only does it allow natural mechanisms to appear, but when you allow these natural mechanisms to function, they permit the formation of a certain price that Boisguilbert[3] will call the "natural" price, the physiocrats will call the "good price,"[4] and that will later be called the "normal price,"[5] that is to say, a certain price—natural, good, normal, it's not important—which will adequately express the relationship, a definite, adequate relationship between the cost of production and the extent of demand. When you allow the market to function by itself according to its nature, according to its natural truth, if you like, it permits the formation of a certain price which will be called, metaphorically, the true price, and which will still sometimes be called the just price, but which no longer has any connotations of justice. It is a certain price that fluctuates around the value of the product.

The importance of economic theory—I mean the theory constructed in the discourse of the *économistes* and formed in their brains—the importance

---

* In inverted commas in the manuscript.

of the theory of the price-value relationship is due precisely to the fact that it enables economic theory to pick out something that will become fundamental: that the market must be that which reveals something like a truth. This does not mean that prices are, in the strict sense, true, and that there are true prices and false prices. But what is discovered at this moment, at once in governmental practice and in reflection on this governmental practice, is that inasmuch as prices are determined in accordance with the natural mechanisms of the market they constitute a standard of truth which enables us to discern which governmental practices are correct and which are erroneous. In other words, it is the natural mechanism of the market and the formation of a natural price that enables us to falsify and verify governmental practice when, on the basis of these elements, we examine what government does, the measures it takes, and the rules it imposes. In this sense, inasmuch as it enables production, need, supply, demand, value, and price, etcetera, to be linked together through exchange, the market constitutes a site of veridiction, I mean a site of verification-falsification for governmental practice.[6] Consequently, the market determines that good government is no longer simply government that functions according to justice. The market determines that a good government is no longer quite simply one that is just. The market now means that to be good government, government has to function according to truth. In this history and formation of a new art of government, political economy does not therefore owe its privileged role to the fact that it will dictate a good type of conduct to government. Political economy was important, even in its theoretical formulation, inasmuch as (and only inasmuch as, but this is clearly a great deal) it pointed out to government where it had to go to find the principle of truth of its own governmental practice. In simple and barbaric terms, let's say that from being a site of jurisdiction, which it remained up to the start of the eighteenth century, the market, through all the techniques I discussed last year with regard to scarcity and grain markets, etcetera,[7] is becoming what I will call a site of veridiction. The market must tell the truth (*dire le vrai*); it must tell the truth in relation to governmental practice. Henceforth, and merely secondarily, it is its role of veridiction that will command, dictate, and prescribe the jurisdictional mechanisms, or absence of such mechanisms, on which [the market] must be articulated.

When I spoke of the coupling carried out in the eighteenth century between a regime of truth and a new governmental reason, and the connection of this with political economy, in no way did I mean that there was the formation of a scientific and theoretical discourse of political economy on one side, and then, on the other, those who governed who were either seduced by this political economy, or forced to take it into account by the pressure of this or that social group. What I meant was that the market—which had been the privileged object of governmental practice for a very long time and continued to be in the sixteenth and seventeenth centuries under the regime of *raison d'État* and a mercantilism which precisely made commerce one of the major instruments of the state's power—was now constituted as a site of veridiction. And this is not simply or so much because we have entered the age of a market economy—this is at once true, and says nothing exactly—and it is not because people wanted to produce the rational theory of the market—which is what they did, but it was not sufficient. In fact, in order to reach an understanding of how the market, in its reality, became a site of veridiction for governmental practice, we would have to establish what I would call a polygonal or polyhedral relationship between: the particular monetary situation of the eighteenth century, with a new influx of gold on the one hand, and a relative consistency of currencies on the other; a continuous economic and demographic growth in the same period; an intensification of agricultural production; the access to governmental practice of a number of technicians who brought with them both methods and instruments of reflection; and finally a number of economic problems being given a theoretical form.

In other words, I do not think we need to look for—and consequently I do not think we can find—*the* cause* of the constitution of the market as an agency of veridiction. If we want to analyze this absolutely fundamental phenomenon in the history of Western governmentality, this irruption of the market as a principle of veridiction, we should simply establish the intelligibility of this process[8] by describing the connections between the different phenomena I have just referred to. This would involve showing how it became possible—that is to say, not

* Foucault repeats the words, stressing the article: *the* cause

showing that it was necessary, which is a futile task anyway, nor showing that it is *a* possibility (*un possible*), one possibility in a determinate field of possibilities ... Let's say that what enables us to make reality intelligible is simply showing that it was possible; establishing the intelligibility of reality consists in showing its possibility. Speaking in general terms, let's say that in this history of a jurisdictional and then veridictional market we have one of those innumerable intersections between jurisdiction and veridiction that is undoubtedly a fundamental phenomenon in the history of the modern West.

It has been around these [questions] that I have tried to organize a number of problems—with regard to madness, for example. The problem was not to show that psychiatry was formed in the heads of psychiatrists as a theory, or science, or discourse claiming scientific status, and that this was concretized or applied in psychiatric hospitals. Nor was it to show how, at a certain moment, institutions of confinement, which had existed for a long time, secreted their own theory and justifications in the discourse of psychiatrists. The problem was the genesis of psychiatry on the basis of, and through institutions of confinement that were originally and basically articulated on mechanisms of jurisdiction in the very broad sense—since there were police type of jurisdictions, but for the present, at this level, it is not very important—and which at a certain point and in conditions that precisely had to be analyzed, were at the same time supported, relayed, transformed, and shifted by process of veridiction.

In the same way, studying penal institutions meant studying them first of all as sites and forms where jurisdictional practice was predominant and we can say autocratic. [It meant studying] how a certain practice of veridiction was formed and developed in these penal institutions that were fundamentally linked to a jurisdictional practice, and how this veridictional practice—supported, of course, by criminology, psychology, and so on, but this is not what is essential—began to install the veridictional question at the very heart of modern penal practice, even to the extent of creating difficulties for its jurisdiction, which was the question of truth addressed to the criminal: Who are you? When penal practice replaced the question: "What have you done?" with the question: "Who are you?" you see the jurisdictional function of the penal system being transformed, or doubled, or possibly undermined, by the question of veridiction.

In the same way, studying the genealogy of the object "sexuality" through a number of institutions meant trying to identify in things like confessional practices, spiritual direction, the medical relationship, and so on, the moment when the exchange and cross-over took place between a jurisdiction of sexual relations, defining the permitted and the prohibited, and the veridiction of desire, in which the basic armature of the object "sexuality" currently appears.

You can see that all these cases—whether it is the market, the confessional, the psychiatric institution, or the prison—involve taking up a history of truth under different angles, or rather, taking up a history of truth that is coupled, from the start, with a history of law. While the history of error linked to a history of prohibitions has been attempted fairly frequently, I would propose undertaking a history of truth coupled with a history of law. Obviously, a history of truth should not be understood in the sense of a reconstruction of the genesis of the true through the elimination or rectification of errors; nor a history of the true which would constitute a historical succession of rationalities established through the rectification or elimination of ideologies. Nor would this history of truth be the description of insular and autonomous systems of truth. It would involve the genealogy of regimes of veridiction, that is to say, the constitution of a particular right (*droit*) of truth on the basis of a legal situation, the law (*droit*) and truth relationship finding its privileged expression in discourse, the discourse in which law is formulated and in which what can be true or false is formulated; the regime of veridiction, in fact, is not a law (*loi*) of truth, [but] the set of rules enabling one to establish which statements in a given discourse can be described as true or false.

Undertaking the history of regimes of veridiction—and not the history of truth, the history of error, or the history of ideology, etcetera—obviously means abandoning once again that well-known critique of European rationality and its excesses, which has been constantly taken up in various forms since the beginning of the nineteenth century. From romanticism to the Frankfurt School,[9] what has always been called into question and challenged has been rationality with the weight of power supposedly peculiar to it. Now the critique* of knowledge I would propose does not in fact consist in denouncing what is continually—I was going to say monotonously—oppressive under reason, for after all, believe me, insanity (*déraison*) is just as oppressive. Nor would this political critique of knowledge consist in flushing out the presumption of power in every truth affirmed, for again, believe me, there is just as much abuse of power in the lie or error. The critique I propose consists in determining under what conditions and with what effects a veridiction is exercised, that is to say, once again, a type of formulation falling under particular rules of verification and falsification. For example, when I say that critique would consist in determining under what conditions and with what effects a veridiction is exercised, you can see that the problem would not consist in saying: Look how oppressive psychiatry is, because it is false. Nor would it consist in being a little more sophisticated and saying: Look how oppressive it is, because it is true. It would consist in saying that the problem is to bring to light the conditions that had to be met for it to be possible to hold a discourse on madness—but the same would hold for delinquency and for sex—that can be true or false according to the rules of medicine, say, or of confession, psychology, or psychoanalysis.

In other words, to have political significance, analysis does not have to focus on the genesis of truths or the memory of errors. What does it matter when a science began to tell the truth? Recalling all the erroneous things that doctors have been able to say about sex or madness does us a fat lot of good ... I think that what is currently politically important is to determine the regime of veridiction established at a given moment that is precisely the one on the basis of which you can now recognize, for example, that doctors in the nineteenth century said so many stupid things about sex. What is important is the determination of the regime of veridiction that enabled them to say and assert a number of things as truths that it turns out we now know were perhaps not true at all. This is the point, in fact, where historical analysis may have a political significance. It is not so much the history of the true or the history of the false as the history of veridiction which has a political

---

* The manuscript adds, p. 10bis: "political"

significance. That is what I wanted to say regarding the question of the market or, let's say, of the connecting up of a regime of truth to governmental practice.

Now let's consider the second question, the second point on which I would like to refine a little what I said to you last week. I said, you recall, that governmentality in the regime of pure *raison d'État*, or at least its tendency, was interminable, without an end. In a sense, governmentality was unlimited. This was precisely the main characteristic of what was called at the time police and which at the end of the eighteenth century will be called, already with a backward glance, the police state. The police state is a government that merges with administration, that is entirely administrative, and an administration which possesses, which has behind it, all the weight of a governmentality.

I have tried to show how this complete governmentality, this governmentality with a tendency to be unlimited, had in fact, not exactly a limit, but a counter-weight in the existence of judicial institutions and magistrates, and in juridical discourses focusing precisely on the problem of the nature of the sovereign's right to exercise his power and the legal limits within which the sovereign's action can be inserted. So, governmentality was not completely unbalanced and unlimited in *raison d'État*, but there was a system of two parts relatively external to each other.

I also pointed out that in the new system of governmental reason perfected in the eighteenth century, frugal government, or the reason of the least state, entailed something very different. This was a limitation on the one hand, and an internal limitation on the other. Nevertheless we should not think that the nature of this internal limitation is completely different from law. In spite of everything it is always a juridical limitation, the problem being precisely how to formulate this limitation in legal terms in the regime of this new, self-limiting governmental reason. As you can see, this is a different problem. In the old system of *raison d'État* there was a governmentality with its tendency to be unlimited on one side, and then a system of law opposing it from outside, but within concrete and well-known political limits: the contrast was between royal power [on one side], and those upholding the judicial institution on the other. In the new system we are dealing with a different problem: How can the necessary self-limitation of governmentality be formulated in law without government being paralyzed, and also—and this is the real problem—without stifling the site of truth which is exemplified by the market and which must be respected as such? In clear terms, the problem raised at the end of the eighteenth century is this: If there is political economy, what is its corresponding public law? Or again: What bases can be found for the law that will structure the exercise of power by public authorities when there is at least one region, but no doubt others too, where government non-intervention is absolutely necessary, not for legal, but for factual reasons, or rather, for reasons of truth? Limited by respect for the truth, how will power, how will government be able to formulate this respect for truth in terms of laws which must be respected?* After all, the fact that for a long time, until recently, faculties of law in France were also faculties of political economy—to the great discomfort of economists and jurists—is only the extension, no doubt excessive in historical terms, of an original fact, which was that you could not think of political economy, that is to say, the freedom of the market, without at the same time addressing the problem of public law, namely that of limiting the power of public authorities.

A number of precise and concrete things are proof of this moreover. After all, the first economists were at the same time jurists and people who addressed the problem of public law. Beccaria, for example, who was a theorist of public law, basically in the form of penal law, was also an economist.[10] You only have to read *The Wealth of Nations*, and not even his other works, to see that the problem of public law runs through all of Adam Smith's work.[11] Bentham, a public law theorist, was at the same time an economist and wrote books on political economy.[12] In addition to these facts, which show the original link between the problem of political economy and the problem of limiting the power of public authorities, there is ample proof in the problems raised during the nineteenth and twentieth centuries concerning economic legislation, the separation of government and administration, the constitution of

* Foucault adds: This coupling between political economy and public law, which now seems very bizarre to us ... *[unfinished sentence]*

administrative law, whether specific administrative courts are needed,[13] and so on. So, when I spoke last week of the self-limitation of governmental reason I was not referring to a disappearance of law, but to the problem raised by the juridical limitation of an exercise of political power which problems of truth were making it necessary to determine.

So, there is a shift of the center of gravity of public law. The fundamental problem of public law will no longer be the foundation of sovereignty, the conditions of the sovereign's legitimacy, or the conditions under which the sovereign's rights can be exercised legitimately, as it was in the seventeenth and eighteenth centuries. The problem becomes how to set juridical limits to the exercise of power by a public authority. Schematically, we can say that at the end of the eighteenth and the beginning of the nineteenth century there were basically two ways of resolving this. The first I will call the axiomatic, juridico-deductive approach, which was, up to a point, the path taken by the French Revolution—we could also call it Rousseau's approach.* In what does it consist? It does not start from government and its necessary limitation, but from law in its classical form. That is to say, it tries to define the natural or original rights that belong to every individual, and then to define under what conditions, for what reason, and according to what ideal or historical procedures a limitation or exchange of rights was accepted. It also consists in defining those rights one has agreed to cede and those, on the other hand, for which no cession has been agreed and which thus remain imprescriptible rights in all circumstances and under any possible government or political regime. Finally, on this basis, and only on this basis, having thus defined the division of rights, the sphere of sovereignty, and the limits of the right of sovereignty, you can then deduce from this only what we can call the bounds of governmental competence, but within the framework determined by the armature constituting sovereignty itself. In other words, put clearly and simply this approach consists in starting from the rights of man in order to arrive at the limitation of governmentality by way of the constitution of the sovereign. I would say that, broadly speaking, this is the revolutionary approach. It is a way of posing right from the start the problem of legitimacy and the

* In the manuscript, the other way is called (p. 15), "the inductive and residual way."

inalienability of rights through a sort of ideal or real renewal of society, the state, the sovereign, and government. Consequently, you can see that if, historically and politically, this is the revolutionaries' approach, we can call it a retroactive, or retroactionary approach inasmuch as it consists in taking up the problem of public law that the jurists had constantly opposed to the *raison d'État* of the seventeenth and eighteenth centuries. In this respect there is continuity between the seventeenth century theorists of natural law and the jurists and legislators of the French Revolution.

The other approach does not start from law but from governmental practice itself. It starts from government practice and tries to analyze it in terms of the de facto limits that can be set to this governmentality. These de facto limits may derive from history, from tradition, or from an historically determined state of affairs, but they can and must also be determined as desirable limits, as it were, as the good limits to be established precisely in terms of the objectives of governmentality, of the objects with which it has to deal, of the country's resources, population, and economy, etcetera. In short, this approach consists in the analysis of government: its practice, its de facto limits, and its desirable limits. On this basis, it distinguishes those things it would be either contradictory or absurd for government to tamper with. Better still, and more radically, it distinguishes those things that it would be pointless for government to interfere with. Following this approach means that government's sphere of competence will be defined on the basis of what it would or would not be useful for government to do or not do. Government's limit of competence will be bounded by the utility of governmental intervention. The question addressed to government at every moment of its action and with regard to each of its institutions, old or new, is: Is it useful? For what is it useful? Within what limits is it useful? When does it stop being useful? When does it become harmful? This is not the revolutionary question: What are my original rights and how can I assert them against any sovereign? But it is the radical question, the question of English radicalism; the problem of English radicalism is the problem of utility.

Don't think that English political radicalism is no more than the projection of a utilitarian ideology on the level of politics. It is, rather, an attempt to define the sphere of competence of government in terms of utility on the basis of an internal elaboration of governmental practice which is nevertheless fully thought through and always endowed and permeated with philosophical, theoretical, and juridical elements. In this respect utilitarianism appears as something very different from a philosophy or an ideology. Utilitarianism is a technology of government, just as public law was the form of reflection, or, if you like, the juridical technology with which one tried to limit the unlimited tendency of *raison d'État.*

A comment with regard to this word "radicalism" or "radical." The word "radical," which I think dates from the end of the seventeenth and the start of the eighteenth century, was employed in England to designate—and it is this that is quite interesting—the position of those who, faced with the sovereign's real or possible abuses, wanted to assert those famous original rights supposedly possessed by the Anglo-Saxons prior to the Norman invasion (I talked about this two or three years ago[14]). This is radicalism. So it consisted in the assertion of original rights in the sense of basic rights identified by the historical reflections of public law. However, for English radicalism, "radical" designates a position which involves continually questioning government, and governmentality in general, as to its utility or non-utility.

So, there are two approaches: the revolutionary approach, basically structured around traditional positions of public law, and the radical approach, basically structured around the new economy of government reason. These two approaches imply two conceptions of the law. In the revolutionary, axiomatic approach, the law will be seen as the expression of a will. So there will be a system of will-law. The problem of the will is, of course, at the heart of all the problems of right, which again confirms the fact that this is a fundamentally juridical problematic. The law is therefore conceived as the expression of a collective will indicating the part of right individuals have agreed to cede, and the part they wish to hold on to. In the other problematic, the radical utilitarian approach, the law is conceived as the effect of a transaction that separates the sphere of intervention of public authorities from that of the individual's independence. This leads us to another distinction which is also very important. On one side you have a juridical conception of freedom: every individual originally has in his possession a certain freedom, a part of which he will or will not cede. On the other side, freedom is not conceived as the exercise of some basic rights, but simply as the independence of the governed with regard to government. We have therefore two absolutely heterogeneous conceptions of freedom, one based on the rights of man, and the other starting from the independence of the governed. I am not saying that the two systems of the rights of man and of the independence of the governed do not intertwine, but they have different historical origins and I think they are essentially heterogeneous or disparate. With regard to the problem of what are currently called human rights, we would only need look at where, in what countries, how, and in what form these rights are claimed to see that at times the question is actually the juridical question of rights, and at others it is a question of this assertion or claim of the independence of the governed vis-à-vis governmentality.

So, we have two ways of constituting the regulation of public authorities by law, two conceptions of the law, and two conceptions of freedom. This ambiguity is a characteristic feature of, let's say, nineteenth and also twentieth century European liberalism. When I say two routes, two ways, two conceptions of freedom and of law, I do not mean two separate, distinct, incompatible, contradictory, and mutually exclusive systems, but two heterogeneous procedures, forms of coherence, and ways of doing things. We should keep in mind that heterogeneity is never a principle of exclusion; it never prevents coexistence, conjunction, or connection. And it is precisely in this case, in this kind of analysis, that we emphasize, and must emphasize a non-dialectical logic if want to avoid being simplistic. For what is dialectical logic? Dialectical logic puts to work contradictory terms within the homogeneous. I suggest replacing this dialectical logic with what I would call a strategic logic. A logic of strategy does not stress contradictory terms within a homogeneity that promises their resolution in a unity. The function of strategic logic is to establish the possible connections between disparate terms which remain disparate. The logic of strategy is the logic of connections between the heterogeneous and not the logic of the homogenization of the contradictory. So let's reject the logic of the dialectic and try to see—this is what I will try to show in these lectures—the connections which succeeded in holding together and conjoining the fundamental axiomatic of the rights of man and the utilitarian calculus of the independence of the governed.

I wanted to add something to this, but I think it would take too long; I will come back to it later.* I would like to return for a moment to what I said at the start with regard to the market—and it is a point to which I will come back later.[15] Still, just now, I would like to stress that between these two heterogeneous systems—that of the revolutionary axiomatic, of public law and the rights of man, and that of the empirical and utilitarian approach which defines the sphere of independence of the governed on the basis of the necessary limitation of government—there is, of course, a ceaseless connection and a whole series of bridges, transits, and joints. Consider the history of property rights, for example.† But it is quite clear (I will talk about this in the lectures) that of the two systems, one has been strong and has held out, while the other has receded. The one that has been strong and has stood fast is, of course, the radical approach which tried to define the juridical limitation of public authorities in terms of governmental utility. This tendency will characterize not only the history of European liberalism strictly speaking, but the history of the public authorities in the West. Consequently, this problem of utility—of individual and collective

---

* Foucault passes quickly over pages 18-20 of the manuscript:
"Obviously we would find many examples of this in the discourse of the American revolutionaries. And maybe revolutionary thought is precisely this: to think at the same time the utility of independence and the axiomatic of rights (American revolution).

[p. 18a] Contemporaries were perfectly aware of this heterogeneity. Bentham, Dumont, the Rights of Man. And it remained perceptible for two centuries, since it has proved impossible to find a genuine coherence and equilibrium between these procedures. Overwhelmingly, and not without some reversals, regulation of the public authorities in terms of utility prevails over the axiomatic of sovereignty in terms of original rights. Collective utility (rather than collective will) as general axis of the art of government.

[p. 19] General tendency, but which does not cancel the other. Especially since they produce similar, although undoubtedly not superimposable, effects. For the axiomatic of sovereignty is led to mark imprescriptible rights so strongly that it cannot in fact find any place for an art of government and the exercise of power by a public authority, unless the juridical constitution of the sovereign as the collective will is so strong that the exercise of basic rights are reduced to pure ideality. Totalitarian orientation. But the radicalism of utility, on the basis of the distinction individual utility/collective utility, will also be led to emphasize general utility over individual utility and infinitely reduce the independence of the governed as a consequence.

[p. 20] Orientation of indefinitely extended governmentality."

† Foucault adds: you will see it function very well in the two *[inaudible word]* and in a way *[inaudible word]*

utility, the utility of each and all, the utility of individuals and the general utility—will be the major criteria for working out the limits of the powers of public authorities and the formation of a form of public law and administrative law. Since the beginning of the nineteenth century we have been living in an age in which the problem of utility increasingly encompasses all the traditional problems of law.

So, on the basis of this I would like to make a remark. With regard to the market, we found that one of the points of anchorage of the new governmental reason was an understanding of the market as a mechanism of exchange and a site of veridiction regarding the relationship between value and price. Now we find a second point of anchorage of the new governmental reason. This is the elaboration of the powers of public authorities and the measure of their interventions by reference to the principle of utility. So, we have exchange on the side of the market, and utility on the side of the public authorities. Exchange value and spontaneous veridiction of economic processes, measures of utility and internal jurisdiction of acts of the public authorities. Exchange for wealth and utility for the public authorities: this is how governmental reason articulates the fundamental principle of its self-limitation. Exchange on one side and utility on the other: obviously, the general category covering both or for thinking both—that is, exchange which must be respected in the market since the market is veridiction, and utility to limit the power of the public authorities since it must only be exercised where it is positively and exactly useful—is, of course, interest, since interest is the principle of exchange and interest is the criterion of utility. Governmental reason in its modern form, in the form established at the beginning of the eighteenth century with the fundamental characteristic of a search for the principle of its self-limitation, is a reason that functions in terms of interest. But this is no longer the interest of an entirely self-referring state which only seeks its own growth, wealth, population, and power, as was the state of *raison d'État.* In the principle to which governmental reason must conform, interest is now interests, a complex interplay between individual and collective interests, between social utility and economic profit, between the equilibrium of the market and the regime of public authorities, between basic rights and the independence of the governed. Government, at any rate, government in this new governmental reason, is something that works with interests.

More precisely, we can say that it is through interests that government can get a hold on everything that exists for it in the form of individuals, actions, words, wealth, resources, property, rights, and so forth. We can put this more clearly, if you like, with a very simple question: On what did the sovereign, the monarch, the state have a hold in the previous system, and on what was its right to exercise this hold based, legitimized, and founded? It was things, lands. The king was often, not always, considered to be the owner of the realm, and it was as such that he could intervene. Or at any rate he owned an estate. He could exercise a hold over the subjects since, as subjects, they had a personal relation to the sovereign that meant that whatever the rights of the subjects themselves he could exercise a hold over everything. In other words, there was a direct hold of power in the form of the sovereign, in the form of his ministers, a direct hold of government over things and people.

On the basis of the new governmental reason—and this is the point of separation between the old and the new, between *raison d'État* and reason of the least state—government must no longer intervene, and it no longer has a direct hold on things and people; it can only exert a hold, it is only legitimate, founded in law and reason, to intervene, insofar as interest, or interests, the interplay of interests, make a particular individual, thing, good, wealth, or process of interest for individuals, or for the set of individuals, or for the interest of a given individual faced with the interest of all, etcetera. Government is only interested in interests. The new government, the new governmental reason, does not deal with what I would call the things in themselves of governmentality, such as individuals, things, wealth, and land. It no longer deals with these things in themselves. It deals with the phenomena of politics, that is to say, interests, which precisely constitute politics and its stakes; it deals with interests, or that respect in which a given individual, thing, wealth, and so on interests other individuals or the collective body of individuals.

I think we have a striking example of this in the penal system. I have tried to show how in the penal system of the seventeenth century, and still at the start of the eighteenth century, basically when the sovereign punished he intervened himself, and this was the true reason for the torture and execution (*la supplice*); he intervened individually so to speak, or anyway as the sovereign, but physically on the individual's body, and this gave him the right of public torture and execution: it was the manifestation of the sovereign himself over someone who had committed a crime and who, by committing a crime, had of course wronged some people, but above all had struck the sovereign in the very body of his power.[16] This was the site of the formation, justification, and even foundation of public torture and execution.

From the eighteenth century the well-known principle of mildness of punishment appears (you can see it very clearly in Beccaria[17]) which, once again, was not the expression of something like a change in people's sensibility. If you wanted to analyze it better than I have done, on what was this moderation of punishments based? Something is interposed between the crime, on the one hand, and the sovereign authority with the right to punish, possibly with death, on the other. This is the thin phenomenal theme of interests, which henceforth is the only thing on which governmental reason can have a hold. As a result, punishment appeared as having to be calculated in terms of the injured party's interests, in terms of redress for damages, etcetera. Punishment will be rooted only in the play of the interests of others, of the family circle, of society, and so on. Is it worthwhile punishing? What interest is there in punishing? What form must punishment take for it to be in society's interests to punish? Is there an interest in torturing, or is it more worthwhile to re-educate, and if so, how and up to what point? How much will it cost? The insertion of this thin phenomenal film of interest as the only sphere, or rather, as the only possible surface of government intervention, is what explains these changes, all of which must be referred back to this reorganization of governmental reason.

In its new regime, government is basically no longer to be exercised over subjects and other things subjected through these subjects. Government is now to be exercised over what we could call the phenomenal republic of interests. The fundamental question of liberalism is: What is the utility value of government and all actions of government in a society where exchange determines the true value of things?* I think

* Foucault adds: Utility value of government faced with a system in which exchange determines the true value of things. How is this possible?

this question encapsulates the fundamental questions raised by liberalism. With this question liberalism posed the fundamental question of government, which is whether all the political, economic, and other forms which have been contrasted with liberalism can really avoid this question and avoid formulating this question of the utility of a government in a regime where exchange determines the value of things.

---

1. In the "Course summary" Foucault refers to Benjamin Franklin (see below, p. 322). See, for example, the letter from Franklin to Charles de Weissenstein of 1 July 1778 in A.H. Smyth, ed., *The Writings of Benjamin Franklin* (New York: Macmillan, 1905-1907) vol. VII, p. 168, quoted in D.R. McCoy, "Benjamin Franklin's vision of a republican political economy for America," *The William and Mary Quarterly*, 3rd series, vol. 35 (4), October 1978, p. 617: "A virtuous and laborious people could always be 'cheaply governed' in a republican system."
2. The just price (*justum pretium*) was fixed as the ideal model of transactions by medieval scholasticism on the basis of the Aristotelian doctrine of commutative justice (*Nicomachean Ethics*, Book V). See S.L. Kaplan, *Bread, Politics and Political Economy in the Reign of Louis XV* (The Hague: Martinus Nijhoff, 1976), Volume One, pp. 58-59: "Lieutenants general of police, commissaires, inspectors, grain measurers and local officials repeatedly invoked the 'just price' which they construed as their obligation to assure ... The just price was a price which would neither 'disgust' merchants nor 'wound' consumers. It was predicated upon an ideal of moderation which tended to vary with the circumstances. A price was thought just when merchants settled for a moderate profit and the bulk of the people, who lived in a state of chronic misery, did not suffer immoderately, that is to say, more than they did usually. In untroubled moments the just price was simply the current price (as the theologians had recommended), fixed by common estimation rather than imposed by merchant maneuvers or governmental fiat." See J.W. Baldwin, *The Medieval Theories of the Just Price: Romanists, canonists and theologians in the twelfth and thirteenth centuries* (Philadelphia: American Philosophical Society, 1959); Joseph A. Schumpeter, *History of Economic Analysis*, edited from a manuscript by E. Boody Schumpeter (London and Boston: Allen & Unwin, 1982) pp. 60-61, and pp. 88-89. See the complementary bibliography given in S.L. Kaplan, *Bread, Politics and Political Economy*, p. 59, note 14. On the question of price, see *Les Mots et les Choses* (Paris: Gallimard, 1966) ch. 6, section 4; English translation by A. Sheridan, *The Order of Things. An Archeology of the Human Sciences* (London: Tavistock and New York: Pantheon, 1970) ch. 6, section 4: "The pledge and the price" (where the question of price is essentially treated in relation to the function of money).
3. Pierre Le Pesant, seigneur de Boisguilbert (1646-1714), the author notably of *Détail de la France* (1695) and the *Traité de la nature, culture, commerce et intérêt des grains* (1707). He is seen as being the precursor of the physiocrats. See Joseph A. Schumpeter, *History of Economic Analysis*, p. 215 note 1, and especially A. Sauvy, *Pierre de Boisguilbert, ou la Naissance de l'économie politique* (Paris: INED, 1966) 2 volumes. However, it seems that Boisguilbert does not use the concept of "natural price." He sometimes speaks of "price of proportion" (or "proportional" price) without a precise analytical content (buyers and sellers draw the same advantage) and "price *de rigueur*," with reference to (minimum acceptable) cost of production.
4. See, E. Depitre, introduction to Dupont de Nemours, *De l'exportation et de l'importation des grains* (1764), (Paris: P. Geuthner, 1911) pp. xxiii-xxiv: "In the physiocratic system nothing is easier to determine than the good price: it is *the common and hardly varying price of the general market*, the one *established by competition between freely trading nations*." See also, *Sécurité, Territoire, Population*, lecture of 5 April 1978, note 25; *Security, Territory, Population*, p. 361.
5. See A. Marshall, *Principles of Economics* (London: Macmillan and Co., 1890), and Joseph A. Schumpeter, *History of Economic Analysis*, p. 189 and p. 220.
6. On this new definition of the market as site of veridiction or of the truth of prices, see, for example, E. [Bonnot de] Condillac, *Le Commerce et le Gouvernement considérés relativement l'un à l'autre* (Amsterdam-Paris: Jombert & Cellot, 1776) Part 1, ch. 4: "Des marchés ou des lieux où se rendent ceux qui ont besoin de faire des échanges." See especially p. 23 of the 1795 edition (reprinted, Paris-Geneva: Slatkine, 1980): "[ ... ] prices can only be regulated in markets, because it is only there that the gathered citizens, by comparing their interests in exchanging, can judge the value of things relative to their needs. They can only do that there because it is only in markets that everything is put on view: it is only in markets that

one can judge the relationship of abundance and scarcity between things that determines their respective prices."

7. See *Sécurité, Territoire, Population*, lecture of 18 January 1978, p. 33 *sq*; *Security, Territory, Population*, p. 30 *sq*.
8. This expression had already been employed by Foucault in the lecture delivered in May 1978 at the Société française de philosophie, "Qu'est-ce que la critique?" *Bulletin de la Société française de philosophie*, 84th year, no. 2, April-June 1990, p. 51, with regard to the difference between genealogy and the procedures of explanatory history: "Let's say roughly that, in contrast with a genesis orientated towards the unity of an originating cause pregnant with a multiple descent, it would be a matter of a genealogy, that is to say something which tries to reconstruct the conditions of appearance of a singularity on the basis of multiple determining elements, from which it arises not as the product, but as the effect. Establishing intelligibility (*mise en intelligibilité*), therefore, but in which we should see that it does not function according to a principle of closure." Foucault had already dwelt on this problem of intelligibility in history in *Sécurité, Territoire, Population*, lecture 8 March 1978, p. 244; *Security, Territory, Population*, pp. 238-239. On the distinction between genesis and genealogy, see ibid., lecture of 8 February 1978, p. 121; pp. 116-117.
9. On Foucault's relationship with the Frankfurt School, see: "Qu'est-ce que la critique?" pp. 42-43; "'*Omnes et singulatim*': Toward a Critique of Political Reason" in *Essential Works of Foucault, 1954-1984, Vol. 3: Power*, ed. James D. Faubion (New York: The New Press, 2000) p. 299; French translation by P.E. Dauzat, "'Omnes et singulatim': vers une critique de la raison politique" in *Dits et Écrits*, 4, p. 135; "Space, Knowledge, and Power," *Essential Works, 3*, pp. 357-358; French translation by F. Durand-Bogaert, "Espace, savoir et pouvoir," *Dits et Écrits*, 4, p. 279; "Structuralisme et post-structuralisme," interview with G. Raulet, *Dits et Écrits*, 4, pp. 438-441; English translation by Jeremy Harding, amended, "Structuralism and Post-structuralism," *Essential Works of Foucault, 1954-1984, Vol 2: Aesthetics, Method, and Epistemology*, ed. James D. Faubion (New York: The New Press, 1998) pp. 440-443.
10. Author of the famous treatise *Dei delitti e delle pene* (*An Essay on Crimes and Punishments*) which was published in Livorno in 1764, Cesare Bonesana, marquis de Beccaria (1738-1794) in 1769 obtained the chair of cameral and economic sciences established shortly before at Milan (he renamed it the chair of political economy), which he left after two years for employment in the Milan administration. His lecture notes were published for the first time in 1804 by P. Custodi, with the title *Elementi di economia pubblica (Scrittori italiani di economia politica: Parte Moderna*, vol. XI and XII) (Milan: G.G. Destefanis, 1804). See also the *Discours de M. le Marqui Cesare Beccaria Bonesana. ... professeur royal de la chaire nouvellement établie par ordre de S.M. impériale pour le commerce et l'administration publique, prononcé à son installation dans les écoles Palatines*, trans. J.A. Comparet (Lausanne: F. Grasset, 1769) [translated from the original Italian edition, *Prolusione letta dal regio professore Marchese Cesare Beccaria Bonesana nell'apertura della nuova cattedra di scienze camerali ultimamente comendata da S.M.I.R.A.* (Florence: G. Allegrini e comp., 1769)] and, *Principes d'économie politique appliqués à l'agriculture par l'auteur du "Traité des délits et des peines"* (Paris: V[ve] Bouchard-Huzard, 1852). "The bulk of his economic writings consisted of those government reports" (Joseph A. Schumpeter, *History of Economic Analysis*, p. 179); Schumpeter describes Beccaria as the "Italian A. Smith," ibid. See, *Atti di governo* by Beccaria, being published in the projected seventeen volumes of the *Edizione nazionale* (five volumes so far published: vol. VI-X, 1987-2000). These writings address very diverse questions: money, mines, weights and measures, manufacture and commerce, fairs and markets, etcetera. I owe these clarifications to the recent thesis of Ph. Audegean, "Philosophie réformatrice, Cesare Beccaria et la critique des savoirs de son temps: droit, rhétorique, économie" (University of Paris 1-Sorbonne, 2003).
11. Adam Smith (1723-1790), *An Inquiry into the Nature and Causes of the Wealth of Nations* (London: W. Straham & T. Cadell, 1776), and more recently, (Oxford: Oxford University Press, 1976) in two volumes.
12. See, *Jeremy Bentham's Economic Writings* (see above, lecture of 10 January 1979, note 9), and T.W. Hutchison, "Bentham as an economist," *Economic Journal*, LXVI, 1956, pp. 288-306.

13. Foucault comes back to these points in the lecture of 21 February 1979 (see below, p. 167 *sq*).
14. See, *"Il faut défendre la société,"* lecture of 4 February 1976, p. 84 *sq*; *"Society Must be Defended,"* pp. 98 *sq*. The word "radicalism" is not employed by Foucault here. See the works of Christopher Hill, with which Foucault was very familiar (see A. Fontana and M. Bertani, "Situation du cours"; "Course context," ibid. p. 262; ibid. p. 290).
15. See below, lecture of 28 March 1979, p. 273 *sq*.
16. See *Surveiller et Punir. Naisssance de la prison* (Paris: Gallimard, 1975) pp. 51-58; English translation by Alan Sheridan, *Discipline and Punish. The Birth of the Prison* (London: Allen Lane, and New York: Pantheon, 1977) pp. 48-57. See also the 1972-1973 course, "La Société punitive," course summary in *Dits et Écrits*, 2, pp. 456-470; English translation by Robert Hurley, "The Punitive Society" in *The Essential Works of Michel Foucault 1954-1984, Vol. 1, Ethics: Subjectivity and Truth*, ed. Paul Rabinow (New York: The New Press, 1997) pp. 23-37.
17. French translation by M. Chevallier, *Des délits et des peines* (Geneva: Droz, 1965) § XII, p. 24: "But des châtiments"; English translation, *An Essay on Crimes and Punishments* (Edinburgh: Bell and Bradfute, 1807), ch. XII, "Of the Intent of Punishments," pp. 41-42. See, *Surveiller et Punir*, pp. 106-134, "La douceur des peines"; *Discipline and Punish*, "The gentle way in punishment" pp. 104-131.

# three

## 24 January 1979

*Specific features of the liberal art of government (II): (3) The problem of European balance and international relations. ~ Economic and political calculation in mercantilism. The principle of the freedom of the market according to the physiocrats and Adam Smith: birth of a new European model. ~ Appearance of a governmental rationality extended to a world scale. Examples: the question of maritime law; the projects of perpetual peace in the eighteenth century. ~ Principles of the new liberal art of government: a "governmental naturalism"; the production of freedom. ~ The problem of liberal arbitration. Its instruments: (1) the management of dangers and the implementation of mechanisms of security; (2) disciplinary controls (Bentham's panopticism); (3) interventionist policies. ~ The management of liberty and its crises.*

LAST WEEK I TRIED to clarify what seem to me to be some of the basic characteristics of the liberal art of government. First of all I spoke about the problem of economic truth and of the truth of the market, and then of the problem of the limitation of governmentality by the calculus of utility. I would now like to deal with a third aspect which I think is also fundamental, that of international equilibriums, or Europe and the international space in liberalism.

You remember that when last year we talked about *raison d'État*,[1] I tried to show you that there was a kind of equilibrium, a system of counterweights between what could be called unlimited objectives within the state, on the one hand, and limited external objectives, on the other. The unlimited objectives within the state were pursued through the mechanism of the police state, that is to say, an always more emphatic, accentuated, fine, and subtle governmentality of regimentation with no predetermined limits. So, internally there were unlimited objectives, and then limited objectives externally inasmuch as at the same time as the formation of *raison d'État* and the organization of the police state was taking place there was also the pursuit and real organization of what is called European balance, the principle of which is the following: to see to it that no state prevails over the others so as to reconstitute imperial unity in Europe; to see to it, consequently, that no state dominates all the others, or prevails over its neighbors to such an extent that it can dominate them, etcetera. It is quite easy to see and understand the connection between these two mechanisms of unlimited objectives with the police state, and limited objectives with European balance, inasmuch as if the raison d'être, purpose, and objective of the police state, or of the internal mechanisms which endlessly organize and develop the police state, is the strengthening of the state itself, then the target of each state is to strengthen itself endlessly, that is to say its aim is an unlimited increase of its power in relation to the others. In clear terms, competition to be the best in this competitive game will introduce into Europe a number of inequalities, which will increase, which will be sanctioned by an imbalance in the population, and consequently in military strength, and you will end up with the well-known imperial situation from which European balance, since the Treaty of Westphalia, wished to free Europe. The balance was established to avoid this situation.

More precisely, in mercantilist calculation and in the way in which mercantilism organizes the economic-political calculation of forces, it is clear that a European equilibrium is actually unavoidable if you want to prevent the realization of a new imperial configuration. For mercantilism, competition between states assumes that everything by which one state is enriched can, and in truth must, be deducted from the wealth of other states. What one state acquires must be taken from the other; one can only enrich itself at the cost of the others. In other words, what I think is important is that for the mercantilists the economic game is a zero sum game. It is a zero sum game quite simply because of the monetarist conception and practice of mercantilism. There is a certain amount of gold in the world. Since gold defines, measures, and constitutes the wealth of each state, it is understood that whenever one state gets richer it will take from the common stock of gold and consequently impoverish the others. The monetarist character of mercantilist policy and calculation consequently entails that competition can only be conceived in the form of a zero sum game and so of the enrichment of some at the expense of others.[2] To avoid the phenomenon of having one and only one winner in this zero sum game, to avoid this political consequence of competition thus defined, strict economic logic requires the establishment of something like an equilibrium which will allow the game to be interrupted, as it were, at a given moment. That is to say, the game will be halted when there is a danger of the difference between the players becoming too great, and it is precisely in this that European equilibrium consists. This is exactly—well, up to a point—Pascal's problem:[3] in a zero sum game, what happens when you interrupt the game and divide out the winnings between the players? Interrupting the game of competition with the diplomacy of European equilibrium is necessarily entailed by the monetarist conception and practice of the mercantilists. This is the starting point.

Now, what happens in the middle of the eighteenth century, in that period I have talked about and tried to locate the formation of a new governmental reason? Things will, of course, be completely different in this new *raison d'État*, or in this new reason of the least state which finds the core of its veridiction in the market and its de facto jurisdiction in utility. In fact, for the physiocrats, but also for Adam Smith, the freedom of the market can and must function in such a way that what they call the natural price or the good price will be established through and thanks to this freedom. Anyway, this natural price or good price is such that it must always be profitable to whom? It will be profitable to the seller, but also to the buyer; to both buyer and seller. That is to say, the beneficial effects of competition will not be divided unequally between them and necessarily to the advantage of one at the expense of the other. The legitimate game of natural competition, that is to say, competition under conditions of freedom, can only lead to a dual profit. The fluctuation of the price around the value, which last week I showed that according to the physiocrats and Adam Smith was assured by the freedom of the market, brings into play a mechanism of mutual enrichment: maximum profit for the seller, minimum expense for the buyers. So we find this idea, which will be at the center of the economic game as defined by the liberals, that actually the enrichment of one country, like the enrichment of one individual, can only really be established and maintained in the long term by a mutual enrichment. My neighbor's wealth is important for my own enrichment, and not in the sense that the mercantilists said my neighbor must possess gold in order to buy my products, which will enable me to impoverish him by enriching myself. My neighbor must be rich, and he will be rich to the same extent as I enrich myself through my commerce and our mutual commerce. Consequently there is a correlative enrichment, an enrichment en bloc, a regional enrichment: either the whole of Europe will be rich, or the whole of Europe will be poor. There is no longer any cake to be divided up. We enter an age of an economic historicity governed by, if not unlimited enrichment, then at least reciprocal enrichment through the game of competition.

I think something very important begins to take shape here, the consequences of which are, as you know, far from being exhausted. What is taking shape is a new idea of Europe that is not at all the imperial and Carolingian Europe more or less inherited from the Roman Empire and referring to quite specific political structures. Nor is it any longer the classical Europe of balance, of an equilibrium between forces established in such a way that the force of one never prevails too decisively over the other. It is a Europe of collective enrichment; Europe as a collective subject that, whatever the competition between states, or rather through the competition between states, has to advance in the form of unlimited economic progress.

This idea of progress, of a European progress, is a fundamental theme in liberalism and completely overturns the themes of European equilibrium, even though these themes do not disappear completely. With this conception of the physiocrats and Adam Smith we leave behind a conception of the economic game as a zero sum game. But if it is no longer to be a zero sum game, then permanent and continuous inputs are still necessary. In other words, if freedom of the market must ensure the reciprocal, correlative, and more or less simultaneous enrichment of all the countries of Europe, for this to function, and for freedom of the market to thus unfold according to a game that is not a zero sum game, then it is necessary to summon around Europe, and for Europe, an increasingly extended market and even, if it comes to it, everything in the world that can be put on the market. In other words, we are invited to a globalization of the market when it is laid down as a principle, and an objective, that the enrichment of Europe must be brought about as a collective and unlimited enrichment, and not through the enrichment of some and the impoverishment of others. The unlimited character of the economic development of Europe, and the consequent existence of a non-zero sum game, entails, of course, that the whole world is summoned around Europe to exchange its own and Europe's products in the European market.

Of course, I do not mean that this is the first time that Europe thinks about the world, or thinks the world. I mean simply that this may be the first time that Europe appears as an economic unit, as an economic subject in the world, or considers the world as able to be and having to be its economic domain. It seems to me that it is the first time that Europe appears in its own eyes as having to have the world for its unlimited market. Europe is no longer merely covetous of all the world's riches that sparkle in its dreams or perceptions. Europe is now in a state of permanent and collective enrichment through its own competition, on condition that the entire world becomes its market. In short, in the time of mercantilism, *raison d'État*, and the police state, etcetera, the calculation of a European balance enabled one to block the consequences of an economic game conceived as being over.* Now, the opening up of a world market allows one to continue the economic game and consequently to avoid the conflicts which derive from a finite market. But this opening of the economic game onto the world clearly implies a difference of both kind and status between Europe and the rest of the world. That is to say, there will be Europe on one side, with Europeans as the

* The manuscript adds, p. 5: "by halting the game when the losses and gains of the different players diverge too much from the situation at the start of the game (Pascal's problem of the interruption of the game)."

players, and then the world on the other, which will be the stake. The game is in Europe, but the stake is the world.

It seems to me that we have in this one of the fundamental features of this new art of government that is indexed to the problem of the market and market veridiction. Obviously, this organization, or at any rate this reflection on the reciprocal positions of Europe and the world, is not the start of colonization. Colonization had long been underway. Nor do I think this is the start of imperialism in the modern or contemporary sense of the term, for we probably see the formation of this new imperialism later in the nineteenth century. But let's say that we have the start of a new type of global calculation in European governmental practice. I think there are many signs of this appearance of a new form of global rationality, of a new calculation on the scale of the world. I will refer to just some of these.

Take, for example, the history of maritime law in the eighteenth century, and the way in which, in terms of international law, there was an attempt to think of the world, or at least the sea, as a space of free competition, of free maritime circulation, and consequently as one of the necessary conditions for the organization of a world market. The history of piracy—the way in which it was at once used, encouraged, combated, and suppressed, etcetera—could also figure as one of the aspects of this elaboration of a worldwide space in terms of a number of legal principles. We can say that there was a juridification of the world which should be thought of in terms of the organization of a market.

Yet another example of this appearance of a governmental rationality that has the entire planet for its horizon is the eighteenth century projects for peace and international organization. If you consider those that existed in the seventeenth century, you will see that these projects for peace were essentially based on European equilibrium, that is to say, on the exact balance of reciprocal forces between different states; between the different powerful states, or between different coalitions of states, or between the powerful states and a coalition of the smaller states, and so on. From the eighteenth century, the idea of perpetual peace and the idea of international organization are, I think, articulated completely differently. It is no longer so much the limitation of internal forces that is called upon to guarantee and found a perpetual peace, but rather the unlimited nature of the external market. The larger the external market, the fewer its borders and limits, the more you will have a guarantee of perpetual peace.

If you take Kant's text on the project of perpetual peace, for example, which dates from 1795,[4] right at the end of the eighteenth century, there is a chapter entitled "On the Guarantee of a Perpetual Peace."[5] How does Kant conceive of this perpetual peace? He says: What fundamentally is it in history that guarantees this perpetual peace and promises us that one day it really will take shape and form in history? Is it men's will and their mutual understanding, the political and diplomatic devices that they will have been able to construct, or the organization of rights that they will have been able to install between them? Not at all. It is nature,[6] just as in the physiocrats it was nature that guaranteed the good regulation of the market. And how does nature guarantee perpetual peace? It is very simple, Kant says. Nature after all has done some absolutely marvelous things, since it has managed, for example, to get not only animals, but even peoples to live in lands completely scorched by the Sun or frozen by eternal sheets of ice.[7] There are people who manage to live there in spite of everything, which proves that there is nowhere in the world where human beings cannot live.[8] But for people to be able to live they must be able to feed themselves, to produce their food, have a social organization, and exchange their products between themselves or with people from other regions. Nature intended the entire world, the whole of its surface, to be given over to the economic activity of production and exchange. And on that basis, nature has prescribed a number of obligations that are juridical obligations for man,[9] but which nature has in a way dictated to him secretly, which she has, as it were, marked out in the very arrangement of things, of geography, the climate, and so on. What are these arrangements?

First, that men can have relations of exchange with each other individually, supported by property, etcetera, and this prescription or precept of nature will be taken up in legal obligations and become civil law.[10]

Second, nature determined that men be distributed across the world in distinct regions and that within each of these regions they have privileged relationships with each other that they do not have with the inhabitants of other regions, and men have taken up this precept in legal terms by forming separate states which maintain certain legal relationships between them. This will become international law.[11] But in addition, nature has wished that there are not only juridical relationships between these states, guaranteeing their independence, but also commercial relationships that cross the borders between states and consequently make the juridical independence of each state porous, as it were.[12] Commercial relationships cross the world, just as nature intended and to the same extent as nature intended the whole world to be populated, and this will constitute cosmopolitan law or commercial law. This edifice of civil law, international law, and cosmopolitan law is nothing other than man's taking up of a precept of nature as obligations.[13] So we can say that law, inasmuch as it resumes the precept of nature, will be able to promise what was in a way already outlined in the first action of nature when it populated the entire world:* something like perpetual peace. Perpetual peace is guaranteed by nature and this guarantee is manifested in the population of the entire world and in the commercial relationships stretching across the whole world. The guarantee of perpetual peace is therefore actually commercial globalization.

A number of things should no doubt be added to this, but in any case I should answer an objection straightaway. When I say that a new form of political calculation on an international scale emerges in the thought of the physiocrats, Adam Smith, of Kant too, and of eighteenth century jurists, I do not in any way mean that every other form of reflection, calculation, and analysis, that every other governmental practice disappears. For, if it is true that something like a worldwide, global market is discovered in this period, if at this moment the privileged position of Europe in relation to the world is asserted, and if it is also asserted at this time that competition between European states is a factor in their common enrichment, this does not mean of course—as all history proves—that we enter into a period of European peace and the peaceful globalization of politics. In fact, with the nineteenth century we enter the worst period of customs barriers, forms of economic protectionism, of national economies and political nationalism, and the biggest wars the world has ever known. What I wanted to show you was simply that a

* Foucault adds: it promises already

particular form of reflection, analysis, and calculation appeared at this time which is integrated as it were into political practices that may perfectly well conform to a different type of calculation, a different system of thought, and a different practice of power. We would only have to look at what happened at the Congress of Vienna, for example.[14] It could be said that this is the most striking manifestation of what was sought after in the seventeenth and eighteenth centuries, namely a European balance. What were its concerns in fact? Its task was to put an end to what appeared to be the resurrection of the imperial idea with Napoleon. Because the historical paradox of Napoleon is that if, at the level of internal policy, he was manifestly hostile to the idea of a police state, and his problem was really how to limit governmental practice internally[15]—and this is clear from his interventions in the Council of State and the way in which he reflected on his own governmental practice[16]—on the other hand, we can say that Napoleon was completely archaic in his external policy, inasmuch as he wanted to reconstitute something like the imperial configuration against which the whole of Europe had been ranked since the seventeenth century. In truth, Napoleon's imperial idea, so far as it can be reconstructed, in spite of the astounding silence of historians on this theme, seems to have corresponded to three objectives.

First (and I think I talked about this last year),[17] if we go by what the historians and jurists of the eighteenth century said about the Carolingian Empire,[18] in terms of internal policy, the Empire guaranteed freedoms. In its opposition to the monarchy, the Empire did not represent more power but rather less power and less governmentality. On the other hand—and probably on the basis of the limitlessness of the revolutionary objectives, that is to say, to revolutionize the whole world—the Empire was a way of taking up the revolutionary project that irrupted in France in 1792-1793, and of taking it up in the then archaic idea of imperial domination inherited from Carolingian forms or from the form of the Holy Roman Empire. This mixture of the idea of an Empire which internally guarantees freedoms, of an Empire which will give a European form to the unlimited revolutionary project, and finally of an Empire which will reconstitute the Carolingian, or German, or Austrian form of Empire, made up the hotchpotch of Napoleon's imperial politics.

The problem of the Congress of Vienna was, of course, to close off, as it were, that imperial limitlessness. It was, of course, to re-establish the equilibrium of Europe, but basically with two different objectives: the Austrian objective and the English objective. The Austrian objective was to reconstitute a European equilibrium in the old form of the seventeenth and eighteenth centuries, ensuring that no country can prevail over the others in Europe. Austria was absolutely tied to this kind of project inasmuch as it only had an administrative government, being made up of a number of different states and only organizing these in the form of the old police state. This plurality of police states at the heart of Europe meant that Europe itself was basically modeled on this old schema of a balanced multiplicity of police states. Europe had to be in the image of Austria for Austria to remain as it was. To that extent, we can say that, for Metternich,[19] the calculation of European equilibrium was still and remained that of the eighteenth century. On the other hand, what kind of equilibrium was sought by England* and imposed together with Austria at the Congress of Vienna? It was a way of regionalizing Europe, of limiting, of course, the power of each of the European states, but so as to allow England a political and economic role as economic mediator between Europe and the world market, so as to globalize the European economy through the mediation, the relay of England's economic power. So we have here a completely different calculation of European equilibrium founded on the principle of Europe as a particular economic region faced with, or within, a world that must become its market. The calculation of European equilibrium for [Austria]† at the Congress of Vienna is completely different. So you can see that within a single historical reality you may very well find two entirely different types of rationality and political calculation.

I will stop these speculations here and before moving on to the analysis of present day liberalism in Germany and America, I would like to summarize a little what I have said about these fundamental features of liberalism, or at any rate of an art of government which emerges in the eighteenth century.

---

* The manuscript clarifies, p. 10: "Castelreagh" [Henry Robert Stewart Castelreagh (1762-1822), Tory foreign secretary from 1812 to 1822, who played an important role at Vienna checking the ambitions of Russia and Prussia].

† M.F.: England

So, I have tried to indicate three features: veridiction of the market, limitation by the calculation of governmental utility, and now the position of Europe as a region of unlimited economic development in relation to a world market. This is what I have called liberalism.

Why speak of liberalism, and why speak of a liberal art of government, when it is quite clear that the things I have referred to and the features I have tried to indicate basically point to a much more general phenomenon than the pure and simple economic doctrine, or the pure and simple political doctrine, or the pure and simple economic-political choice of liberalism in the strict sense? If we take things up a bit further back, if we take them up at their origin, you can see that what characterizes this new art of government I have spoken about would be much more a naturalism than liberalism, inasmuch as the freedom that the physiocrats and Adam Smith talk about is much more the spontaneity, the internal and intrinsic mechanics of economic processes than a juridical freedom of the individual recognized as such. Even in Kant, who is much more a jurist than an economist, you have seen that perpetual peace is not guaranteed by law, but by nature. In actual fact, it is something like a governmental naturalism which emerges in the middle of the eighteenth century. And yet I think we can speak of liberalism. I could also tell you—but I will come back to this[20]—that this naturalism, which I think is fundamental or at any rate original in this art of government, appears very clearly in the physiocratic conception of enlightened despotism. I will come back to this at greater length, but, in a few words, what conclusions do the physiocrats draw from their discovery of the existence of spontaneous mechanisms of the economy which must be respected by every government if it does not want to induce effects counter to or even the opposite of its objectives? Is it that people must be given the freedom to act as they wish? Is it that governments must recognize the essential, basic natural rights of individuals? Is it that government must be as little authoritarian as possible? It is none of these things. What the physiocrats deduce from their discovery is that the government must know these mechanisms in their innermost and complex nature. Once it knows these mechanisms, it must, of course, undertake to respect them. But this does not mean that it provide itself with a juridical framework respecting individual freedoms and the basic rights of individuals. It means, simply, that it arm its politics with a precise, continuous, clear and distinct knowledge of what is taking place in society, in the market, and in the economic circuits, so that the limitation of its power is not given by respect for the freedom of individuals, but simply by the evidence of economic analysis which it knows has to be respected.[21] It is limited by evidence, not by the freedom of individuals.

So, what we see appearing in the middle of the eighteenth century really is a naturalism much more than a liberalism. Nevertheless, I think we can employ the word liberalism inasmuch as freedom really is at the heart of this practice or of the problems it confronts. Actually, I think we should be clear that when we speak of liberalism with regard to this new art of government, this does not mean* that we are passing from an authoritarian government in the seventeenth century and at the start of the eighteenth century to a government which becomes more tolerant, more lax, and more flexible. I do not want to say that this is not the case, but neither do I want to say that it is. It does not seem to me that a proposition like that has much historical or political meaning. I did not want to say that there was a quantitative increase of freedom between the start of the eighteenth century and, let's say, the nineteenth century. I have not said this for two reasons. One is factual and the other is a reason of method and principle.

The factual reason first of all. What sense is there in saying, or simply wondering, if an administrative monarchy like that of France in the seventeenth and eighteenth centuries, with all its big, heavy, unwieldy, and inflexible machinery, with its statutory privileges which had to be recognized, with the arbitrariness of decisions left to different people, and with all the shortcomings of its instruments, allowed more or less freedom than a regime which is liberal, let's say, but which takes on the task of continuously and effectively taking charge of individuals and their well-being, health, and work, their way of being, behaving, and even dying, etcetera? So, comparing the quantity of freedom between one system and another does not in fact have much sense. And we do not see

---

* Foucault adds: we should not understand

what type of demonstration, what type of gauge or measure we could apply.

This leads us to the second reason, which seems to me to be more fundamental. This is that we should not think of freedom as a universal which is gradually realized over time, or which undergoes quantitative variations, greater or lesser drastic reductions, or more or less important periods of eclipse. It is not a universal which is particularized in time and geography. Freedom is not a white surface with more or less numerous black spaces here and there and from time to time. Freedom is never anything other—but this is already a great deal—than an actual relation between governors and governed, a relation in which the measure of the "too little"* existing freedom is given by the "even more"† freedom demanded. So when I say "liberal"‡ I am not pointing to a form of governmentality which would leave more white spaces of freedom. I mean something else.

If I employ the world "liberal," it is first of all because this governmental practice in the process of establishing itself is not satisfied with respecting this or that freedom, with guaranteeing this or that freedom. More profoundly, it is a consumer of freedom. It is a consumer of freedom inasmuch as it can only function insofar as a number of freedoms actually exist: freedom of the market, freedom to buy and sell, the free exercise of property rights, freedom of discussion, possible freedom of expression, and so on. The new governmental reason needs freedom therefore, the new art of government consumes freedom. It consumes freedom, which means that it must produce it. It must produce it, it must organize it. The new art of government therefore appears as the management of freedom, not in the sense of the imperative: "be free," with the immediate contradiction that this imperative may contain. The formula of liberalism is not "be free." Liberalism formulates simply the following: I am going to produce what you need to be free. I am going to see to it that you are free to be free. And so, if this liberalism is not so much the imperative of freedom as the management and organization of

---

* In inverted commas in the manuscript, p. 13.

† In inverted commas in the manuscript, p. 13.

‡ In inverted commas in the manuscript, p. 13.

the conditions in which one can be free, it is clear that at the heart of this liberal practice is an always different and mobile problematic relationship between the production of freedom and that which in the production of freedom risks limiting and destroying it. Liberalism as I understand it, the liberalism we can describe as the art of government formed in the eighteenth century, entails at its heart a productive/destructive relationship [with]* freedom [ ... ].† Liberalism must produce freedom, but this very act entails the establishment of limitations, controls, forms of coercion, and obligations relying on threats, etcetera.

Clearly, we have examples of this. There must be free trade, of course, but how can we practice free trade in fact if we do not control and limit a number of things, and if we do not organize a series of preventive measures to avoid the effects of one country's hegemony over others, which would be precisely the limitation and restriction of free trade? All the European countries and the United States encounter this paradox from the start of the nineteenth century when, convinced by the economists of the end of the eighteenth century, those in power who want to establish the order of commercial freedom come up against British hegemony. American governments, for example, who used this problem of free trade as a reason for revolt against England, established protectionist tariffs from the start of the nineteenth century in order to save a free trade that would be compromised by English hegemony. Similarly, there must be freedom of the internal market, of course, but again, for there to be a market there must be buyers as well as sellers. Consequently, if necessary, the market must be supported and buyers created by mechanisms of assistance. For freedom of the internal market to exist, the effects of monopolies must be prevented, and so anti-monopoly legislation is needed. There must be a free labor market, but again there must be a large enough number of sufficiently competent, qualified, and politically disarmed workers to prevent them exerting pressure on the labor market. We have then the conditions for the creation for a formidable body

---

* Manuscript. M.F.: in relation to

† An inaudible passage on the recording; [ ... ] a relation [ ... ] of consumption/annulment of freedom.

of legislation and an incredible range of governmental interventions to guarantee production of the freedom needed in order to govern.

Broadly speaking, in the liberal regime, in the liberal art of government, freedom of behavior is entailed, called for, needed, and serves as a regulator, but it also has to be produced and organized. So, freedom in the regime of liberalism is not a given, it is not a ready-made region which has to be respected, or if it is, it is so only partially, regionally, in this or that case, etcetera. Freedom is something which is constantly produced. Liberalism is not acceptance of freedom; it proposes to manufacture it constantly, to arouse it and produce it, with, of course, [the system]* of constraints and the problems of cost raised by this production.

What, then, will be the principle of calculation for this cost of manufacturing freedom? The principle of calculation is what is called security. That is to say, liberalism, the liberal art of government, is forced to determine the precise extent to which and up to what point individual interest, that is to say, individual interests insofar as they are different and possibly opposed to each other, constitute a danger for the interest of all. The problem of security is the protection of the collective interest against individual interests. Conversely, individual interests have to be protected against everything that could be seen as an encroachment of the collective interest. Again, the freedom of economic processes must not be a danger, either for enterprises or for workers. The freedom of the workers must not become a danger for the enterprise and production. Individual accidents and events in an individual's life, such as illness or inevitable old age, must not be a danger either for individuals or for society. In short, strategies of security, which are, in a way, both liberalism's other face and its very condition, must correspond to all these imperatives concerning the need to ensure that the mechanism of interests does not give rise to individual or collective dangers. The game of freedom and security is at the very heart of this new governmental reason whose general characteristics I have tried to describe. The problems of what I shall call the economy of power peculiar to liberalism are internally sustained, as it were, by this interplay of freedom and security.

---

* Conjecture: inaudible words

Broadly speaking, in the old political system of sovereignty there was a set of legal and economic relations between the sovereign and the subject which committed, and even obliged the sovereign to protect the subject. But this protection was, in a way, external. The subject could demand the protection of his sovereign against an external or internal enemy. It is completely different in the case of liberalism. It is no longer just that kind of external protection of the individual himself which must be assured. Liberalism turns into a mechanism continually having to arbitrate between the freedom and security of individuals by reference to this notion of danger. Basically, if on one side—and this is what I said last week—liberalism is an art of government that fundamentally deals with interests, it cannot do this—and this is the other side of the coin—without at the same time managing the dangers and mechanisms of security/freedom, the interplay of security/freedom which must ensure that individuals or the community have the least exposure to danger.

A number of consequences follow from this. First, we can say that the motto of liberalism is: "Live dangerously." "Live dangerously," that is to say, individuals are constantly exposed to danger, or rather, they are conditioned to experience their situation, their life, their present, and their future as containing danger. I think this kind of stimulus of danger will be one of the major implications of liberalism. An entire education and culture of danger appears in the nineteenth century which is very different from those great apocalyptic threats of plague, death, and war which fed the political and cosmological imagination of the Middle Ages, and even of the seventeenth century. The horsemen of the Apocalypse disappear and in their place everyday dangers appear, emerge, and spread everywhere, perpetually being brought to life, reactualized, and circulated by what could be called the political culture of danger in the nineteenth century. This political culture of danger has a number of aspects. For example, there is the campaign for savings banks at the start of the nineteenth century;[22] you see the appearance of detective fiction and journalistic interest in crime around the middle of the nineteenth century; there are the campaigns around disease and hygiene; and then think too of what took place with regard to sexuality and the fear of degeneration:[23] degeneration of the individual, the family, the race, and the human species. In short, everywhere you see this stimulation of the fear of danger which is, as it were, the condition, the internal psychological and cultural correlative of liberalism. There is no liberalism without a culture of danger.

The second consequence of this liberalism and liberal art of government is the considerable extension of procedures of control, constraint, and coercion which are something like the counterpart and counterweights of different freedoms. I have drawn attention to the fact that the development, dramatic rise, and dissemination throughout society of these famous disciplinary techniques for taking charge of the behavior of individuals day by day and in its fine detail is exactly contemporaneous with the age of freedoms.[24] Economic freedom, liberalism in the sense I have just been talking about, and disciplinary techniques are completely bound up with each other. At the beginning of his career, or around 1792-1795, Bentham presented the famous Panopticon as a procedure for institutions like schools, factories, and prisons which would enable one to supervise the conduct of individuals while increasing the profitability and productivity of their activity.[25] At the end of his life, in his project of the general codification of English legislation,[26] Bentham will propose that the Panopticon should be the formula for the whole of government, saying that the Panopticon is the very formula of liberal government.[27] What basically must a government do? It must give way to everything due to natural mechanisms in both behavior and production. It must give way to these mechanisms and make no other intervention, to start with at least, than that of supervision. Government, initially limited to the function of supervision, is only to intervene when it sees that something is not happening according to the general mechanics of behavior, exchange, and economic life. Panopticism is not a regional mechanics limited to certain institutions; for Bentham, panopticism really is a general political formula that characterizes a type of government.

The third consequence (the second being the conjunction between the disciplines and liberalism), is the appearance in this new art of government of mechanisms with the function of producing, breathing life into, and increasing freedom, of introducing additional freedom through additional control and intervention. That is to say, control is no longer just the necessary counterweight to freedom, as in the case of panopticism: it becomes its mainspring. And here again we have examples of this, such as what took place in England and the United States in the twentieth century, in the 1930s say, when not only the economic but also the political consequences of the developing economic crisis were immediately detected and seen to represent a danger to a number of what were thought to be basic freedoms. Roosevelt's welfare policy, for example, starting from 1932,[28] was a way of guaranteeing and producing more freedom in a dangerous situation of unemployment: freedom to work, freedom of consumption, political freedom, and so on. What was the price of this? The price was precisely a series of artificial, voluntarist interventions, of direct economic interventions in the market represented by the basic Welfare measures, and which from 1946, and even from the start moreover, were described as being in themselves threats of a new despotism. In this case democratic freedoms are only guaranteed by an economic interventionism which is denounced as a threat to freedom. So we arrive, if you like—and this is also an important point to keep hold of—at the idea that in the end this liberal art of government introduces by itself or is the victim from within [of]* what could be called crises of governmentality. These are crises which may be due, for example, to the increase in the economic cost of the exercise of these freedoms. Consider, for example, how, in the texts of the [Trilateral][29] in recent years, there has been an attempt to project the effects of political freedom on the economic level of cost. So there is a problem, or crisis, if you like, or a consciousness of crisis, based on the definition of the economic cost of the exercise of freedom.

Another form of crisis would be due to the inflation of the compensatory mechanisms of freedom. That is to say, for the exercise of some freedoms, like that of the freedom of the market and anti-monopoly legislation, for example, you could have the formation of a legislative straitjacket which the market partners experience as excessive interventionism and excessive constraint and coercion. At a much more local level, you have everything which takes on the appearance of revolt and rejection of the world of the disciplines. Finally, and above all, there are processes of clogging such that the mechanisms for producing freedom, precisely

---

* M.F.: by

those that are called upon to manufacture this freedom, actually produce destructive effects which prevail over the very freedom they are supposed to produce. This is, if you like, the ambiguity of all the devices which could be called "liberogenic,"* that is to say, devices intended to produce freedom which potentially risk producing exactly the opposite.

This is precisely the present crisis of liberalism. All of those mechanisms which since the years from 1925 to 1930 have tried to offer economic and political formulae to secure states against communism, socialism, National Socialism, and fascism, all these mechanisms and guarantees of freedom which have been implemented in order to produce this additional freedom or, at any rate, to react to threats to this freedom, have taken the form of economic interventions, that is to say, shackling economic practice, or anyway, of coercive interventions in the domain of economic practice. Whether German liberals of the Freiburg School from 1927 to 1930,[30] or present day, so-called libertarian American liberals,[31] in both cases the starting point of their analysis and the cornerstone of their problem is this: mechanisms of economic intervention have been deployed to avoid the reduction of freedom that would be entailed by transition to socialism, fascism, or National Socialism. But is it not the case that these mechanisms of economic intervention surreptitiously introduce types of intervention and modes of action which are as harmful to freedom as the visible and manifest political forms one wants to avoid? In other words, Keynesian kinds of intervention will be absolutely central to these different discussions. We can say that around Keynes,[32] around the economic interventionist policy perfected between 1930 and 1960, immediately before and after the war, all these interventions have brought about what we can call a crisis of liberalism, and this crisis manifests itself in a number of re-evaluations, re-appraisals, and new projects in the art of government which were formulated immediately before and after the war in Germany, and which are presently being formulated in America.

To summarize, or conclude, I would like to say that if it is true that a feature of the contemporary world, or of the modern world since the

* "*libérogènes*": in inverted commas in the manuscript.

eighteenth century, really has been the constant presence of phenomena of what may be called crises of capitalism, couldn't we also say that there have been crises of liberalism, which are not, of course, independent of these crises of capitalism? The problem of the thirties I have just been referring to is indeed the proof of this. But crises of liberalism are not just the pure and simple or direct projection of these crises of capitalism in the political sphere. You can find crises of liberalism linked to crises of the capitalist economy. But you can also find them with a chronological gap with regard to these crises, and in any case the way in which these crises manifest themselves, are handled, call forth reactions, and prompt re-organizations is not directly deducible from the crises of capitalism. It is the crisis of the general apparatus (*dispositif*) of governmentality, and it seems to me that you could study the history of these crises of the general apparatus of governmentality which was installed in the eighteenth century.

That is what I will try to do this year, but approaching things retrospectively, as it were. That is to say, I will start with the way in which the elements of this crisis of the apparatus of governmentality have been set out and formulated over the last thirty years, and [I will try]* to find in the history of the nineteenth century some of the elements which enable us to clarify the way in which the crisis of the apparatus of governmentality is currently experienced, lived, practiced, and formulated.

* M.F.: trying

---

1. See *Sécurité, Territoire, Population*, lecture of 22 March 1978, p. 295 *sq.*; *Security, Territory, Population*, p. 287 *sq.*
2. See this formula of a journalist, de Law, in the *Mercure de France*, April 1720, with regard to foreign trade: "One can usually only win if the other loses," quoted by C. Larrère, *L'Invention de l'économie au XVIII^e siècle* (Paris: PUF, 1992) p. 102, with regard to the mercantilist conception of foreign trade.
3. Foucault is alluding to the method of rational calculation of chance set out by Pascal in 1654 and, more precisely, to the problem of the "proportion of the last or first rounds": "In a game of *n* rounds, what rule enables one to determine the fraction of the other's money that should be given to player A if the game is stopped *just before its conclusion*" or "*just after the first round won.*" C. Chevalley, *Pascal. Contingence et probabilités* (Paris: PUF, 1995) p. 88. See Blaise Pascal, Letters to Fermat from 29 July to 24 August 1654, in *Œuvres complètes*, ed. L. Lafuma (Paris: Le Seuil, 1963) pp. 43-49.
4. I. Kant, *Zum ewigen Frieden* (Königsberg: Friedrich Nicolovius, 1795; Berlin: Akademie Ausgabe, 1912) vol. VIII, pp. 341-386; French translation by J. Gibelin, *Projet de paix perpétuelle* (Paris: Vrin, 1984, 5th ed.), Foucault used the first, 1948 edition of this translation; English translation by H.B. Nisbet, "Perpetual Peace: A Philosophical Sketch" in Hans Reiss, ed., *Kant's Political Writings* (Cambridge: Cambridge University Press, 1970).
5. *Projet de paix perpétuelle*, First supplement, "De la garantie de la paix perpétuelle," pp. 35-48; "Perpetual Peace: A Philosophical Sketch," First supplement "On the Guarantee of a Perpetual Peace," pp. 108-114.
6. Ibid. p. 35; English, ibid. p. 108: "Perpetual peace is *guaranteed* by no less an authority than the great artist [*Künstlerin*] *Nature* herself (*natura daedala rerum*). The mechanical process of nature visibly exhibits the purposive plan ( ... )."
7. Ibid. pp. 38-39; English ibid. p. 110: "It is in itself wonderful that moss can still grow in the cold wastes around the Arctic Ocean; the *reindeer* can scrape it out from beneath the snow, and can thus itself serve as nourishment or as a draft animal for the Ostiaks or Samoyeds. Similarly the sandy salt deserts containing the *camel*, which seems as if it had been created for travelling over them in order that they might not be left unutilised."
8. Ibid. p. 38; English pp. 109-110: "Firstly, she has taken care that human beings are able to live in all the areas where they are settled."
9. Ibid.; English ibid. p. 110: "[The third provisional arrangement of nature is] she has compelled them by the same means to enter into more or less legal relationships." Foucault does not mention the means by which, according to Kant, nature has achieved her ends of populating inhospitable regions and establishing juridical bonds, namely: war.
10. Ibid. pp. 43-46; English ibid. pp. 112-113.
11. Ibid. pp. 46-47; English ibid. p. 113: "The idea of international right presupposes the separate existence [*Absonderung*] of many independent adjoining States."
12. Ibid. pp. 47-48; English ibid. p. 114: "Thus nature wisely separates the nations, although the will of each individual State, even basing its argument on international right, would gladly unite them under its own sway by force or by cunning. On the other hand, nature also unites nations which the concept of cosmopolitan right would not have protected from violence and war, and does so by means of their mutual self-interest. For the *spirit of commerce* sooner or later takes hold of every people, and it cannot exist side by side with war."
13. Ibid. p. 43; English ibid. p. 112: "And how does nature guarantee that what man *ought* to do by the laws of his freedom (but does not do) will in fact be done through nature's compulsion, without prejudice to the free agency of man? This question arises, moreover, in all three areas of public right—in *political*, *international* and *cosmopolitan right*."
14. The conference in Vienna from September 1814 to June 1815 which brought together the major powers allied against France (Russia, Great Britain, Austria, and Prussia). Its aim was to establish a lasting peace after the Napoleonic wars and to redraw the political map of Europe. See, C.K. Weber, *The Congress of Vienna: 1814-1815* (London and New York: H. Milford, Oxford University Press, 1919; reprinted, London: Thames and Hudson, 1963).

15. See the interview of 1982, "Space, Knowledge, and Power," *Essential Works of Foucault*, 3, p. 351, in which Foucault claims that Napoleon can be placed "almost exactly at the break between the old organization of the eighteenth-century police state ( ... ) and the forms of the modern state, which he invented." In *Surveiller et Punir*, p. 219; *Discipline and Punish*, p. 217, however, Foucault places the Napoleonic figure "at the point of junction of the monarchical, ritual exercise of sovereignty and the hierarchical, permanent exercise of indefinite discipline." See the quotation, on the same page, taken from J.B. Treilhard, *Exposé des motifs des lois composant le code de procédure criminelle* (Paris: 1808) p. 14.
16. See A. Marquiset, *Napoléon sténographié au Conseil d'État* (Paris: H. Champion, 1913); J. Bourdon, *Napoléon au Conseil d'État*, unpublished notes and verbal proceedings of J.-G. Locré, secretary general of the Council of State (Paris: Berger-Levrault, 1963); C. Durand, *Études sur le Conseil d'État napoléonien* (Paris: PUF, 1947); C. Durand, "Le fonctionnement du Conseil d'État napoléonien," *Bibliothèque de l'université d'Aix-Marseille*, series I, Cap, Impr. Louis Jean, 1954; C. Durand, "Napoléon et le Conseil d'État pendant la seconde moitié de l'Empire," *Études et Documents du Conseil d'État*, no. XXII, 1969, pp. 269-285.
17. Foucault did not deal with this point in the 1978 lectures, but in those of 1976, *"Il faut défendre la société,"* lecture of 3 March 1976, pp. 179-181; *"Society Must Be Defended,"* pp. 199-202, on the basis of J.-B. Dubos, *Histoire critique de l'établissement de la monarchie française dans les Gaules* (Paris, 1734).
18. See, for example, Mably, *Observations sur l'histoire de France* (Geneva: 1765) Book VIII, ch. 7: "( ... ) will a new Charlemagne come among us? We must wish for it, but we cannot hope so," in Mably, *Sur la théorie du pouvoir politique*, selected texts (Paris: Éditions sociales, 1975) p. 194.
19. Klemenz Wenzel Nepomuk Lotar, prince de Metternich-Winneburg, called Metternich (1773-1859), Austrian foreign minister from the Congress of Vienna.
20. Foucault does not return to this subject in these lectures.
21. On evidence (*évidence*) as the principle of governmental self-limitation, see *Sécurité, Territoire, Population*, lecture of 5 April 1978, p. 361; *Security, Territory, Population*, p. 350.
22. The first savings bank, conceived as a preventive remedy for the improvidence of the lower classes, was founded in Paris in 1818. See R. Castel, *Le Métamorphoses de la question sociale* (Paris: Fayard, 1995; re-published Gallimard, 1999) pp. 402-403.
23. See, *Les Anormaux. Cours au Collège de France, 1974-1975*, eds. V. Marchetti and A. Salomoni (Paris: Gallimard-Le Seuil, 1999) Lecture of 19 March 1975, pp. 297-300; English translation by Graham Burchell, *Abnormal. Lectures at the Collège de France, 1974-1975*, English series editor, Arnold I. Davidson (New York: Picador, 2003) pp. 315-318.
24. We recall the way in which, the previous year, Foucault corrected his previous analysis of the relations between disciplinary techniques and individual freedoms (see *Sécurité, Territoire, Population*, lecture of 18 January 1978, pp. 49-50; *Security, Territory, Population*, pp. 48-49). The present argument extends this clarification, making freedom "the correlative ( ... ) of apparatuses of security."
25. It is worth recalling that the Panopticon, or Inspection-House, was not just a model of prison organization, but the idea of a new principle of construction which can be applied to all sorts of establishments. See the complete title of the first edition: *"Panopticon": or, the Inspection-House; containing the idea of a new principle of construction applicable to any sort of establishment, in which persons of any description are to be kept under inspection; and in particular to Penitentiary-houses, Prisons, Houses of industry, Workhouses, Poor Houses, Manufactories, Madhouses, Lazarettos, Hospitals, and Schools; with a plan of management adapted to the principle; in a series of letters, written in 1787, from Crechoff in White Russia, to a friend in England* (in one volume, Dublin: Thomas Byrne, 1791; and in two volumes, London: T. Payne, 1791), included in Jeremy Bentham, *Works*, ed. John Bowring (Edinburgh: W. Tait, 1838-1843) vol. IV, pp. 37-66 (see especially letters 16 to 21). The most recent, and readily available, edition of the Panopticon Letters is Jeremy Bentham, *The Panopticon Writings*, ed. M. Božovič (New York and London: Verso, 1995); French translation by M. Sissung in J. Bentham, *Le Panoptique* (Paris: Belfond, 1977) pp. 97-168. The French translation of 1791 did not include the 21 letters and its title was less explicit: *Panoptique, Mémoire sur un nouveau principe pour construire des maisons d'inspection, et nommément des maisons de force*

(Paris: Imprimerie nationale). See *Le Pouvoir psychiatrique. Cours au Collège de France, 1973-1974*, ed. J. Lagrange (Paris: Gallimard-Le Seuil, 2003), lecture of 28 November 1973, pp. 75-76; English translation by Graham Burchell, *Psychiatric Power. Lectures at the Collège de France 1973-1974*, English series ed. Arnold I. Davidson (London: Palgrave Macmillan, 2006) pp. 73-75.

26. Foucault is no doubt referring to the *Constitutional Code* in *The Collected Works of Jeremy Bentham*, eds. F. Rosen and J.H. Burns (Oxford: Clarendon Press, 1983) vol. 1, although this is not, strictly speaking, a codification of English legislation. Bentham develops his theory of liberal government in this book, whose genesis goes back to the 1820s (see *Codification Proposal, Addressed to All Nations Professing Liberal Opinions*, London: J. M'Creery, 1822), and the first volume of which appeared in 1830 (*Constitutional Code for Use of all Nations Professing Liberal Opinions*, London: R. Heward).
27. It seems that this phrase is not Bentham's, but translates Foucault's fairly free interpretation of Bentham's political-economic thought after 1811 (date of the failure of the Panopticon). Foucault seems to make a kind of short-cut between the distinction *agenda/non-agenda* referred to several times in the lectures (see the lectures of 10 January 1979, above p. 12, 14 February 1979, below p. 133, and 7 March, below p. 195) and the principle of inspection, or supervision, applied to government. In the *Constitutional Code*, however, government itself is the object of inspection on the part of the "tribunal of public opinion." (See *Le Pouvoir psychiatrique*, lecture of 28 November 1973, p. 78; *Psychiatric Power*, p. 77, with regard to the democratization of the exercise of power in terms of the panoptic apparatus: the accent is put on visibility, not on control through "publicity"). What's more, it is not clear that Bentham, in his economic writings or in the *Constitutional Code*, is a partisan of economic laissez-faire, as Foucault suggests here (see L.J. Hume, "Jeremy Bentham and the nineteenth-century revolution in government," *The Historical Journal*, vol. 10 (3), 1967, pp. 361-375). Compare however with the *sponte acta* defined in the text of 1801-1804 (see above, lecture of 10 January, note 9).
28. This was, of course, the economic and social program of struggle against the crisis, the New Deal, developed by Franklin Roosevelt immediately after his election as President of the U.S. in November 1932.
29. Foucault says, "the Tricontinental." Founded in 1973, the *Trilateral Commission*, which brought together representatives of North America (the U.S. and Canada), Europe, and Japan, with the objective of strengthening cooperation between these three major zones to confront the new challenges of the end of the century. The "Tricontinental," on the other hand, is the name of the conference called by Fidel Castro in Havana, from December 1965 to January 1966, to facilitate a face to face encounter between revolutionary organizations of the Old and New Worlds.
30. See below, lectures of 31 January, and 7, 14, and 21 February 1979.
31. See below, lectures of 14 and 21 March 1979.
32. See below, lecture of 31 January 1979, note 10.

# four

## 31 JANUARY 1979

*Phobia of the state. ~ Questions of method: sense and stakes of the bracketing off of a theory of the state in the analysis of mechanisms of power. ~ Neo-liberal governmental practices: German liberalism from 1948 to 1962; American neo-liberalism. ~ German neo-liberalism (I). ~ Its political-economic context. ~ The scientific council brought together by Erhard in 1947. Its program: abolition of price controls and limitation of governmental interventions. ~ The middle way defined by Erhard in 1948 between anarchy and the "termite state." ~ Its double meaning: (a) respect for economic freedom as condition of the state's political representativity; (b) the institution of economic freedom as basis for the formation of political sovereignty. ~ Fundamental characteristic of contemporary German governmentality: economic freedom, the source of juridical legitimacy and political consensus. ~Economic growth, axis of a new historical consciousness enabling the break with the past. ~ Rallying of Christian Democracy and the SPD to liberal politics. ~ The principles of liberal government and the absence of a socialist governmental rationality.*

I AM SURE YOU have all heard of the art historian, Berenson.[1] He was almost one hundred years old, approaching death, when he said something like: "God knows I fear the destruction of the world by the atomic bomb, but there is at least one thing I fear as much, and that is the invasion of humanity by the state."[2] I think this is the purest, clearest expression of a state-phobia one of the most constant features of which is its coupling with fear of the atomic bomb. The state and the atomic bomb, or rather the bomb than the state, or the state is no better than the bomb, or the state entails the bomb, or the bomb entails and necessarily calls for the state: this familiar theme is not that recent since Berenson expressed it around 1950-1952. This state-phobia runs through many contemporary themes and has undoubtedly been sustained by many sources for a long time: the Soviet experience of the 1920s, the German experience of Nazism, English post-war planning, and so on. The phobia has also had many agents and promoters, from economics professors inspired by Austrian neo-marginalism,[3] to political exiles who, from 1920, 1925 have certainly played a major role in the formation of contemporary political consciousness, and a role that perhaps has not been studied closely. An entire political history of exile could be written, or a history of political exile and its ideological, theoretical, and practical effects. Political exile at the end of the nineteenth century was certainly one of the major agents of the spread of socialism, and I think twentieth century political exile, or political dissidence, has also been a significant agent of the spread of what could be called anti-statism, or state-phobia.

To tell the truth, I do not want to talk about this state-phobia directly and head on, because for me it seems above all to be one of the signs of the crises of governmentality I was talking about last week, of those crises of governmentality of the sixteenth century, which I spoke about last year,[4] and of the second half of the eighteenth century, which manifests itself in that immense, difficult, and tangled criticism of despotism, tyranny, and arbitrariness. Well, just as at the end of the eighteenth century there was a criticism of despotism and a phobia about despotism—an ambiguous phobia about despotism—so too today there is a phobia about the state which is perhaps also ambiguous. Anyway, I would like to take up this problem of the state, or the question of the state, or state-phobia, on the basis of the analysis of governmentality that I have already talked about.

You will, of course, put to me the question, or make the objection: Once again you do without a theory of the state. Well, I would reply, yes, I do, I want to, I must do without a theory of the state, as one can and must forgo an indigestible meal. What does doing without a theory of the state mean? If you say that in my analyses I cancel the presence and the effect of state mechanisms, then I would reply: Wrong, you are mistaken or want to deceive yourself, for to tell the truth I do exactly the opposite of this. Whether in the case of madness, of the constitution of that category, that quasi-natural object, mental illness, or of the organization of a clinical medicine, or of the integration of disciplinary mechanisms and technologies within the penal system, what was involved in each case was always the identification of the gradual, piecemeal, but continuous takeover by the state of a number of practices, ways of doing things, and, if you like, governmentalities. The problem of bringing under state control, of 'statification' (*étatisation*) is at the heart of the questions I have tried to address.

However, if, on the other hand, "doing without a theory of the state" means not starting off with an analysis of the nature, structure, and functions of the state in and for itself, if it means not starting from the state considered as a sort of political universal and then, through successive extension, deducing the status of the mad, the sick, children, delinquents, and so on, in our kind of society then I reply: Yes, of course, I am determined to refrain from that kind of analysis. There is no question of deducing this set of practices from a supposed essence of the state in and for itself. We must refrain from this kind of analysis first of all because, quite simply, history is not a deductive science, and secondly, for another no doubt more important and serious reason: the state does not have an essence. The state is not a universal nor in itself an autonomous source of power. The state is nothing else but the effect, the profile, the mobile shape of a perpetual statification (*étatisation*) or statifications, in the sense of incessant transactions which modify, or move, or drastically change, or insidiously shift sources of finance, modes of investment, decision-making centers, forms and types of control, relationships between local powers, the central authority, and so on. In short, the state has no heart, as we well know, but not just in the sense that it has no feelings, either good or bad, but it has no heart in the sense that it has no interior. The state is nothing else but the mobile effect of a regime of multiple governmentalities. That is why I propose to analyze, or rather to take up and test this anxiety about the state, this state-phobia, which seems to me a typical feature of common themes today, not by trying to wrest from the state the secret of what it is, like Marx tried to extract the secret of the commodity, but by moving outside and questioning the problem of the state, undertaking an investigation of the problem of the state, on the basis of practices of governmentality.

Having said that, in this perspective, and continuing with the analysis of liberal governmentality, I would like to see how it appears and reflects on itself, how at the same time it is brought into play and analyzes itself, how, in short, it currently programs itself. I have indicated some of what seem to me to be the, as it were, first characteristics of liberal governmentality as it appeared in the middle of the eighteenth century. So I will skip two centuries, because obviously I do not claim to be able to undertake the overall, general, and continuous history of liberalism from the eighteenth to the twentieth century. Starting from how liberal governmentality is currently programming itself, I would just like to pick out and clarify some problems which recur from the eighteenth to the twentieth century. More or less, and subject to the qualification that I may change the plan—because, as you know, I am like the crawfish and advance sideways—I think, I hope we can study successively the problem of *law and order*,* the opposition between the state and civil society, or rather the way in which this opposition functioned and was employed, and then, finally, if I am lucky, we will come to the problem of biopolitics and the problem of life. Law and order, the state and civil society, and politics of life: these are the three themes that I would like to pick out in this broad and lengthy history of two centuries of liberalism.[5]

So, let's take things as they stand now. What is the nature of today's liberal, or, as one says, neo-liberal program? You know that it is identified in two main forms, with different cornerstones and historical contexts. The German form is linked to the Weimar Republic, the crisis of 1929, the development of Nazism, the critique of Nazism, and, finally, post-war reconstruction. The other, American form, is a neo-liberalism defined by reference to the New Deal, the criticism of Roosevelt's[6]

---

* In English in original; G.B.

policies, and which, especially after the war, is developed and organized against federal interventionism, and then against the aid and other programs of the mainly Democrat administrations of Truman,[7] Kennedy,[8] Johnson,[9] etcetera. There are, of course, a number of connections between these two forms of neo-liberalism, which I have cut out with somewhat arbitrary slices. First of all there is the main doctrinal adversary, Keynes,[10] the common enemy, which ensures that criticism of Keynes will pass back and forth between these two neo-liberalisms. Second, they share the same objects of repulsion, namely, the state-controlled economy, planning, and state interventionism on precisely those overall quantities to which Keynes attached such theoretical and especially practical importance. Finally, a series of persons, theories, and books pass between these two forms of neo-liberalism, the main ones referring to the Austrian school broadly speaking, to Austrian neo-marginalism, at any rate to those who came from there, like von Mises,[11] Hayek,[12] and so on. I would like to talk above all about the first, about, to put it very roughly, German neo-liberalism, both because it seems to me to be more important theoretically than the others for the problem of governmentality, and also because I am not sure I will have enough time to talk about the Americans.

So let's take the example of German neo-liberalism.[13] It's April 1948—fine, I'm ashamed to remind you of things so well known—and throughout Europe economic policies governed by a series of well-known requirements reign almost unchallenged:

First, the requirement of reconstruction, that is to say, the conversion of a war economy back into a peace economy, the reconstruction of destroyed economic potential, and also the integration of new technological information which appeared during the war, and new demographic and geopolitical facts.

The second requirement is that of planning as the major instrument of reconstruction. Planning is required both due to internal necessities and also because of the weight represented by America and American policy and the existence of the Marshall plan,[14] which practically entailed—except precisely for Germany and Belgium, to which we will return shortly—the planning of each country and a degree of coordination between the different plans.

Finally, the third requirement is constituted by social objectives that were considered to be politically indispensable in order to avoid the renewal of fascism and Nazism in Europe. In France this requirement was formulated by the CNR.[15]

With these three requirements—reconstruction, planning, and, broadly speaking, socialization and social objectives—all of which entailed an interventionist policy on the allocations of resources, price stability, the level of savings, the choice of investments, and a policy of full employment, we are, in short—and once again, please forgive all these banalities—in the middle of a fully-fledged Keynesian policy. Now, in April 1948, a Scientific Council[16] formed alongside the German economic administration in what was called the Bi-Zone, that is to say, the Anglo-American zone, presented a report which laid down the following principle: "The Council is of the view that the function of the direction of the economic process should be assured as widely as possible by the price mechanism."[17] It turned out that this resolution or principle was accepted unanimously. And the Council voted by a simple majority for drawing the following consequence from this principle: We call for the immediate deregulation of prices in order [to bring prices in line with]* world prices. So, broadly speaking, there is the principle of no price controls and the demand for immediate deregulation. We are in the realm of decisions, or of demands anyway, a realm of proposals that, in its elementary simplicity, calls to mind what the physiocrats called for or what Turgot decided in 1774.[18] This took place on 18 April 1948. Ten days later, the 28th, at the meeting of the Council at Frankfurt,[19] Ludwig Erhard[20]—who was not in charge of the Scientific Council, for it had come together around him, but of the economic administration of the Anglo-American zone, or at any rate of the German part of the economic administration of the zone—gave a speech in which he took up the conclusions of this report.[21] That is to say, he laid down the principle of no price controls and called for gradual deregulation, but he accompanied this principle, and the conclusion he drew from it, with a number of important considerations. He says: "We must free the

---

* M.F.: to obtain a tendential alignment with

economy from state controls."[22] "We must avoid," he says, "both anarchy and the termite state," because "only a state that establishes both the freedom and responsibility of the citizens can legitimately speak in the name of the people."[23] You can see that this economic liberalism, this principle of respect for the market economy that was formulated by the Scientific Council, is inscribed within something much more general, and this is a principle according to which interventions by the state should generally be limited. The borders and limits of state control should be precisely fixed and relations between individuals and the state determined. Ludwig Erhard's speech clearly differentiates these liberal choices, which he was about to propose to the Frankfurt meeting, from some other economic experiments that managed to be undertaken at this time despite the *dirigiste*, interventionist, and Keynesian ambiance in Europe. That is to say, a liberal policy was also adopted in Belgium, and partially too in Italy where, spurred on by Luigi Einaudi,[24] who was then the director of the Bank of Italy, a number of liberal measures were adopted. But in Belgium and Italy these were specifically economic interventions. In Erhard's speech, and in the choices he proposed at that time, there was something quite different. What was at stake, and the text itself says this, was the legitimacy of the state.

What does Ludwig Erhard mean when he says that we must free the economy from state controls while avoiding anarchy and the termite state, because "only a state that establishes both the freedom and responsibility of the citizens can legitimately speak in the name of the people"? Actually, it is fairly ambiguous, in the sense that I think it can and should be understood at two levels. On the one hand, at a trivial level, if you like, it is simply a matter of saying that a state which abuses its power in the economic realm, and more generally in the realm of political life, violates basic rights, impairs essential freedoms, and thereby forfeits its own rights. A state cannot exercise its power legitimately if it violates the freedom of individuals; it forfeits its rights. The text does not say that it forfeits all its rights. It does not say, for example, that it is stripped of its rights of sovereignty. It says that it forfeits its rights of representativity. That is to say, a state which violates the basic freedoms, the essential rights of citizens, is no longer representative of its citizens. We can see what the precise tactical objective of this kind of statement is in reality: it amounts to saying that the National Socialist state, which violated all these rights, was not, could not be seen retrospectively as not having exercised its sovereignty legitimately. That is to say, roughly, that the orders, laws, and regulations imposed on German citizens are not invalidated and, as a result, the Germans cannot be held responsible for what was done in the legislative or regulatory framework of Nazism. However, on the other hand, it was and is retrospectively stripped of its rights of representativity. That is to say, what it did cannot be considered as having been done in the name of the German people. The whole, extremely difficult problem of the legitimacy and legal status to be given to the measures taken [under] Nazism are present in this statement.

But there is [also] a broader, more general, and at the same time more sophisticated meaning to Ludwig Erhard's statement that only a state that recognizes economic freedom and thus makes way for the freedom and responsibility of individuals can speak in the name of the people. Basically, Erhard is saying that in the current state of affairs—that is to say, in 1948, before the German state had been reconstituted, before the two German states had been constituted—it is clearly not possible to lay claim to historical rights for a not yet reconstituted Germany and for a still to be reconstituted German state, when these rights are debarred by history itself. It is not possible to claim juridical legitimacy inasmuch as no apparatus, no consensus, and no collective will can manifest itself in a situation in which Germany is on the one hand divided, and on the other occupied. So, there are no historical rights, there is no juridical legitimacy, on which to found a new German state.

But—and this is what Ludwig Erhard's text says implicitly—let's suppose an institutional framework whose nature or origin is not important: an institutional framework *x*. Let us suppose that the function of this institutional framework *x* is not, of course, to exercise sovereignty, since, precisely, there is nothing in the current situation that can found a juridical power of coercion, but is simply to guarantee freedom. So, its function is not to constrain, but simply to create a space of freedom, to guarantee a freedom, and precisely to guarantee it in the economic domain. Let us now suppose that in this institution *x*—whose function is not the sovereign exercise of the power to constrain, but simply to establish a space of freedom—any number of individuals freely agree to play this game of economic freedom guaranteed by the institutional framework. What will happen? What would be implied by the free exercise of this freedom by individuals who are not constrained to exercise it but who have simply been given the possibility of exercising it? Well, it would imply adherence to this framework; it would imply that consent has been given to any decision which may be taken to guarantee this economic freedom or to secure that which makes this economic freedom possible. In other words, the institution of economic freedom will have to function, or at any rate will be able to function as a siphon, as it were, as a point of attraction for the formation of a political sovereignty. Of course, I am adding to Ludwig Erhard's apparently banal words a whole series of implicit meanings which will only take on their value and effect later. I am adding a whole historical weight that is not yet present, but I will try to explain how and why this meaning, which is at once theoretical, political, and programmatic, really was in the minds of those who wrote this discourse, if not in the mind of the one who actually delivered it.

I think this idea of a legitimizing foundation of the state on the guaranteed exercise of an economic freedom is important. Of course, we must take up this idea and its formulation in the precise context in which it appears, and straightaway it is easy to see tactical and strategic shrewdness. It was a matter of finding a juridical expedient in order to ask from an economic regime what could not be directly asked from constitutional law, or from international law, or even quite simply from the political partners. Even more precisely, it was an artful move with regard to both the Americans and Europe, since by guaranteeing economic freedom to a Germany in the process of reconstruction and prior to any state apparatus, the Americans, and let's say different American lobbies were assured that they could have the free relationships that they could choose with this German industry and economy. Secondly, both Western and Eastern Europe were reassured by ensuring that the institutional embryo being formed presented absolutely none of the dangers of the strong or totalitarian state they had experienced in the previous years. But beyond these immediate tactical imperatives, and beyond the immediate context and situation of 1948, I think there was the formulation in this discourse of something which will remain a fundamental feature of contemporary German governmentality*: we should not think that economic activity in contemporary Germany, that is to say, for thirty years, from 1948 until today, has been only one branch of the nation's activity. We should not think that good economic management has had no other effect and no other foreseen and calculated end than that of securing the prosperity of all and each. In fact, in contemporary Germany, the economy, economic development and economic growth, produces sovereignty; it produces political sovereignty through the institution and institutional game that, precisely, makes this economy work. The economy produces legitimacy for the state that is its guarantor. In other words, the economy creates public law, and this is an absolutely important phenomenon, which is not entirely unique in history to be sure, but is nonetheless a quite singular phenomenon in our times. In contemporary Germany there is a circuit going constantly from the economic institution to the state; and if there is an inverse circuit going from the state to the economic institution, it should not be forgotten that the element that comes first in this kind of siphon is the economic institution. There is a permanent genesis, a permanent genealogy of the state from the economic institution. And even this is not saying enough, for the economy does not only bring a juridical structure or legal legitimization to a German state that history had just debarred. This economic institution, the economic freedom that from the start it is the role of this institution to guarantee and maintain, produces something even more real, concrete, and immediate than a legal legitimization; it produces a permanent consensus of all those who may appear as agents within these economic processes, as investors, workers, employers, and trade unions. All these economic partners produce a consensus, which is a political consensus, inasmuch as they accept this economic game of freedom.

Let's say that in leaving people free to act, the German neo-liberal institution lets them speak, and to a large extent it lets them act because

---

* Foucault adds: for there is here, I think, one of the essential features on which we should reflect and the programming of which seems to me to be one of the fundamental features of this German neo-liberalism.

it wants to let them speak; but what does it let them say? Well, it lets them say that one is right to give them freedom to act. That is to say, over and above juridical legitimation, adherence to this liberal system produces permanent consensus as a surplus product, and, symmetrically to the genealogy of the state from the economic institution, the production of well-being by economic growth will produce a circuit going from the economic institution to the population's overall adherence to its regime and system.

If we believe historians of the sixteenth century, like Max Weber,[25] it would seem that the enrichment of an individual in sixteenth century protestant Germany was a sign of God's arbitrary election of that individual. What did wealth signify? Wealth was a sign that God really had granted his protection to that individual and that he showed by this the certainty of a salvation which could not be guaranteed by anything in the individual's real and concrete works. You will not be saved because you have tried to enrich yourself as you should, but if in actual fact you have become rich, this is a sign sent to you on earth by God that you will be saved. So, enrichment enters into a system of signs in sixteenth century Germany. In twentieth century Germany, an individual's enrichment will not be the arbitrary sign of his election by God, but general enrichment will be the sign of something else: not, of course, of God's election, [but] the daily sign of the adherence of individuals to the state. In other words, the economy always signifies, but not at all in the sense that it endlessly produces those signs of the equivalence and exchange value of things, which, in its illusory structures, or its structures of the simulacrum, has nothing to do with the use of things. The economy produces political signs that enable the structures, mechanisms, and justifications of power to function. The free market, the economically free market, binds and manifests political bonds. A strong Deutschmark, a satisfactory rate of growth, an expanding purchasing power, and a favorable balance of payments are, of course, the effects of good government in contemporary Germany, but to a certain extent this is even more the way in which the founding consensus of a state—which history, defeat, or the decision of the victors had just outlawed—is constantly manifested and reinforced. The state rediscovers its law, its juridical law, and its real foundation in the existence and practice of economic freedom. History had said no to the German state, but now the economy will allow it to assert itself. Continuous economic growth will take over from a malfunctioning history. It will thus be possible to live and accept the breach of history as a breach in memory, inasmuch as a new dimension of temporality will be established in Germany that will no longer be a temporality of history, but one of economic growth. A reversal of the axis of time, permission to forget, and economic growth are all, I think, at the very heart of the way in which the German economic-political system functions. Economic freedom is jointly produced through growth, well-being, the state, and the forgetting of history.

In contemporary Germany we have what we can say is a radically economic state, taking the word "radically" in the strict sense, that is to say, its root is precisely economic. As you know, Fichte—and this is generally all that is known about Fichte—spoke of a closed commercial state.[26] I will have to come back to this a bit later.[27] I will just say, making a somewhat artificial symmetry, that we have here the opposite of a closed commercial state. We have a state-forming commercial opening. Is this the first example in history of a radically economic state? We would have to ask historians who have a much better understanding of history than I do. Was Venice a radically economic state? Can we say that the United Provinces in the sixteenth century, and still in the seventeenth century, were an economic state? Anyway, we are dealing with something new in comparison with everything that since the eighteenth century constituted the functioning, justification, and programming of governmentality. If it is true that we are still dealing with a liberal type of governmentality, you can see the shift that has been carried out in relation to the liberalism programmed by the physiocrats, Turgot, and the economists of the eighteenth century, for whom the problem was exactly the opposite. The problem they had to resolve was the following: given the existence of a legitimate state, which is already functioning in the fully and completely administrative form of a police state, how can we limit this existing state and, above all, allow for the necessary economic freedom within it? The problem the Germans had to resolve was the exact opposite: given a state that does not exist, how can we get it to exist on the basis of this non-state space of economic freedom?

I think this is the kind of commentary we can give on the apparently banal little sentence of the future Chancellor Erhard on 28 April 1948 (once again, giving a lot of extra weight to this phrase, but extra weight which I will try to show is not arbitrary). Obviously, this idea, this formulation of 1948, could only take on this historical depth by being very quickly inscribed in a sequence of subsequent decisions and events.

So, on 18 April there is the report of the Scientific Council; on 28 April Erhard's discourse; on 24 June 1948,[28] abolition of price controls on industrial products, then of price controls on food, and then progressively, but relatively slowly, of all price controls. In 1952 price controls are abolished on coal and electricity, which is, I think, one of the last price controls to be abolished in Germany. And it is only in 1953 that there is removal of exchange controls for foreign trade that reaches the level of around 80%-95%. So, in 1952-1953 liberalization is more or less established.

Another thing to note is that this policy of liberalization, more or less explicitly supported by the Americans for the reasons I mentioned, aroused considerable mistrust on the part of the other occupying powers, particularly the English who were in a period of fully-fledged Labour Party Keynesianism.[29] It aroused considerable resistance in Germany itself, since, of course, prices began to rise as soon as the first price controls were abolished. The German socialists demanded Erhard's resignation in August 1948 and in November of the same year there was a general strike against Erhard's economic policy and a call for a return to a state-controlled economy. The strike failed and prices stabilized in December 1948.[30]

The third series of important facts for pinpointing the way in which the neo-liberal program I have been talking about was inscribed in reality was a rallying of support for it on the part of a number of organizations and people. First of all, and very early on, there was support from the Christian Democrats, in spite of its stronger links with a Christian, social economy than with a liberal type of economy. With the Christian

Democrats came Christian theorists of the social economy and in particular those of Munich, the famous Jesuit Oswald Nell-Breuning,[31] who taught political economy at Munich.[32] The support of the labor unions was, of course, much more important. The first major, most official and most manifest case of adherence to the program being that of Theodor Blank,[33] who was vice president of the miners' union and who declared that the liberal order constitutes a valid alternative to capitalism and economic planning.[34] It could be said that this phrase is completely hypocritical or naively plays on a number of ambiguities: in fact, in saying that the liberal order constituted an alternative to capitalism and economic planning, you can see the asymmetries on which he was playing, since the liberal order never claimed, or was certainly not claiming through the mouth of the future chancellor Erhard to be an alternative to capitalism, but was indeed a particular way of making capitalism work. And if it is true that he was opposed to planning, someone like Theodor Blank, as a trade union representative on the one hand, and with his social Christian origins and ideology, etcetera, on the other, could not criticize it all that directly. And, in fact, what he meant was that in neo-liberalism there was the finally fulfilled promise of a middle way or third order between capitalism and socialism. Once again, this was not what was at stake at all. The phrase was simply [intended] to get the Christian inspired trade unions of the time to swallow the pill.

Finally and above all, the SPD, social democracy, came over to the program, although obviously it did so much more slowly than the others since practically until 1950 German social democracy remained faithful to most of what had been its general principles of Marxist inspired socialism since the end of the nineteenth century. At the Hanover Congress,[35] and again at the Bad Dürkheim Congress in 1949, the German Socialist Party still recognized the historical and political validity of the class struggle and had the socialization of the means of production as its objective.[36] Fine, this is still how things stand in 1949, in 1950. In 1955, Karl Schiller,[37] who will later become Minister of the Economy and Finance in federal Germany,[38] writes a book that will cause a big stir since it bears the significant title *Socialism and Competition*,[39] that is to say, not socialism or competition, but socialism *and* competition. I don't know if he states it for the first time in this book, but anyway he gives the greatest publicity to what will become the formula of German socialism: "as much competition as possible and as much planning as necessary."[40] This is in 1955. In 1959, at the Bad Godesberg congress,[41] German social democracy first renounced the principle of transition to the socialization of the means of production and, secondly and correlatively, recognized that not only was private ownership of the means of production perfectly legitimate, but that it had a right to state protection and encouragement.[42] That is to say, one of the state's essential and basic tasks is to protect not only private property in general, but private property in the means of production, with the condition, adds the motion of the congress, of compatibility with "an equitable social order." Finally, third, the congress approved the principle of a market economy, here again with the restriction, wherever "the conditions of genuine competition prevail."[43]

Clearly, for anyone who thinks in Marxist terms, or on the basis of Marxism, or on the basis of the tradition of German socialism, what is important in these motions is obviously the series of renunciations—desertions, heresies, betrayals, as you like—of the class struggle, of the social appropriation of the means of production, and so on. From an orthodox Marxist perspective it is these renunciations which are important and all the rest, all these vague little restrictions like aiming for an equitable social order, or realizing the conditions of genuine competition, is just so much hypocrisy. But for someone who hears these same phrases with a different ear or on the basis of a different theoretical "background," these words—"equitable social order," "condition of genuine economic competition"—resonate very differently because they indicate—and here again is something that I would like to explain next week—adherence to a doctrinal and programmatic whole which is not simply an economic theory on the effectiveness and utility of market freedom: it is adherence to a type of governmentality that was precisely the means by which the German economy served as the basis for the legitimate state.

Why did German social democracy finally come over, albeit somewhat late, but fairly easily, to these theses, practices, and programs of neo-liberalism? There are at least two reasons. One, of course, was a necessary and indispensable reason of political tactics. You can see that as long as the SPD, under the leadership of the old Schumacher,[44] maintained the traditional attitude of a socialist party—on the one hand accepting the system of the state, of the constitution and juridical structures of the so-called liberal democratic regime, while, on the other, rejecting in theory the principles of the capitalist economic system, thus adopting the task within this legal framework, seen as sufficient for developing the basic role of essential freedoms, of simply correcting the existing system in terms of a number of distant objectives—it could have no place in the new economic-political state that was being born. There could be no place for it precisely because the new state was the opposite of this. It was not a matter of choosing or accepting a legal framework or a given historical framework because it had been formed in that way by the state or by popular consensus, and then working within, economically, at a number of adjustments. It was quite the opposite. In the new German economic-political regime one started by giving oneself a certain economic functioning which was the very basis of the state and of its existence and international recognition. One gave oneself this economic framework, and it is then that the legitimacy of the state emerged as it were. How could a socialist party, whose at least long-term objective is a completely different economic regime, be integrated into this political game, since the givens had been reversed, so to speak, and it was the economic that was radical in relation to the state, and not the state that was primary as the historical-juridical framework for this or that economic choice? Consequently, to enter into the political game of the new Germany, the SPD really had to convert to these neo-liberal theses, if not to the economic, scientific, or theoretical theses, at least to the general practice of this neo-liberalism as governmental practice. Thus the famous Bad Godesberg congress with its absolute renunciation of the most traditional themes of social democracy certainly was the break with Marxist theory, with Marxist socialism, but at the same time it was—and this was not just a betrayal, except, if you like, in general historical terms—the acceptance of what was already in the process of functioning as the economic-political consensus of German liberalism. It was not so much the renunciation of this or that part of the program common to most socialist parties as entry into the game of governmentality. There remains one more step for social democracy to make, and this was the break with the English model and any reference to Keynesian economics. This step was taken by Karl Schiller, him again, in 1963, since he even abandons the formula: "as much competition as possible and as much planning as necessary." In 1963 he asserts the principle that all, even flexible planning is dangerous for the liberal economy.[45] At this point social democracy has arrived; it has entered fully into the type of economic-political governmentality that was adopted by Germany in 1948. It joins in the game so well that six years later Willy Brandt[46] becomes Chancellor of Federal Germany.

This is, for sure, one of the reasons, and not the least, but I think we should try to examine further this problem of the relation between German socialism and the neo-liberal governmentality defined by Erhard in 1948, or at least by his counselors about whom I spoke a little last week. We can try to understand a bit better what happened and why it happened in this way. Actually, there is no doubt another reason than this kind of tactical stranglehold in which the German socialist party found itself after 1948. It is often said, well, at least by those who know his work, that there is no theory of power in Marx, that the theory of the state is inadequate, and that it really is time to produce it. But is it really so important to provide oneself with a theory of the state? After all, the English have not done so badly and, at least until these last few years, have been tolerably well-governed without a theory of the state. At any rate, the last of the theories of the state is found in Hobbes,[47] that is to say, in someone who was both the contemporary and "supporter" of a type of monarchy that the English precisely got rid of at that time. After Hobbes, there is Locke.[48] Locke does not produce a theory of the state; he produces a theory of government. So, we can say that the English political system has never functioned, and liberal doctrine has never functioned on the basis of, or even by providing itself with a theory of the state. They have adopted principles of government.

In short, whether or not there is a theory of the state in Marx is for Marxists to decide. As for myself, I would say that what socialism lacks is not so much a theory of the state as a governmental reason, the definition of what a governmental rationality would be in socialism, that is to say, a reasonable and calculable measure of the extent, modes, and objectives of governmental action. Socialism provides itself with, or anyway proposes, an historical rationality. You know this and there's no point saying anything more about it. It proposes an economic rationality. God knows how much discussion there has been about whether or not this rationality holds up, especially in the years from 1920 to 1930. Around this period the neo-liberals I have talked about, like von Mises, Hayek, and so on, especially von Mises,[49] denied that there was an economic rationality to socialism. Others replied to him, and we will come back to this. Let's say that the problem of the economic rationality of socialism is something about which we can argue. In any case, socialism offers an economic rationality just as it puts forward an historical rationality. We can also say that it possesses, and has shown that it possesses, rational techniques of intervention, of administrative intervention, in domains like those of health, social insurance, and so on. So, it is possible to recognize the existence of an historical rationality, an economic rationality, and an administrative rationality in socialism, or, at any rate, let's say that we can argue about the existence of these rationalities in socialism and we cannot eliminate all these forms of rationality with a wave of the hand. But I do not think that there is an autonomous socialist governmentality. There is no governmental rationality of socialism. In actual fact, and history has shown this, socialism can only be implemented connected up to diverse types of governmentality. It has been connected up to liberal governmentality, and then socialism and its forms of rationality function as counterweights, as a corrective, and a palliative to internal dangers. One can, moreover, [reproach it, as do liberals],* with being itself a danger, but it has lived, it has actually functioned, and we have examples of it within and connected up to liberal governmentalities. We have seen it function, and still see it function, within governmentalities that would no doubt fall more under what last year we called the police state,[50] that is to say, a hyper-administrative state in which there is, so to

* M.F.: liberals reproach it

speak, a fusion, a continuity, the constitution of a sort of massive bloc between governmentality and administration. At that point, in the governmentality of a police state, socialism functions as the internal logic of an administrative apparatus. Maybe there are still other governmentalities that socialism is connected up to; it remains to be seen. But in any case, I do not think that for the moment there is an autonomous governmentality of socialism.

Let's consider things from a different angle. When we cross the border separating the Germany of Helmut Schmidt[51] and the Germany of [Erich Honecker[52]],* the question every good Western intellectual asks himself is, of course: Where is true socialism? Is it where I have just come from, or there where I am going? Is it on the right or the left, on this side or the other? Where is true socialism?† But does this question have any meaning? Basically, should we not say instead that socialism is no more true here than there for the simple reason that socialism does not have to be true. What I mean is that socialism is anyway connected up to a type of governmentality: here it is connected up to this governmentality and there it is connected up to another, yielding very dissimilar fruit in both cases and, in the event of course of a more or less normal or aberrant branch, the same deadly fruit.

But do we address to liberalism the question which is always raised within and with regard to socialism, namely: true or false? A form of liberalism does not have to be true or false. One asks whether a form of liberalism is pure, radical, consistent, or mixed, etcetera. That is to say, we ask what rules it adopts for itself, how it offsets compensating mechanisms, how it calculates the mechanisms of measurement it has installed within its governmentality. I think that if we are so strongly inclined to put to socialism this indiscreet question of truth that we never address to liberalism—"Are you true or are you false?"—it is precisely because socialism lacks an intrinsic governmental rationality, and because it replaces this essential, and still not overcome [absence of] an internal governmental rationality, with the relationship of conformity to

---

* M.F.: I have forgotten his name, but it's not important.

† Foucault repeats: Where is true socialism?

a text. The relationship of conformity to a text, or to a series of texts, is charged with concealing this absence of governmental rationality. A way of reading and interpreting is advanced that must found socialism and indicate the very limits and possibilities of its potential action, whereas what it really needs is to define for itself its way of doing things and its way of governing. I think the importance of the text in socialism is commensurate with the lacuna constituted by the absence of a socialist art of government. With regard to all forms of real socialism, of every socialism implemented in policy, we should not ask what text it refers to, whether or not it betrays the text, whether or not it conforms to the text, or whether it is true or false. We should simply and always ask socialism: So, what is this necessarily extrinsic governmentality that makes you function and only within which you can function? And if this kind of question seems to smell too much of resentment, let us put the question in a more general way, and more turned towards the future: What would really be the governmentality appropriate to socialism? Is there a governmentality appropriate to socialism? What governmentality is possible as a strictly, intrinsically, and autonomously socialist governmentality? In any case, we know only that if there is a really socialist governmentality, then it is not hidden within socialism and its texts. It cannot be deduced from them. It must be invented.[53]*

This, then, is the historical framework within which what is called German neo-liberalism takes shape. You can see that we are dealing with a whole set of things that it would be impossible to reduce to a pure and simple calculation of political groups or political personnel of Germany after its defeat, although the existence, pressure, and the possible strategies defined by this situation were absolutely determinant. It is something other than a political calculation, even if it is completely permeated by political calculation. No more is it an ideology, although, of course, there is a whole set of perfectly coherent ideas, analytical principles, and so forth. What is involved in fact is a new programming of liberal governmentality. It is an internal reorganization that, once again,

* In the manuscript Foucault notes: "Socialism is not the alternative to liberalism. They do not exist on the same level, although there are levels at which they come into collision with each other, where things don't go well together. Hence the possibility of their unhappy symbiosis."

does not ask the state what freedom it will leave to the economy, but asks the economy how its freedom can have a state-creating function and role, in the sense that it will really make possible the foundation of the state's legitimacy?

I will stop there.* So, next week I would like to talk about the formation of this neo-liberal doctrine around 1925, and its implementation from around 1952.

---

* Foucault forgoes reading the last pages of the manuscript (pp. 22-25):

"[p. 22] Reversal in comparison with the 'liberalism' defined by d'Argenson or Turgot.
—Take a state: if you want to enrich yourself, then you must not govern too much. Therefore, freedom of the market.
—Take a state that does not exist. How to ensure that it exists just enough. Therefore, a free market.

To get the legality of the state from the veridiction of the market: this is the German miracle.
[p. 23] There has been a precedent, the *Zollverien*, but precisely it was a failure. And German nationalism was constructed against economic liberalism.
—either because it failed to defend itself against French imperialism: Fichte,
—or because, from 1840, the solidarity between economic and political liberalism unravels. The liberal economic policy, from which German unity (against Austria) was expected, turns out to serve England in fact. It is realized that unity can only be brought about by a revolutionary politics and that the economy must be inserted within the nationalist framework. List: *National Ökonomie*.

[p. 24] N.B. Nationalism is only seen as an instrument → the future age of liberalism
—From 1870 economic liberalism/free market economy modeled on free competition was rejected
—in the name of external policy: struggle against England; the free market is an instrument of English domination;
—in the name of internal policy: the proletariat must be reintegrated into German society;
—in the name of the historicist doctrine that rejected the presupposition of nature, of natural law, as the founding principle of an economy. The economy is only ever a dimension of successive historical configurations.
—finally, after 1918, liberalism is rejected.
—by the extension of a war economy and its methods of planning;
—by the development of a *Welfare economy* [English in original; G.B.] that seems to theorize and justify Bismarckian practices on a new basis (or at least their [ ... ])
— [p. 25] finally by the development of the principle of a policy of full employment and state intervention.

In short, an economy of balances [ ... ]
All of this constitutes an enormous burden, taken over by socialism. There had already been attempts to lift it (Lujo Brentano). There were also theoretical instruments (Austrian). But what is interesting is that the Freiburg School did not just develop an economic theory, or even a doctrine. It completely rethought the relation between the economy and politics, the whole of the art of government. And with good reason: it had to grapple with a considerable historical phenomenon. Nazism, in fact, was not just the accumulation and crystallization of all the policies of nationalism, interventionism, and planning that had marginalized liberalism ... " (end of the manuscript).

1. Bernard Berenson (1865-1959), American art collector, expert, and critic of Lithuanian origin, and a specialist in Italian Renaissance painting. Author of: *The Italian Painters of the Renaissance* (London: Phaidon Press, 1953); *Drawings of the Florentine Painters* (Chicago: University of Chicago Press, 1970); and a book of memoirs, *Sketch for a Self-Portrait* (New York: Pantheon, 1949).
2. The quotation is, as Foucault suggests, fairly free. The manuscript contains only: "Berenson: atomic destruction, state invasion."
3. These are named later in the lecture: von Mises, Hayek (see below, note 11).
4. See *Sécurité, Territoire, Population*, lecture of 1 February 1978, p. 105; *Security, Territory, Population*, pp. 101-102.
5. Foucault will only deal with the first two points in the remainder of the course. See above, lecture of 10 January 1979, pp. 21-22, the reasons he gives to justify their analysis, the condition of the intelligibility of the third point ("only when we know what this governmental regime called liberalism was, will we be able to grasp what biopolitics is") and his comment right at the start of the lecture of 7 March 1979 (below p. 185): "I would like to assure you that, in spite of everything, I really did intend to talk about biopolitics, and then, things being what they are, I have ended up talking at length, and maybe for too long, about neo-liberalism, and neo-liberalism in its German form."
6. See above, p. 68.
7. Harry S. Truman (1884-1972), President of the United States from 1945 to 1953.
8. John F. Kennedy (1917-1963), President of the United States from 1961 to 1963.
9. Lyndon B. Johnson (1908-1973), President of the United States from 1963 to 1969.
10. John Maynard Keynes (1883-1946), British economist and author of *A Treatise on Money* (London and New York: Harcourt, Brace & Co., 1930), and especially *The General Theory of Employment, Interest and Money* (London: Macmillan & Co., 1936), French translation by J. de Largentaye, *Théorie générale de l'emploi, de l'intérêt et de la monnaie* (Paris: Payot, 1942). In the latter work, the publication of which marks a crucial date in the history of economic thought (the "Keynesian revolution"), addressing the problem of under-employment and criticizing in particular Pigou's theory of unemployment (A.C. Pigou, *The Theory of Unemployment*, London: Macmillan, 1933), Keynes explained the contemporary crisis of capitalism by the fall in marginal efficiency of capital and the excessively high rate of interest entailing a decline in investment. This analysis led him to advocate state intervention with a view to assuring full employment, through measures encouraging consumption (leaving the gold standard, increasing private and public investment). The traditional "microeconomic" vision, based on the interaction between prices and wages, thus had to be replaced by a "macroeconomic" vision based on relations between aggregates, or overall quantities, which can be influenced by economic policy, such as the national revenue, total consumption, the volume of savings and investment. Appointed as deputy governor of the Bank of England, in 1944 Keynes took part in the Bretton Woods conference which resulted in the creation of the International Monetary Fund and the World Bank for economic reconstruction and development.
11. Ludwig Edler von Mises (1881-1973). After studying law at the University of Vienna, he turned to political economy under the influence of C. Menger and his disciples, F. von Wieser and E. von Böhm-Bawerk (the "Austrian school"). In 1927 he founded with Hayek the *Österreichisches Institut für Konjunkturforschung* in Vienna. Appointed in 1934 to the University Institute for higher international studies in Geneva, he left for New York in 1940. His main works are: *Die Gemeinwirtschaft, untersuchungen über den Sozialismus* (Jena: G. Fischer, 1922); French translation by P. Bastier, A. Terrasse and F. Terrasse, with a preface by F. Perroux (Paris: Librairie de Médicis, 1938); English translation by J. Kahane, *Socialism: An Economic and Sociological Analysis* (London: Cape, 1936), in which he demonstrates that "in the absence of a market for factors of production these could not be rationally allocated to industrial plants and that, in consequence, a centrally directed economy could not function" (Michael Polanyi, *The Logic of Liberty. Reflections and Rejoinders* [London: Routledge and Kegan Paul, 1951] p. 123) *Liberalismus* (Jena: G. Fischer, 1927); English translation, *Liberalism: The Classical Tradition* (Indianapolis, Ind.: The Liberty Fund, 2005); *Nationalökonomie, Theorie des Handelns und Wirtschaftens* ([no place of publication]: Éditions

Union, 1940); and *Human Action: A treatise on economics* (Yale University Press: 1949; third, revised and corrected edition, Chicago: Contemporary Books, Inc., 1966); French translation by R. Audouin (Paris: PUF, 1985).

12. See below, lecture of 7 February 1979, note 24.
13. On this current of thought, see P.-A. Kunz, *L'Expérience néo-libérale allemande dans le contexte international des idées*, doctoral thesis in political science (Lausanne: University of Geneve, Imprimerie central, 1962), and especially F. Bilger, *La Pensée économique libérale de l'Allemagne contemporaine* (Paris: Librairie Générale de Droit, 1964) and J. François-Poncet, *La Politique économique de l'Allemagne ocidentale* (Paris: Sirey, 1970), works used extensively by Foucault, as can be seen from his preparatory notes.
14. The European Recovery Program proposed in 1947 by the American Secretary of State G. Marshall, and adopted in 1948 by 16 Western European countries.
15. The National Council of Resistance (*Conseil national de la Résistance*, CNR) was formed in the Spring of 1943 in order to unite the different and politically divided resistance movements. It was presided over by Jean Moulin and then by Georges Bidault. "During their plenary meeting, all came to an agreement to remain united after Liberation. The Resistance Charter, which resulted from these deliberations, discussed and approved by the different groups making up the CNR, contained a bold social and economic program. Amongst other reforms, it called for 'a complete plan of social security aiming to guarantee every citizen the means of existence, when they cannot procure these through work, with management entrusted to the representatives of the different interests and the state'" (H.G. Galant, *Histoire politique de la sécurité sociale française, 1945-1952* (Paris: Librairie A. Colin, 1955) p. 24). See below, lecture of 7 March 1979, note 25 on the French plan for social security in 1945.
16. Formed on 19 December 1947, one half of this Scientific Council (*wissenschaftliche Beirat*) was made up of representatives of the Freiburg School (W. Eucken, F. Böhm, A. Müller, L. Miksch, A. Lampe, O. Veit, ... ), and the other by representatives of Christian-social doctrines, such as the Jesuit O. von Nell-Breuning, and socialists, such as K. Schiller, G. Weisser, H. Peter.
17. Quoted by F. Bilger, *La Pensée économique libérale de l'Allemagne contemporaine*, p. 211. See, *Der wissenschaftliche Beirat beim Bundeswirtschaftsministerium* (Göttingen: Schwartz, 5 volumes 1950-1961).
18. Controller General of Finances from 1774 to 1776 under Louis XVI, Turgot, in line with the doctrine of the *économistes* and the physiocrats, decreed free trade in grains (decree of September 1774). See G. Weulersse, *La Physiocratie sous le ministère de Turgot et de Necker (1774-1781)* (Poitiers: Impr. de Poitou, 1925; republished Paris: PUF, 1950). See F. Bilger, *La Pensée économique libérale de l'Allemagne contemporaine*, p. 215: "( ... ) if Erhard was not a party man, he was the Turgot of an economic doctrine."
19. According to F. Bilger, *La Pensée économique libérale*, p. 211, the fourteenth plenary meeting of the Council was held on 21 April and not, as Foucault says, the 28th.
20. Ludwig Erhard (1897-1977). Assistant and then director of the Institute of Economic Observation attached to the Nuremberg College of commerce, he steered clear of Nazism during the Third Reich and devoted himself to economic research. He directed the economic administration of the Anglo-American zone from February 1948. As a Christian Democrat deputy he contributed to a large extent to the adhesion of the CDU (*Christlich-Demokratische-Union*) to the principles of the "social market economy." From 1948, at the time of the fourteenth plenary meeting of the Council, he traced out the major orientations of his political future (the primacy of monetary policy and the policy of growth, alignment of prices on the supply of commodities, equitable and gradual distribution of increasing material well-being). He was chosen as Minister of the Economy by Adenauer in 1951 and is considered to be the father of the "German economic miracle (*Wirtschaftswunder*)." See J. François-Poncet, *La Politique économique de l'Allemagne occidentale*, pp. 74-75. On these neo-liberal councilors, see N. Pietri, *L'Allemagne de l'Ouest (1945-1969)* (SEDES, 1987) pp. 44-45; D.L. Bark and D.R. Gress, *Histoire de l'Allemagne depuis 1945* (Paris: R. Laffont, 1992) pp. 199-200. See his main work, *Wohlstand für alle* (Düsseldorf: Econ Verlag, 1957); French translation by F. Brière with preface by J. Rueff, *La prosperité pour tous* (Paris: Plon, 1959), and *Deutsche Wirtschaftspolitik, der Weg der sozialen Marktwirtschaft*

(Frankfurt am Main: Knapp, 1962); French translation by L. Mozère, *Une politique de l'abundance* (collection of articles and speeches 1945-1962) (Paris: R. Laffont, 1963); English translation by Edith Temple Roberts and John B. Wood, *Prosperity Through Competition* (London: Thames and Hudson, 1958).

21. *Rede vor der 14. Vollersammlung der Wirtschaftsrates des Vereinigten Wirtschaftsgebietes am 21*, Frankfurt am Main, April 1948. The speech is reproduced in L. Erhard, *Deutsche Wirtschaftspolitik*, and in W. Stützel and others, eds., *Grundtexte zur Sozialen Marktwirtschaft. Zeugnisse aus zweihundert Jahren ordnungspolitischer Diskussion* (Bonn-Stuttgart-New York: Ludwigh-Erhard-Stiftung, 1981) pp. 39-42.
22. Ibid. (*Grundtexte*) p. 40: "Wenn auch nicht im Ziele völlig einig, so ist doch die Richtung klar, die wir einzuschlagen haben—die Befreiung von der staatlichen Befehlswirtschaft, die alle Menschen in das Entwürdigende Joch einer alles Leben überwuchernden Bürokratie zwingt ( ... )." See F. Bilger, *La Pensée économique libérale*, p. 211 ("freedom of the economy from State controls").
23. Ibid.: "Es sind aber weder die Anarchie noch der Termitenstaat als menschliche Lebensformen geeignet. Nur wo Freiheit und Bindung zum verpflichtenden Gesetz werden, findet der Staat die sittliche Rechtfertigung, im Namen des Volkes zu sprechen und zu handeln." French translation in F. Bilger, *La Pensée économique libérale*, p. 211: "Neither anarchy nor the termite-state are worthy forms of life. Only a state establishing both the freedom and responsibility of its citizens can legitimately speak in the name of the people." It would be better to translate *Termitenstaat* as "state of termites," an expression already used in 1944 by Wilhelm Röpke in *Civitas Humana: Grundfragen der Gesellschafts- und Wirtschaftsreform* (Erlenbach-Zurich: E. Rentsch, 1944); English translation by Cyril Spencer Fox, *Civitas Humana. A Humane Order of Society* (London: William Hodge, 1948) with regard to the "mortal danger" of "Collectivism" p. 2: "this resulting insect State [*Termitenstaat*] would not only destroy most institutions and values which comprise a development of three thousand years and which, with a conscious pride, we designate Occidental civilisation ... it would take from the life of the individual just that essential purpose which only freedom can bestow."
24. Luigi Einaudi (1874-1961): Professor of political economy at Turin and Milan. His opposition to fascism and his attachment to liberalism forced him to emigrate to Switzerland (1943-1944). He was Governor of the Bank of Italy (1945), parliamentary deputy (1946), and Minister of Finance (1947). He was elected President of the Republic (1948-1955). See his, *Lezioni di politica economica* (Turin: G. Einaudi, 1944).
25. See Max Weber, *Die protestantische Ethik und der "Geist" des Kapitalismus* (1905), in *Gesammelte Aufsätze zur Religionssociologie* (Tübingen: J.C.B. Mohr, 1920) vol. 1, pp. 1-236; English translation by Stephen Kalberg, *The Protestant Ethic and the Spirit of Capitalism* (Oxford: Blackwell, 2002).
26. See *Sécurité, Territoire, Population*, lecture of 11 January 1978, p. 17 and p. 27 n. 26; *Security, Territory, Population*, p. 15 and p. 26, note 26.
27. Foucault does not refer to Fichte again in the rest of the lectures. However, with reference to Zollverein, he mentions him in pages of the manuscript that he did not use which correspond to the end of this lecture (see above, footnote *, p. 00).
28. 24 June 1948, which is actually a decisive turning point in the history of post-war Germany (Erhard, armed with the authorization of the Economic Council, abolishes all price controls without asking for the prior agreement of the military governments), should be linked with 18 June, "J day," which, thanks to monetary reform (creation of the Deutsche Mark), marks the first stage, and the determinant condition, of this process of transformation. See D.R. Bark and D.L. Gress, *Histoire de l'Allemagne depuis 1945*, pp. 191-194; N. Pietri, *L'Allemagne de l'Ouest*, pp. 46-48. As Erhard writes in *Wohlstand für alle*, p. 21; *Prosperity Through Competition*, p. 12: "The big chance for Germany came in 1948: it depended on linking the currency reform with an equally resolute economic reform." The law of 24 June 1948 bears the name, moreover, of "law on the principles of management and prices policy after monetary reform." See G. Schneilin and H. Schumacher, *Économie de l'Allemagne depuis 1945* (Paris: A. Colin, 1992) p. 24; J. François-Poncet, *La Politique économique*, pp. 71-73. This point is all the more important as monetary stability represents, after the fundamental principle ("realization of a system of prices of perfect competition"),

the major principle of the neo-liberal program. See below, lecture of 14 February 1979, pp. 138-139.

29. Churchill, beaten in the 1945 election, was replaced by C.R. Attlee, leader of the Labour Party since 1935. His government (1945-1951) was marked by a strong state hold on the economy (nationalizations, austerity plan, social security).
30. On the general strike, see Erhard, *Wohlstand für alle*, pp. 24-32; *Prosperity Through Competition*, pp. 15-22.
31. Oswald von Nell-Breuning (1890-1991), s.j., was a member of the Scientific Council in the ministry for the Economy from 1948 to 1965. He was a theoretician of a "genuinely Christian socialism," based on the social encyclicals of Popes Leo XIII and Pious XI. He was the drafter of the encyclical *Quadragesimo Anno* (15 May 1931): see O. von Nell-Breuning, *Die soziale Enzyklika. Erläuterungen zum Weltrundschreiben Papst Pius' XI. über die gesellschaftsordnung* (Cologne: Hermann, 1932); he published *Gesellschaftsordnung. Wesensbild und Ordnungsbild der menschlichen Gesellschaft* (Nuremberg-Bamberg-Passau: Glock & Lutz, 1947) and, with H. Sacher, *Beiträge zu einem Wörterbuch der Politik*, Heft 2: *Zur christlichen Staatslehre* (Fribourg-en-Brisgau: Herder, 1948), as well as several articles (on wage justice, the concept of the proletariat, etcetera) extending the teaching of the encyclical *Quadragesimo Anno*. "( ... ) Convinced of the intrinsic justice of socialism, [he] asserted that modern man could only lead a satisfying life if he participated in the management of his enterprise, which did not mean only co-management but, in the short term, labor union control of all private industry" (D.J. Bark and D.R. Gress, *Histoire d'Allemagne*, p. 145); see F. Bilger, *La Pensée économique liberale*, pp. 248-253 (on the combination of competition and corporative organization recommended by Nell-Breuning). His, very relative, "rallying" to the neo-liberal program is expressed in particular in the article "Neoliberalismus und katholische Soziallehre," in P.M. Boarman, ed., *Der Christ und die soziale Marktwirtschaft* (Stuttgart-Cologne: Kohlhammer, 1955) pp. 101-122.
32. It is not at Munich, but at the Johann-Wolfgang-Goethe-Universität in Frankfurt that Oswald von Nell-Breuning takes on various teaching responsibilities from 1948.
33. Theodor Blank (1905-1972), CDU deputy, and Catholic union leader. On 26 October 1950, Adenauer entrusted him with the direction of what would become the Ministry of Defense, with the title "general councilor of the federal chancellor responsible for matters concerning the increase of allied forces."
34. See F. Bilger, *La Pensée économique libérale*, p. 211: "Christian trade unionist, vice president of the miners' union, he became acquainted with the works of the Freiburg School and accepted that the liberal order was a valid alternative to capitalism and economic planning, both of which he rejected."
35. 9-11 May 1946, the first Congress of the SPD (*Sozialdemokratische Partei Deutschlands*). Schumacher was confirmed as president.
36. See the texts quoted by F. Bilger, *La Pensée libérale*, p. 271.
37. Karl Schiller (1911-1994), professor of economics at the University of Hamburg, was an SPD member of the Hamburg parliament (1949-1957), rector of his university (1958-1959), then senator responsible for the economy in West Berlin (1961-1965), deputy in the Bundestag (1965-1972), and federal minister of the Economy (see the following note). From 1947 he was a member of the Scientific Council of economic administration brought together by Erhard.
38. In the government of the "grand coalition" bringing together the CDU/CSU and the SPD, formed by the Christian Democrat Kiesinger in December 1966. He exercised this function until 1972 (combining the portfolios of the Economy and Finance from 1971 to 1972). On his economic policy, see D.L. Bark and D.R. Gress, *Histoire de l'Allemagne*, pp. 584-586.
39. K. Schiller, *Sozialismus und Wettbewerb* (Hamburg: Verlagsges. deutscher Konsumgenossenschaften, 1955).
40. D.L. Bark and D.R. Gress, *Histoire d'Allemagne*, pp. 428-429: "In 1953 he forged an expression with regard to the social market economy defining the alterations that the social democrats could bring to it: 'As much competition as possible, as much planning as necessary.' See H. Körner and others, *Wirtschaftspolitik, Wissenschaft und politische Aufgabe* (Bern: Paul Haupt, 1976) p. 86." He formulated the famous slogan during a session of the SPD on economic policy that took place at Bochum in February 1953. The formula was taken up

again in the program of the SPD in 1959 (see the following note; D.L. Bark and D.R. Gress, ibid. p. 430). See F. Bilger, *La Pensée économique libérale*, the Preface by D. Villey, p. xiv, and pp. 257-258.

41. Meeting at an extraordinary congress from the 13 to 15 November 1959 at Bad Godesberg, by a majority of 324 to 16 the SPD adopted the "basic program" (*Grundsatzprogram*) which, breaking with the Marxist inspired Heidelberg program of 1925, marked a decisive turning point in the party's line.
42. "Private ownership of the means of production deserves protection and encouragement insofar as it is not an obstacle to an equitable social order. Small and medium enterprises deserve to be consolidated so that they can assert themselves against big enterprises on the economic plane" (*Basic program of the German Social Democratic Party*, quoted by D.L. Bark and D.R. Gress, *Histoire de l'Allemagne*, p. 430. See F. Bilger, *La Pensée économique libérale*, p. 273, which refers here to the article by W. Kreiterling, "La social-démocratie révise sa doctrine," *Documents. Revue des questions allemandes*, 1959, p. 652 *sq*.
43. "A totalitarian or dictatorial economy destroys freedom. That is why the German Social Democratic Party approves a free market economy wherever competition exists. However, where the markets are dominated by individuals or groups, measures must be taken to preserve the freedom of the economy. Competition as much as possible—planning as much as necessary" (*Basic program*, quoted by D.L. Bark and D.R. Gress, *Histoire de l'Allemagne*, p. 430). See F. Bilger, *La Pensée économique libérale*, p. 273.
44. Kurt Schumacher (1895-1952) was deputy in the Reichstag between 1930 and 1933 and president of the SPD from 1932 until the prohibition of the party a year later. He spent ten years in a concentration camp under the Nazis. From 1945 he re-established the headquarters of the revived SPD, declaring: "Either we succeed in making Germany a socialist country in the economic domain and democratic in the political domain, or we will cease being a German people" (quoted by D.L. Bark and D.R. Gress, *Histoire de l'Allemagne*, p. 188).
45. See F. Bilger, *La Pensée économique libérale*, p. 275: "At the end of 1961, Professor Schiller was called by Willy Brandt to take up the office of 'Wirtschaftssenator' [economic senator, i.e., Minister of Economic Affairs] in West Berlin and it is generally thought that he will become Minister of Economic Affairs in an eventual socialist federal government. In his new functions, Schiller systematically applied a liberal policy and one of his last speeches in an 'economics' session of the SPD at Essen in October 1963 provoked a real sensation throughout Germany with the extremely clear affirmation of his adherence to the market economy and the categorical rejection of even flexible planning."
46. Karl Herbert Frahm Brandt, known as Willy Brandt (1913-1992). SPD deputy in the Bundestag from 1950 to 1957, and then Mayor of West Berlin from 1957 to 1966, in 1966 he became Minister of Foreign Affairs in the coalition government of Kiesinger and was elected Chancellor in 1969.
47. Thomas Hobbes (1588-1679), *Leviathan* (London: A. Crooke, 1651).
48. John Locke (1632-1704), *Two Treatises of Government*, written around 1680-1683, they were published in 1690 (London: A. Churchill).
49. See L. von Mises, *Die Gemeinswirtschaft, Untersuchungen über den Sozialismus*; *Socialism: An Economic and Sociological Analysis*.
50. See *Sécurité, Territoire, Population*; *Security, Territory, Population*, lectures of 29 March and April 1978.
51. See above, lecture of 10 January 1979, note 18.
52. Erich Honecker (1912-1994), named First Secretary in 1971 after the retirement of Walter Ulbricht.
53. In continuity with these analyses, in 1983 Foucault conceived of a project of a report on socialist politics: "Do the socialists have a problematic of government, or do they only have a problematic of the state" (quoted by Daniel Defert, "Chronologie," *Dits et Écrits*, 1, p. 62). Apart from some reading by Foucault at this time (Jaurés, Blum, Mitterand), it seems that this project did not get beyond a dossier of press cuttings.

# five

## 7 FEBRUARY 1979

*German neo-liberalism (II).* ~ *Its problem: how can economic freedom both found and limit the state at the same time?* ~ *The neo-liberal theorists: W. Eucken, F. Böhm, A. Müller-Armack, F. von Hayek.* ~ *Max Weber and the problem of the irrational rationality of capitalism. The answers of the Frankfurt School and the Freiburg School.* ~ *Nazism as necessary field of adversity to the definition of the neo-liberal objective.* ~ *The obstacles to liberal policy in Germany since the nineteenth century: (a) the protectionist economy according to List; (b) Bismarck's state socialism; (c) the setting up of a planned economy during the First World War; (d) Keynesian interventionism; (e) the economic policy of National Socialism.* ~ *The neo-liberal critique of National Socialism on the basis of these different elements of German history.* ~ *Theoretical consequences: extension of this critique to the New Deal and to the Beveridge plans; interventionism and the growth of the power of the state; massification and uniformization, effects of state control.* ~ *The stake of neo-liberalism: its novelty in comparison with classical liberalism. The theory of pure competition.*

TODAY I WOULD LIKE to try to finish what I began to say about post-war German neo-liberalism, that is to say, the contemporary neo-liberalism which actually involves us.

I have tried to show you the problem which the question of the market raised for the eighteenth century. The problem was how, within a given state whose legitimacy could not be questioned, could you allow for a market freedom which was both historically and juridically new insofar as in the eighteenth century kind of police state freedom was almost only ever defined as the freedom of privilege, as a reserved freedom, as freedom linked to status, profession, or a concession of power, and so on? How was freedom of the market, as the freedom of laissez-faire, possible within a police state? This was the problem, and the answer given by the eighteenth century was ultimately simple and consisted in saying that what will give a place to market freedom and allow its insertion within *raison d'État* and the police state is quite simply that left to itself and governed by laissez-faire the market will be a source of the state's enrichment, growth, and therefore power. The answer of the eighteenth century was, in sum, that you will move towards more state by less government.

The problem posed to Germany in 1945, or more precisely in 1948 if we take those texts and decisions I talked about last week as our reference point, was clearly a very different and opposite problem (this is what I tried to explain last week). The problem was: given a state that does not exist, if I can put it like that, and given the task of giving existence to a state, how can you legitimize this state in advance as it were? How can you make it acceptable on the basis of an economic freedom which will both ensure its limitation and enable it to exist at the same time? This was the problem, the question that I tried to outline last week and which constitutes, if you like, the historically and politically first objective of neo-liberalism. I would now like to try to examine the answer more closely. How can economic freedom be the state's foundation and limitation at the same time, its guarantee and security? Clearly, this calls for the re-elaboration of some of the basic elements of liberal doctrine—not so much in the economic theory of liberalism as in liberalism as an art of government or, if you like, as a doctrine of government.

I will break a bit from my habits and give a few biographical details about these people who were grouped around the future Chancellor Erhard and who programmed this new economic policy, this new way of connecting the economy and politics that is a characteristic feature of the present German Federal Republic. Who were these people? In the scientific commission I have talked about, and which was brought together by Erhard in 1948, there were a number of people, among the main ones being, first of all, Walter Eucken,[1] a professional economist who at the start of the century was a student of Alfred Weber, the brother of Max Weber. Eucken was appointed professor of political economy at Freiburg in 1927 where he met Husserl,[2] encountered phenomenology, and met a number of the jurists who were eventually so important in the theory of law in twentieth century Germany, who themselves came into contact with phenomenology and who tried to re-elaborate a theory of law that tried to avoid both the constraints of nineteenth century historicism and Kelsen's formalist, axiomatic, statist conception.[3] In 1930, 1933, I am not sure of the date, Eucken wrote an article, which caused a big stir at the time, against the possible application of Keynesian methods to resolve the crisis in Germany.[4] These methods were being advocated at the time by people like Lautenbach[5] and Doctor Schacht.[6] Eucken remained silent during the Nazi period.[7] He was still professor at Freiburg. In 1936 he founded a journal with the name *Ordo*[8] and in 1940 published a book with the somewhat paradoxical title of *Grundlagen der Nationalökonomie*,[9] which in reality is not about national economy but precisely something which doctrinally and politically is fundamentally opposed to national economy. It was Eucken who formed the school of economists called the Freiburg School or the "ordoliberals" around the journal *Ordo* which he directed. He, then, was one of the scientific advisors, no doubt the main one, brought together by Erhard[10] in 1948. So, there was Eucken, and there was also Franz Böhm,[11] who was one of the jurists at Freiburg, a phenomenologist by training, or at least a disciple of Husserl, up to a point. Franz Böhm later became a deputy in the Bundestag and in the seventies he had a decisive influence on German economic policy. There was also Müller-Armack[12] in the commission, who was an economic historian, I think a professor at Freiburg,[13] but I am not absolutely sure, and who in 1941 wrote a very interesting book with the curious title of *Genealogy of Economic Style*[14] in which, outside of pure economic theory and outside of pure economic policy, he tries to define something that in a way would be an art of economic government, of governing economically, which he calls economic style.[15] Müller-Armack became Ludwig Erhard's Secretary of State when the latter was Minister for the Economy and was one of the negotiators of the Rome Treaty. These, along with others, are some of the characters of this scientific commission.

Behind these, we should also refer to some other people who also [played an important role in]* this new definition of liberalism, of the liberal art of government. They were not members of the scientific commission, but some of them at least were people who inspired it, the main one being obviously Wilhelm Röpke,[16] an economist in the Weimar period. He was one of Schleicher's[17] counselors and [should have become] one of his ministers if Schleicher had not been dismissed in favor of Hitler at the start of 1933. Röpke was also an anti-Keynesian and was forced into exile in 1933. He went to Istanbul[18] and then settled in Geneva[19] where he remained until the end of his career. In 1950 he published a little book entitled *The Orientation of German Economic Policy*,[20] with a preface by Adenauer, which in a way represents the clearest, simplest, and most clear-cut manifesto for this new economic policy. Others should be added. With regard to Röpke, I should add that during and just after the war he wrote a kind of great trilogy which, together with the *Grundlagen der Nationalökonomie*, is a kind of bible of this neo-liberalism. It is a work in three volumes, the first of which bears the title of *Gesellschaftskrisis (The Crisis of Society)*,[21] a term whose sad fate in contemporary political vocabulary you are familiar with, and which explicitly refers of course to Husserl's *The Crisis of European Sciences*.[22] There was also Rüstow.[23] There was someone who is clearly very important who also was not a member of the scientific commission, but whose career and trajectory was ultimately very important for the definition of contemporary neo-liberalism. This is the Austrian von Hayek.[24] He came from Austria and from neo-liberalism; he emigrated at the time of, or just before, the Anschluss. He went to England and also to the United States. He was very clearly one of the inspirations of contemporary American liberalism, or of American anarcho-capitalism if you like, and he returned to Germany in 1962 where he was appointed professor at Freiburg, thus closing the circle.

---

* M.F.: had a direct importance on

I have mentioned these small biographical details for a number of reasons. The first is that it is clear that those in Germany in 1948 who grappled with and tried to resolve the problem of how to link together the legitimacy of a state and the freedom of economic partners, while accepting that the second must found the first, or serve as its guarantee, had already been dealing with this problem for a long time. The problem had already arisen within and at the time of the Weimar Republic,[25] whose state legitimacy was constantly challenged and which had to struggle with well-known economic problems, and in the years between 1925 and 1930 people like Eucken, Böhm, and Röpke had to struggle with this problem.

I have also given some biographical reference points to show you something which may be worth studying more closely (for those who are interested in contemporary Germany). This is the curious closeness and parallels between what we call the Freiburg School or ordoliberals and their neighbors, as it were, the Frankfurt School. There is a parallel in the dates and equally in their fate, since part at least of the Freiburg School, like the Frankfurt School, was dispersed and forced into exile. There is the same type of political experience and also the same starting point, since broadly speaking both schools started from a problematic, I was going to say a political-university problematic, which was dominant in Germany at the start of the twentieth century and which we can call Weberianism. What I mean is that Max Weber[26] was a starting point for both schools and we could say, to schematize drastically, that he functioned in early twentieth century Germany as the person who, broadly speaking, displaced Marx's problem.[27] If Marx tried to define and analyze what could be summed up as the contradictory logic of capital, Max Weber's problem, and the problem he introduced into German sociological, economic, and political reflection at the same time, is not so much the contradictory logic of capital as the problem of the irrational rationality of capitalist society. I think, again very schematically, that what characterizes Max Weber's problem is this movement from capital to capitalism, from the logic of contradiction to the division between the rational and the irrational. And we can say roughly that the Frankfurt School as well as the Freiburg School, Horkheimer[28] as well as Eucken, have simply taken up this problem in two different senses, in two different directions. Again schematically, the problem for the Frankfurt School was to determine what new social rationality could be defined and formed in such a way as to nullify economic irrationality. The decipherment of this irrational rationality of capitalism was also the problem for the Freiburg School, but people like Eucken, Röpke, and others try to resolve it in a different way, not by rediscovering, inventing, or defining the new form of social rationality, but by defining, or redefining, or rediscovering, the economic rationality that will make it possible to nullify the social irrationality of capitalism. So, there were two opposed ways, if you like, for solving the same problem. Rationality or irrationality of capitalism, I don't know. The result anyway was, as you know, that both returned from exile to Germany in 1945, 1947—I am, of course, talking about those who were forced into exile—and history had it that in 1968 the last disciples of the Frankfurt School clashed with the police of a government inspired by the Freiburg School, thus finding themselves on opposite sides of the barricades, for such was the double, parallel, crossed, and antagonistic fate of Weberianism in Germany.

I have mentioned the career details of these people who inspired the programming of neo-liberal politics in Germany for a third, clearly more important reason, which is that the experience of Nazism was at the very heart of their reflections. But I think we can say that Nazism was, in a way, the epistemological and political "road to Damascus"* for the Freiburg School. That is to say, Nazism enabled them to define what I would call the field of adversity that they had to define and cross in order to reach their objective. Putting forward a merely strategic analysis, that is to say, not an exhaustive analysis of their discourse, I would say that basically they had to do three things.

First, they had to define an objective. This objective, which we analyzed last week,[29] was to found the legitimacy of a state on the basis of a space of freedom for the economic partners. This is the objective. It was the objective in 1948. It was basically already the objective around the years 1925-1930, although it was less urgent, less clear, and less clear-cut.

---

* In inverted commas in the manuscript.

Second, they had to define not just the set of adversaries they could come up against in achieving this objective, but, fundamentally, the general system with which this objective and the pursuit of this objective could clash, that is to say, the whole set of obstacles and enemies which broadly speaking constitutes the field of adversity with which they had to deal.

And the third operation they had to carry out to cross this field of adversity and achieve their objective was, of course, the distribution or redistribution of the conceptual or technical resources available to them. I would like to develop the last two points of this "strategic"* analysis a little today.

How did they constitute their field of adversity? That is to say, how did they find the overall logic of the set of enemy obstacles or adversaries with which they had to deal? I think the experience of Nazism was very important here. Of course, German liberal thought, although relatively subdued, was not born with the Freiburg School. For many years there were people, like Lujo Brentano[30] for example, who tried to support and maintain the classical themes of liberalism in a climate that was clearly not very favorable. Very schematically, we can say that from practically the middle of the nineteenth century there were a number of major obstacles to and criticisms of liberalism and liberal politics in Germany, appearing successively on the historical scene. Again, this is very schematic.

First, there was the principle, practically formulated in 1840 by List,[31] that, in Germany at least, national policy and a liberal economy could not be compatible. The failure of the Zollverein[32] to constitute a German state on the basis of an economic liberalism was in a way the proof of this. List and his successors laid down the principle that far from being the general formula universally applicable to any economic policy, liberal economics could only ever be, and was in fact only ever a tactical instrument or strategy for some countries to obtain an economically hegemonic and politically imperialist position over the rest of the world. In clear and simple terms, liberalism is not the general form

---

* M.F. notes: in inverted commas

which every economic policy must adopt. Quite simply, liberalism is English policy; it is the policy of English domination. As a general rule it is also the policy suited to a maritime nation. To that extent, Germany, with its history, with its geographical position, with the whole set of constraints in which it is held, cannot afford a liberal economic policy; it needs a protectionist economic policy.

The second, both theoretical and political obstacle that German liberalism encountered at the end of the nineteenth century, was Bismarckian state socialism: for a unified German nation to exist, it must not only be protected against the outside by a protectionist policy, in addition, internally, everything that could compromise national unity must be brought under control, suppressed, and generally speaking the proletariat, as a threat to the unity of the nation and state, must be effectively reintegrated within a social and political consensus. This is roughly the theme of Bismarckian state socialism, the second obstacle to a liberal politics.

The third obstacle, starting with the war, was obviously the development of a planned economy, that is to say, the technique which Germany was forced to adopt by its wartime situation and which [consisted in] the organization of a centralized economy under an administrative apparatus which took the most important decisions in the economic order—allocating scarce resources, fixing prices, and guaranteeing full employment. Germany did not abandon the planned economy at the end of the war, since planning was then renewed by both socialist and non-socialist governments. Practically from Rathenau[33] until 1933 Germany had an economy in which planning and economic centralization was a recurrent, if not a constant form.

Finally, the fourth obstacle, which arrived later on the scene in Germany, was Keynesian-style interventionism. From 1925 more or less [... *] in 1930, German Keynesians, like Lautenbach[34] for example, make the same kind of criticisms of liberalism as Keynesians in general, and they propose a number of state interventions on the general balances of the economy. So, from before the Nazi seizure of power, we have

* One or two inaudible words.

four elements: a protected economy, state socialism, economic planning, and Keynesian interventionism. These four elements acted as barriers to a liberal policy and from the end of the nineteenth century they were the object of a series of discussions conducted by the few partisans of liberalism living in Germany. In a way the German neo-liberals will be the heirs of this dispersed heritage, of this series of discussions.

I know I am giving a caricature of the situation and that in actual fact there was no discontinuity between these different elements but rather a sort of continuous transition, a sort of continuous network. The movement from economic protectionism to the economy of state aid was quite natural. Rathenau type planning, for example, was more or less re-utilized in a Keynesian perspective at the end of the 1920s and in the 1930s. All of this was connected, of course, but it did not form a system. Now what Nazism finally contributed was the strict coalescence of these different elements, that is to say, the organization of an economic system in which protectionist economics, the economics of state aid, the planned economy, and Keynesian economics formed a firmly secured whole in which the different parts were bound together by the economic administration that was set up. The Keynesian policy of Doctor Schact[35] was taken over in 1936* by the four-year plan for which Göring was responsible[36] and for which, moreover, he was surrounded by some of Rathenau's counselors.[37] Planning had a double objective: on the one hand, to ensure the economic autarchy of Germany, that is to say, an absolute protectionism, and, on the other, a policy of state aid, all, of course, entailing inflationary effects that war preparations (this was, if you like, a militarized economy) enabled to be financed. All this formed a whole.

I would say that, faced with the Nazi system, the theoretical, speculative *coup de force* of the German neo-liberals was not to say, as most people did at the time, and especially the Keynesians: The economic system the Nazis are setting up is a monstrosity. They are combining elements that are actually heterogeneous, which constrict the German economy within an armature of mutually contradictory and disparate

---

* M.F.: 1934

elements. The *coup de force* of the ordoliberals was not to say: Nazism is the product of an extreme state of crisis, the final point towards which an economy and a politics unable to overcome their contradictions are carried, and Nazism as the extreme solution cannot serve as an analytical model for general history, or at any rate for the past history of capitalism* in Europe. The ordoliberals refuse to see Nazism as this monstrosity, this economic hotchpotch, this solution of the last resort at the final point of crisis. They say: Nazism is a truth. Or rather, they say: Nazism is the revelation of the necessary system of relations between these different elements. The neo-liberals say: Take any of these elements, a protected economy or Keynesian-type intervention. These are, of course, apparently different things, but you will never be able to develop one without arriving, in one way or another, at the other. That is to say, the neo-liberals say that these four elements which German economic and political history successively brought onto the scene of governmental action are economically linked to each other and if you adopt one of them you will not escape the other three.

Taking up this schema and principle they successively study different types of economy, like Soviet planning for example. Those, like Hayek, who had a good knowledge of the United States took the example of the New Deal, and others took up the English example and, in particular, the examples of Keynesian policy in the big Beveridge programs worked out during the war.[38] They took all this and said: You can see anyway that, first, these are the same principles at work and, second, each of these elements will attract the other three. It was in this way that, in 1943 or 1944, I no longer remember, Röpke published, not without boldness and nerve, an analysis of the Beveridge plan which had been worked out during the war, and he said to the English: What you are preparing for yourselves with your Beveridge plan is quite simply Nazism. On one side you battle with the Germans militarily, but economically, and so politically, you are in the process of repeating their lessons. English Labour party socialism will lead you to German-style Nazism. The Beveridge plan will lead you to the Göring plan, to the

* Foucault adds: and of its history

four-year plan of 1936.[39] Consequently they tried to pinpoint a sort of economic-political invariant that could be found in political regimes as different as Nazism and parliamentary England, the Soviet Union and America of the New Deal. They tried to identify this relational invariant in these different regimes and they laid down the principle that the important difference was no longer between this or that constitutional structure. The real problem was between a liberal politics and any other form whatsoever of economic interventionism, whether it takes the relatively mild form of Keynesianism or the drastic form of an autarchic plan like that of Germany. So we have an invariant that could be called, if you like, the anti-liberal invariant, which possesses its own logic and internal necessity. This was what the ordoliberals deciphered in the experience of Nazism.

The second lesson they drew from Nazism was the following. What, they said, is Nazism? Essentially and above all it is the unlimited growth of state power. To tell the truth, this claim, which now seems to us a commonplace, presented a paradox and also represented a theoretical or analytical *coup de force*, for when we look at how National Socialist Germany functioned, I think the least we can say is that, at first sight at least, Nazism was the first systematic attempt to initiate the withering away of the state. Nazism is the withering away of the state for a number of reasons. First, this appears in the very juridical structure of National Socialist Germany, since as you know in National Socialist Germany the state lost the status of juridical personality inasmuch as the state could only be defined in law as the instrument of something else which was the true foundation of right, namely the people, the *Volk*.[40] The *Volk* in its community organization, the people as *Gemeinschaft*, is at once the principle of right and the objective behind every organization, behind every juridical institution, the state included. The state may well express the *Volk*, it may well express the *Gemeinschaft*, and it may well be the form in which the *Gemeinschaft* both manifests itself and produces its actions, but the state will be nothing more than this form, or rather, than this instrument.

Second, in Nazism the state is, as it were, disqualified from within, since the principle of the internal operation of all the apparatuses was not an administrative kind of hierarchy with the game of authority and responsibility typical of European administrations since the nineteenth century. It was the principle of the *Fühertum*, the principle of conduction,* to which loyalty and obedience had to correspond, which means that in the form of the state's structure nothing must be preserved of the vertical communication, from below to above and from above to below, between the different elements of this *Gemeinschaft*, of the *Volk*.

Finally, third, the existence of the party and the whole legislative system which governed relations between the administrative apparatus and the party vested essential authority in the party at the expense of the state. The subordinate position of the state is clearly marked by its systematic destruction, or at any rate, its reduction to the pure and simple instrument of the community of the people, which was the Führer principle, which was the existence of the party.

Deciphering this situation, the ordoliberals reply: Don't be deceived. The state is apparently disappearing; it has apparently been subordinated and renounced. Nonetheless it remains the case that if the state is subordinated in this way, it is quite simply because the traditional forms of the nineteenth century state cannot stand up to this new demand for state control that the economic policy of the Third Reich calls for. In fact, if you adopt the economic system I have been talking about, then you will need a sort of super-state to make it work, a supplement to the state which the present organizational and institutional forms we are familiar with cannot assure. Hence the necessity, precisely, for this new state to extend beyond itself in comparison with the forms we know and its need to create these sorts of supplements of the state, these intensifiers of state power represented by the theme of the *Gemeinschaft*, by the principle of obedience to the Führer, and by the existence of the party. So, everything presented by the Nazis as the destruction of the bourgeois and capitalist state are in fact supplements of the state, a state in the process of being born, institutions undergoing statification (*étatisation*). A consequence of this, and what enables the ordoliberals to draw a different conclusion, is that there is in fact a necessary link between this

---

* Foucault first used this term in relation to the practice of conducting conduct in the 1978 lectures, *Security, Territory, Population*. See the lecture of 1 March 1978; G.B.

economic organization and this growth of the state, which means that none of these elements of the economic system can be adopted without the other three arriving gradually in its wake, and to be established and to work, each of these elements calls precisely for the growth of state power. The economic invariant, on the one hand, and, on the other, the growth of the power of the state, even in apparently aberrant forms in comparison with the classical state, are absolutely bound up with each other.

Finally, the third *coup de force* that Nazism allowed the neo-liberals to carry out with regard to the problem they wanted to resolve is the following. The Nazi analysis of capitalist, bourgeois, utilitarian, and individualistic society can be traced back to Sombart,[41] insofar as it was expressed and epitomized by Sombart in his trajectory between 1900 and 1930 from quasi-Marxism to quasi-Nazism. The best summary is in his book *Der deutsche Sozialismus*.[42] What have the bourgeois and capitalist economy and state produced? They have produced a society in which individuals have been torn from their natural community and brought together in the flat, anonymous form of the mass. Capitalism produces the mass. Capitalism consequently produces what Sombart does not exactly call one-dimensionality,[43] but this is precisely what he defines. Capitalism and bourgeois society have deprived individuals of direct and immediate communication with each other and they are forced to communicate through the intermediary of a centralized administrative apparatus. [They have] therefore reduced individuals to the state of atoms subject to an abstract authority in which they do not recognize themselves. Capitalist society has also forced individuals into a type of mass consumption with the functions of standardization and normalization. Finally, this bourgeois and capitalist economy has doomed individuals to communicate with each other only through the play of signs and spectacles.*[44] In Sombart, and in fact already from around 1900,[45] we find that well-known critique which has now become one of the commonplaces of a thought whose articulation and framework we do not know very well: the critique of mass society, of the

* Manuscript: "of the spectacle."

society of one-dimensional man, of authority, of consumption, of the spectacle,[46] and so forth. That is what Sombart said. What's more, it is what the Nazis took up in their own way. And it was indeed in opposition to this destruction of society by the [capitalist]* economy and state that the Nazis proposed to do what they wished to do.

But, say the neo-liberals, what do the Nazis actually do with their organization, their party, and their principle of the *Führertum*? In reality all they do is intensify this mass society, this society of standardizing and normalizing consumption, this society of signs and spectacles. Look at Nazi society as it actually functions. We are dealing entirely with the order of the mass, the masses at Nuremberg, the Nuremberg spectacles, standard consumption for everyone, the idea of the Volkswagen, and so on. All of this is only the renewal and intensification of all those features of bourgeois capitalist society that Sombart had denounced and which the Nazis claimed to be rejecting. And why is this? Why do they only renew what they claim to denounce if not because all these elements are not the effect and product of capitalist society as Sombart claimed and as the Nazis claim after him? Rather, they are the product and effect of a society that economically does not accept liberalism, of a society, or rather of a state, that has chosen a policy of protectionism and planning in which the market does not perform its function and in which the state or para-state administration takes responsibility for the everyday life of individuals. These mass phenomena of standardization and the spectacle are linked to statism, to anti-liberalism, and not to a market economy.

To summarize all this, the decisive point of the Nazi experience for the Freiburg liberals—and this was their choice of adversary, if you like, the way in which they set up the field of adversity necessary for the definition of their strategy—was that, first, they thought they could establish that Nazism was the product of an economic invariant which is indifferent and as it were impervious to the capitalism/socialism opposition and to the constitutional organization of states; second, they thought they could establish National Socialism as an invariant which,

* M.F.: socialist

as both cause and effect, was absolutely bound up with the unlimited growth of state power; and third, that the first major and visible effect of this invariant linked to the growth of the state was a destruction of the network, the tissue of the social community, a destruction which, through a sort of chain reaction, a loop, calls precisely for protectionism, a centrally planned economy, and an increase in the power of the state.

Broadly speaking, everything which opposes liberalism and proposes state management of the economy thus constitutes an invariant whose history can be seen throughout the development of European societies since the end of the nineteenth century and, more precisely, from the start of the twentieth century, that is to say, when the liberal art of government became, so to speak, intimidated by its own consequences and tried to limit the consequences that it ought to have drawn itself from its own development. How did it try to limit them? Well, by a technique of intervention which consisted in applying to society and the economy a type of rationality considered valid within the natural sciences. In short, what we can broadly call technology. Technicization of state management, of control of the economy, and also in the analysis of economic phenomena, is what the ordoliberals call "eternal Saint-Simonism,"[47] and they identify Saint-Simon[48] with the birth of that vertigo which takes hold of the liberal art of government and leads it to seek a principle of limitation, a principle of organization in the application to society of a schema of rationality specific to nature, a principle which ultimately leads to Nazism. So, from Saint-Simon to Nazism there is a cycle of rationality entailing interventions which entail the growth of the state, which entails setting up an administration that itself functions according to technical types of rationality, and this constitutes precisely the genesis of Nazism over two centuries, or at any rate a century and a half, of the history of capitalism.

Making this type of analysis—of course, I am oversimplifying everything they said between 1935 and 1940 or 1950—in putting forward this analysis at the borders of political reflection, economic analysis, and sociology, the ordoliberals launched a fine scathing attack, since a familiar type of discourse and analysis takes off through this kind of analysis: the traditional critiques of bourgeois society and the analysis of bureaucracy; the idea of Nazism we all have in our heads, the theme of Nazism as the revelation and final point of an in some way historically natural development of capitalism; the negative theology of the state as the absolute evil; the possibility of sweeping up events in the Soviet Union and the USA, concentration camps and social security records, into the same critique, and so on. You are familiar with all of this, and I think it originates in this series of theoretical and analytical *coups de force* of ordoliberalism.

But with regard to what I would like to say, this is not for me the most important thing. The essential thing is the conclusion the ordoliberals drew from this series of analyses, namely: since Nazism shows that the defects and destructive effects traditionally attributed to the market economy should instead be attributed to the state and its intrinsic defects and specific rationality, then the analyses must be completely overturned. Our question should not be: Given a relatively free market economy, how should the state limit it so as to minimize its harmful effects? We should reason completely differently and say: Nothing proves that the market economy is intrinsically defective since everything attributed to it as a defect and as the effect of its defectiveness should really be attributed to the state. So, let's do the opposite and demand even more from the market economy than was demanded from it in the eighteenth century. In the eighteenth century the market was called upon to say to the state: Beyond such and such a limit, regarding such and such a question, and starting at the borders of such and such a domain, you will no longer intervene. This is not enough, the ordoliberals say. Since it turns out that the state is the bearer of intrinsic defects, and there is no proof that the market economy has these defects, let's ask the market economy itself to be the principle, not of the state's limitation, but of its internal regulation from start to finish of its existence and action. In other words, instead of accepting a free market defined by the state and kept as it were under state supervision—which was, in a way, the initial formula of liberalism: let us establish a space of economic freedom and let us circumscribe it by a state that will supervise it—the ordoliberals say we should completely turn the formula around and adopt the free market as organizing and regulating principle of the state, from the start of its existence up to the last form of its interventions. In other words: a state under the supervision of the market rather than a market supervised by the state.

I think this kind of reversal, which the ordoliberals were only able to carry out on the basis of their analysis of Nazism, enabled them in 1948 to try to resolve the problem they faced of finding a way of giving legitimacy to a state that did not yet exist and that had to be made acceptable to those who most mistrusted it. Well, let's adopt the free market and we will have a mechanism that will found the state and at the same time, by controlling it, will provide the guarantees demanded by those who have grounds for mistrusting it. This, I think, was the reversal they carried out.

And what is important and decisive in current neo-liberalism can, I think, be situated here. For we should not be under any illusion that today's neo-liberalism is, as is too often said, the resurgence* or recurrence of old forms of liberal economics which were formulated in the eighteenth and nineteenth centuries and are now being reactivated by capitalism for a variety of reasons to do with its impotence and crises as well as with some more or less local and determinate political objectives. In actual fact, something much more important is at stake in modern neo-liberalism, whether this takes the German form I am presently referring to, or the anarcho-liberal American form. What is at issue is whether a market economy can in fact serve as the principle, form, and model for a state which, because of its defects, is mistrusted by everyone on both the right and the left, for one reason or another. Everyone is in agreement in criticizing the state and identifying its destructive and harmful effects. But within this general critique—which is also a confused critique since it can be found with little difference from Sombart to Marcuse—through and in the shadow of this critique, will liberalism in fact be able to bring about its real objective, that is to say, a general formalization of the powers of the state and the organization of society on the basis of the market economy? Can the market really have the power of formalization for both the state and society? This is the important, crucial problem of present-day liberalism and to that extent it represents an absolutely important mutation with regard to traditional liberal projects, those that were born in the eighteenth century. It is not

* M.F.: la resurgescence [?]

just a question of freeing the economy. It is a question of knowing how far the market economy's powers of political and social information extend. This is the stake. Well, in order to give a positive answer and affirm that the market economy really can both inform the state and reform society, or reform the state and inform society, the ordoliberals carried out a number of shifts, transformations, and inversions in traditional liberal doctrine, and it is these transformations that I would now like to explain a little.*

So, the first shift is that of exchange, a shift from exchange to competition in the principle of the market. Putting it again very roughly, how was the market defined in eighteenth century liberalism, or rather on what basis was it described? It was defined and described on the basis of free exchange between two partners who through this exchange establish the equivalence of two values. The model and principle of the market was exchange, and the freedom of the market, the non-intervention of a third party, of any authority whatsoever, and a fortiori of state authority, was of course applied so that the market was valid and equivalence really was equivalence. The most that was asked of the state was that it supervise the smooth running of the market, that is to say, that it ensure respect for the freedom of those involved in exchange. The state did not have to intervene within the market therefore. On the other hand, the state was called upon to intervene in production in the sense that liberal economists in the middle of the eighteenth century said that when you produce something, that is to say, when you are investing work in something, it is necessary that everyone respects the individual ownership of what is produced. It was for this, the necessity of private property for production, that state authority was demanded. But the market must be a cleared space free from intervention.

Now for the neo-liberals, the most important thing about the market is not exchange, that kind of original and fictional situation imagined by eighteenth century liberal economists. The essential thing of the market is elsewhere; it is competition. In this, moreover, the neo-liberals only follow

---

* Foucault pauses at this point to say:
I see that it is late, I don't really know if I will start now ... What do you want? *[Some calls of "yes" are heard.]* Five minutes, no more.

a development of liberal thought, of liberal doctrine and theory, in the nineteenth century. Practically since the end of the nineteenth century, more or less all liberal theory has accepted that the most important thing about the market is competition, that is to say, not equivalence but on the contrary inequality.[49] It is the problem of competition and monopoly, much more than that of value and equivalence, that forms the essential armature of a theory of the market. On this point therefore the ordoliberals do not depart in any way from the historical development of liberal thought. They take up this classical conception and the principle that competition, and only competition, can ensure economic rationality. How does it ensure economic rationality? Well, it ensures it through the formation of prices which, precisely to the extent that there is full and complete competition, can measure economic magnitudes and thus regulate choices.

With regard to this liberalism focused on the problem of competition, this theory of the market focused on competition, the ordoliberals introduce something that I think is specific to them. In fact, the nineteenth and twentieth century marginalist and neo-marginalist conception of the market economy said that since the market can only function through free and full competition, the state must therefore refrain from altering the existing state of competition and carefully avoid introducing elements that will alter this state of competition through phenomena of monopoly, control, and so forth. At the most, it must intervene to prevent competition being distorted by phenomena like monopoly, for example. So the same conclusion is still drawn from this principle of the market economy as was drawn by those of the eighteenth century who defined the market economy by exchange, namely, laissez-faire. In other words, from the principle of the market economy, both eighteenth century and nineteenth* century liberals draw the same conclusion of the necessity of laissez-faire. The former deduce it from exchange, the latter deduce it from competition, but in any case the logical, political consequence of the market economy is laissez-faire.

This is where the ordoliberals break with the tradition of eighteenth and nineteenth century liberalism. They say: Laissez-faire cannot and

---

* M.F.: twentieth

must* not be the conclusion drawn from the principle of competition as the organizing form of the market. Why not? Because, they say, when you deduce the principle of laissez-faire from the market economy, basically you are still in the grip of what could be called a "naive naturalism,"† that is to say, whether you define the market by exchange or by competition you are thinking of it as a sort of given of nature, something produced spontaneously which the state must respect precisely inasmuch as it is a natural datum. But, the ordoliberals say—and here it is easy to spot the influence of Husserl[50]—this is naive naturalism. For what in fact is competition? It is absolutely not a given of nature. The game, mechanisms, and effects of competition which we identify and enhance are not at all natural phenomena; competition is not the result of a natural interplay of appetites, instincts, behavior, and so on. In reality, the effects of competition are due only to the essence that characterizes and constitutes it. The beneficial effects of competition are not due to a pre-existing nature, to a natural given that it brings with it. They are due to a formal privilege. Competition is an essence. Competition is an *eidos*.[51] Competition is a principle of formalization.[52] Competition has an internal logic; it has its own structure. Its effects are only produced if this logic is respected. It is, as it were, a formal game between inequalities; it is not a natural game between individuals and behaviors.

Just as for Husserl a formal structure is only given to intuition under certain conditions, in the same way competition as an essential economic logic will only appear and produce its effects under certain conditions which have to be carefully and artificially constructed. This means that pure competition is not a primitive given. It can only be the result of lengthy efforts and, in truth, pure competition is never attained. Pure competition must and can only be an objective, an objective thus presupposing an indefinitely active policy. Competition is therefore an historical objective of governmental art and not a natural given that must be respected. In this kind of analysis we find, of course, both the influence of Husserl and, in a somewhat Weberian way, the

---

* Foucault repeats: can

† In inverted commas in the manuscript.

possibility of connecting up history with the economy.[53] The ordoliberals go on to say that the task of economic theory is the analysis of competition as a formal mechanism and the identification of its optimum effects. But what actually takes place in the societies we know cannot be analyzed on the basis of this theory of competition. We can only analyze it by taking the real historical systems within which these formal economic processes function and are formed and conditioned. Consequently, we need an historical analysis of the systems that intersect, as it were, as a horizontal intersects a vertical, the formal analysis of economic processes. Economics analyzes the formal processes and history will analyze the systems in which the operation of these formal processes is either possible or impossible.[54]

The third consequence they draw from this is that the relation between an economy of competition and a state can no longer be one of the reciprocal delimitation of different domains. There will not be the market game, which must be left free, and then the domain in which the state begins to intervene, since the market, or rather pure competition, which is the essence of the market, can only appear if it is produced, and if it is produced by an active governmentality. There will thus be a sort of complete superimposition of market mechanisms, indexed to competition, and governmental policy. Government must accompany the market economy from start to finish. The market economy does not take something away from government. Rather, it indicates, it constitutes the general index in which one must place the rule for defining all governmental action. One must govern for the market, rather than because of the market. To that extent you can see that the relationship defined by eighteenth century liberalism is completely reversed. The problem thus becomes, what type of delimitation of government follows from this principle, or rather, what will be the effect on the art of government of this general principle that the market is what ultimately must be produced in government? And like a good serial, this is what I will try to explain next week.

---

1. Walter Eucken (1891-1950): head of the German neo-liberal school (Freiburg School) whose positions were expounded in the journal *Ordo* (see below, note 8). He studied economics at Bonn and Berlin, where he was a student of Heinrich Dietzel, an opponent of the historical school, and of one of the last figures of this school, Hermann Schumacher, the successor of Gustav Schmoller at the University of Berlin. After becoming Schumacher's assistant, Eucken broke with him in 1923, noting the inability of historicism to respond to the problem of inflation. He was nominated professor at Tübingen in 1925, and then at Freiburg in 1927, where he remained until his death. See F. Bilger, *La Pensée économique libérale de l'Allemagne contemporaine*, pp. 39-70.
2. On the relations between Eucken and Husserl, see F. Bilger, ibid., p. 47: "On his arrival in the town, Eucken established a deep friendship with Husserl, spiritually linked to Rudolf Eucken. The two men had frequent contacts, sadly quickly interrupted by the philosopher's death. In his works Eucken acknowledged the influence of the founder of phenomenology on the formation of his economic method. In particular, he often refers to Husserl's great book, *Die logische Untersuchungen* (Halle: S. Niemeyer, 1928); English translation by J.N. Findlay, *Logical Investigations* (London: Routledge, 2001) 2 volumes), the critical and positive aspect of which he transposes into political economy." For a more precise analysis, see R. Klump, "On the phenomenological roots of German *Ordnungstheorie*: what Walter Eucken owes to Edmund Husserl" in P. Commun, ed., *L'Ordolibéralisme allemand: aux sources de l'économie sociale de marche* (University of Cergy-Pontoise, CIRAC/CICC, 2003) pp. 149-162.
3. Among whom Hans Grossmann-Doerth and Franz Böhm (on the latter, see below note 11). See F. Bilger, *La Pensée économique libérale*, pp. 47-48 and 71-74. On Kelsen, see *Sécurité, Territoire, Population*; *Security, Territory, Population*, lecture of 25 January 1978, note 1.
4. W. Eucken, "Staatliche Strukturwandlungen und die Krisis des Kapitalismus" [Structural modifications of the state and crisis of capitalism], *Weltwirtschaftliches Archiv*, Jena, vol. 36 (2), 1932, pp. 297-321.
5. Wilhelm Lautenbach (1891-1948); see especially his article: "Auswirkungen der unmittelbaren Arbeitsbeschaffung," *Wirtschaft und Statistik*, vol. 13, no. 21, 1933, republished in G. Bombach and others, eds., *Der Keynesianismus* (Berlin: Springer, 1981) pp. 301-308, and his posthumous work, *Zins, Kredit und Produktion* (Tübingen: J.C.B. Mohr, 1952).
6. Hjalmar Greely Horace Schacht (1877-1970), first of all President of the Reichsbank, from November 1923 to March 1930, and then Minister for the Economy from July 1934 to November 1937. He was opposed to Göring and to arms expenditure (see below, note 36), but retained the title of Minister without portfolio until 1943. See J. François-Poncet, *La Politique économique de l'Allemagne occidentale*, pp. 21-22.
7. Quite the opposite. From the end of 1933 Eucken took part in a seminar organized by the economist Karl Diehl, which brought together opponents of Nazism from various faculties (among whom were the historian Gerhard Ritter and the theologian Clemens Bauer). He was resolutely committed against the policy directed by Heidegger in the administration of the University of Freiburg. He was a co-founder, with several Catholic and Protestant theologians, of the *Freiburger Konzil*, which was without doubt the only university group of opposition to Nazism after the 1938 pogroms, and during the war he took part in the discussions of the *Arbeitsgemeinschaft Volkwirtschaftslehre*, organized by Erwin von Beckerath, at the heart of *Gruppe IV* (responsible for economic questions) of the *Akademie für Deutsches Recht* founded by the Nazis in 1933-34 with the aim of Germanizing the law. *Gruppe IV* was created in January 1940. Its organizer, Jens Jessen, who became a fervent opponent of National Socialism, was executed in November 1944 for his participation in the July Plot against Hitler. *Gruppe IV* itself, which constituted an underground opposition forum, was suppressed in March 1943, but discussions between economists—especially around the transition economy of the post-war period—continued within a private framework of the "Beckerath circle." Eucken published several articles during this period. See H. Rieter and M. Schmolz, "The ideas of German Ordoliberalism 1938-1945: pointing the way to a new economic order," *The European Journal of the History of Economic Thought*, I (1), Autumn 1993, pp. 87-114; R. Klump, "On the phenomenological roots of German *Ordnungstheorie*" pp. 158-160.

8. Foucault confuses here the date of publication of the preface, co-signed by F. Böhm, W. Eucken, and H. Grossmann-Doerth with the title "Our task," in the first volume of the series *Die Ordnung der Wirtschaft* directed by these three authors (see the English translation with the title "The Ordo Manifesto of 1936" in A. Peacock and H. Willgerodt, eds., *Germany's Social Market Economy: Origins and evolution* [London: Macmillan, 1989] pp. 14-26) and that of the first issue of the journal *Ordo* in 1948. The latter appeared in the form of an annual volume from 1948 to 1974 (Düsseldorf: Helmut Küpper) and from 1975 (Stuttgart: Gustav Fischer).
9. W. Eucken, *Die Grundlagen der Nationalökonomie* (Jena: G. Fischer, 1940, 2nd ed. 1942); English translation by T.W. Hutchison, *The Foundations of Economics: History and theory in the analysis of economic reality* (London: William Hodge, 1950).
10. See above, lecture of 31 January 1979, note 19.
11. Franz Böhm (1895-1977). Legal counselor to the Minister for the Economy from 1925 to 1932. He taught law at the universities of Freiburg and Jena from 1933 to 1938, but had to resign due to his opposition to the anti-Semitic policy. After the war he became Minister of Cultural Affairs in Hesse (1945-1946) and then professor of civil law and economics at the University of Frankfurt. He was a member (CDU) of the Bundestag from 1953 to 1965 and from 1948 to 1977 he played an active role in the Scientific Council of the *Verwaltung für Wirtschaft des Vereinigten Wirtschaftsgebietes* in Frankfurt. In 1965 he became the first German ambassador to Israel. His main works are: *Wettbewerb und Monopolkampf* (Berlin: C. Heymann, 1933); *Die Ordnung der Wirtschaft als geschichtliche Aufgabe und rechtsschöpferische Leistung* (Stuttgart-Berlin: Kohlhammer, 1937); *Wirtschaftsordnung und Staatsverfassung* (Tübingen: J.C.B. Mohr, 1950). See too his *Reden und Schriften* (Karlsruhe: C.F. Müller, 1960). With W. Eucken and H. Grossmann-Doerth, he was one of the co-signatories of the 1936 "Ordoliberal manifesto" (see above, note 8).
12. Alfred Müller-Armack (1901-1978). Assistant in economics at the University of Cologne from 1926, he obtained a professorial chair at Münster in 1940, and then again at Cologne in 1950. He joined the National Socialist Party in 1933 while condemning its racial doctrine (see his book, *Staatsidee und Wirtschaftsordnung im neuen Reich* [Berlin: Junker and Dünnhaupt, 1933]), and he then progressively distanced himself from the party in the name of his religious convictions. From 1952 to 1963 he was appointed ministerial director to the Minister for the Economy and Secretary of State for European problems. In this capacity he took part in the drafting of the Rome Treaty. He resigned in 1963 in order to take up posts in the administrative councils of several big enterprises. In addition, he was a member of the Mont Pèlerin group, created in Switzerland in 1947 on the initiative of F. Hayek, with a view to the defense of free enterprise, and other members of which were L. von Mises, W. Röpke, and M. Friedman. See F. Bilger, *La Pensée économique libérale*, pp. 111-112. His main works (apart from his *Genealogie der Wirtschaftsstile*, see below note 14) are: *Wirtschaftslenkung und Marktwirtschaft* (Düsseldorf: Verlag Wirtschaft und Finanzen, 1946, 2nd ed. 1948); *Diagnose unserer Gegenwart. Zur Bestimmung unseres geistesgeschichtlichen Standortes* (Gütersloh: Bertelsmann, 1949); *Religion und Wirschaft. Geistesgeschichtliche Hintergründe unserer europäischen Lebensform* (Stuttgart: Kohlhammer, 1959).
13. Actually it was Cologne, see the previous note.
14. A. Müller-Armack, *Genealogie der Wirtschaftsstile: die geistesgeschichtlichen Ursprünge der Staats- und Wirtschaftsformen bis zum Augang des 18.Jahrhunderts* (Stuttgart: Alfred Kohlhammer, 1941, 3rd ed. 1944). The author "tried to show that the economic organization of a time is the economic translation of the dominant 'Weltanschauung'" and "deduced [from this] the need to construct a post-war economy in line with a new 'style of life' that the Germans intended to adopt" (F. Bilger, *La Pensée économique libérale*, pp. 109-110).
15. The concept of "economic style" (*Wirtschaftsstil*), designating the overall socio-economic form of a society in a given epoch, was forged by A. Spiethoff ("Die allgemeine Volkswirtschaftslehre als geschichtliche Theorie. Die Wirtschaftsstile," *Schmollers Jahrbuch für Gesetzgebung, Verwaltung und Wirtschaft im Deutschen Reich*, 56, II, 1932) in order to deepen and clarify the concept of "economic system" (*Wirtschaftssystem*), introduced by W. Sombart in the 1920s: *Die Ordnung des Wirtschaftslebens* (Berlin: Julius Springer, 1927); *Die drei Nationalökonomien–Gesischte und System der Lehre von der Wirtschaft* (Berlin: Duncker and Humblot, 1930). It is therefore in partial continuity with the problematic of the German

historical school, while exhibiting a concern for a more rigorous typological analysis. The concept was critically examined by W. Eucken, *Die Grundlagen der Nationalökonomie*, pp. 71-74; *The Foundations of Economics*, pp. 90-93. See H. Möller, "Wirtschaftsordnung, Wirtschaftssystem und Wirtschaftsstil: ein Vegleich der Auffassungen von W. Eucken, W. Sombart und A. Spiethoff," in *Schmollers Jahrbuch für Gesetzgebung, Verwaltung und Volkswirtschaft* (Berlin: Duncker and Humblot, 64, 1940) pp. 75-98. In his articles from the 1950s and 1960s, Müller-Armack frequently uses the concept of style to define the program of action of the social market economy. See, for example, "Stil und Ordnung der sozialen Marktwirtschaft" (1952) in A. Müller-Armack, *Wirtschaftsordnung und Wirtschaftspolitik* (Fribourg-en-Brisgau: Rombach, 1966) pp. 231-242. See S. Broyer, "*Ordnungstheorie* et ordolibéralisme: les leçons de la tradition" in P. Commun, ed., *L'Ordolibéralisme allemand*, pp. 90-95.

16. Wilhelm Röpke (1899-1966): professor of economics at the University of Marbourg, until his dismissal for political reasons. A convinced follower of neo-marginalism, he was designated to be a member of an official commission to study unemployment in 1930-31. See F. Bilger, *La Pensée économique libérale*, pp. 93-103; J. François-Poncet, *La Politique économique*, pp. 56-57.
17. Kurt von Schleicher (1882-1934): Minister of the Reichswehr (June 1932), he became Chancellor after the resignation of von Papen (December 1932) but had to give way to Hitler in January 1933. He was assassinated by the Nazis the following year. It seems that Foucault here mixes up Röpke and Rüstow (see below, note 23). It was actually to the latter that Schleicher wanted to give the Ministry of Economic Affairs in January 1933.
18. ... where he meets the sociologist Alexander Rustöw, who was also an émigré.
19. In 1937. He taught there at the Institut des hautes études internationales. He also presided over the Mont-Pèlerin Society (see above, note 12) from 1960 to 1962.
20. W. Röpke, *Ist die deutsche Wirtschaftspolitik richtig? Analyse und Kritik* (Stuttgart: Kohlhammer, 1950) (see F. Bilger, *La Pensée économique libérale*, p. 97); republished in W. Stützel and others, eds., *Grundtexte zur sozialen Marktwirtschaft*, pp. 49-62 (see above, lecture of 31 January 1979, note 21).
21. W. Röpke, *Die Gesellschaftskrisis der Gegenwart* (Erlanbach-Zurich: E. Rentsch, 1942, 4th ed. 1945); French translation by H. Faesi and Ch. Reichard, *La Crise de notre temps* (Neuchâtel: Éd. de La Baconnière, 1945, edition with reduced annotations and no index; republished, Paris: "Petite Bibliothèque Payot," 1962); English translation by Annette and Peter Schiffer Jacobsohn, (Roepke) *The Social Crisis of Our Time* (London: William Hodge, 1950). The work was banned in Germany shortly after publication (see the *Völkische Beobachter* of 11 July 1942). The other volumes completing this book are, *Civitas Humana: Grundfragen der Gesellschafts- und Wirtschaftsreform* (Erlenbach-Zurich: E. Rentsch, 1944); French translation by P. Bastier, *Civitas Humana, ou les Questions fondamentales de la Réforme économique et sociale: capitalisme, collectivisme, humanisme économique, État, société, économie* (Paris: Librairie de Médicis, 1946); English translation by Cyril Spencer Fox, *Civitas Humana. A Humane Order of Society* (London: William Hodge, 1948), and *Internationale Ordnung* (Erlenbach-Zurich: E. Rentsch, 1945); French translation [anon.], *La Communauté internationale* (Geneva: C. Bourquin, 1947); English translation, *International Order and Economic integration* (Dordrecht: Reidel, 1959). In 1947 Röpke also published a book on the "German question," *Die deutsche Frage* (Erlenbach-Zurich: E. Rentsch); English translation by E.W. Dickes, *The German Question* (London: George Allen & Unwin, 1946), in which he recommends a constitutional monarchy as a way of re-establishing the *Rechtsstaat.*
22. E. Husserl, *Die Krisis der europäischen Wissenschaften und die transzendentale Phänomenologie* (W. Biemel: 1954); English translation by D. Carr, *The Crisis of European Sciences and Transcendental Phenomenology* (Evanston Ill.: Northwestern University Press, 1970). If the definitive version belongs to Husserl's posthumous works, the first part, which was the material of two lectures in Vienna and Prague in 1935, was published in Belgrade in 1936, in Arthur Liebert's journal, *Philosophia*. It is therefore possible that Röpke knew of the text. However he makes no explicit reference to it. His source, or his implicit reference, is religious rather than philosophical. See *Civitas Humana*, p. xvii: "( ... ) a careful reader of the celebrated but much misunderstood papal Encyclical 'Quadragesimo Anno' will find a social and economic philosophy expressed therein which at heart comes to much the same

conclusion [as *Die Gesellschaftskrisis der Gegenwart; The Social Crisis of Our Time*]." On this encyclical, see above, lecture of 31 January 1979, note 31.

23. Alexander Rüstow (1885-1963), son of Prussian general officer. As a radical socialist he belonged to the first generation of the *Jugendbewegung*. After the First World War he was employed in the Ministry for the economy and in 1924 he became scientific counselor of the *Verein deutscher Maschinenbauanstalten* (VDMA, The Confederation of German Machine Constructors). His adoption of a position favorable to social liberalism made him the target of Communists and National Socialists. After his exile in 1933, with Röpke's help, he obtained a post as professor of economic and social history at Istanbul, where he remained until 1947. In 1950 he succeeded Alfred Weber in the chair of economic sociology. His main works are: *Das Versagen des Wirtschaftsliberalismus als religionsgeschichtliches Problem* [The failure of economic liberalism, a problem of religious history] (Istanbul, 1945) and his monumental trilogy: *Ortsbestimmung der Gegenwart* [Determination of the place of the present] (Erlenbach-Zurich: E. Rentsch) volume 1: *Ursprung der Herrschaft* [The origin of domination], 1950; volume 2: *Weg der Freiheit* [The road of freedom], 1952; and volume 3: *Herrschaft oder Freiheit*, 1955, [abridged English translation by Salvator Attanasio, *Freedom or Domination: a Historical Critique of Civilisation*, ed. A. Dankwart (Princeton: Princeton University Press, 1980)], see the review by C.J. Friedrich, "The political thought of Neoliberalism," *The American Political Science Review*, 49 (2) June 1955, pp. 514-525.
24. Friedrich von Hayek: born in Vienna 8 May 1899; studies law and political sciences at Vienna where he follows F. von. Wieser's (1851-1926) courses on political economy and takes part in the informal seminars organized in his office by Ludwig von Mises, then a functionary in the Chamber of Commerce. Hayek, who still leans towards the socializing thought of the Fabians, soon adheres to the ultra-liberal theses defended by Mises in his book *Socialism* (see lecture of 31 January 1979, note 11). Director of the Viennese Institute for economic research (the vice president of which is Mises), he leaves Austria for London in 1931. Appointed professor of social and moral sciences at the University of Chicago in 1952, he returns to Germany in 1962 to finish his career at the University of Freiburg. Apart from the works cited in notes (see above, lecture of 10 January 1979, note 3, and below, this lecture, note 33), Hayek is the author of: *Prices and Production* (London: George Routledge and Sons, 1931); *Individualism and Economic Order* (Chicago and London: University of Chicago Press—Routledge and Kegan Paul, 1949); *The Counter-Revolution of Science: Studies of the abuse of reason* (Glencoe, Ill.: Free Press, 1952); *Law, Legislation and Liberty*, vol. 1: *Rules and Order*; vol. 2: *The Mirage of Social Justice*; vol. 3: *The Political Order of a Free People* (Chicago and London: University of Chicago Press—Routledge and Kegan Paul, 1973-1979).
25. Proclaimed on 9 November 1918, following the announcement of the abdication of William II, endowed with a constitution in 1919, the Weimar Republic (1919-1933) had to confront considerable economic difficulties due, in particular, to inflation accentuated by the costs of reparations and to the shock of the 1929 crisis that encouraged the development of extremist movements.
26. Max Weber (1864-1920). It is not clear that Foucault is referring here to Weber's great work, *Wirtschaft und Gesellschaft* (Tübingen: J.C.B. Mohr, 1922; 4th ed. by J. Winckelmann, 1956); partial French translation J. Chavy and E. de Dampierre (Paris: Plon, 1971); English translation by Ephraim Fischoff and others, *Economy and Society. An Outline of Interpretive Sociology* (Berkeley and London: University of California Press, 1979) or rather to *The Protestant Ethic and The Spirit of Capitalism* already referred to (see above, lecture of 31 January 1979, note 25).
27. On the abundant literature on the relation of Weber to Marx, and the contradictory points of view it contains, see C. Colliot-Thélène, "Max Weber et l'héritage de la conception matérialiste de l'histoire," in *Études wébériennes* (Paris: PUF, 2001) pp. 103-132.
28. Max Horkheimer (1895-1973), co-founder of the *Institut für Sozialforschung* (Institute for Social Research), created at Frankfurt in 1923, which he reorganizes from 1931. Dismissed in 1933, he directed the Genevan annex of the Institute and then settled in New York in 1934. He returned to Germany in April 1948.
29. See above, lecture of 31 January 1979, pp. 82-84.
30. Ludwig Joseph (Lujo) Brentano (1844-1931): member of the Young Historical School guided by Gustav von Schmoller (1838-1917). See Joseph A. Schumpeter, *History of*

*Economic Analysis*, p. 809. F. Bilger, *La Pensée économique libérale*, pp. 25-26, presents him as "the founder of German liberalism": "He preached a liberalism that had to distinguish itself from English liberalism by a program that was not only negative, but also positive, particularly in the social domain. The state must therefore intervene, and Brentano was part of the 'Verein für Sozialpolitik' founded by the state socialists; he supported the social policy carried out by the Empire, and he approved the formation of workers' unions that, according to him, enabled equilibrium to be reestablished between forces on the labor market."

31. Friedrich List (1789-1846), *Das nationale System der politischen Ökonomie* (Stuttgart-Tübingen: Cotta, 1841); French translation by H. Richelot, *Système nationale d'économie politique* (Paris: Capelle, 1857; republished "Tel," 1998). On List's role in the genesis of the "protection of infant industries," see W. Röpke (Roepke), *The Social Crisis of our Time*, pp. 55-62.
32. *Deutscher Zollverein*: Customs union of the German States carried out in the nineteenth century under Prussian direction. Initiated in 1818, extended in 1854 to almost all of Germany, it made a strong contribution to the transformation of Germany into a major economic power. On this subject see Foucault's comments in the last pages of the manuscript for the preceding lecture (above p. 95).
33. Walther Rathenau (1867-1922): Jewish industrialist who, from 1915, was in charge of the organization of the German war economy. Minister of Foreign Affairs in 1922, he was assassinated by two nationalists of the extreme right. See, W. Röpke, *Civitas Humana*, p. 79, note 1 to p. 63: "Eternal Saint-Simonism which inherits from its founder the ideas of a planning hungering for power meets us again in the tragic figure of *Walter Rathenau*, the great German industrialist and engineer, himself a victim of a most tragic period, who, together with other engineer friends invented if not the thing itself at least the phrase 'Planned Economy' (Planwirtschaft). He also became what a little later was called a 'Technocrat.'" See too F. Hayek, *The Road to Serfdom* (Chicago: University of Chicago Press; London: Routledge, 1944) p. 129, which underlines the influence of his ideas on the economic options of the Nazi regime.
34. See above, this lecture note 5.
35. See above, this lecture note 6.
36. The four-year plan asserted the absolute priority of rearmament. On the role and organization of the office of the four-year plan directed by Göring, see F. Neuman, *Behemoth: The structure and practice of National Socialism* (Oxford: Oxford University Press, 1944) pp. 247-254, with table on p. 253. For a synthesis of the most recent work on this moment of German economic policy, see I. Kershaw, *Nazi Dictatorship: Problems and perspectives of interpretation* (London and New York: E. Arnold, 1996) pp. 59-61. See also H. James, *The German Slump: Politics and economics, 1924-1936* (Oxford: Clarendon Press; New York: Oxford University Press, 1986).
37. See F. Hayek, *The Road to Serfdom*, p. 129: "Through his writings he [Rathenau] has probably, more than any other man, determined the economic views of the generation which grew up in Germany during and immediately after the last war; and some of his closest collaborators were later to form the backbone of the staff of Göring's Five Year Plan administration."
38. Appointed by Churchill, in 1940, president of an inter-ministerial committee responsible for proposing improvements to the English system of social protection. William Beveridge (1879-1963) published a first report in 1942, *Social Insurance and Allied Services* (New York: Agathon Press, 1969), in which he recommended a generalized, unified, and centralized system of social protection, as well as the creation of a health service free and accessible to all, and then a second report in 1944, *Full Employment in a Free Society* (London: George Allen & Unwin, 1944), that broadly helped to popularize Keynesian theses. The first report was never fully translated into French (on the syntheses, commentaries, and analyses published in French in the 1940s, see N. Kerschen, "L'influence du rapport Beveridge sur le plan français de sécurité sociale in 1945," *Revue française de science politique*, vol. 45 (4), August 1995, p. 571). See R. Servoise, *Le Premier Plan Beveridge, le Second Plan Beveridge* (Paris: Domat-Montchrestien, 1946). Foucault refers to the Beveridge plan in various lectures and interviews. See especially, "Crise de la médecine our crise de l'antimédicine?"

(1976) *Dits et Écrits*, 3, pp. 40-42; "Un système fini face à une demande infinie" (1983), *Dits et Écrits*, 4, p. 373; English translation by Alan Sheridan as "Social Security" in *Michel Foucault. Politics, Philosophy, Culture. Interviews and other writings 1977-1984*, ed. Lawrence D. Kritzman, translated by Alan Sheridan and others (New York and London: Routledge, 1988) p. 166.

39. W. Röpke, "Das Beveridgeplan," *Schweizerische Monatshefte für Politik und Kultur*, June-July 1943. This criticism of the Beveridge plan is summarized by Röpke in *Civitas Humana*, pp. 142-149 (see above, lecture of 7 March 1979, note 5). Referring to Foucault's comments in this passage, K. Tribe, in his *Strategies of Economic Order, German Economic Discourse 1750-1950* (Cambridge: Cambridge University Press, 1995) p. 240, notes: "There is some artistic licence at work here: for Röpke does not seem to have committed himself in so many words."
40. On the juridical structure of the National Socialist State, Foucault had read, notably, the works of M. Cot, *La Conception hitlérienne du droit*, doctoral thesis (Toulous: Impr. du Commerce, 1938), and R. Bonnard, *Le Droit et l'État dans la doctrine national-socialist* (Paris: Librairie Générale de Droit et de Jurisprudence, 1936, 2nd ed. 1939).
41. Werner Sombart (1863-1941): with A. Spiethoff and M. Weber, he was one of the main representatives of the last generation of the German historical school. Professor of economics at Berlin from 1917. His first major work, *Der moderne Kapitalismus* (Leipzig: Duncker & Humblot, 1902) is a continuation of Marx's theses and wins him a socialist reputation. In 1924 he adheres to the program of the conservative revolution and in 1933 becomes a member of the *Akademie für deutsches Recht*. Despite his adherence to the *Führer* principle, he does not subscribe to the National Socialist racial theories. His last books, including, *Deutscher Sozialismus* were badly received by the regime.
42. *Deutscher Sozialismus* (Berlin-Charlottenburg: Buchholz und Weisswange, 1934); English translation by K.F. Geiser as, *A New Social Philosophy* (Princeton and London: Princeton University Press, 1934); French translation by G. Welter as *Le Socialisme allemand: une théorie nouvelle de la société* (Paris: Payot, 1938), republished with a Preface by A. de Benoist (Paris: Pardès "Révolution conservatrice," 1990).
43. See H. Marcuse, *One-dimensional Man: Studies in the ideology of advanced industrial societies* (Boston: Beacon Press, 1964).
44. W. Sombart, *A New Social Philosophy*, Part One: "The economic era" ch. 2, "The Reconstruction of Society and the State" and ch. 3, "The Intellectual life" pp. 16-41.
45. W. Sombart, *Der Moderne Kapitalismus*; French translation by S. Jankélévitch as *L'Apogée du capitalisme* (Paris: Payot, 1932) Part III, ch. 53, and *Das Proletariat* (Frankfurt am Main: Rütter und Loening, 1906) in which he denounced the solitude and uprooting of workers produced by the "economic era."
46. See G. Debord, *La Société du spectacle* (Paris: Buchet-Chastel, 1967). The books by Marcuse and Debord to which Foucault alludes here were the two major references of the Situationist critique from the end of the 1960s (see already the final lecture of the previous year's lectures, *Sécurité, Territoire, Population*; *Security, Territory, Population*, lecture of 5 April 1978, p. 338, and note 15).
47. See W. Röpke, *Civitas Humana*: "His success rests on the fact that from 'scientism' he drew the final consequences for politics and the life of society and thus inevitably arrived by these means at the only possible destination, namely Collectivism. This represents the scientific elimination of the Human element in political and economic practice. His dubious glory it is that he created the model for a world and social outlook which may be described as *eternal Saint-Simonism*; that attitude of mind which is the outcome of a mixture of the hubris of the natural scientist and engineer mentality of those who, with the cult of the 'Colossal' combine their egotistical urge to assert themselves; those who would construct and organise economics, the State and society according to supposedly scientific laws and blueprints, whilst mentally reserving for themselves the principal *porte-feuilles*."
48. Claude Henri de Rouvroy, comte de Saint-Simon (1760-1825), French philosopher, economist, and social reformer, who, in *Du système industriel* (1821) (Paris: Anthropos, 1966), to remedy the crisis opened up by the Revolution, presented a plan of "general overhaul of the social system" (p. 11) replacing the old "feudal and military system" (p. 12) with the "industrial system" founded on the domination of industrialists and scientists and

organizing the whole of society in terms of the "industrial aim" (p. 19). See also *Catéchisme des industriels* (Paris: Impr. de Sétier, 1824-1825) in four volumes, the third volume of which was redrafted by Auguste Comte. After his death, his disciples—Rodrigues, Enfantin, and Bazard—were organized in a Society around the journal *Le Producteur.* Their movement played an important role in the colonial policy of the July monarchy, the construction of the first railways, and building the Suez canal.

49. See below, lecture of 21 February 1979, p. 166, the more explicit reference to Walras, Marshall, and Wicksell.
50. Reference to the Husserlian eidetic reduction is found in Eucken from 1934 in the essay, "Was leistet die nationalökonomische Theorie?" published as an introduction to his *Kapitaltheoretische Untersuchungen* (Jena: Fischer, 1934), in which he theorizes his method for the first time—a procedure of abstraction effectuated by the "Reduktion des tatsächlich Gegebenen auf reine Fälle" (the reduction of the factual given to pure cases) p. 21.
51. On the intuition of the essence, or *eidos*, in opposition to empirical intuition, see E. Husserl, *Ideas. General Introduction to Pure Phenomenology*, translated by W.R. Boyce Gibson (London/New York: George Allen and Unwin/Humanities Press, 1969).
52. See F. Bilger, *La Pensée économique libérale*, p. 155: "The liberals do not see the theory of perfect competition as a positive theory, but as a normative theory, an ideal type that one must strive to achieve."
53. See above, this lecture, p. 105.
54. See F. Bilger, *La Pensée économique libérale*, p. 52: "According to Walter Eucken, economic morphology [i.e., the typological analysis of economic systems] offers 'a strong link between the empirical view of historical events and the general theoretical analysis necessary for the comprehension of relations.'" On the connection between the morphological analysis of the framework and the theoretical analysis of economic processes within this, see, ibid. pp. 54-55.

six

# 14 February 1979

*German neo-liberalism (III).* ~ *Usefulness of historical analyses for the present.* ~ *How is neo-liberalism distinguished from classical liberalism?* ~ *Its specific stake: how to model the global exercise of political power on the principles of a market economy, and the transformations that derive from this.* ~ *The decoupling of the market economy and policies of laissez-faire.* ~ *The Walter Lippmann colloquium (26 to 30 August 1938).* ~ *The problem of the style of governmental action. Three examples: (a) the question of monopolies; (b) the question of "conformable actions (*actions conformes*)." The bases of economic policy according to W. Eucken. Regulatory actions and organizing actions (*actions ordonnatrices*); (c) social policy. The ordoliberal critique of the welfare economy.* ~ *Society as the point of application of governmental interventions. The "policy of society" (*Gesellschaftspolitik*).* ~ *First aspect of this policy: the formalization of society on the model of the enterprise.* ~ *Enterprise society and judicial society; two faces of a single phenomenon.*

TODAY I WOULD LIKE to continue with what I began to say about German neo-liberalism. When you talk about contemporary neo-liberalism, whether German or any other kind, you generally get three types of response.

The first is that from the economic point of view neo-liberalism is no more than the reactivation of old, secondhand economic theories.

The second is that from the sociological point of view it is just a way of establishing strictly market relations in society.

And finally, the third response is that from a political point of view neo-liberalism is no more than a cover for a generalized administrative intervention by the state which is all the more profound for being insidious and hidden beneath the appearances of a neo-liberalism.

You can see that these three types of response ultimately make neo-liberalism out to be nothing at all, or anyway, nothing but always the same thing, and always the same thing but worse. That is to say: it is just Adam Smith revived; second, it is the market society that was decoded and denounced in Book I of *Capital*; and third, it is the generalization of state power, that is to say, it is Solzhenitsyn on a world scale.[1]

Adam Smith, Marx, Solzhenitsyn, laissez-faire; society of the market and spectacle, the world of the concentration camp and the Gulag: broadly speaking these are the three analytical and critical frameworks with which this problem of neo-liberalism is usually approached, and which therefore enable it to be turned into practically nothing at all, repeating the same type of critique for two hundred, one hundred, or ten years. Now what I would like to show you is precisely that neo-liberalism is really something else. Whether it is of great significance or not, I don't know, but assuredly it is something, and I would like to try to grasp it in its singularity. If it is true that important and even invaluable political effects can be produced by historical analyses which present themselves precisely as historical and which seek to detect types of practice, institutional forms, etcetera, which exist and function for a time in certain places, if it is important to show what a [mechanism like]* the prison was at a given moment and to see what effect this purely historical type of analysis produces in a present situation, this absolutely never consists in saying, either implicitly or with more reason explicitly, that what existed then is the same as what exists now. The problem is to let knowledge of the past work on the experience of the present. It is

---

* Conjecture: inaudible word

not at all a matter of coating the present in a form that is recognized in the past but still reckoned to be valid in the present. It is this transfer of the political effects of an historical analysis in the form of a simple repetition that is undoubtedly what is to be avoided at any cost, and that is why I stress this problem of neo-liberalism in order to try to detach it from these critiques made on the basis of the pure and simple transposition of historical moulds. Neo-liberalism is not Adam Smith; neo-liberalism is not market society; neo-liberalism is not the Gulag on the insidious scale of capitalism.

So, what is this neo-liberalism? Last week I tried to indicate at least its theoretical and political principle. I tried to show you how the problem of neo-liberalism was not how to cut out or contrive a free space of the market within an already given political society, as in the liberalism of Adam Smith and the eighteenth century. The problem of neo-liberalism is rather how the overall exercise of political power can be modeled on the principles of a market economy. So it is not a question of freeing an empty space, but of taking the formal principles of a market economy and referring and relating them to, of projecting them on to a general art of government. This, I think, is what is at stake, and I tried to show you that in order to carry out this operation, that is to say, to discover how far and to what extent the formal principles of a market economy can index a general art of government, the neo-liberals had to subject classical liberalism to a number of transformations.

The first of these, which I tried to show you last week, was basically that of dissociating the market economy from the political principle of laissez-faire. I think this uncoupling of the market economy and laissez-faire policies was achieved, or was defined, at any rate, its principle was laid down, when the neo-liberals put forward a theory of pure competition in which competition was not presented as in any way a primitive and natural given, the very source and foundation of society that only had to be allowed to rise to the surface and be rediscovered as it were. Far from it being this, competition was a structure with formal properties, [and] it was these formal properties of the competitive structure that assured, and could assure, economic regulation through the price mechanism. Consequently, if competition really was this formal structure, both rigorous in its internal structure but fragile in its real, historical existence, then the problem of liberal policy was precisely to develop in fact the concrete and real space in which the formal structure of competition could function. So, it is a matter of a market economy without laissez-faire, that is to say, an active policy without state control. Neo-liberalism should not therefore be identified with laissez-faire, but rather with permanent vigilance, activity, and intervention.

This is very clear in most of the neo-liberal texts,* and there is one to which I refer you (if you can find it, for it is not easy to find; it was strangely lost by the Bibliothèque nationale, but you will certainly find it at the Musée social[2]). This text is the summary of the contributions made in 1939, on the eve of the war, in a colloquium called the "Walter Lippmann Colloquium."[3] It was held in France[4] following the publication of Lippmann's book which was translated into French with the title *La Cité [libre*† *]*.[5] It is a curious book because, on the one hand, it takes up the themes of classical liberalism in the form of a pure and simple reactivation, but, on the other hand, in a number of respects it also presents elements that form part of neo-liberalism. His book had just appeared in the United States, was translated into French, and a colloquium was held in Paris in which Walter Lippmann himself took part along with old liberals of the classical tradition, some French people like Baudin,[6] for example,[7] and then some of the German or Austrian neo-liberals, those precisely who formed part of the Freiburg School, some of whom who were exiled from Germany and others silenced in Germany, and for whom the colloquium was an opportunity for them to express their point of view. Röpke,[8] Rüstow, Hayek, and von Mises took part in the colloquium.[9] And then there were the intermediaries: Jacques Rueff,[10] Marjolin,[11] who is nonetheless important in the post-war French economy, and the general secretary of the congress, Raymond Aron,[12] who did not speak, or, at least, does not appear in the proceedings. Following the colloquium—I just signal this, because there are people who are particularly interested in the structures of the signifier—it is decided, in July 1939,[13] to form a permanent committee that will be

* M.F.: neo-positivist
† M.F.: future

called "Comité international d'étude pour le renouveau du libéralisme," CIERL.[14] In the course of this colloquium the specific propositions peculiar to neo-liberalism are defined. (You will find this in the summary, sprinkled with other theses and themes of classical liberalism.) And one of the participants, I no longer know which one,[15] proposes the extremely significant expression "positive liberalism" as the name for the neo-liberalism being formulated. Positive liberalism, then, is an intervening liberalism. It is a liberalism about which Röpke, in the *Gesellschaftskrisis*, which he published shortly after the Lippmann colloquium, says: "The free market requires an active and extremely vigilant policy."[16] In all the texts of the neo-liberals you find the theme that government is active, vigilant, and intervening in a liberal regime, and formulae that neither the classical liberalism of the nineteenth century nor the contemporary American anarcho-capitalism could accept. Eucken, for example, says: "The state is responsible for the result of economic activity."[17] Franz Böhm says: "The state must master economic development."[18] Miksch says: "In this liberal policy"—and here the phrase is important—"there may be as many economic interventions as in a policy of planning, but their nature is different."[19] Well, I think this problem of the nature of the interventions gives us a starting point for approaching what is specific in neo-liberal policy. As you know, broadly speaking the problem of the liberalism of the eighteenth century and the start of the nineteenth century was to distinguish between actions that must be taken and actions that must not be taken, between domains in which one can intervene and domains in which one cannot intervene. This was the distinction between the *agenda* and the *non-agenda*.[20] This is a naive position in the eyes of the neo-liberals, for whom the problem is not whether there are things that you cannot touch and others that you are entitled to touch. The problem is how you touch them. The problem is the way of doing things, the problem, if you like, of governmental style.

I will take three examples to locate how the neo-liberals define the style of governmental action. I will be schematic, brief, and stark, but you will see that these are things with which you are certainly familiar, since we are in fact immersed in them. I would just like to point out schematically three things: first, the question of monopoly; second, the problem of what the neo-liberals call a conformable economic action (*action économique conforme*); and third, the problem of social policy. Then, on the basis of this, I will try to indicate some of what seem to me to be specific features of this neo-liberalism which absolutely oppose them to everything one generally thinks one is criticizing when one criticizes the liberal policy of neo-liberalism.

First, then, I will take the question of monopolies. Once again, forgive me, this is very banal, but I think we need to go back over this, at least to bring some problems up to date. Let's say that in the classical conception, or one of the classical conceptions of the economy, monopoly is seen as a semi-natural, semi-necessary consequence of competition in a capitalist regime, that is to say, competition cannot be left to develop without monopolistic phenomena appearing at the same time, which precisely have the effect of limiting, attenuating, and even nullifying competition. Thus, a feature of the historico-economic logic of competition would be for it to suppress itself, this implying, of course, that any liberal who wants to assure the operation of free competition must in fact intervene within the economy on those economic mechanisms that facilitate, bring with them, and determine monopolistic phenomena. That is to say, if you want to save competition from its own effects, then there are times when you must act on economic mechanisms. This is the paradox of monopoly for a liberal economics which raises the problem of competition and at the same time accepts the idea that monopoly is actually part of the logic of competition. Of course, as you can imagine, the position of the neo-liberals will be completely different, and their problem will be to demonstrate that monopoly, the monopolistic tendency is not in fact part of the economic and historical logic of competition. Röpke, in the *Gesellschaftskrisis*, says that monopoly is "a foreign body in the economic process" and does not develop within it spontaneously.[21] To support this thesis, the neo-liberals deploy a number of arguments that I will pick out for you just for information.

First, there are arguments of an historical type, namely that monopoly, far from being a sort of ultimate, final phenomenon in the history of the liberal economy, is an archaic phenomenon the source of which is the intervention of public authorities in the economy. After all, if there is monopoly it is because the public authorities, or those who at the time assured the functions and exercise of public power, granted privileges to corporations and workshops, it is because states and sovereigns granted monopolies to individuals or families in exchange for financial services in the form of a sort of derivative or concealed tax system. This was the case, for example, with the monopoly granted to the Fugger family by Maximilian I in exchange for financial services.[22] In short, the development in the Middle Ages of a tax system that was itself a condition of the growth of centralized power brought about the creation of monopolies. Monopoly is an archaic phenomenon and a phenomenon of intervention.

There is also a juridical analysis of the conditions whereby the law functioned to allow or facilitate monopoly. How were inheritance practices, the existence of a law of joint-stock companies, the problem of patent rights, and so on, able to give rise to phenomena of monopoly, not for economic reasons, but due to the functioning of law? Here the neo-liberals raised a whole series of problems that are more historical and institutional than specifically economic, but which opened the way to very interesting research on the political-institutional framework of the development of capitalism, and from which the American neo-liberals benefited. The ideas of North[23] on the development of capitalism, for example, are directly in line with this opening up made by the neo-liberals, the problematic of which appears clearly in several contributions to the Lippmann colloquium.

Another argument to show that the monopolistic phenomenon does not belong in principle or logically to the economics of competition is found in political analyses of the link between the existence of a national economy, protectionist customs barriers, and monopoly. Von Mises, for example, analyzed this a number of times.[24] He shows how monopolistic phenomena are facilitated by division into national markets which, by reducing economic units to relatively small dimensions, effectively allow the existence, within this framework, of monopoly phenomena which would not remain in a world economy.[25] More positively and directly he shows how protectionism, in fact decided on by a state, can only be effective inasmuch as you create or call for the existence of cartels or monopolies which are capable of controlling production, foreign sales, price levels, and so on.[26] This was, broadly speaking, Bismarck's policy.

Third, economically, the neo-liberals say that classical analysis is true when it says that in capitalism the necessary increase in fixed capital is an undeniable support for the tendency towards concentration and monopoly. However, they say, in the first place this tendency does not necessarily and inevitably result in monopoly. There is, of course, an optimum level of concentration around which the capitalist regime tends to balance, but between this optimum of concentration and the maximum represented by the fact of monopoly there is a threshold that cannot be crossed spontaneously as the direct effect of competition, as the direct effect of economic processes. There must be what Rüstow calls "predatory neo-feudalism"[27] which must also receive "the support of the state, laws, courts, and public opinion" in order to pass from optimum concentration to the maximum of monopoly. And then, Röpke says, in any case, even if the phenomenon of monopoly exists, it is not in itself stable.[28] That is to say, in the medium term, if not in the short term, in the economic process there are always either modifications of productive forces, or technical modifications, or massive increases in productivity, or again the appearance of new markets. And all this means that the evolution towards monopoly can only be one variable which functions for a certain time among other variables which will be dominant at other times. In its overall dynamic, the economy of competition includes a series of variables in which the tendency to concentration is always counter-balanced by other tendencies.

Finally—and it is still von Mises reasoning in this way[29]—what is it, fundamentally, that is important, or rather disturbing about the phenomenon of monopoly with regard to the functioning of the economy? Is it the fact that there is only one producer? Absolutely not. Is it the fact that there is only one enterprise with the right to sell? Absolutely not. Monopoly has a disturbing effect inasmuch as it acts on prices, that is to say, on the regulatory mechanism of the economy. Now we can very well imagine, and it regularly happens in fact, that the monopoly price, that is to say, a price which can rise without either a fall in sales or profits, is not and cannot be applied by monopolies themselves, because as a result of applying the monopoly price they are always exposed to the appearance of competition which will take advantage of the existence of these abusive prices in order to hit back at the monopoly. Consequently, if a monopoly wishes to retain its monopolistic power it will have to apply, not the monopoly price, but a price identical, or at any rate close to the price of competition. That is to say it will act as if there were competition. And then it will not disrupt the market, it will not disrupt the price mechanism and the monopoly will not be important. The structure that is so important and the determinant phenomenon in competition is made to function by practicing this competitive "policy of the as if,"[30] and to that extent it is basically not relevant whether or not there is a monopoly.

All this merely situates how the neo-liberals want to pose the problem. In a way, they are freed from this problem of the handicap of monopoly. They can say: You can see that there is no need to intervene directly in the economic process, since the economic process, as the bearer in itself of a regulatory structure in the form of competition, will never go wrong if it is allowed to function fully. What constitutes the specific property of competition is the formal rigor of its process. But what guarantees that this formal process will not go wrong is that in reality, if one lets it function, nothing will come from competition, from the economic process itself, that is of such a nature that it will change the course of this process. Consequently, non-intervention is necessary at this level. Non-intervention is necessary on condition, of course, that an institutional framework is established to prevent either individuals or public authorities intervening to create a monopoly. And thus you find an enormous anti-monopolistic institutional framework in German legislation, the function of which is not at all to intervene in the economic field to prevent the economy itself from producing the monopoly, but whose function is to prevent external processes from intervening and creating monopolistic phenomena.*

The second important point in this neo-liberal program is the question of conformable actions (*actions conformes*).[31] This theory of conformable actions, this programming of conformable actions, is essentially found in a text which was actually one of the great charters of

---

* Foucault here leaves out pages 8-10 of the manuscript devoted to the German anti-cartel legislation of 1957.

contemporary German policy. It is a posthumous text by Eucken which appeared in 1951 or 1952, called *Grundsätze der Wirtschaftspolitik* (the foundations of economic policy)[32] and which is, as it were, the other, practical side of the text called *Grundlagen der Nationalökonomie* published a dozen years earlier, which was the theoretical side.[33] In this *Foundations*, these *Fundamental principles of economic policy*, Eucken tells us that liberal government, which must be perpetually vigilant and active, must intervene in two ways: first, through regulatory actions (*actions régulatrices*) and second, through organizing actions (*actions ordonnatrices*).[34]

Regulatory actions first of all. We should not forget that Eucken is the son of Eucken, the neo-Kantian Nobel prize-winner of the beginning of the twentieth century.[35]* As a good Kantian, Eucken says: How should government intervene? It should intervene in the form of regulatory actions, that is to say, it must intervene in fact on economic processes when intervention is imperative for conjunctural reasons. "The economic process always leads to temporary frictions, to modifications which risk giving rise to exceptional situations with difficulties of adaptation and more or less serious repercussions on some groups."[36] It is necessary then, he says, not to intervene on the mechanisms of the market economy, but on the conditions of the market.[37] Rigorously following the Kantian idea of regulation, intervening on the conditions of the market would mean identifying, accepting, and giving free play to the three typical and fundamental tendencies in the market, but in order to encourage these tendencies and somehow push them to their limit and full reality. These three tendencies are: the tendency to the reduction of costs, the tendency to the reduction of the profit of the enterprise, and finally, the provisional, localized tendency to increased profit, either through a decisive and massive reduction of prices, or by an improvement in production.[38] These are the three tendencies that regulation of the market, that regulatory action must take into account, inasmuch as they are themselves tendencies of the regulation of the market.

In clear terms this means first of all that the main objective of regulatory action will necessarily be price stability, understood not as fixed

---

* A short partially audible sentence follows: Neo-Kantianism ( ... ) literature.

prices but as control of inflation. Consequently all other objectives apart from price stability can only be secondary and, so to speak, adjuncts. At any rate, they can never be the primary objective. In particular, the primary objectives must not be the maintenance purchasing power, the maintenance of full employment, or even balancing the balance of payments.

Second, what does this mean for the instruments to be used? It means first of all using the policy of credit, that is to say, establishing the discount rate. It means using foreign trade by reducing the credit balance when you want to contain the rise in foreign prices. Shifts in taxation will also be employed, but always moderate ones, when seeking to act on saving or investment. But none of the kind of instruments used by planning will be resorted to, namely: price control, support for a particular sector of the market, systematic job creation, or public investment. All these forms of intervention must be rigorously banished and replaced by the pure market instruments I have just mentioned. The neo-liberal policy with regard to unemployment in particular is perfectly clear. Whatever the rate of unemployment, in a situation of unemployment you absolutely must not intervene directly or in the first place on the unemployment, as if full employment should be a political idea and an economic principle to be saved at any cost. What is to be saved, first of all and above all, is the stability of prices. Price stability will in fact allow, subsequently no doubt, both the maintenance of purchasing power and the existence of a higher level of employment than in an unemployment crisis, but full employment is not an objective and it may be that a reserve of unemployment is absolutely necessary for the economy. As, I think it was Röpke said, what is an unemployed person? He is not someone suffering from an economic disability; he is not a social victim. He is a worker in transit. He is a worker in transit between an unprofitable activity and a more profitable activity.[39] These then, are the regulatory actions.

Organizing actions are more interesting, however, because they bring us closer to the specific object. What are organizing actions? Well, [they are] actions with the function of intervening on conditions of the market, but on more fundamental, structural, and general conditions of the market than those I have just been talking about. In fact, we should never forget the principle that the market is a general social and economic regulator, but this does not mean it is a natural given to be found at the very basis of society. Rather, it constitutes—forgive me for saying it once again—a sort of fine and very reliable mechanism on condition that it functions well and nothing disturbs it. Consequently, the main and constant concern of governmental intervention, apart from these conjunctural moments I have just spoken about, must be the conditions of existence of the market, that is to say, what the ordoliberals call the "framework."[40]

What is a framework policy? I think it will appear clearly if we consider a text from Eucken's *Grundsätze*, that is to say, from 1952, where he takes up the problem of German agriculture, although he says the same arguments apply to most of European agriculture.[41] Basically, he says, agriculture has never been normally, fully, and exhaustively integrated within the market economy. It has not been integrated within the market economy because of protective customs that, throughout Europe, have marked off, and cut out the spaces of European agriculture. These protective customs were made indispensable both by technical differences and generally by the technical inadequacy of each country's agriculture. These differences and inadequacies were entirely linked to an over-population that made intervention, the insertion of technical improvements, pointless and, in truth, undesirable. So, what must be done if we want European agriculture to function within a market economy? The text is from 1952. We will have to act on facts that are not directly economic facts, but which are conditioning facts for a possible market economy. So on what will it be necessary to act? Not on prices, and certainly not on a particular sector, ensuring support for a scarcely profitable sector, since these are bad interventions. What will good interventions act on? Well, on the framework. That is to say, first, on the population. The agricultural population is too large, so it will have to be reduced by interventions enabling population transfers, migration, and so on. We will also have to intervene at the level of techniques, by making implements available, by the technical improvement of elements like fertilizers, etcetera, and also by the training and education given to farmers, which will enable them to modify [agricultural] techniques. Third, we will also modify the legal framework of farms, and in particular the laws governing inheritance, governing tenant farms and the location of estates, trying to find the means to get the legislation, structures, and institutions of society to play a part through action in agriculture, and so on. Fourth, as far as possible we will modify the allocation of the soil and the extent, nature, and exploitation of the soil available. Finally, if necessary, we will have to be able to intervene on the climate.[42]

You can see that none of these elements—population, technology, training and education, the legal system, the availability of land, the climate—are directly economic and they do not affect market mechanisms directly, but for Eucken they are conditions for agriculture to be able to function as a market, for agriculture to be able to function within a market. The idea was not, given the state of things, how can we find the economic system that will be able to take account of the basic facts peculiar to European agriculture? It was, given that economic-political regulation can only take place through the market, how can we modify these material, cultural, technical, and legal bases that are given in Europe? How can we modify these facts, this framework so that the market economy can come into play? You can see here something that I will return to shortly, which is that to the same extent that governmental intervention must be light at the level of economic processes themselves, so must it be heavy when it is a matter of this set of technical, scientific, legal, geographic, let's say, broadly, social factors which now increasingly become the object of governmental intervention. What is more, you can see in passing that this 1952 text programs, even if in a completely rough and ready way, what will become the Common Agricultural Market of the next decade. The text is from 1952. The Mansholt plan[43] is already in Eucken, or it is in part in Eucken, in 1952. So there you are for conformable actions, for conjunctural actions and organizing actions at the level of the framework. This is what they call the organization of a market order, of an order of competition.[44] And this is actually what European agricultural policy is: How to reconstruct a competitive order that will regulate the economy?

The third aspect is social policy. Here again I will have to be allusive, because for reasons of both time and competence I cannot go into details. However, we should agree to a number of things that are, if you like, banal and boring, but which enable us to locate some important elements. What is a social policy in a welfare economy, that is to say, in the kind of economy programmed by Pigou[45] and then taken up in one way or another by Keynesian economists, the New Deal, the Beveridge plan, and by European post-war plans? A social policy is broadly speaking a policy with the objective of everybody having relatively equal access to consumer goods.

How is this social policy conceptualized in a welfare economy? First of all, it is conceptualized as a counterweight to unrestrained economic processes which it is reckoned will induce inequality and generally destructive effects on society if left to themselves. So, the nature of social policy should be a kind of counterpoint to economic processes. Second, what should the major instrument of social policy be in a welfare economy? It should be socialization of some elements of consumption; the appearance of a form of what is called socialized or collective consumption: medical consumption, cultural consumption, etcetera. A second instrument is the transfer of elements of income in the form of family allowances [ ... *]. Finally, third, a social policy in a welfare economy is acceptance of the principle that stronger growth should entail a more active, intense, [and] generous social policy as a kind of reward and compensation.

Ordoliberalism very quickly raised doubts about these three principles. In the first place, they say that if you really want to integrate social policy into economic policy, and if you do not want social policy to be destructive in relation to economic policy, then it cannot serve as a counterweight and must not be defined as compensation for the effects of economic processes. In particular, relative equalization, the evening out of access to consumer goods cannot in any case be an objective. It cannot be an objective in a system where economic regulation, that is to say, the price mechanism, is not obtained through phenomena of equalization but through a game of differentiations which is characteristic of every mechanism of competition and which is established through fluctuations that only perform their function and only produce their regulatory

* Some inaudible words follow, ending with: certain categories, etcetera.

effects on condition that they are left to work, and left to work through differences. In broad terms, for regulations to take effect there must be those who work and those who don't, there must be big salaries and small salaries, and also prices must rise and fall. Consequently, a social policy with the objective of even a relative equalization, even a relative evening out, can only be anti-economic. Social policy cannot have equality as its objective. On the contrary, it must let inequality function and, I no longer recall who it was, I think it was Röpke, who said that people complain of inequality, but what does it mean? "Inequality," he said, "is the same for all."[46] This formula may seem enigmatic, but it can be understood when we consider that for the ordoliberals the economic game, along with the unequal effects it entails, is a kind of general regulator of society that clearly everyone has to accept and abide by. So, there is no equalization and, as a consequence and more precisely, no transfer of income from some to others. [More particularly, a transfer of income is dangerous when it is withdrawn from the part of income that generates saving and investment.]* This deduction would thus mean withdrawing a part of income from investment and transferring it to consumption. The only thing one can do is deduct from the highest incomes a part that would in any case be devoted to consumption, or, let's say, to over-consumption, and transfer this part of over-consumption to those who find themselves in a state of under-consumption due to permanent disability or unforeseen events. But nothing more. So you can see that social transfers are of a very limited character. Broadly speaking it is not a matter of maintaining purchasing power but merely of ensuring a vital minimum for those who, either permanently or temporarily, would not be able to ensure their own existence.† It involves only the marginal transfer from a maximum to a minimum; it is absolutely not the establishment of or regulation around an average.

Second, the instrument of this social policy, if it can be called a social policy, will not be the socialization of consumption and income. On the

---

* Manuscript, p. 16. There is an inaudible passage on the recording: [ ... ] from the part of income a section that would normally be directed towards saving or investment.

† The manuscript adds: "But as one cannot define it [the vital minimum], it will no doubt be the subdivision of the transfers of possible consumption."

contrary, it can only be privatization. That is to say, society as a whole will not be asked to guarantee individuals against risks, whether these are individual risks, like illness or accidents, or collective risks, like damage, for example; society will not be asked to guarantee individuals against these risks. Society, or rather the economy, will merely be asked to see to it that every individual has sufficient income to be able, either directly and as an individual, or through the collective means of mutual benefit organizations, to insure himself against existing risks, or the risks of life, the inevitability of old age and death, on the basis of his own private reserves. That is to say, social policy will have to be a policy which, instead of transferring one part of income to another part, will use as its instrument the most generalized capitalization possible for all the social classes, the instrument of individual and mutual insurance, and, in short, the instrument of private property. This is what the Germans call an "individual social policy," as opposed to a socialist social policy.[47] It involves an individualization of social policy and individualization through social policy, instead of collectivization and socialization by and in social policy. In short, it does not involve providing individuals with a social cover for risks, but according everyone a sort of economic space within which they can take on and confront risks.

This leads us to the conclusion that there is only one true and fundamental social policy: economic growth. The fundamental form of social policy must not be something that works against economic policy and compensates for it; social policy must not follow strong economic growth by becoming more generous. Economic growth and only economic growth should enable all individuals to achieve a level of income that will allow them the individual insurance, access to private property, and individual or familial capitalization with which to absorb risks. This is what Müller-Armack, Chancellor Erhard's counselor, around 1952-1953, called "the social market economy,"[48] which is also the name for German social policy. I add immediately that in fact this drastic program of social policy defined by the neo-liberals was not and could not be strictly applied in Germany for a whole range of reasons. German social policy was ballasted by a wide range of elements, some of which derived from Bismarckian state socialism, others from Keynesian economics, and others from the Beveridge plans or European social security plans, so that on this point the neo-liberals, the German ordoliberals, could not fully recognize themselves in German policy. However, I want to emphasize two points. First of all, it was starting from this and from the rejection of this social policy that American anarcho-capitalism developed, and second, it is also important to see that, in spite of everything, social policy increasingly tends to follow this program, at least in those countries increasingly aligned with neo-liberalism. The idea of a privatization of insurance mechanisms, and the idea at any rate that it is up to the individual [to protect himself against risks] through all the reserves he has at his disposal, either simply as an individual, or through mutual benefit organizations and suchlike, is the objective you can see at work in the neo-liberal policies currently being pursued in France.[49] This is the tendency: privatized social policy.

Forgive me for being so prolix and banal on all this history, but I think it was important in order to bring out now a number of things that seem to me [to form] the, how to put it, original armature of neo-liberalism. The first point to underline is that, as you can see, and as the neo-liberals have always said, neo-liberal governmental intervention is no less dense, frequent, active, and continuous than in any other system. But what is important is to see what the point of application of these governmental interventions is now. Since this is a liberal regime, it is understood that government must not intervene on effects of the market. Nor must neo-liberalism, or neo-liberal government, correct the destructive effects of the market on society, and it is this that differentiates it from, let's say, welfare or suchlike policies that we have seen [from the twenties to the sixties].* Government must not form a counterpoint or a screen, as it were, between society and economic processes. It has to intervene on society as such, in its fabric and depth. Basically, it has to intervene on society so that competitive mechanisms can play a regulatory role at every moment and every point in society and by intervening in this way its objective will become possible, that is to say, a general regulation of society by the market. So this will not be the kind of economic government imagined by the physiocrats,[50] that is to say, a

* M.F.: in the years 1920-1960

government which only has to recognize and observe economic laws; it is not an economic government, it is a government of society. What's more, one of the participants in the Lippmann colloquium, who, in 1939, was looking for this new definition of liberalism, said: Could we not call it a "sociological liberalism"?[51] In any case, it is a government of society; what the neo-liberals want to construct is a policy of society. Moreover, Müller-Armack gave Erhard's policy the significant term of *Gesellschaftspolitik*:[52] a policy of society. The words mean however what they [say],* and the trajectory of the words actually indicates the processes that they can. In 1969-1970, Chaban presented his economic and social policy as a project of society, that is to say, he quite clearly identifies society as the target and objective of governmental practice.[53] At this point we pass from a, broadly speaking, Keynesian type of system, which had more or less lingered on in Gaullist policy, to a new art of government, which will be taken up by Giscard.[54] This is the point of fracture: the object of governmental action is what the Germans call "*die soziale Umwelt*":[55] the social environment.

So, what does this sociological government want to do in relation to this society that has now become the object of governmental intervention and practice? It wants, of course, to make the market possible. To play the role of general regulator, of principle of political rationality, the market must be possible. But what does it mean to introduce market regulation as regulatory principle of society? Does it mean establishing a market society, that is to say, a society of commodities, of consumption, in which exchange value will be at the same time the general measure and criterion of the elements, the principle of communication between individuals, and the principle of the circulation of things? In other words, does this neo-liberal art of government involve normalizing and disciplining society on the basis of the market value and form? Does this not return us to the model of mass society, of the society of consumption, of commodities, the spectacle, simulacra, and speed that Sombart defined for the first time in 1903?[56] I don't think so in fact. It is not market society that is at stake in this new art of government; it is not a

* M.F.: mean (*veulent dire*).

question of reconstructing that kind of society. The society regulated by reference to the market that the neo-liberals are thinking about is a society in which the regulatory principle should not be so much the exchange of commodities as the mechanisms of competition. It is these mechanisms that should have the greatest possible surface and depth and should also occupy the greatest possible volume in society. This means that what is sought is not a society subject to the commodity-effect, but a society subject to the dynamic of competition. Not a supermarket society, but an enterprise society. The *homo œconomicus* sought after is not the man of exchange or man the consumer; he is the man of enterprise and production. We find ourselves here at an important point to which I will try to come back to next week. It is a point of intersection of a whole series of things.

First, of course, is the analysis of the enterprise that developed from the nineteenth century: to a considerable extent the historical, economic, and moral analysis of the nature of the enterprise, and the series of works on the enterprise by Weber,[57] Sombart,[58] and Schumpeter[59] actually support the neo-liberal analysis or project. So, if there is something like a return in neo-liberal politics, it is certainly not a return to the governmental practice of laissez-faire, and it is not a return to the kind of market society that Marx denounced at the beginning of Book I of *Capital*. There is an attempt to return to a sort of social ethic of the enterprise, of which Weber, Sombart, and Schumpeter tried to write the political, cultural, and economic history. More concretely, if you like, in 1950 Röpke wrote a text entitled *The Orientation of German Economic Policy*, which was published with a preface by Adenauer.[60] What does Röpke identify in this text, this charter, as the object, the final aim, the ultimate objective of governmental action? I will list the objectives he fixes: first, to enable as far as possible everyone to have access to private property; second, the reduction of huge urban sprawls and the replacement of large suburbs with a policy of medium-sized towns, the replacement of the policy and economics of large housing blocks with a policy and economics of private houses, the encouragement of small farms in the countryside, and the development of what he calls non-proletarian industries, that is to say, craft industries and small businesses; third, decentralization of places of residence, production, and management, correction of the effects of specialization and the division of labor, and the organic reconstruction of society on the basis of natural communities, families, and neighborhoods; finally, generally organizing, developing, and controlling possible effects of the environment arising either from people living together or through the development of enterprises and centers of production. Broadly speaking, Röpke says in 1950, it is a question of "shifting the center of gravity of governmental action downwards."[61]

You will recognize this text; it has been repeated 25,000 times for the last 25 years. In fact, it currently constitutes the theme of governmental action and it would certainly be false to see it as no more than a cover, a justification and a screen behind which something else is going on. At any rate, we should try to take it as it is given, that is to say, well and truly as a program of rationalization, and of economic rationalization. What does this involve? Well, when we look a bit more closely, we may of course hear it as a kind of more or less Rousseauesque return to nature, something that Rüstow called, moreover, with a very ambiguous word, a "*Vitalpolitik*," a politics of life.[62] But what is this *Vitalpolitik* that Rüstow talks about, and of which this is an expression? Actually, as you can see, it is not a matter of constructing a social fabric in which the individual would be in direct contact with nature, but of constructing a social fabric in which precisely the basic units would have the form of the enterprise, for what is private property if not an enterprise? What is a house if not an enterprise? What is the management of these small neighborhood communities [ ... *] if not other forms of enterprise? In other words, what is involved is the generalization of forms of "enterprise" by diffusing and multiplying them as much as possible, enterprises which must not be focused on the form of big national or international enterprises or the type of big enterprises of a state. I think this multiplication of the "enterprise" form within the social body is what is at stake in neo-liberal policy. It is a matter of making the market, competition, and so the enterprise, into what could be called the formative power of society.

---

* Two or three inaudible words.

To that extent, you can see that we are at the crossroads where a number of old themes are revived concerning family life, co-ownership, and a whole range of recurrent themes criticizing market society and standardization through consumption. And it is in this sense that we see a convergence—without this being anything like a recuperation, a word which has no meaning strictly speaking—between the Sombartian style of criticism of around 1900 against standardizing market society, etcetera, and the objectives of current governmental policy. They actually want the same thing. Quite simply, those who denounce a "Sombartian" society, in inverted commas, I mean that standardizing, mass society of consumption and spectacle, etcetera, are mistaken when they think they are criticizing the current objective of governmental policy. They are criticizing something else. They are criticizing something that was certainly on the explicit or implicit horizon, willed or not, of the arts of government [from the twenties to the sixties].* But we have gone beyond that stage. We are no longer there. The art of government programmed by the ordoliberals around the 1930s, and which has now become the program of most governments in capitalist countries, absolutely does not seek the constitution of that type of society. It involves, on the contrary, obtaining a society that is not orientated towards the commodity and the uniformity of the commodity, but towards the multiplicity and differentiation of enterprises.

That is the first thing I wanted to say. The second—but I really don't think I have time now—the second consequence of this liberal art of government is profound changes in the system of law and the juridical institution. For in fact there is a privileged connection between a society orientated towards the form of the enterprise [ ... †] and a society in which the most important public service is the judicial institution. The more you multiply enterprises, the more you multiply the centers of formation of something like an enterprise, and the more you force governmental action to let these enterprises operate, then of course the more you multiply the surfaces of friction between each of these enterprises, the more you multiply opportunities for disputes, and the more you multiply the

* M.F.: 1920-1960

† Some words that are difficult to hear: at once (made denser?) and (multiplied?)

need for legal arbitration. An enterprise society and a judicial society, a society orientated towards the enterprise and a society framed by a multiplicity of judicial institutions, are two faces of a single phenomenon.

This is something of what I would like to stress next week in developing other consequences, other formations in the neo-liberal art of government.*

---

* Foucault adds:
Ah yes, wait, I have something else to tell you, I'm sorry. The seminar will begin Monday the 26th. Those of you who come know that this seminar always creates problems. A seminar is usually something where you could work with 10, 20 or 30 people. Its nature, and consequently its object and form change when there are 80 or 100 people. So I would have a little indication to make, that is for those who do not really feel directly involved, that if they would be so kind ... good. Second, the main question in the seminar will be the analysis of the transformations of juridical mechanisms and judicial institutions, and of legal thought, at the end of the nineteenth century. However, I would like to devote the first seminar to some problems of method and possibly some discussion on the things I am talking about in the lectures. So what I would suggest, for those, but only for those who have some time and who it interests, etcetera, that if they want to ask me some questions that they write them for me here during the week. I will get the letters then next Wednesday and on Monday 26th I will try to answer those who have asked me questions. And then the following Monday, at the seminar, we will talk about themes in the history of law.

---

1. Alexander Isayevich Solzhenitsyn (born 1918), the Russian writer, author of a considerable body of work including, among the most well-known: *One Day in the Life of Ivan Denisovitch* (1962), *The First Circle* (1968), *Cancer Ward* (1968), and *The Gulag Archipelago* (1974). The publication of the latter (translation by Thomas P. Whitney, New York/London: Harper and Row/Collins, 1974), an "experiment in literary investigation," devoted to a detailed description of the Soviet world of concentration camps, earned its author arrest, deprivation of Soviet citizenship, and forced exile. It aroused a wide debate in the West on the repressive nature of the Soviet system. See in particular, A. Glucksmann, *La Cuisinière et le Mangeur d'hommes. Essai sur les rapports entre l'État, le marxisme et les camps de concentration* (Paris: Le Seuil, 1975) to which Foucault refers in his review of Glucksmann's *Maîtres penseurs* (English translation as *The Master Thinkers*) in 1977: "The frightened scholars went back from Stalin to Marx, as to their tree. Glucksmann had the effrontery to come back down to Solzhenitsyn"; "Le grande colère des faits," *Dits et Écrits*, 3, p. 278. In the first edition of *Surveiller et Punir*, in 1975, Foucault used the expression "carceral archipelago" (p. 304; *Discipline and Punish*, p. 298) in homage to Solzhenitsyn. See "Questions à M. Foucault sur la géographie" (1976), *Dits et Écrits*, 3, p. 32; English translation by Colin Gordon, "Questions on Geography" in Michel Foucault, *Power/Knowledge. Selected Interviews and Other Writings 1972-1977*, ed. Colin Gordon, translations by Colin Gordon and others (Brighton: The Harvester Press, 1980), p. 68. Solzhenitsyn's name is evoked here as a metonym for the concentration camp world and the Gulag.
2. Founded in 1894, in order to bring together books, pamphlets, and periodicals useful for knowledge of the "social question," the Musée social brings together collections covering the social domain in the widest sense of the term. It is found at 5 rue Las Cases, Paris, in the 7th arondissement. This address was chosen as the registered office of the Centre d'études created as a result of the colloquium (see below, this lecture, note 14).
3. *Compte rendu des séances du colloque Walter Lippmann (26-30 août 1938)*, Travaux du Centre international d'études pour la rénovation du libéralisme, vol. I, Preface by L. Rougier (Paris: Librairie de Médicis, 1939). See P.-A. Kunz, *L'Expérience néo-libérale allemande*, pp. 32-33.
4. On the initiative of Louis Rougier (see below, lecture of 21 February 1979, p. 161).
5. Walter Lippmann (1889-1974), *An Enquiry into the Principles of the Good Society* (Boston: Little, Brown, 1937); French translation by G. Blumberg as, *La Cité libre*, preface by A. Maurois (Paris: Librairie de Médicis, 1938). In an article published more than twenty years after the colloquium, L. Rougier presented the book of the "great American columnist" (for thirty years he wrote the column "Today and Tomorrow" in the *Herald Tribune*) in the following way: "This work rejected the identification of liberalism with the physiocrat and Manchester doctrine of *laisser-faire, laisser-passer*. He established that the market economy was not the spontaneous result of a natural order, as the classical economists thought, but that it was the result of a legal order postulating a legal interventionism of the state"; L. Rougier, "Le libéralisme économique et politique," *Les Essais*, 11, 1961, p. 47. See the quotation from W. Lippmann used as an epigraph to the second volume of Karl Popper's, *The Open Society and its Enemies, The High Tide of Prophecy* (London: Routledge & Kegan Paul, 1966): "To the débâcle of liberal science can be traced the moral schism of the modern world which so tragically divides enlightened men."
6. Louis Baudin (1887-1964): French economist, director of the series of "Great Economists," and author of *La Monnaie. Ce que tout le monde devrait en savoir* (Paris: Librairie de Médicis, 1938); *La Monnaie et la Formation des prix* (Paris: Sirey, 1947); *Précis d'histoire des doctrines économiques* (Paris: F. Loviton, 1941) and *L'Aube d'un nouveau libéralisme* (Paris: M.-T. Génin, 1953).
7. The other French members of the colloquium, apart from those cited, were R. Auboin, M. Bourgeois, A. Detœuf, B. Lavergne (author of *Essor et Décadence du capitalisme* [Paris: Payot, 1938] and *La Crise et ses remèdes* [Paris: Librairie de Médicis, 1938]), E. Mantoux, L. Marlio (author of *Le Sort du capitalisme* [Paris: Flammarion, 1938]), Mercier, and A. Piatier. W. Eucken was invited but did not obtain permission to leave Germany.

8. See above, lecture of 7 February 1979, notes 16 and 21.
9. See above, lecture of 31 January 1979, note 11. The translation of the book by von Mises, *Le Socialisme* had just appeared in the Librairie de Médicis (publishers of W. Lippmann's book).
10. Jacques Rueff (1896-1978): student of the École polytechnique, Treasury auditor, director of the Mouvement général des fonds (predecessor of the direction of the Treasury) at the time of the Popular Front. A liberal economist, who established experimentally the link between unemployment and the high cost of labor (the "Rueff law"), Rueff thought that a system of stable and effective prices was the central element of a developed economy and that in order to defend this economic policy had to combat its two main obstacles, the absence of competition and inflation. Before the colloquium he published *La Crise du capitalisme* (Paris: Éditions de la "Revue Bleue," 1935). His *Épitre aux dirigistes* (Paris: Gallimard, 1949) takes up and develops some of the conclusions of the colloquium. His main work is *L'Ordre social* (Paris: Librairie de Resueil Sirey, 1945). See his autobiography, *De l'aube au crépuscule* (Paris: Plon, 1977). Foucault met him several times.
11. Robert Marjolin (1911-1986): French economist, general commissioner of the Monnet Plan for Modernization and Equipment in 1947, then general secretary of the Organization for European Economic Cooperation (OEEC) from 1948 until 1955. See his memoirs *Le Travail d'une vie*, with collaboration of Ph. Bauchard, (Paris: R. Laffont, 1986).
12. Raymond Aron (1905-1983): philosopher and sociologist who after 1945, in the name of his rejection of communism, had to assert himself as one of the most committed defenders of liberal thought. At this time he had only published *La Sociologie allemande contemporaine* (Paris: Félix Alcan, 1935), and his two theses, *Introduction à la philosophie de l'histoire* (Paris: Gallimard, 1938) and *La Philosophie critique de l'histoire* (Paris: Vrin, 1938).
13. More exactly, 30 August 1938 (see the *Colloque W. Lippmann*, p. 107).
14. More exactly: Centre international d'études pour la rénovation du libéralism (the initials CIRL were adopted at the end of the colloquium (see p. 110), but the record of the colloquium is published under the initials CRL). See the extract of the statutes published in the record of the colloquium: "The object of research of the *Centre International d'Études pour la Rénovation du Libéralisme* is to determine and make known how the fundamental principles of liberalism, and principally the price mechanism, by maintaining a contractual regime of production and exchanges that do not exclude interventions arising from the duties of the state, in contrast with the directives of planned economies, enable men to be assured of the maximum satisfaction of their needs and society to be assured of the necessary conditions of its stability and duration." The International Center was inaugurated at the Musée social on 8 March 1939, with an address on neo-liberalism from its president, Louis Marlio, member of the Institut, and a lecture by Louis Rougier on "Le planisme économique, ses promesses. ses résultats." These texts are reproduced, with the stenographic records of several contributions from later sessions, in the 12th number of the journal, *Les Essais*, 1961: *Tendances modernes du libéralisme économique*.
15. It was L. Rougier, in *Colloque W. Lippmann*, p. 18: "It is only after having resolved these two prior questions [(1) without state intervention, is the decline of liberalism inevitable as the result of its laws of development? and (2) can economic liberalism satisfy the social requirements of the masses?] that we will be able to tackle the specific tasks of what we may call *positive liberalism*." See also, L. Marlio, ibid. p. 102: "I am in agreement with M. Rueff, but I would not like to use the expression 'left liberalism' [see J. Rueff, ibid. p. 101: '(M. Lippmann's text) establishes the bases of a policy that I, for my part, would describe as left liberal politics, because it tends to give the greatest possible well-being to the most deprived classes'] for this does not seem to me to be right and I think that there is at present more or less the same views on the left and right. [ ... ] I would prefer us to call this doctrine 'positive liberalism,' 'social liberalism,' or 'neo-liberalism,' but not the word 'left' which suggests a political position."
16. W. Röpke, *The Social Crisis of Our Time*, Part II, ch. 3, p. 228: "The freedom of the market in particular necessitates a very watchful and active economic policy which at the same time must also be fully aware of its goal and the resulting limits to its activity, so that it does not transgress the boundaries which characterize a compatible form of intervention."

17. Quoted, without reference, by F. Bilger, *La Pensée économique libérale de l'Allemagne contemporaine*, p. 182.
18. F. Böhm, *Die Ordnung der Wirtschaft als geschichtliche Aufgabe und rechgtsschöpferische Leistung* (Stuttgart-Berlin: Kohlhammer, 1937) p. 10: "The principal requirement of any economic system worthy of the name is that political direction becomes mistress of the economy in its totality as in its parts; the economic policy of the state must master the whole of economic development both intellectually and materially" (translated and quoted by F. Bilger, *La Pensée économique libérale*, p. 173).
19. Foucault apparently reproduces fairly freely here a phrase of Leonhard Miksch taken from an article of 1949, "Die Geldschöpfung in der Gleichgewichtstheorie," *Ordo*, II, 1949, p. 327, quoted by F. Bilger, ibid. p. 188: "Even if the number of apparently necessary corrective interventions should turn out to be so many such that from this point of view there would no longer any quantitative difference with regard to the planners, the principle expressed here would not lose its value."
20. See above, lecture of 10 January 1979, p. 12.
21. W. Röpke, *The Social Crisis of Our Time*, Part II, ch. 3, p. 228: "Not only are monopolies socially intolerable but they also interfere with the economic process and act as a brake on productivity as a whole."
22. See W. Röpke, ibid. p. 302: " ... we must remember that in the great majority of cases it was the State itself which through its legislative, administrative and judicial activities first created conditions favorable to the formation of monopolies ... That the State acted as midwife is quite clear in those cases where a monopoly was expressly granted by a special charter, a procedure which is particularly characteristic of the early history of European monopolies. Even then, however, the grant of monopolies appears to have been a sign of the State's weakness since the State in this way usually tried to free itself from debt, as for example when in Germany Maximilian I granted monopolies to the Fuggers."
23. Douglass Cecil North (born in 1920), *The Rise of the Western World*, in collaboration with R.-P. Thomas (Cambridge: Cambridge University Press, 1973); French translation by J.-M. Denis, *L'Essor du monde occidental: une nouvelle histoire économique* (Paris: Flammarion, 1980). See H. Lepage, *Demain le capitalisme* (Paris: Librairie Générale Francaise, 1978; republished "Pluriel") p. 34 and chapters 3 and 4 (this book was one of the sources used by Foucault in the last of these 1979 lectures).
24. See, *Colloque W. Lippmann*, pp. 36-37.
25. L. von Mises, ibid. p. 36: "Protectionism has divided up the economic system into a multitude of distinct markets, and by reducing the extent of the economic units, has provoked the creation of cartels."
26. L. von Mises, ibid.: "Protectionism can only have effective results on a national market, where production already exceeds demand, by the constitution of a cartel able to control production, foreign sales, and prices."
27. A. Rüstow, ibid. p. 41: "The tendency to exceed the economic optimum of concentration clearly cannot be a tendency of an economic order, in the sense of the competitive system. It is rather a predatory, neo-feudal, monopolizing tendency which cannot succeed without the support of the state, laws, courts, magistrates, and public opinion."
28. W. Röpke, *The Social Crisis of Our Time*, Part I, ch. 3, p. 136 *sq*; the author deploys a number of technical arguments against the thesis that "technical development ... manifestly leads to ever larger industrial and commercial aggregates."
29. *Colloque W. Lippmann*, p. 41.
30. On this policy of the "as if" (*Als-ob Politik*), theorized by one of Eucken's disciples, Leonhard Miksch, in his *Wettbewerb als Aufgabe* [Competition as duty] (Stuttgart-Berlin: W. Kohlhammer, 1937, 2nd ed. 1947), which enables the ordoliberal program not to be confused with the demand for a realization of perfect competition, see F. Bilger, *La Pensée économique libérale* p. 82, p. 155, and the whole of chapter 3 of Part 2: "La politique économique," pp. 170-206; J. François-Poncet, *La Politique économique de l'Allemagne occidentale*, p. 63.
31. On the distinction between "conformable" and "non-conformable" actions ("*actions conformes*" and "*non-conformes*") see W. Röpke, *Die Gesellschaftskrisis der Gegenwart* (5th ed. 1948) pp. 258-264; *The Social Crisis of Our Time*, pp. 159-163; *Civitas Humana*, p. 29. See

F. Bilger, *La Pensée économique libérale*, pp. 190-192 ("static" conformity and "dynamic" conformity in relation to the model according to Röpke). [The notions "*actions conformes*" and "*non-comformes*" are translated as "compatible" and "incompatible" interventions in *The Social Crisis of Our Time*, but as "conformable" and "non-conformable" in *Civitas Humana*. I have opted for the latter translation throughout; G.B.]

32. W. Eucken, *Die Grundsätze der Wirtschaftspolitik* (Bern-Tübingen: Francke & J.C.B. Mohr, 1952).
33. See above, lecture of 7 February 1979, note 9. See F. Bilger, *La Pensée économique libérale*, p. 62: "Thus this book is like the exact opposite of the first; after political economy, economic policy."
34. This distinction is not formulated explicitly in the *Grundsätze* (on the *Ordungspolitik*, see p. 242 *sq*). Foucault relies on F. Bilger, *La Pensée économique libérale*, pp. 174-188.
35. Rudolf Eucken (1846-1926): professor at the University of Basle in 1871, then at Jena, in 1874, where he taught until his retirement. He won the Nobel Prize for literature in 1908. Among his main works are: *Geistige Strömungen der Gegenwart* (Berlin: Verleger, 1904); French translation by H. Buriot and G.-H. Luquet, with a foreword by E. Boutroux, *Les Grands Courants de la pensée contemporaine* (Paris: Alcan, 1912); English translation by R. Eucken, *Main Currents of Modern Thought* (London: Unwin, 1912); *Hauptprobleme der Religionsphilosophie der Gegenwart* (Berlin: Reuther und Reichard, 1907); French translation by Ch. Rognard, *Problèmes capitaux de la philosophie de la religion au temps présent* (Lausanne: Payot, 1910); *Der Sinn und Wert des Lebens* (Leipzig: Quelle & Meyer, 1908) French translation by M.-A. Hullet and A. Leicht, with a foreword by H. Bergson, *Le Sens et la Valeur de la vie* (Paris: F. Alcan, 1912); English translation by Lucy Judge Gibson, *The Meaning and Value of Life* (London: Adam & Charles Black, 1909). The description "neo-Kantian," taken no doubt from F. Bilger's presentation in *La Pensée économique libérale*, pp. 41-42, imperfectly defines his "philosophy of activity," which is linked rather to the movement of vitalist spiritualism, tinged with religiosity, that was then opposed to intellectualism and scientism in Germany. See G. Campagnolo, "Les trois sources philosophiques de la réflexion ordolibérale" in P. Commun, ed., *L'Ordolibéralisme allemand*, pp. 138-143. The link Foucault suggests with neo-Kantianism no doubt refers to the Kantian distinction between "constitutive principles" and "regulatory principles" in the *Critique of Pure Reason*, trans. Norman Kemp Smith (London: Macmillan, 1978) 1st Division, Book 2, ch. 2, section 3 ("Analogies of Experience") pp. 210-211.
36. The quotation is in fact from Röpke (as the manuscript indicates), *The Social Crisis of Our Time*, Part II, ch. 2, p. 186: "In addition there is a no less important task [than working out the program of the 'third way']. Within the legal and institutional permanent framework the economic process will always produce certain frictions which are temporary by nature, changes which will bring hardship to certain groups, states of emergency and difficulties of adjustment."
37. See W. Eucken, *Grundsätze*, Book V, ch. 19, p. 336: "Die wirtschaftspolitische Tätigkeit des Staates sollte auf die Gestaltung der Ordnungsformen der Wirtschaft gerichtet sein, nicht auf die Lenkung des Wirtschaftsprozesses."
38. It is a matter here of the "restrictive definition of conformable intervention" according to F. Böhm, "that which does not run counter to three fundamental 'tendencies' of the market: the tendency to the reduction of costs, the tendency to the progressive reduction of profits of the enterprise, and the provisional tendency to an increase of profits in the case of a decisive reduction of costs and improvement in productivity" (F. Bilger, *La Pensée économique libérale*, pp. 190-191).
39. The attribution of this phrase to Röpke seems mistaken. We can find no trace of it either in the Lippmann colloquium or in Bilger's work.
40. On this notion, see F. Bilger, *La Pensée économique libérale*, pp. 180-181: "To the same extent that the 'ordoliberals' seek to restrict interventions in the process [object of regulatory actions], so they are favorable to the extension of the state's activity on the framework. For the process functions more or less well according as the framework is more or less well adapted. ( ... ) The framework is the specific domain of the state, the public domain, in which it can fully exercise its 'organizing (*ordonnatrice*)' function. It contains all that does not arise spontaneously in economic life: thus it contains realities which, in virtue of the

general interdependence of social facts, determine economic life or conversely suffer its effects: human beings and their needs, natural resources, the active and inactive population, technical and scientific knowledge, the political and legal organization of society, intellectual life, geographical data, social classes and groups, mental structures, and so forth."

41. In the manuscript, Foucault refers here, following Bilger (*La Pensée économique libérale*, p. 181), to W. Eucken, *Grundsätze*, pp. 377-378. However, the reference is inexact, and Eucken does not deal specially with agricultural questions in this section of his work.

42. See Bilger, *La Pensée économique libérale*, p. 185: "Agriculture must be prepared for the free market by seeing to it that all the measures taken lead it to this end and do not have immediate harmful consequences on the other markets. To arrive at the final result, the state will be able to intervene on the facts previously listed and determining agricultural activity: the population occupied in agriculture, the technology employed, the legal framework of farms, the soil available, even the climate, and so forth." See also the quotation on p. 181, taken from Eucken's *Grundsätze*, p. 378: "There is no doubt a limit to the action of economic policy on global facts. But each of them can be influenced. Even the climate of a country can be modified by human intervention (*Selbst das Klima eines Landes kann durch menschliches Eingreifen verändert werden*). *A fortiori* other factors, like the size of the population, its knowledge, and its capabilities, etcetera. The broadest field of action is offered by the sixth fact, the legal and social order."

43. Dutch politician, Sicco Leendert Mansholt (1908-1995), vice president (1967-1972), and then President of the European Commission (1972-1973), worked from 1946 on the construction of the Benelux countries and then on the Common Market. He developed two agricultural plans, the first in 1953, aiming to replace national policies with a common agricultural policy, and the second in 1968, in which he proposed a program for the restructuring of community agriculture (the "Mansholt plan"). See the *Rapport de la Commission des Communautés européenes (Plan Mansholt ... )* (Brussels: Secretary General of the EEC, 1968).

44. On this notion of "order of competition" (*Wettbewerbsordnung*), see W. Eucken, "Die Wettbewerbsordnung und ihre Verwicklichung," *Ordo*, vol. 2, 1949, and the 4th book, with the same title, of the *Grundsätze*, pp. 151-190.

45. Arthur Cecil Pigou (1877-1959), British economist who opposed a welfare economy, defined by the maximum increase in individual satisfactions, to a wealth economy. He was the author of *Welfare and Wealth* (London: Macmillan and Co., 1912), which was profoundly revised in a 1920 re-publication under the title *The Economics of Welfare* (London: Macmillan). See K. Pribram, *A History of Economic Reasoning* (Baltimore, Md.: Johns Hopkins University Press, 1983): "Conceived of as a 'realistic' positive theory, economic welfare was to be studied in terms of quantities of values and their distribution. In a more or less axiomatic manner, Pigou assumed that—with the exception of some special circumstances—welfare was increased when the volume of aggregate real income was enlarged, the steadiness of its flow better assured, the dissatisfaction caused by its production reduced, and the distribution of the national dividend changed in favor of the poor."

46. The attribution of this formula remains uncertain and is not found in any of the writings by Röpke consulted by Foucault.

47. See F. Bilger, *La Pensée économique libérale*, p. 198: "The 'ordoliberals' do not consider it less 'social' to put forward an individualist rather than a socialist social policy."

48. See A. Müller-Armack, "Soziale Marktwirtschaft," in E. von Beckerath and others, *Handwörterbuch der Sozialwissenschaften*, vol. 9, (Stuttgart-Tübingen-Göttingen: G. Fischer, J.C.B. Mohr, Vandenhoeck & Ruprecht, 1956); republished in A. Müller-Armack, *Wirtschaftsordnung und Wirtschaftspolitik*; English translation, "The meaning of the social market economy" in A. Peacock and H. Willgerodt, *Germany's Social Market Economy*, pp. 82-86. Müller-Armack uses the term for the first time in 1947 in a report to the Chambers of Industry and Commerce of Nordrhein-Westfalen (reprinted in his book, *Genealogie der sozialen Marktwirtschaft* [Berne: Paul Haupt, 1974] pp. 59-65). It really enters into circulation after being included in the program of the Christian Democratic Union for the first election campaigns for the Bundestag (*Düsseldorfer Leitsätze über Wirtschaftspolitik, Sozialpolitik und Wohnungsbau* of 15 July 1949).

49. On neo-liberal policies undertaken in France in the seventies, see below, lecture of 7 March 1979.

50. On the physiocratic concept of "economic government," see *Sécurité, Territoire, Population*; *Security, Territory, Population*, lecture of 25 January 1978, note 40, and lecture of 1 February 1978, note 23.
51. This expression is not found in the proceedings of the *Colloque W. Lippmann* (Foucault possibly confuses it with the expression used by L. Marlio on p. 102 ("social liberalism," see above, this lecture, note 15). On the other hand, it is used by W. Röpke in *Civitas Humana*, p. 36: "This *primary* Liberalism might be described as *sociological*. The arms forged for the attack on the old purely economic form are blunted in the face of the new."
52. See F. Bilger, *La Pensée économique libérale*, p. 111 (which does not identify the source). The term *Gesellschaftspolitik* seems only to appear in Müller-Armack's work from 1960. See, "Die zweite Phase der socialen Marktwirtschaft. Ihre Ergänzung durch das Leitbild einer neuren Gesellschaftspolitik," 1960 (republished in A. Müller-Armack, *Wirtschaftsordnung und Wirtschaftspolitik*, pp. 267-291, and in W. Stützel and others, eds., *Grundtexte der socialen Marktwirtschaft* pp. 63-78), and, "Das gesellschaftspolitische Leitbild de socialen Marktwirtschaft," 1962 (republished in *Wirtschaftsordnung* pp. 293-317). He defines then the program, on the level of internal policy, of the second phase of the construction of the social market economy.
53. Jacques Chaban-Delmas (1915-2000): Prime Minister under the presidency of Georges Pompidou from 1969 to 1972. His project of a "new society," presented in his inaugural speech of 16 September 1969 and inspired by his two collaborators, Simon Nora and Jacques Delors, provoked much resistance from the conservative side. Denouncing "the weakness of our industry," he notably declared: "But here the economy joins up with the political and the social. In fact, the defective working of the state and the archaism of our social structures are obstacles to the economic development we need. ( ... ) The new leaven of youth, creativity, and invention which is shaking our old society can ferment new and richer forms of democracy and participation in all the social bodies, as in a flexible, decentralized state. We can therefore undertake the construction of a new society" [from: www.assemblée-nat.fr].
54. Valéry Giscard d'Estaing (born 1926): elected President of the Republic in May 1974. See below, lecture of 7 March 1979, p. 194 and note 20.
55. An expression of Müller-Armack, quoted by F. Bilger, *La Pensée économique libérale*, p. 111. See, "Die zweite Phase der socialen Marktwirtschaft," in W. Stützel and others, eds., *Grundtexte der socialen Marktwirtschaft*, p. 72.
56. The date given by Foucault is no doubt based on the references Sombart gives to his earlier works in *Le Socialisme allemand*, French translation (see above, lecture of 7 February 1979, note 42), 1990 edition, p. 48, note 1, concerning the destructive effects of the "economic age" on "the men of our times" in the domain of "spiritual life": "See my works: *Deutsche Volkswirtschaft* (1903) [*Die deutsche Volkswirtschaft im 19.Jahrhundert und im Anfang des 20.Jahrhundert* (Berlin: G. Bondi)], *Das Proletariat* (1906), *Der Bourgeois* (1913) [*Der Bourgeois. Zur Geistesgeschichte des modernen Wirtschaftsmenschen* (Munich-Leipzig: Duncker & Humblot)], *Händler und Helden* (1915) [*Händler und Helden. Patriotische Besinnungen* (Munich-Leipzig: Duncker & Humblot)]." See also, *Der moderne Kapitalismus*, Part 3, ch. 53; *L'Apogée du capitalisme*, vol. 2, pp. 404-435: "The dehumanization of the enterprise." On the different characteristics of capitalist society described by Foucault, see in particular, *Le Socialisme allemand*, pp. 49-52 and p. 56.
57. See above, lecture of 7 February 1979, note 26.
58. See W. Sombart, *Der moderne Kapitalismus*, Part 1, ch. 1-2; *L'Apogée du capitalisme*, vol. 1, pp. 24-41: "The role of the head of the capitalist enterprise" and "The new leaders"; *Gewerbewesen*, 1: *Organisation und Geschichte des Gewerbes*, 2: *Das Gewerbe im Zeitalter des Hochkapitalismus* (Leipzig: 1904; 2nd revised edition, Berlin: W. De Gruyter, 1929); and, "Der kapitalistische Unternehemer," *Archiv für Sozialwissenschaft und Sozialpolitik*, 29, 1909, pp. 689-758.
59. Joseph A. Schumpeter (1883-1950): it is in his *Theorie der wirtschaftlichen Entwicklung*, published in 1912 (republished Munich: Duncker & Humblot, 1934; English translation by Redvers Opie, *The Theory of Economic Development* [New Brunswick N.J. and London: Transaction Books, 1983]; French translation by J.-J. Anstett, *La Théorie de l'évolution économique* [Paris: Librairie Dalloz, 1935] with a long introduction by F. Perroux, "The

economic thought of Joseph Schumpeter"), that the author of the monumental *History of Economic Analysis* sets out for the first time his conception of the creator of enterprise who, through his pioneer spirit and innovative capability, was the real agent of economic development. See also his article, "Unternehmer" in, *Handwörterbuch der Staatwissenschaften* (Jena: 1928) vol. VIII. This theory of entrepreneurial boldness is the basis of the pessimistic finding in 1942 in *Capitalism, Socialism and Democracy* (London: Unwin, 1987) (see in particular, pp. 131-134, "The Obsolescence of the Entrepreneurial Function") in which he predicts the coming of the planned economy. See below, lecture of 21 February 1979, pp. 176-178.

60. W. Röpke, *Ist die deutsche Wirtschaftspolitik richtig?* (see above, lecture of 7 February 1979, note 20).

61. Ibid., and in W. Stützel and others, eds., *Grundtexte zur sozialen Marktwirtschaft*, p. 59. The list of measured proposed by Röpke, however, do not correspond exactly to that given by Foucault: "Die Maßnahmen, die hier ins Auge zu fassen sind [für eine grundsätzliche Änderung sociologischer Grundlagen (Entmassung und Entroletarisierung)], betreffen vor allem die Förderung der wirtschaftlichen und sozialen Dezentralisation im Sinne einer die Gebote der Wirtschaftlichkeit beachtenden Streuung des kleinen und mittleren Betriebes, der Bevölkerungsverteilung zwischen Stadt und Land und zwischen Industrie und Landwirtschaft, einer Auflockerung der Großbetriebe und eiener Förderung des Kleineigentums der Massen und sonstiger Umstände, die die Verwurzelung des heutigen Großstadt- und Industrie-nomaden begünstigen. Es ist anzustreben, das Proletariat im Sinne einer freien Klasse von Beziehern kurzfristigen Lohneinkommens zu beseitigen und eine neue Klasse von Arbeiten zu schaffen, die durch Eigentum, Reserven, Einbettung in Natur und Gemeinschaft, Mitverantwortung un ihren Sinn in sich selbst tragende Arbeit zu vollwertigen Bürgen einer Gesellschaft freier Menschen werden." See *Civitas Humana*, p. 154: "decentralisation in the widest and most comprehensive sense of the word; to the restoration of property; to a shifting of the social centre of gravity from above downwards; to the organic building-up of society from natural and neighbourly communities in a closed gradation starting with the family through parish and county to the nation; to a corrective for exaggerations in organisation, in specialisation, and in division of labour ... ; to the bringing back of all dimensions and proportions from the colossal to the humanly reasonable; to the development of fresh non-proletarian types of industry, that is to say to forms of industry adapted to peasants and craftsmen; to the natural furtherance of smaller units of factories and undertakings ... ; to the breaking-up of monopolies of every kind and to the struggle against concentrations of businesses and undertakings, where and whenever possible; ... to a properly directed country-planning having as its aim a dencentralisation of residence and production."

62. Rüstow defined this *Vitalpolitik* thus: " ... a policy of life, which is not essentially orientated to increased earnings and reduced hours of work, like traditional social policy, but which takes cognizance of the worker's whole vital situation, his real, concrete situation, from morning to night and from night to morning," material and moral hygiene, the sense of property, the sense of social integration, etcetera, being in his view as important as earnings and hours of work (quoted by F. Bilger, *La Pensée économique libérale*, p. 106, which refers only to "an article in *Wirtschaft ohne Wunder*," which is no doubt "Soziale Marktwirtschaft als Gegenprogramm gegen Kommunismus und Bolschewismus," in A. Hunold, ed., *Wirtschaft ohne Wunder* [Erlenbach-Zürich: E. Rentsch, 1953] pp. 97-108). See also, by the same author, "Sozialpolitik oder Vitalpolitik," *Mitteilungen der Industrie- und Handelskammer zu Dortmund*, 11, November 1951, Dortmund, pp. 453-459; "Vitalpolitik gegen Vermassung," in A. Hunold, ed., *Masse und Demokratie, Volkswirtschaftliche Studien für das Schweizer Institut für Auslandsforschung* (Erlenbach-Zürich: E. Rentsch, 1957) pp. 513-514. On the contrast between *Vitalpolitik* and *Sozialpolitik*, see C.J. Friedrich, "The political thought of Neo-liberalism," pp. 513-514. It is A. Müller-Armack who connects the measures concerning the whole of the environment ("die Gesamtheit der Umwelt") with the *Vitalpolitik*: "Die hier erhobene Forderung dürfte in etwa dem Wunsche nach einer Vitalpolitik im Sinne von Alexander Rüstow entsprechen, einer Politik, die jenseits des Ökonomischen aud die Vitale Einheit des Menschen gerichtet ist" ("Die zweite Phase der sozialen Marktwirtschaft" p. 71).

# seven

## 21 February 1979

*Second aspect of the "policy of society" according to the neo-liberals: the problem of law in a society regulated according to the model of the competitive market economy. ~ Return to the Walter Lippmann colloquium. ~ Reflections based on a text by Louis Rougier. ~ (1) The idea of a juridical-economic order. Reciprocity of relations between economic processes and institutional framework. ~ Political stake: the problem of the survival of capitalism. ~ Two complementary problems: the theory of competition and the historical and sociological analysis of capitalism. ~ (2) The question of legal interventionism. ~ Historical reminder: the Rule of law (*l'État de droit*) in the eighteenth century, in opposition to despotism and the police state. Re-elaboration of the notion in the nineteenth century: the question of arbitration between citizens and public authorities. The problem of administrative courts. ~ The neo-liberal project: to introduce the principles of the Rule of law into the economic order. ~ Rule of law and planning according to Hayek. ~ (3) Growth of judicial demand. ~ General conclusion: the specificity of the neo-liberal art of government in Germany. Ordoliberalism faced with the pessimism of Schumpeter.*

LAST WEEK I TRIED to show you how ordoliberalism necessarily entailed a *Gesellschaftspolitik*, as it was called, that is to say, a policy of society and a social interventionism that is at the same time active, multiple, vigilant, and omnipresent. So, on the one hand there is a market economy, and on the other an active, intense, and interventionist social policy. But we should again carefully underline that this social policy in ordoliberalism is not to function like a compensatory mechanism for absorbing or nullifying the possible destructive effects of economic freedom on society or the social fabric. In actual fact, if there is a permanent and multiform social interventionism, it is not directed against the market economy or against the tendency of the market economy. On the contrary, this interventionism is pursued as the historical and social condition of possibility for a market economy, as the condition enabling the formal mechanism of competition to function so that the regulation the competitive market must ensure can take place correctly without the negative effects that the absence of competition would produce. The *Gesellschaftspolitik* must not nullify the anti-social effects of competition; it must nullify the possible anti-competitive mechanisms of society, or at any rate anti-competitive mechanisms that could arise within society.

This is what I tried to underline last week, and to give content to this *Gesellschaftspolitik* I think the ordoliberals laid stress on two major axes. On the one hand is the formalization of society on the model of the enterprise, and I have pointed out the importance of this notion of enterprise, and will return to it later.[1] A whole history could be written of these economic, historical, and social notions of the entrepreneur and the enterprise, with the derivation of one from the other from the end of the nineteenth to the middle of the twentieth century. So, there is formalization of society on the model of the enterprise. On the other hand, the second aspect, which I would like to talk about today, is the redefinition of the juridical institution and of the necessary rules of right in a society regulated on the basis of and in terms of the competitive market economy: the problem then, broadly speaking, of law.

To situate this a little, I would like to return to the Walter Lippmann colloquium I spoke about one or two weeks ago, I no longer recall,[2] which was a fairly important event in the history of contemporary neo-liberalism, since in 1939, right on the eve of the Second World War, we see at this colloquium the intersection of old traditional liberalism, the protagonists of German ordoliberalism, like Röpke, Rüstow, and so on, and then people like Hayek and von Mises who will be intermediaries between German ordoliberalism and American neo-liberalism which gives rise to the anarcho-liberalism of the Chicago School,[3] Milton Friedman,[4] etcetera. So, all these people—not Milton Friedman, but Hayek and von Mises, who will be agents of transmission in a way—came together in 1939. The colloquium was introduced and organized by someone you know, Louis Rougier,[5] one of the rare and very good post-war French epistemologists who is especially known in history for having been the intermediary between Pétain and Churchill in the summer of 1940.[6] So Louis Rougier is the organizer of the Walter Lippmann colloquium in the summer of 1939, in May or June I think.[7] He introduces the whole of the colloquium and the different contributions, and I think his introduction is quite remarkable with regard to the general principles of this neo-liberalism. This is what he says concerning, precisely, the legal problem: "The liberal regime is not just the result of a spontaneous natural order as the many authors of the *Natural codes* declared in the eighteenth century; it is also the result of a legal order that presupposes juridical intervention by the state. Economic life takes place [in fact]* within a juridical framework which fixes the regime of property, contracts, patents, bankruptcy, the status of professional associations and commercial societies, the currency, and banking, none of which are given by nature, like the laws of economic equilibrium, but are contingent creations of legislation. There is then no reason to suppose that the current, historically existing legal institutions are definitively and permanently the best suited for safeguarding the freedom of transactions. The question of the legal framework best suited to the supplest, most efficient, and fair operation of the market has been neglected by classical economists and deserves to be the object of an *International Center of Studies for the Renewal of Liberalism*. To be liberal, therefore, is not at all to be conservative, in the sense of the maintenance of de facto privileges resulting from past legislation. On the contrary, it is to be essentially progressive in the sense of a constant adaptation of the legal order to scientific discoveries, to the progress of economic organization

* Words added by Foucault.

and technique, to changes in the structure of society, and to the requirements of contemporary consciousness. Being liberal is not like the 'Manchester' attitude, allowing vehicles to circulate in any direction, according to whim, with the consequence of endless congestion and accidents; and it is not that of the 'planners,' fixing the hours of use and routes to be followed for every vehicle: it means imposing a *Highway Code*, while accepting that at a time of faster means of transport this code will not necessarily be the same as in the time of stagecoaches. Today we understand better than the great classics what a truly liberal economy consists in. It is an economy subject to a double arbitration: the spontaneous arbitration of consumers, who decide between the goods and services they are offered on the market according to their preferences through the plebiscite of prices, and [, on the other hand,]* the common arbitration of the state ensuring the freedom, honesty, and efficiency of the market†."[8]

This text contains a number of elements. Straightaway we can put aside some propositions that would clearly be unacceptable to the ordoliberals; everything concerning the natural character of the mechanisms of competition. When Rougier says that the liberal regime is not only the result of a natural order but also the result of a legal order, the ordoliberals would obviously say: "Not true, the natural order, what is understood by the natural order, what the classical economists or, at any rate, those of the eighteenth century understood by a natural order, is nothing other than the effect of a particular legal order." So we can leave these elements at the turning point of classical liberalism and neo-liberalism, or of this form of neo-liberalism, and move on to the more important elements in this text, those specific to neo-liberalism.

First of all, I think we should note that for Rougier, as for the ordoliberals moreover, the juridical is clearly not part of the superstructure. That is to say, they do not conceive of the juridical as being in a relation of pure and simple expression or instrumentality to the economy. The economy does not purely and simply determine a juridical

---

* Words added by Foucault.

† Rougier says: "of the markets."

order that would both serve it and be constrained by it. The juridical gives form to the economic, and the economic would not be what it is without the juridical. What does this mean? I think we can identify three levels of meaning. First, a theoretical meaning. You can see that the theoretical meaning, I am embarrassed to point it out, is that instead of distinguishing between an economic belonging to the infrastructure and a juridical-political belonging to the superstructure, we should in reality speak of an economic-juridical order. In this, Rougier, and then the ordoliberals, place themselves strictly in line with Max Weber's important perspective. That is to say, like Max Weber, they situate themselves from the outset at the level of the relations of production rather than at the level of the forces of production. At that level they grasp in one hand, as it were, both history and economics, both law and the economy strictly speaking, and, placing themselves in this way at the level of the relations of production they do not consider the economic to be a set of processes to which a legal system is added which is more or less adapted or more or less obsolete in relation to these processes. In actual fact, the economic must be considered as a set of regulated activities from the very beginning: it is a set of regulated activities with rules of completely different levels, forms, origins, dates, and chronologies; rules which may comprise a social habitus, a religious prescription, an ethics, a corporative regulation, and also a law. In any case, the economic is not a mechanical or natural process that one can separate out, except by abstraction a posteriori, by means of a formalizing abstraction.[9] The economic can only ever be considered as a set of activities, which necessarily means regulated activities. It is this economic-juridical ensemble, this regulated set of activities that Eucken calls—in a perspective which is more phenomenological than Weberian—the "system."[10] What is the system? It is a complex whole including economic processes the specifically economic analysis of which is a matter for pure theory and a formalization which may take the form of the formalization of mechanisms of competition, for example, but these economic processes only really exist, in history, insofar as an institutional framework and positive rules have provided them with their conditions of possibility.[11] This is what this common analysis, this combined analysis of the relations of production means historically.

What does this mean, historically? It means that we should guard against thinking that at a given moment there was the literal and simple economic reality of capitalism, or of capital and the accumulation of capital, which with its own necessity would have come up against old rules of right, like the right of primogeniture, for example, or ancient feudal right, etcetera, and then created, in accordance with its own logic and requirements and somehow by pressure from below, new and more favorable rules of right, whether property rights, legislation on joint-stock companies, patent law, and so on. This is not how we should view things in fact. We should keep in mind that historically we are dealing with a singular figure in which economic processes and institutional framework call on each other, support each other, modify and shape each other in ceaseless reciprocity. Capitalism was not a process from below which comes up against the law of primogeniture, for example. In fact, we can only understand the historical figure of capitalism if we consider the role that was actually played by the rule of primogeniture, for example, in its formation and genesis. The history of capitalism can only be an economic-institutional history. And from this stemmed a whole series of studies of economic history, of juridical-economic history, which were very important in a theoretical debate, but also, and this is what I want to come to, from a political point of view, because it is quite clear that the problem and stake of this theoretical and historical analysis of capitalism, and of the role played by the juridical institution, was of course political.

What is this political stake? Well, it's very simple. It is quite simply the problem of the survival of capitalism, of the possibility and the field of possibilities still open for capitalism. Because if we accept that in a Marxist type of analysis, in the broadest sense of the term, it is the economic logic of capital and its accumulation that is determinant in the history of capitalism, then you can see that in fact there can only be one capitalism since there is only one logic of capital. There can only be one capitalism which is defined precisely by the single necessary logic of its economy and regarding which all we can say is that this institution has favored it and this other institution has impeded it. We have either a flourishing capitalism or a shackled capitalism, but in any case we have Capitalism (*le* capitalisme). The capitalism we know in the West is capitalism tout court, merely modulated by favorable or unfavorable elements. And, as a further consequence, the current impasses of capitalism are clearly historically definitive impasses insofar as they are ultimately, in the last instance, determined by the logic of capital and its accumulation. In other words, when you link all the historical figures of capitalism to the logic of capital and its accumulation, the end of capitalism is revealed in the historical impasses it is currently manifesting.

If, on the other hand, what economists call "capital"* is actually only a process which falls within the domain of pure economic theory and which only has, and can only have historical reality within an economic-institutional capitalism, then you can see that the historical capitalism we know is not deducible as the only possible and necessary figure of the logic of capital. In actual fact, historically, we have a capitalism with its singularity, but which, in virtue of this very singularity, may give rise to institutional and consequently economic transformations, to economic-institutional transformations, which open up a field of possibilities for it. In the first type of analysis, which refers entirely to the logic of capital and its accumulation, there is a single capitalism and so, before long, no more capitalism at all. In the other possibility you have an historical singularity of an economic-institutional figure before which a field of possibilities opens up (if, at least, you take a bit of historical distance and use a bit of economic, political, and institutional imagination). That is to say, in this battle around the history of capitalism, around the history of the role of the institution of law, of the rule in capitalism, we are actually dealing with a whole political stake.

We can consider this question in a different way if we look at how things appear to the ordoliberals. On a fairly rough analysis, we can say that their problem was to demonstrate that capitalism was still possible and could survive if a new form was invented for it. If this was their final objective, then we can say that basically they had to demonstrate two things. First, they had to demonstrate that the specifically economic logic of capitalism, the logic of the competitive market, was possible and non-contradictory. I talked about their attempt to do this last week.

---

* In inverted commas in the manuscript ("*le capital*").

Then they had to show that this non-contradictory and so reliable economic logic had a set of juridical-economic relations in the concrete, real, historical forms of capitalism and that these were such that by inventing a new institutional functioning it was possible to overcome the effects—contradictions, impasses, irrationalities—which were typical of capitalist society but which, rather than being due to the logic of capitalism, were simply the effects of a precise and particular figure of this economic-juridical complex.

You can see, therefore, that in Germany these two great problems which dominated economic theory, on the one hand, and economic history, or economic sociology, on the other, were completely bound up with each other. One problem was the theory of competition. If the economists of this time—Walras,[12] Marshall[13] in England, Wicksell[14] in Sweden, and all those who followed them—attached so much importance to the theory of competition, it was because it was a question of determining whether or not the formal mechanism of the market was contradictory, and also the extent to which the competitive market did or did not lead to phenomena which were liable to nullify it, namely to monopoly. So there is this set of problems, which are problems of economic theory if you like. And then there's the, let's say, Weberian set of problems of economic history and sociology, which are actually only the other aspect, the counterpart of the first question, and which concern whether it really is possible to identify an economic-institutional ensemble in the history of capitalism which can account both for the singularity of capitalism and the impasses, contradictions, difficulties, and mixtures of rationality and irrationality presently being observed. Analyzing the history of the role of the protestant ethic and of the religious prescriptions linked to it,[15] for example, and developing the pure theory of competition, were two different aspects, or two complementary ways of posing and trying to resolve in a particular way the problem of whether or not capitalism could survive. This is one aspect of the questions, I think, and of Rougier's text, of the propositions by which he tries to show that economic process cannot be dissociated from an institutional ensemble, from a juridical ensemble, which is not just its more or less deferred or matching effect or expression, but which is really united with it in an economic system, that is to say, roughly, in a set of regulated economic practices.

The other aspect of the text that I have just read concerns what we could call "legal interventionism," which is the consequence of the first aspect. If we accept that we are not dealing with an essential Capitalism deriving from *the* logic of Capital, but rather with a singular capitalism formed by an economic-institutional ensemble, then we must be able to act on this ensemble and intervene in such a way as to invent a different capitalism. We do not have to carry on with capitalism so much as invent a new one. But where and by what route will this irruption of innovation be able to take place within capitalism? Clearly innovation will not come from the laws of the market, it will not take place in the market itself since economic theory shows that, by definition, the market must function in such a way that its pure mechanisms are in themselves regulative of the whole. So we do not touch the laws of the market but act so that institutions are such that these laws, and only these laws, really are the principle of general economic regulation and, as a consequence, of social regulation. The consequence of this is no economic interventionism, or a minimum of economic interventionism, and maximum legal interventionism. In what is, I think, a significant formula, Eucken says that we must "move on to a conscious economic law."[16] I think this formula should be set term by term against the banal Marxist formulation in which the economic is always that which escapes historians' consciousness when they are pursuing their analyses. For Eucken, the historians' unconscious is not the economic but the institutional; or rather, the institutional is not so much the historians' unconscious as the economists' unconscious. What eludes economic theory and economists' analyses is the institution, and we must move on to a level of conscious economic law both by using historical analysis, which will show in what respects and how the institution and rules of law exist in reciprocally conditioning relationships with the economy, and then, thanks to this, by becoming aware of the possible modifications to be introduced into this economic-juridical complex. So the problem is this: By what route will we be able to introduce the institutional corrections and innovations which will permit an economically regulated social order to be established on the market economy? How are we to arrive at what the ordoliberals call the *Wirtschaftsordnung*,[17] or "the economic constitution"? The answer given by the ordoliberals—and I want now to focus on this—is to say, quite simply, that the institutional innovation we must now adopt is the application to the economy of what is called the *Rechtsstaat* in the German tradition and the Rule of law in English, or *l'État de droit* in French. At this point the ordoliberal analysis no longer follows the line of the economic theory of competition defined by Walras, Wicksell, and Marshall, and the sociological history of the economy defined by Weber; it follows a line of legal theory, the theory of state law (*droit de l'État*), which was very important in the history of both German legal thought and German institutions.

I would like to say a couple of words about this. What do we understand by *Rechtsstaat*, by this Rule of law (*l'État de droit*) which you have no doubt heard so much talk about just by reading the newspapers over the last year?[18] With regard to the Rule of law I think we need to begin very schematically, so you will forgive the completely bald and sketchy character of what I am going to say. This notion of the Rule of law, of *l'État de droit*, appeared in German political and legal theory at the end of the eighteenth and the beginning of the nineteenth century.[19] What is the *Rechtsstaat*? Well, in this period it is defined in opposition to two things.

First, it is defined in opposition to despotism understood as a system that makes the particular or general will of the sovereign the principle of the obligation of each and all with regard to the public authorities. Despotism is that which identifies the obligatory character and form of the injunctions of the public authority with the sovereign's will.

Second, the Rule of law is also opposed to something different from despotism, and this is the *Polizeistaat*, the police state. The police state is different from despotism, although concretely they overlap, or aspects of them overlap. What is understood by police state, by *Polizeistaat*? It is a system in which there is no difference of kind, origin, validity, and consequently of effect, between, on the one hand, the general and permanent prescriptions of the public authorities—roughly, if you like, what we will call the law—and, on the other hand, the conjunctural, temporary, local, and individual decisions of these same public authorities—if you like, the level of rules and regulations. The police state establishes an administrative continuum that, from the general law to the particular measure, makes the public authorities and the injunctions they give one and the same type of principle, according it one and the same type of coercive value. Despotism, then, refers any injunction made by the public authorities back to the sovereign's will and to it alone, or, rather, it makes it originate in this will. The police state, on the other hand, establishes a continuum between every possible form of injunction made by the public authorities, whatever the origin of their coercive character.

The Rule of law represents an alternative position to both despotism and the police state. This means, first, that the Rule of law is defined as a state in which the actions of the public authorities will have no value if they are not framed in laws that limit them in advance. The public authorities act within the framework of the law and can only act within the framework of the law. Therefore the principle and origin of the coercive character of the public authorities is not the sovereign or his will; it will be the form of the law. Where there is the form of the law, and in the space defined by the form of the law, the public authorities may legitimately become coercive. This is the first definition of the Rule of law, of *l'État de droit.* Second, in the Rule of law there is a difference of kind, effect, and origin between, on the one hand, laws, which are universally valid general measures and in themselves acts of sovereignty, and, on the other hand, particular decisions of the public authorities. In other words, the Rule of law is a state in which legal dispositions, the expression of sovereignty, on the one hand, and administrative measures, on the other, are distinguished in their principle, effects, and validity. Broadly speaking, at the end of the eighteenth and the beginning of the nineteenth century this theory of the public authorities and of the law of public authorities organized what is called the theory of the Rule of law, against the forms of power and public law that operated in the eighteenth century.

This double theory or these two aspects of the Rule of law, one in opposition to despotism and the other opposed to the police state, can be found in a whole series of texts at the beginning of the nineteenth century. The main text, and the first, I think, to produce the theory of the Rule of law (*l'État de [droit]**) is by Welcker, *The Ultimate Principles*

* M.F.: police

*of Law, the State, and Punishment*, which appeared in 1813.[20] Jumping ahead a bit, in the second half of the nineteenth century you find another definition, or rather a more extensive working out of this notion of the Rule of law. The Rule of law then appears as a state in which every citizen has the concrete, institutionalized, and effective possibility of recourse against the public authorities. That is to say, the Rule of law is not just a state that acts in accordance with the law and within the framework of the law. It is a state in which there is a system of law, that is to say, of laws, but it also means a system of judicial arbitration between individuals and the public authorities. This is quite simply the problem of administrative courts. So, in the second half of the nineteenth century you see in German theory and policy the development of a whole series of discussions about whether the Rule of law means a state in which citizens can and must have recourse against the public authority through specialized administrative courts responsible precisely for this function of arbitration, or, alternatively, a state in which citizens can have recourse against the public authority through the ordinary courts. Some theorists, like Gneist[21] for example, reckon that the administrative court, as the legal instance of arbitration between the state and citizens, between the public authorities and citizens, is indispensable for the constitution of the Rule of law. Others, like Bähr*[22] for example, object that since an administrative court emanates from the public authorities and is basically only one of its forms, it cannot be a valid arbiter between the state and citizens, and that only justice, the apparatus of ordinary justice inasmuch as it is really or supposedly independent of the public authorities, can arbitrate between citizens and the state. At any rate, this is the English thesis, and in all the English analyses at the end of the nineteenth century[23] the Rule of law is clearly defined as a state in which the state itself does not organize administrative courts which arbitrate between citizens and the public authorities; the Rule of law is a state in which citizens can appeal to ordinary justice against the public authorities. The English say: If there are administrative courts, then we are not living under the Rule of law. The proof for

---

* M.F.: von Bähr (manuscript: "v. Bähr").

the English that the Rule of law does not exist in France is the existence of administrative courts and the Council of State.[24] According to English theory, the Council of State excludes the possibility of the existence of the Rule of law.[25] This, in short, is the second definition of the Rule of law: the possibility of judicial arbitration, by one or another institution, between citizens and the public authorities.

This is the starting point for the liberals' attempt at defining a way to renew capitalism. The way will be to introduce the general principles of the Rule of law into economic legislation. This idea of asserting the principles of a Rule of law in the economy was, of course, a concrete way of challenging the Hitlerite state, even though the Hitlerite state was undoubtedly not the target in the first instance in this search for an economic Rule of law. In truth, what was challenged, and was in fact challenged in Hitlerite practice was the whole of the people's economic Rule of law (*tout l'État de droit économique du people*),* precisely because the state had ceased to be a legal subject in this state, the people, not the state, being the origin of the law, and the state could only be the instrument of the people's will, which totally excluded the state from being a legal subject in the sense of the source of law, or as a legal personality which could be called before any kind of court. In actual fact, the search for a Rule of law in the economic order was directed at something completely different. It was directed at all the forms of legal intervention in the economic order that states, and democratic states even more than others, were practicing at this time, namely the legal economic intervention of the state in the American New Deal and, in the following years, in the English type of planning. What does applying the principle of the Rule of law in the economic order mean? Roughly, I think it means that the state can make legal interventions in the economic order only if these legal interventions take the form solely of the introduction of formal principles. There can only be formal economic legislation. This is the principle of the Rule of law in the economic order.

What does it mean to say that legal interventions have to be formal? I think Hayek, in *The Constitution of Liberty*,[26] best defines what should

---

* *Sic.* The meaning of this expression is somewhat unclear.

be understood by the application of the principles of *l'État de droit*, or of the *Rule of law*,* in the economic order. Basically, Hayek says, it is very simple. The Rule of law, or formal economic legislation, is quite simply the opposite of a plan.[27] It is the opposite of planning. What is a plan? An economic plan is something which has an aim:[28] the explicit pursuit of growth, for example, or the attempt to develop a certain type of consumption or a certain type of investment, or reducing the gap between the earnings of different social classes. In short, a plan means the adoption of precise and definite economic ends. Second, a plan always allows for the possibility of introducing corrections, rectifications, the suspension of measures, or the adoption of alternative measures at the opportune moment depending on whether or not the sought-after effect is obtained. Third, in a plan, the public authorities have a decision-making role. They replace individuals as the source of decisions and consequently force individuals into one thing or another, such as not exceeding a given level of remuneration, for example. Or else they perform the decision-making function by becoming an economic agent themselves, by investing in public works, for example. So, in a plan, public authorities play the role of decision-maker.[29] Finally, a plan presupposes that the public authorities can be a subject capable of mastering all the economic processes. That is to say, the great state decision-maker is someone who has a clear awareness or who should have the clearest possible awareness of all the economic processes. He is the universal subject of knowledge in the order of the economy.[30] This is a plan.

Now, says Hayek, if we want the Rule of law to operate in the economic order, it must be the complete opposite of this. That is to say, the Rule of law will have the possibility of formulating certain measures of a general kind, but these must remain completely formal and must never pursue a particular end. It is not for the state to say that the gap between earnings should be reduced. It is not for the state to say that it wants an increase in a certain type of consumption. A law in the economic order must remain strictly formal. It must tell people what they must and must not do; it must not be inscribed within an overall economic choice.

* In English in the original; G.B.

Second, if a law is to respect the principles of the Rule of law in the economic order, then it must be conceived a priori in the form of fixed rules and must never be rectifiable by reference to the effects produced. Third, it must define a framework within which economic agents can freely make their decisions, inasmuch as, precisely, every agent knows that the legal framework is fixed in its action and will not change. Fourth, a formal law is a law which binds the state as much as it binds others, and consequently it must be such that everyone knows how the public authorities will behave.[31] Finally, and thereby, you can see that this conception of the Rule of law in the economic order basically rules out the existence of any universal subject of economic knowledge who could have, as it were, a bird's eye view of all of the economic processes, define their ends, and take the place of this or that agent so as to take this or that decision. In actual fact, the state must be blind to the economic processes. It must not be expected to know everything concerning the economy, or every phenomenon concerning the economy.[32] In short, both for the state and for individuals, the economy must be a game: a set of regulated activities—you can see that we have come back to what we were saying at the start—but in which the rules are not decisions which someone takes for others. It is a set of rules which determine the way in which each must play a game whose outcome is not known by anyone. The economy is a game and the legal institution which frames the economy should be thought of as the rules of the game. The Rule of law and *l'État de droit* formalize the action of government as a provider of rules for an economic game in which the only players, the only real agents, must be individuals, or let's say, if you like, enterprises. The general form taken by the institutional framework in a renewed capitalism should be a game of enterprises regulated internally by a juridical-institutional framework guaranteed by the state. It is a rule of the economic game and not a purposeful economic-social control. Hayek describes this definition of the Rule of law, or of *l'État de droit* in economic matters in a very clear sentence. The plan, he says, is precisely the opposite of *l'État de droit* or the Rule of law, "it shows how the resources of society must be consciously directed in order to achieve a particular end. The Rule of law, on the other hand, sets out the most rational framework within which individuals engage in their activities in line with their personal plans."[33] Or again, Polanyi, in his *The Logic of Liberty*, writes: "The main function of a system of jurisdiction is to govern the spontaneous order of economic life. The system of law must develop and reinforce the rules according to which the competitive mechanism of production and distribution operates."[34] We have therefore a system of laws as the rules of the game, and then a game which, through the spontaneity of its economic processes, displays a certain concrete order. *Law and order**: these two notions, [to which] I will try to return next week and whose destiny in the thought of the American Right you are familiar with, are not just slogans for a stubborn American extreme Right born in the Midwest.[35] *Law and order* originally had a very precise meaning which can be traced back well beyond the liberalism I am talking about.† *Law and order* means that the state, the public authorities, will only ever intervene in the economic order in the form of the law and, if the public authorities really are limited to these legal interventions, within this law an economic order will be able to emerge which will be at the same time both the effect and principle of its own regulation.

This is the other aspect I wanted to stress with regard to the text from Rougier I quoted. So, first of all, an essential Capitalism (*le* capitalisme), with its logic, contradictions, and impasses does not exist. Second, it now becomes perfectly possible to invent or devise a capitalism different from the first, different from the capitalism we have known, and whose essential principle would be a reorganization of the institutional framework in terms of the Rule of law, and which would consequently discard the whole system of administrative or legal interventionism which states have assumed the right to impose, be it in the form of the nineteenth century protectionist economy or of the planned economy of the twentieth century.

The third aspect is inevitably what could be called the growth of judicial demand, because in fact this idea of law in the form of a rule of the game imposed on players by the public authorities, but which is only imposed on players who remain free in their game, implies of course a revaluation of the juridical, but also a revaluation of the

* In English and French in original; G.B.
† Foucault adds: since already in the nineteenth century ... *[unfinished sentence]*. In short

judicial. You know that one of the problems of liberalism in the eighteenth century was the maximum reinforcement of a juridical framework in the form of a general system of laws imposed on everyone in the same way. But the idea of the primacy of law that was so important in eighteenth century thought entailed as a result a reduction of the judicial, or of the jurisprudential, inasmuch as the judicial institution was in principle confined to the pure and simple application of the law. Now, on the other hand, if it is true that the law must be no more than the rules for a game in which each remains master regarding himself and his part, then the judicial, instead of being reduced to the simple function of applying the law, acquires a new autonomy and importance. Concretely, in this liberal society in which the true economic subject is not the man of exchange, the consumer or producer, but the enterprise, in this economic and social regime in which the enterprise is not just an institution but a way of behaving in the economic field—in the form of competition in terms of plans and projects, and with objectives, tactics, and so forth—you can see that the more the law in this enterprise society allows individuals the possibility of behaving as they wish in the form of free enterprise, and the greater the development of multiple and dynamic forms typical of this "enterprise" unit, then at the same time so the number and size of the surfaces of friction between these different units will increase and occasions of conflict and litigation multiply. Whereas economic regulation takes place spontaneously, through the formal properties of competition, the social regulation of conflicts, irregularities of behavior, nuisance caused by some to others, and so forth, calls for a judicial interventionism which has to operate as arbitration within the framework of the rules of the game. If you multiply enterprises, you multiply frictions, environmental effects, and consequently, to the extent that you free economic subjects and allow them to play their game, then at the same time the more you detach them from their status as virtual functionaries of a plan, and you inevitably multiply judges. The reduction of the number of functionaries, or rather, the de-functionarization of the economic action of plans, together with the increased dynamic of enterprises, produces the need for an ever-increasing number of judicial instances, or anyway of instances of arbitration.

The problem—but this is a question of organization—of whether this arbitration should be inserted within already existing judicial institutions, or whether it is necessary to create new institutions, is one of the fundamental problems in liberal societies where there is a multiplication of the judicial and instances of and the need for arbitration. Solutions vary from one country to another. Next week I will try to talk about this[36] with regard to France and problems which have arisen in the present French judicial institution, the magistrates' association, and so on.[37] Anyway, with regard to this creation of an intensified and increased judicial demand, I would just like to quote this text of Röpke, who said: "It is now advisable, to make courts, more than in the past, organs of the economy and to entrust to their decision tasks that were previously entrusted to administrative authorities."[38] In short, the more the law becomes formal, the more numerous judicial interventions. And to the extent that governmental interventions of the public authority are more and more formalized, and to the extent that administrative intervention recedes, then to the same extent justice tends to become, and must become, an omnipresent public service.

I will stop there on this description of the ordoliberal program formulated by the Germans from 1930 up until the foundation and development of the modern German economy. However, I would like to take a further thirty seconds, well, two minutes, to indicate—how can I put it?—a possible way of reading these problems. So, ordoliberalism envisions a competitive market economy accompanied by a social interventionism that entails an institutional reform around the revaluation of the "enterprise" unit as the basic economic agent. I do not think that this is merely the pure and simple consequence and projection of the current crisis of capitalism in ideology, economic theory, or political choice. It seems to me that we are seeing the birth, maybe for a short period or maybe for a longer period, of a new art of government, or at any rate, of a renewal of the liberal art of government. I think we can grasp the specificity of this art of government and its historical and political stakes if we compare them with Schumpeter[39] (and I would like to dwell on this for a few moments and then I will let you go). Basically, all these economists, Schumpeter, Röpke, or Eucken, all start (I have stressed this, and I come back to it) from the Weberian problem of the rationality or irrationality of capitalist society. Schumpeter, like the ordoliberals, and the ordoliberals like Weber, think that Marx, or at any rate, Marxists, are wrong in looking for the exclusive and fundamental origin of this rationality/irrationality of capitalist society in the contradictory logic of capital and its accumulation. Schumpeter and the ordoliberals think that there is no internal contradiction in the logic of capital and its accumulation and consequently that capitalism is perfectly viable from an economic and purely economic point of view. This, in brief, is the set of theses shared by Schumpeter and the ordoliberals.

The differences begin at this point. For Schumpeter, if it is true that capitalism is not at all contradictory [on the level of] the purely economic process, and if, consequently, the economic in capitalism is always viable, in actual fact, Schumpeter says, historically, concretely, capitalism is inseperable from monopolistic tendencies. This is not due to the economic process, but to the social consequences of the process of competition. That is to say, the very organization of competition, and the dynamic of competition, will call for, and necessarily so, an increasingly monopolistic organization. So the monopolistic phenomenon is, for Schumpeter, a social phenomenon consequent upon the dynamic of competition, but not inherent to the economic process of competition itself. There is a tendency to centralization; there is a tendency to an incorporation of the economy in increasingly closely connected decision-making centers of the administration and the state.[40] This, then, is the historical condemnation of capitalism. But it is not a condemnation in terms of contradiction; it is condemnation in terms of historical inevitability. For Schumpeter, capitalism cannot avoid this concentration; it cannot avoid a sort of transition to socialism being brought about within its own development, since this, for Schumpeter, is what defines socialism: "a system in which a central authority will be able to control the means of production and production itself."[41] So the transition to socialism is not inscribed in the historical necessity of capitalism by virtue of an illogicality or irrationality specific to the capitalist economy, but due to the organizational and social necessity entailed by the competitive market. So we will develop into socialism, with, of course, a political price, which Schumpeter says is undoubtedly heavy, but not one that it is absolutely impossible to pay. That is to say, the political price is not absolutely unbearable and is not impossible to correct, so that we will advance towards socialist society with a political structure which will obviously have to be strictly supervised and worked out so as to avoid the political price of, broadly speaking, totalitarianism.[42] Totalitarianism can be avoided, but not without effort. We can say, broadly speaking, that, for Schumpeter, it won't be much fun, but it will happen. It will come about and, if we take great care, it may not be as bad as we might think.

With regard to Schumpeter's analysis—both as an analysis of capitalism and as an historical-political prediction—with regard to this kind of pessimism, or what we can call Schumpeter's pessimism, the ordoliberals reply by, as it were, reassembling his analysis and saying that, first of all, unlike Schumpeter, we should not think that the political price he says we will have to pay, this loss of freedom, if you like, when we arrive at a socialist regime, is acceptable. And why is it not acceptable? It is not acceptable because it is not in fact just a matter of drawbacks which accompany a planned economy. In actual fact, a planned economy cannot avoid being politically costly; that is to say, it cannot avoid being paid for with the loss of freedom. Consequently, there is no possible correction. No possible adjustment would be able to circumvent the loss of freedom which is the necessary political consequence of planning. And why is this complete loss of freedom inevitable with planning? Quite simply, it is because planning involves a series of basic economic errors and it will constantly have to make up for these errors; and you will only be able to make up for the intrinsic error or irrationality of planning by the suppression of basic freedoms. Now, they say, how can we avoid the error of planning? Precisely by seeing to it that the tendency Schumpeter identifies in capitalism towards the organization, centralization, and absorption of the economic process within the state, which he saw was not a tendency of the economic process but of its social consequences, is corrected, and corrected precisely by social intervention. At this point, social intervention, the *Gesellschaftspolitik*, legal interventionism, the definition of a new institutional framework of the economy protected by a strictly formal legislation like that of the *Rechtsstaat* or the Rule of law, will make it possible to nullify and absorb the centralizing tendencies which are in fact immanent to capitalist society and not to the logic of capital. This is what will enable us to maintain the logic of capital in its purity and get the strictly competitive market to work without the risk of it ending up in the phenomena of monopoly, concentration, and centralization observable in modern society. As a result, this is how we will be able to mutually adapt to each other, on the one hand, a competitive type of economy, as defined or at least problematized by the great theorists of the competitive economy, and, on the other, an institutional practice whose importance was demonstrated in the great works of historians or sociologists of the economy, like Weber. Broadly speaking, according to the ordoliberals the present historical chance of liberalism is defined by a combination of law, an institutional field defined by the strictly formal character of interventions by the public authorities, and the unfolding of an economy whose processes are regulated by pure competition.

This analysis, political project, and historical wager of the ordoliberals has, I think, been very important, forming the framework of modern German policy. And if there really is a German model, it is not the frequently invoked model of the all-powerful state, of the police state, which, as you know, has so frightened our compatriots. The German model being diffused is not the police state; it is the Rule of law (*l'État de droit*). And I have not made these analyses just for the pleasure of engaging in a bit of contemporary history, but so as to try to show you how it was possible for this German model to spread, on the one hand, in contemporary French economic policy, and, on the other, in a number of liberal problems, theories, and utopias like those we see developing in the United States. So, next week I will talk about some aspects of Giscard's economic policy and then about American liberal utopians.*

---

* Foucault adds:
I will not give my lecture next Wednesday, simply for reasons of tiredness and so I can take a bit of a breath. Forgive me. So, I will resume the lectures in two weeks' time. The seminar next Monday, but the lecture in two weeks' time.

---

1. See above, this lecture, p. 175.
2. See above, lecture of 14 February 1979.
3. See below, lectures of 21 and 28 March 1979.
4. Milton Friedman (1912-2006): founder of the American neo-liberal movement, Nobel Prize-winner for economics in 1976, became known at the end of the 1950s through his rehabilitation of the quantitative theory of money (the so-called "monetarist" theory). Partisan of an intransigent liberalism and the main inspirer of United States economic policy from the 1970s (he was the economic advisor of Nixon and Reagan during their candidatures for the Presidency), he is the author of a number of works, including *Capitalism and Freedom* (Chicago: The University of Chicago Press, 1962) in which he claims that the market mechanism is sufficient to regulate most of the economic and social problems of our times. See, H. Lepage, *Demain le capitalisme*, pp. 373-412: "Milton Friedman or the death of Keynes."
5. Louis Rougier (1889-1982), the author notably of: *La Matière et l'Énergie, suivant la théorie de la relativité et la théorie des quanta* (Paris: Gauthier-Villars, 1919); *Les Paralogismes du rationalisme. Essai sur la théorie de la connaissance* (Paris: F. Alcan, 1920); *La Philosophie géométrique de Henri Poincaré* (Paris: F. Alcan, 1920); *La Structure des théories déductives* (Paris: F. Alcan, 1921); and *La Matière et l'Énergie* (Paris: Gauthier-Villars, 2nd edition, 1921). He was a representative of the Vienna Circle in Paris and was responsible for the organization of the major international colloquium of scientific philosophy that took place in Paris in 1935. On the economic level, he wrote *La Mystique démocratique: ses origines, ses illusions* (Paris: Flammarion, 1929; republished Paris: Albatros, 1983, with a Preface by A. de Benoist); *La Mystique soviétique* (Brussels: Équilibres, 1934), and had just published *Les Mystiques économiques* (Paris: Librairie de Médicis, 1938) in which he proposed to show "how liberal democracies turn into totalitarian regimes by ill-considered social reforms and abusive interventions by public authorities, encouraged by theoreticians of the planned economy," the latter being the "new Mysticism that creates the intellectual climate favorable to the establishment of dictatorships" (pp. 8-9). See, M. Allais, *Louis Rougier, prince de la pensée* (Lyon: Fondation de Lourmarin, printed by Tixier et fils, 1990) bibliography pp. 55-71, and F. Denord, "Aux origines du néo-libéralisme en France. Louis Rougier et le Colloque Walter Lippmann de 1938," *Le Mouvement social*, 195, April-June 2001, pp. 9-34.
6. On this controversial episode, see R.O. Paxton, *Vichy France: Old guard and new order 1940-1944* (New York: A.A. Knopf, 1972): "The Franco-British negotiations at Madrid from September 1940 to February 1941 between the two ambassadors—M. Robert de la Baume followed by François Piétri, facing Sir Samuel Hoare—were the real link between Vichy and London. Few aspects of Vichy policy have been more subject to postwar mystification than this. Two unofficial links, Professor Louis Rougier of the University of Besançon and Jacques Chevalier, Vichy minister of education and then of health in 1940-41, claimed after the war to have negotiated secret Churchill-Pétain 'accords.' Although Professor Rougier did go to London in November 1940, the notations on his document are not in the handwriting of Winston Churchill, as he claimed." See also, J. Lacouture, *De Gaulle* (Paris: Le Seuil, 1984) vol. 1, pp. 453-455.
7. The colloquium was held at the Institut international de coopération intellectuelle from 26 to 30 August 1938 (see above, lecture of 14 February, note 3).
8. *Colloque W. Lippmann*, pp. 16-17.
9. On "isolating abstraction," as a condition of economic morphology according to Eucken, distinct from the "generalizing abstraction" put to work by Weber in the formation of ideal types, see F. Bilger, *La Pensée économique libérale*, p. 52.
10. See, F. Bilger, ibid., pp. 57-58.
11. See ibid., p. 58. "The basic idea of Walter Eucken, the idea that enabled him to resolve the antinomy [between history and economic theory], is the distinction between the framework, which is in history, and the process, which, in the expression of L. Miksch, is 'non-history.' The process is an eternal recommencement that also has a time, an internal time as it were. But the framework, the ensemble of facts, is subject to real, historical time, and evolves in a certain direction."

12. Léon Walras (1834-1910) was a student of the Paris École des mines and became a journalist and then professor of political economy at Lausanne from 1870. He was concerned to reconcile free competition and social justice at the same time as Jevons (*Theory of Political Economy*, 1871) and Menger (*Grundsätze der Volkwirtschatslehre*, 1871) but according to his own axiomatic approach, and he developed a new theory of value based on the principle of marginal utility ("marginalist revolution" of 1871-1874). He constructed a mathematical model postulating the perfectly "rational" behavior of the set of agents, which should enable the general equilibrium of prices and exchanges to be determined in a system of pure competition. Main works: *L'Économie politique et la Justice* (Paris: Guillaumin, 1860); *Éléments d'économie politique pure, ou Théorie de la richesse sociale* (Lausanne: 1874-1887); English translation by William Jaffé, *Elements of Pure Economics* (London: George Allen & Unwin, 1954); *Théorie mathématique de la richesse sociale* (Lausanne: 1883); *Études d'économie sociale* (Lausanne-Paris, 1896) and, *Études d'économie appliquée* (Lausanne-Paris: 1898); English translation by Jan van Daal, *Studies in Applied Economics: Theory of the Production of Social Wealth* (London: Routledge, 2005).
13. Alfred Marshall (1842-1924): British economist, professor at Cambridge, and author of famous textbook: *Principles of Economy* (London: Macmillan & Co., 1890). Seeking to realize the synthesis of classical political economy and marginalism, he underlined the importance of time as a crucial element in the functioning of the process of equilibrium (distinction between short and long periods).
14. Johann Gustav Knut Wicksell (1851-1926): Swedish economist, professor at the University of Lund. He tried to go beyond the Walrasian theory of general equilibrium in his work on fluctuations of the average level of prices. He is the author of: *Über Wert, Kapital und Rente nach den neueren nationalökonomischen Theorien* (Jena: G. Fischer, 1893); *Geldzins und Güterpreise* (Jena: G. Fischer, 1898); *Vorlesungen über Nationalökonomie auf Grundlage des Marginalprinzips* (Jena: G. Fischer, 1928). None of these works is translated into French. In English see, translated by J.M. Buchanan, *A New Principle of Just Taxation* (The International Economic Association, 1958); translated by E. Classen, *Lectures on Political Economy* (London: George Routledge and Sons, 1934); translated by R.F. Kahn, *Interest and Prices* (London: Macmillan, 1936); *Selected Papers on Economic Theory* (London: George Allen & Unwin, 1958).
15. See above, lecture of 31 January 1979, note 25.
16. It seems that this expression is taken from the following phrase in F. Bilger, *La Pensée économique libérale*, p. 65, with regard to the scientific politics recommended by Eucken on the basis of his economic morphology: " ... after having refuted evolutionist philosophy, Eucken recalls that most groups in history are not formed from technical necessity, but thanks to the absence of a real conscious economic law."
17. On this notion of *Wirtschaftsordnung*, see W. Eucken, *Die Grundlagen der Nationalökonomie*, pp. 57-58; *The Foundations of Economics*, pp. 83-85, [where it is translated as "'economic constitution' ... the decision as to the general ordering of the economic life of a community"; G.B.] See also the title of the book by Müller-Armack, *Wirtschaftsordnung und Wirtschaftspolitik*.
18. Is this an allusion to the polemics provoked by the expulsion of Klaus Croissant, the lawyer for the Baader group? On this event, which caused a considerable stir in France, see *Sécurité, Territoire, Population*; *Security, Territory, Population*, lecture of 15 March 1978, note 28 (on Jean Genet), and the "Situation des cours," ibid. (French) p. 385; "Course context," ibid. (English) p. 372. See, for example, the article by O. Wormser, French ambassador to Bonn from 1974 to 1977, "Connaître avant de juger," *Le Monde*, 5 November 1977: "What did Andreas Baader and his friend want by kidnapping M. Schleyer? Above all, to exchange their freedom for that of the president of the employers' association and at the same time to cause the federal government to lose face; subsidiary to this, if the federal government did not agree to this exchange, to lead it to give up the 'Rule of Law (*l'État de droit*)' established long ago with the support of the Western powers, so as to return to a 'state' where violence would replace law, in a word to an authoritarianism close to Nazism."
19. See H. Mohnhaupt, "L'État de droit en Allemagne: histoire, notion, fonction," *Cahiers de philosophie politique et juridique*, no. 24, 1993: "L'État de droit," pp. 75-76: "The notion of the

Rule of law (*l'État de droit*) in Germany was directed, on the one hand, against the police state, that is to say, state administration in the sense of the Welfare State, and on the other, against the arbitrary state of absolutism. The combination of the two words *droit* and *État* appeared for the first time in Germany in 1798, in Johann Wilhelm Petersen who, under the name of Placidus [*Literatur der Staats-Lehre. Eine Versuch*, 1 (Strasbourg: 1798) p. 73], described with this formula the philosophical juridical doctrine of Kant which he entitled 'the critique or the school of the doctrine of the Rule of law (*l'État de droit*)' [*die kritische oder die Schule der Rechts-Staats-Lehre*]." See M. Stolleis, "Rechtsstaat," in *Handwörterbuch zur deutschen Rechtsgeschichte*, vol. IV (Berlin: E. Schmidt, 1990) col 326, and by the same author, *Geschichte des öffentlichen Rechts in Deutschland* (Munich: C.H. Beck, 1988) vol. 1, p. 326; French translation by M. Senellart as *Histoire du droit public en Allemagne, 1600-1800* (Paris: PUF, 1998) p. 490.

20. C. Th. Welcker, *Die letzten Gründe von Recht, Staat und Strafe* (Giessen: Heyer, 1813), pp. 13-26. See H. Mohnhaupt, "L'État de droit in Allemagne: histoire, notion, fonction," p. 78: "[He traced] the following stages of the development of the state: despotism, as state of sensibility, theocracy as state of belief, and, as the supreme development the 'Rule of Law (*État de droit*)' as 'state of reason'." The manuscript, p. 12, adds the following references: "Von Mohl, studies on the United States and federal law (*Bundesstaatsrecht*) [= *Das Bundes-Staatsrecht der Vereinigten Staaten von Nord-Amerika* (Stuttgart: 1824)], *Polizeiwissenschaft nach den Grundsätzen des Rechtsstaates* ([Tubingen: Laupp] 2 vol., 1832[-1833]); F.J. Stahl, *Philosophie des Rechts* [= *Die Philosophie des Rechts nach geschichtlicher Ansicht* (Heidelberg: J.C.B. Mohr, 1830-1837) 2 vol]."
21. Rudolf von Gneist, *Der Rechtsstaat* (Berlin: J. Springer, 1872); 2nd edition with the title *Der Rechtsstaat und die Verwaltungsgerichte in Deutschland* (Berlin: J. Springer, 1879). Foucault relies here on F. Hayek, to whom he refers later, *The Constitution of Liberty*, 1976 ed., p. 200 (ch. 13: "Liberalism and Administration: The '*Rechtsstaat*'").
22. Otto Bähr, *Der Rechtsstaat. Eine publizistische Skizze* (Cassel: Wigand, 1864), republished (Aalen: Scientia Verlag, 1961). See Hayek, *The Constitution of Liberty*, p. 200 on this "justicialist" conception of the *Rechtsstaat*. On this point, see M. Stolleis, *Geschichte des öffentlichen Rechts in Deutschland* (Munich: C.H. Beck, 1992) p. 387.
23. F. Hayek, *The Constitution of Liberty*, pp. 203-204, refers here to the classic work of A.V. Dicey, *Lectures Introductory to the Study of the Law of the Constitution* (London: Macmillan & Co., 1886), which he reproaches for "completely misunderstanding the use of the term [*Rule of Law/Rechtsstaat*] on the continent" ibid. p. 484, n. 35.
24. The heir of the old *Conseil du roi*, the *Conseil d'État* was created by the Constitution of Year VIII (15 December 1799) and is the highest jurisdictional organ in France. "Since the reform of 1953, it has recognized three types of disputed appeal: in the first instance, against certain important administrative acts, such as decrees, in appeal against all judgments made by administrative courts, and in cassation against the rulings of administrative jurisdictions deliberating in the final instance. The rulings of the Council of State all enjoy the definitive authority of the matter judged" (*Encyclopaedia Universalis*, Thesaurus, t. 18, 1974, p. 438).
25. Hayek, after remarking that Dicey, ignoring the German evolution of administrative law, only had knowledge of the French system, observes that, in relation to the latter "his severe strictures may then have been somewhat justified, although even at that time the Conseil d'État had already initiated a development which, as a modern observer has suggested [M.A. Sieghart, *Government by Decree* (London: Stevens, 1950) p. 221] 'might in time succeed in bringing all discretionary powers of the administration ... within the range of judicial control'" *The Constitution of Liberty*, p. 204. He adds, however, that Dicey later recognized that he was partly mistaken, in his article, "*Droit administratif* in Modern French Law," *Law Quarterly Review*, vol. XVII, 1901.
26. F.A. Hayek, *The Constitution of Liberty*. Actually, Foucault's references are not to this book but to *The Road to Serfdom*. See ch. 5, pp. 54-65: "Planning and the Rule of Law" which could be linked with ch. 15 of *The Constitution of Liberty*: "Economic policy and the Rule of Law."
27. Ibid. (ch. VI) p. 55: "Economic planning of the collectivist kind necessarily involves the very opposite of this [the Rule of Law]."

28. Ibid.: "Under the second [direction of economic activity by a central authority] the government directs the use of the means of production to particular ends."
29. Ibid.: "The planning authority ... must constantly decide questions which cannot be answered by formal principles only, and in making these decisions it must set up distinctions of merit between the needs of different people."
30. Ibid. p. 36: "What [the supporters of central planning] generally suggest is that the increasing difficulty of obtaining a coherent picture of the complete economic process makes it indispensable that things should be co-ordinated by some central agency if social life is not to dissolve in chaos."
31. Ibid. p. 54: "government in all its actions is bound by rules fixed and announced beforehand—rules which make it possible to foresee with fair certainty how the authority will use its coercive powers in given circumstances," and, "under the Rule of Law the government is prevented from stultifying individual efforts by *ad hoc* action."
32. Ibid. p. 36 (on the impossibility of having a "synoptic view" of the whole of the economic process): "As decentralisation has become necessary because nobody can consciously balance all the considerations bearing on the decisions of so many individuals, the co-ordination can clearly not be effected by 'conscious control,' but only by arrangements which convey to each agent the information he must possess in order effectively to adjust his decisions to those of others." On this necessary blindness of the state with regard to economic processes, see Foucault's reading of Adam Smith's "invisible hand" below, lecture of 28 March 1979, pp. 279-281.
33. The manuscript refers here to *Road of Serfdom [sic]*, but the quotation is undoubtedly a fairly free adaptation of the text. See p. 55: "Under the first [the Rule of Law] the government confines itself to fixing rules determining the conditions under which the available resources may be used, leaving to the individuals the decision for what ends they are to be used. Under the second [central planning] the government directs the use of the means of production to particular ends."
34. Michael Polanyi (1891-1976): chemist, economist, and philosopher originally from Hungary (the brother of the historian Karl Polanyi). He was professor of chemistry at Manchester University from 1933 to 1948, and then professor of social sciences at the same university from 1948 to 1958. The quotation is taken from *The Logic of Liberty: Reflections and rejoinders* (London: Chicago University Press, 1951) p. 185: " ... the main function of the existing spontaneous order of jurisdiction is to govern the spontaneous order of economic life. A *consultative* system of law develops and enforces the rules under which the *competitive* system of production and distribution operates. No marketing system can function without a legal framework which guarantees adequate proprietary powers and enforces contracts."
35. See "Le citron et le lait" (October 1978) in *Dits et Écrits*, 3, p. 698; English translation by Robert Hurley, "Lemon and Milk" in *Essential Works of Foucault*, 3, p. 438: "*Law and Order* is not simply the motto of American conservatism ( ... ). Just as people say milk or lemon, we should say law *or* order. It is up to us to draw lessons for the future from that incompatibility."
36. Foucault does not return to this subject in the next lecture.
37. In 1977, Foucault participated in the days of reflection of the magistrate's union and discussed the work *Liberté, Libertés* (1976), directed by R. Badinter; he criticized "the increased role that the Socialist Party assigned to judges and judicial power as a means of social regulation" (Daniel Defert, "Chronologie," *Dits et Écrits*, 1, p. 51). The text appeared posthumously in the Union's journal, *Justice*, no. 115, June 1984, pp. 36-39 (not reproduced in *Dits et Écrits*).
38. W. Röpke, *The Social Crisis of Our Times*, Part II, chapter 2, p. 193: "Indeed, the law courts of a country are the last citadel of the authority of the state and of trust in the state, and no state is completely lost where this citadel is still intact. This leads us to urge more insistently than has ever been done before that the law courts should be made organs of national economic policy and that they should be given jurisdiction over matters which up to now have been left to the administrative agencies." He sees the American anti-trust legislation, since the Sherman Act of 2 July 1890, as an example allowing one to see how "such a judicially directed economic policy is likely to work in practice."

39. See above, lecture of 14 February 1979, note 59.
40. See Joseph A. Schumpeter, *Capitalism, Socialism and Democracy*, Part II: "Can Capitalism Survive?" and in particular pp. 139-142, "The Destruction of the Institutional Framework of Capitalist Society."
41. Ibid. p. 167: "By socialist society we shall designate an institutional pattern in which the control over the means of production and over production itself is vested with a central authority—or, as we may say, in which, as a matter of principle, the economic affairs of society belong to the public and not to the private sphere."
42. See ibid, Part IV, pp. 232-302: "Socialism and Democracy." See in particular the conclusion, pp. 296-302, on the problem of democracy in a socialist regime: "No responsible person can view with equanimity the consequences of extending the democratic method, that is to say the sphere of 'politics,' to all economic affairs. Believing that democratic socialism means precisely this, such a person will naturally conclude that democratic socialism must fail. But this does not necessarily follow. As has been pointed out before, extension of the range of public management does not imply corresponding extension of the range of political management. Conceivably, the former may be extended so as to absorb a nation's economic affairs while the latter still remains within the boundaries set by the limitations of the democratic method."

# eight

## 7 March 1979

*General remarks: (1) The methodological scope of the analysis of micro-powers. (2) The inflationism of state phobia. Its links with ordoliberalism. ~ Two theses on the totalitarian state and the decline of state governmentality in the twentieth century. ~ Remarks on the spread of the German model, in France and in the United States. ~ The German neo-liberal model and the French project of a "social market economy." ~ The French context of the transition to a neo-liberal economics. ~ French social policy: the example of social security. ~ The separation of the economic and the social according to Giscard d'Estaing. ~ The project of a "negative tax" and its social and political stakes. "Relative" and "absolute" poverty. Abandonment of the policy of full employment.*

I WOULD LIKE TO assure you that, in spite of everything, I really did intend to talk about biopolitics, and then, things being what they are, I have ended up talking at length, and maybe for too long, about neo-liberalism, and neo-liberalism in its German form. I must however explain a little this change to the direction I wanted to give these lectures. Obviously, I have not spoken at such length about neo-liberalism, and worse, about the German form of neo-liberalism, because I wanted to trace the historical or theoretical "background"* of German Christian

* In English in the original; G.B.

Democracy. Nor was it so as to denounce what is not socialist in the governments of Willy Brandt or Helmut Schmidt.[1] I have dwelt so long on this problem of German neo-liberalism first of all for methodological reasons, because, continuing what I began to say last year, I wanted to see what concrete content could be given to the analysis of relations of power—it being understood, of course, and I repeat it once again, that power can in no way be considered either as a principle in itself, or as having explanatory value which functions from the outset. The term itself, power, does no more than designate a [domain]* of relations which are entirely still to be analyzed, and what I have proposed to call governmentality, that is to say, the way in which one conducts the conduct of men, is no more than a proposed analytical grid for these relations of power.

So, we have been trying out this notion of governmentality and, second, seeing how this grid of governmentality, which we may assume is valid for the analysis of ways of conducting the conduct of mad people, patients, delinquents, and children, may equally be valid when we are dealing with phenomena of a completely different scale, such as an economic policy, for example, or the management of a whole social body, and so on. What I wanted to do—and this was what was at stake in the analysis—was to see the extent to which we could accept that the analysis of micro-powers, or of procedures of governmentality, is not confined by definition to a precise domain determined by a sector of the scale, but should be considered simply as a point of view, a method of decipherment which may be valid for the whole scale, whatever its size. In other words, the analysis of micro-powers is not a question of scale, and it is not a question of a sector, it is a question of a point of view. Good. This, if you like, was the methodological reason.

A second reason for dwelling on these problems of neo-liberalism is what I would call a reason of critical morality. Actually, going by the recurrence of certain themes, we could say that what is currently challenged, and from a great many perspectives, is almost always the state: the unlimited growth of the state, its omnipotence, its bureaucratic

* M.F.: term

development, the state with the seeds of fascism it contains, the state's inherent violence beneath its social welfare paternalism ... I think there are two important elements which are fairly constant in this theme of the critique of the state.

First, there is the idea that the state possesses in itself and through its own dynamism a sort of power of expansion, an intrinsic tendency to expand, an endogenous imperialism constantly pushing it to spread its surface and increase in extent, depth, and subtlety to the point that it will come to take over entirely that which is at the same time its other, its outside, its target, and its object, namely: civil society. The first element which seems to me to run through all this general theme of state phobia is therefore this intrinsic power of the state in relation to its object-target, civil society.

The second element which it seems to me is constantly found in these general themes of state phobia is that there is a kinship, a sort of genetic continuity or evolutionary implication between different forms of the state, with the administrative state, the welfare state, the bureaucratic state, the fascist state, and the totalitarian state all being, in no matter which of the various analyses, the successive branches of one and the same great tree of state control in its continuous and unified expansion. These two ideas, which are close to each other and support each other—namely, [first], that the state has an unlimited force of expansion in relation to the object-target, civil society, and second, that forms of state give rise to each other on the basis of a specific dynamism of the state—seem to me to form a kind of critical commonplace frequently found today. Now it seems to me that these themes put in circulation what could be called an inflationary critical value, an inflationary critical currency. Why inflationary?

In the first place, it is inflationary because I think the theme encourages the growth, at a constantly accelerating speed, of the interchangeability of analyses. As soon as we accept the existence of this continuity or genetic kinship between different forms of the state, and as soon as we attribute a constant evolutionary dynamism to the state, it then becomes possible not only to use different analyses to support each other, but also to refer them back to each other and so deprive them of their specificity. For example, an analysis of social security and the administrative apparatus on which it rests ends up, via some slippages and thanks to some plays on words, referring us to the analysis of concentration camps. And, in the move from social security to concentration camps the requisite specificity of analysis is diluted.[2] So, there is inflation in the sense of an increasing interchangeability of analyses and a loss of specificity.

This critique seems to me to be equally inflationary for a second reason, which is that it allows one to practice what could be called a general disqualification by the worst. Whatever the object of analysis, however tenuous or meager it is, and whatever its real functioning, to the extent that it can always be referred to something which will be worse by virtue of the state's intrinsic dynamic and the final forms it may take, the less can always be disqualified by the more, the better by the worst. I am not taking an example of the better, obviously, but think, for example, of some unfortunate who smashes a cinema display case and, in a system like ours, is taken to court and sentenced rather severely; you will always find people to say that this sentence is the sign that the state is becoming fascist, as if, well before any fascist state, there were no sentences of this kind—or much worse.

The third factor, the third inflationary mechanism which seems to me to be characteristic of this type of analysis, is that it enables one to avoid paying the price of reality and actuality inasmuch as, in the name of this dynamism of the state, something like a kinship or danger, something like the great fantasy of the paranoiac and devouring state can always be found. To that extent, ultimately it hardly matters what one's grasp of reality is or what profile of actuality reality presents. It is enough, through suspicion and, as François Ewald would say, "denunciation,"[3] to find something like the fantastical profile of the state and there is no longer any need to analyze actuality. The elision of actuality seems to me [to be] the third inflationary mechanism we find in this critique.

Finally, I would say that this critique in terms of the mechanism and dynamism of the state is inflationary inasmuch as it does not carry out a criticism or analysis of itself. That is to say, it does not seek to know the real source of this kind of anti-state suspicion, this state phobia that currently circulates in such varied forms of our thought. Now it seems to me—and this is why I have laid such stress on the neo-liberalism of

1930-1950—that this kind of analysis, this critique of the state, of its intrinsic and irrepressible dynamism, and of its interlinking forms that call on each other, mutually support each other, and reciprocally engender each other is effectively, completely, and already very clearly formulated in the years 1930-1945. At this time it was quite precisely localized and did not have the force of circulation it has now. We find it precisely localized within the neo-liberal choices being developed at this time. You find this critique of the polymorphous, omnipresent, and all-powerful state in these years when, liberalism or neo-liberalism, or even more precisely, ordoliberalism was engaged in distinguishing itself from the Keynesian critique and at the same time undertaking the critique of New Deal and Popular Front policies of state control and intervention, of National Socialist economics and politics, of the political and economic choices of the Soviet Union, or, in a word, of socialism generally. It is in this context, in this German neo-liberal school, and taking things in their narrowest or almost petty form, that we find both this analysis of the necessary and as it were inevitable kinship between different forms of the state, and also this idea that the state has a specific, intrinsic dynamism which means that it can never halt its expansion and complete takeover of the whole of civil society.

I would just like to quote two texts that testify to the precocity of these two ideas which seem so contemporary, alive, and actual to us. I will quote Röpke's reaction, in June-July 1943 in a Swiss journal,[4] in which he criticizes the recently published Beveridge plan and says: the Beveridge plan leads to "ever more social insurance, ever more social bureaucracy, ever more upheaval of incomes, ever more stamps to stick and seals to affix, ever more subscriptions and contributions, ever more concentration of power, national income, and responsibility in the hands of the state that, in any case, embraces everything, regulates everything, concentrates and controls everything with the single certain result of exercising on society an even more centralized action of proletarianization and state control that destroys the middle class."[5] At exactly the same time, in England in 1943, and again in reaction to the post-war plans being constructed by the Anglo-Americans, and especially the English, Hayek wrote the following: "it is Germany whose fate we are in some danger of repeating."[6] He did not say this because of the danger of a German invasion of England, which had been definitively averted by then. In 1943, experiencing Germany's fate meant for Hayek adopting the Beveridge system of socialization, interventionist economics, planning, and social security. Moreover, he clarified by adding: We are not close to Hitler's Germany exactly, but to the Germany of the previous war. As in the latter case, there is the wish "[to preserve]* for productive ends the organization which was developed for purposes of national defense."[7] There is a refusal to "recognize that the rise of Fascism and Nazism was not a reaction against the socialist trends of the preceding period, but a necessary outcome of those tendencies."[8] So, with regard to the Beveridge plan Hayek said that we are close to Germany. It is true that he was referring to Wilhelmine Germany, to the Germany anyway of the 1914 war, but this Germany, with its interventionist practices, its planning techniques, and its socialist choices, was what really engendered Nazism, and in drawing close to the Germany of 1914-1918 we also draw close to Nazi Germany. The dangers of German invasion are far from being definitively averted. The English socialists, the Labour Party, and the Beveridge plan will be the real agents of the Nazification of England through the excess and growth of state control. So, you can see that these are all old and localized themes, and I take them in their 1945 formulation. You find them in 1939, in 1933, and even before.[9]

Well, against this inflationary critique of the state, against this kind of laxness, I would like to suggest some theses which have been present, roughly, in what I have already said, but on which I would like to take a bit of a bearing. In the first place is the thesis that the welfare state has neither the same form, of course, nor, it seems to me, the same root or origin as the totalitarian state, as the Nazi, fascist, or Stalinist state. I would also like to suggest that the characteristic feature of the state we call totalitarian is far from being the endogenous intensification and extension of the mechanisms of the state; it is not at all the exaltation but rather a limitation, a reduction, and a subordination of the autonomy of the state, of its specificity and specific functioning—but in relation to what? In relation to something else, which is the party. In other

* M.F.: to consider

words, the idea would be that we should not look for the principle of totalitarian regimes in the intrinsic development of the state and its mechanisms: the totalitarian state is not the eighteenth century administrative state, the nineteenth century *Polizeistaat* pushed to the limit, it is not the administrative state, the bureaucratized nineteenth century state pushed to its limits. The totalitarian state is something else. We should not look for its principle in the "statifying" or "statified" (*étatisante ou étatisée*) governmentality born in the seventeenth and eighteenth centuries; we should look for it in a non-state governmentality, precisely in what could be called a governmentality of the party. The party, this quite extraordinary, very curious, and very new organization, this very new governmentality of the party which appeared in Europe at the end of the nineteenth century is probably—well, in any case this is what I may try to show you next year, if I still have these ideas in mind[10]—at the historical origin of something like totalitarian regimes, of something like Nazism, fascism, or Stalinism.

Another thesis I would like to put forward—and this is, in short, the other side of what I have just been saying—is that what is presently at issue in our reality, what we see emerging in our twentieth century societies, is not so much the growth of the state and of *raison d'État*, but much more its reduction, and in two forms. One of these is precisely the reduction of state governmentality through the growth of party governmentality, and the other form of reduction is the kind we can observe in regimes like our own in which there is an attempt to find a liberal governmentality. I add straightaway that in saying this I am not trying to make a value judgment. In speaking of liberal governmentality, in using this word "liberal," I do not want to make sacred or immediately attach value to this type of governmentality. Nor do I mean that it is not legitimate, if one wishes, to hate the state. But what I think we should not do is imagine we are describing a real, actual process concerning ourselves when we denounce the growth of state control, or the state becoming fascist, or the establishment of a state violence, and so on. All those who share in the great state phobia should know that they are following the direction of the wind and that in fact, for years and years, an effective reduction of the state has been on the way, a reduction of both the growth of state control and of a "statifying" and "statified" (*étatisante et étatisée*) governmentality. I am not saying at all that we delude ourselves on the faults or merits of the state when we say "this is very bad" or "this is very good"; that is not my problem. I am saying that we should not delude ourselves by attributing to the state itself a process of becoming fascist which is actually exogenous[11] and due much more to the state's reduction and dislocation. I also mean that we should not delude ourselves about the nature of the historical process which currently renders the state both so intolerable and so problematic. It is for this reason that I would like to study more closely the organization and diffusion of what could be called this German model. It is understood, of course, that the model as I have described it and in some of the forms of its diffusion which I would now like to show you, is not the model—so often discredited, dismissed, held in contempt, and loathed—of the Bismarckian state becoming the Hitler state. The German model which is being diffused, debated, and forms part of our actuality, structuring it and carving out its real shape, is the model of a possible neo-liberal governmentality.

We could follow the spread of the German model in two ways. Today I will try to look at its spread in France, and maybe, if I don't change my mind, I will do the same for the USA next week. What we could call the diffusion of the German model in France has taken place slowly, insidiously, and creakingly with, I think, three characteristics. First of all, we should not forget that the diffusion of the German neo-liberal model has taken place in France on the basis of a strongly state-centered, interventionist, and administrative governmentality, with precisely all the problems this entails. Second, the attempt to introduce and implement the German neo-liberal model in France takes place in a context of an initially relatively limited, and now acute economic crisis which is the motive, pretext, and reason for the introduction and implementation of the model and, at the same time, what checks it. Finally, for the reasons I have just mentioned, the third characteristic is that the agents of the spread and implementation of this model are precisely those who administer and direct the state in this context of crisis. Because of all this, the implementation of the German model in France involves a whole range of difficulties and a sort of awkwardness mixed with hypocrisy, examples of which we will see.

In the United States, the diffusion of the German model takes on a completely different appearance. And first of all, can we really speak of a diffusion of the German model? After all, liberalism, the liberal tradition, the constant renewal of liberal politics, has been a constant in the United States, which means that what we are now seeing, or what was seen in reaction to the New Deal, is not necessarily the diffusion of the German model. It can also be seen as a phenomenon which is absolutely endogenous to the United States. We would have to undertake more precise studies on the role played by German emigrants like Hayek, for example, in the United States. Fine. Between American neo-liberalism and the German neo-liberal model, basically formed around the Freiburg people, there is a whole range of historical relationships which are undoubtedly difficult to unravel.

The second characteristic of the diffusion of the German model in the United States is that it too takes place in a context of crisis, but of a completely different crisis than the one experienced in France, since it is an economic crisis, of course, but with a completely different form and undoubtedly less acute. It develops within a political crisis in which the problem of the influence, action, and intervention of the federal government, the problem of its political credibility and so forth, had already been posed at the time of the New Deal, and all the more so with Johnson, Nixon,[12] and Carter.[13]

Finally, the third characteristic of this diffusion of neo-liberalism in the United States is that instead of being in a sense the almost exclusive property of governmental personnel and advisors, as is the case in France, neo-liberal governmentality appears, at least in part, as a sort of major economic-political alternative which, at a certain moment at any rate, takes the form of, if not a mass movement, at least a widespread movement of political opposition within American society. All this means that it is completely impossible to deal with the diffusion of the German model in France and the American neo-liberal movement at the same time. The two phenomena are not completely overlapping and cannot be superimposed on each another, although there is, of course, a whole system of exchanges and supports between them.

So, today I would like to speak a little about what we could call neo-liberalism in France and the existence of the German model. To tell the truth, for a long time I have been a bit uneasy because I honestly believe that it is not possible to read—for they must be read—the speeches, writings, and texts of Giscard, Barre,[14] [or] his advisors, without being immediately struck in a clear, but simply intuitive way, by a kinship between what they say and the German model, German ordoliberalism and the ideas of Röpke, Müller-Armack, etcetera. Now it is very difficult to find just the act of acknowledgement, the statement that would permit one to say: There you are, this really is what they are doing, and they know it. It was very difficult until very recently and almost until a few weeks ago. Right at the end of 1978, in December I think, a book by Christian Stoffaës appeared, entitled *La Grande Menace industrielle*.[15] Stoffaës being one of the closest advisors to the present government, an economic advisor with special reference to industrial questions,[16] I thought that maybe I would find in this book what I was looking for, but I was quickly disappointed, for on the back cover of the book one reads that the author, "rejecting the temptation to hurriedly transpose the German and Japanese models, sets out the bases for an original industrial policy."[17] I said to myself: Once again I will not find what I want. But what is funny, the curious thing which is quite revealing of the clear reasons why these things cannot be said, is that if this statement is found on the back cover of the book, in the concluding chapter which summarizes the whole analysis, the final or penultimate paragraph I think, summarizing what the book has proposed, begins in this way: "Ultimately what is involved is the model of the *social market economy*"—so, the phrase is uttered—with simply, the author adds, "a little more revolutionary boldness than across the Rhine."[18] In fact, he says, it is a question of constructing both an efficient market economy open to the world and an advanced social project.[19]

There is no question of giving you an overall analysis of the policy of Giscard,[20] or of Giscard-Barre, first of all because I am not capable of doing this and secondly because there is no doubt that it would not interest you. I would just like to consider some of its aspects. First, to put things back in their context a bit I will give some information about what we could call the economic context which has speeded up the introduction and implementation of this model over the last few years. Let's summarize very schematically. Let's say that following the great crisis of the 1930s, all in all, every government of whatever type knew that the economic elements which they had to take into consideration—whatever the nature of their options, whatever their choices and objectives—were full employment, stable prices, equilibrium of the balance of payments, growth of the GNP, the redistribution of income and wealth, and the provision of social services. Roughly speaking, this constitutes the list of what Bentham would have called, in his terms, the economic *agenda* of government, the things it must concern itself with, whatever the way it may choose to do so.[21] Let's say that in this set of objectives, the German neo- or ordoliberal formula, you recall, consisted in adopting price stability and the balance of payments as the primary objective, with growth and all the other elements being in some way the consequence of these primary, absolute objectives. On the other hand, England and France—France at the time of the Popular Front and then after Liberation, England at the time of the development of the Beveridge plan and the victory of the Labour Party in 1945—adopted full employment rather than price stability as the primary and absolute objective, the provision of social services rather than the balance of payments, and assuring full employment and the provision of social services obviously implied a voluntarist kind of extensive, strong, and sustained growth.

Let's leave aside the problem of why, all things considered, the pursuit of these objectives in England failed or revealed their drastic limits in the period from 1955 to 1975, while in France the same policy led to some positive results. Let's say that this was the situation at the start and the reason why, attenuated by a range of liberal type measures, these interventionist objectives and methods, and these planning procedures focused on full employment and the distribution of social services, were basically still maintained under De Gaulle, as the 5th Plan clearly shows.[22] Simplifying considerably, we can say that from 1970 to 1975, or anyway in the decade now coming to a close, the problem arises of the final liquidation of these objectives and forms of economic-political priority. It is in this decade that the problem arises of the overall transition to a neo-liberal economy, that is to say, roughly, catching up and inserting the German model. The reasons, the immediate economic pretexts and incentives were of course the crisis, which appeared before 1973 in a pre-crisis characterized by a constant rise in unemployment since 1969, a fall from credit balance in the balance of payments, and increasing inflation: all those signs which, according to the economists, did not indicate a Keynesian type of crisis situation, that is to say, a crisis of under consumption, but actually a crisis concerning the regime of investment. That is to say, roughly, it was thought that the crisis was due to errors in investment policy, to insufficiently rationalized and programmed investment choices. It was against this pre-crisis background that what was called the oil crisis broke, which was in fact an increase in the cost of energy that was due not to the formation of a cartel of sellers fixing a price which was too high, but rather to the reduction of the economic and political influence of the cartel of buyers and the formation of a market price for both oil and energy generally, or at any rate, a tendency for the price of energy to fall in line with market prices. So, in this context—please excuse the absolutely schematic character of all this—it is easy to see how economic liberalism could appear, and actually did appear, as the only solution to this pre-crisis and its acceleration through the increasing cost of energy. Liberalism, that is to say, the total, unrestricted integration of the French economy in an internal, European, and world market, was the choice which appeared, first of all, as the only way to be able to rectify the erroneous investment choices made in the previous period because of interventionist objectives, techniques, and so on; so, liberalism was the only means of correcting these investment errors by taking into account the new factor of the high cost of energy, which was in reality only the formation of a market price for energy. The general insertion of the French economy in the market in order to correct the errors of investment, on the one hand, and in order to adjust the French economy to the new cost of energy, on the other, seemed then to be the self-evident solution.

You will say that this is, after all, only an episode in those regular and sometimes rapid swings which France has experienced since the war, since 1920, between a rather interventionist, *dirigiste*, protectionist policy interested in overall balances and concerned about full employment, and a liberal policy more open to the outside world and more concerned about exchange and the currency. The swings, if you like, that marked the Pinay government in 1951-1952,[23] the Rueff reform of 1958,[24] also represent inflections towards liberalism. Now, what I think is presently in question, and for which the economic crisis, whose aspects I have very briefly tried to define, has served as the pretext, is not just one of those swings from interventionism to a bit more liberalism. In fact, it seems to me that the question today is the entire stakes of a policy that would be neo-liberal overall. Once again, since I do not intend to describe this policy in every aspect, I would just like to consider an aspect which does not concern the economy strictly speaking, or the direct and immediate insertion of the French economy in a world market economy; I would like to consider [this policy]* in another aspect, that of social policy. In the present government, in the present governmentality which was virtually entailed with the arrival in power of Giscard and his policy, what has social policy been, what could it be, and towards what is it directed? This is what I would now like to talk about.

Let's say once again, in a few schematic historical remarks, that the post-Liberation social policy which had been programmed during the war was dominated in France and England by two problems and a model. The two problems were, first, the maintenance of full employment as the main economic and social priority, because the 1929 economic crisis was attributed to the absence of full employment. The absence of full employment was also blamed for all the political consequences it had in Germany and in Europe generally. So, the first problem was the maintenance of full employment for economic, social, and therefore political reasons. The second problem was to avoid the effects of a devaluation made necessary by a policy of growth. To maintain full employment and attenuate the effects of devaluation which makes saving and individual capitalization ineffective it was thought necessary to establish a policy of social security coverage of risks. The model for the techniques for achieving these objectives was war, that is to say, the model of national solidarity which consists in not asking people why what happened to them happened, nor to what economic category they belong. Anything that happens to an individual in terms of shortage, accident, or unknown causes must be taken care of by the whole

* M.F.: consider it

community in the name of national solidarity. These two objectives and this model explain why the English and French social policies were policies of collective consumption assured by a permanent redistribution of income, by a collective consumption and permanent redistribution which has to concern the whole population, with just some privileged sectors. In France, due to policies directed at increasing the birthrate, the family was seen as one of the sectors which had to be especially privileged, but generally speaking it was thought that it was up to the entire community to provide cover for the risks faced by individuals. Once these objectives have been fixed and this model for achieving them has been chosen, the question arises, of course, of whether such a policy, presented as a social policy, is necessarily an economic policy at the same time. In other words, does not this policy bring with it willy-nilly a whole series of economic effects which are in danger of introducing unforeseen consequences and, as it is said, perverse effects on the economy itself, which will disrupt the economic system and the social system?

Several answers have been given to this question. Some say yes. Of course, this kind of policy will produce economic effects, but these are precisely the effects we are looking for. That is to say, for example, the redistribution of income and the equalization of income and consumption is precisely the effect sought, and social policy only has real meaning if it introduces some corrections and leveling within the economic regime which liberal policy itself and economic mechanisms in themselves could not guarantee. Others say, not at all. The social policy we envisage setting up, or which has been established since 1945,[25] actually has no direct effect on the economy, or its effect on the economy is so adjusted to, so in conformity with the mechanisms of the economy themselves that it cannot disrupt them. It is very interesting to note that Laroque,[26] the man who did not invent social security in France but who was behind its organization and devised its mechanism, in a text from 1947 or '48,[27] I no longer remember, gave precisely this explanation and justification of social security. Precisely at the time that it was being set up, he said: Don't worry, Social Security is not designed to produce and cannot have any economic effects other than beneficial ones.[28] He defined social security in the following way: It is no more than a technique to ensure that each "can provide for himself and those for whom he is responsible in every circumstance."[29] What does providing for himself and those for whom he is responsible mean? It means, simply, establishing a mechanism such that social security contributions are deducted solely from wages, in other words, that there will be a virtual wage in addition to the wage really paid in monetary form. In truth this is not an addition, but in fact you will have a total wage part of which will be in the form of a wage strictly speaking, and the other part will be in the form of social benefits. In other words, social security costs are paid for by the wage itself, by the mass of wages, and by nothing else. This is not a solidarity imposed on non-wage-earners for the benefit of wage-earners, it is "a solidarity imposed on the mass of wage-earners" for their own advantage, "to the advantage," says Laroque, "of their children and the aged."[30] So this Social Security cannot be said to put a strain on the economy, to overburden it, or increase the costs of the economy. In fact, Social Security was just a particular way of paying what is no more than a wage; it does not put a strain on the economy. Even better, basically it enables us not to raise wages, and consequently its effect is to reduce the costs of the economy by pacifying social conflicts by enabling wage claims to be less steep and pressing. This is what Laroque said in 1947, '48, to explain the mechanism of Social Security that he had himself perfected.[31]

Thirty years later, in 1976, a report appeared in the *Revue française des affaires sociales* which is very interesting because it was written by some ENA* students as a study-appraisal of thirty years of Social Security,[32] and these students made the following observation. In the first place, they say, Social Security has a considerable economic impact and this is linked, moreover, to the very way in which the basis for assessing contributions was defined. The impact, in fact, is on the cost of labor. Due to Social Security labor becomes more expensive. When labor costs more, it is obvious that there will be a restrictive effect on employment, so there will be an increase in unemployment due directly to the increase in the cost of labor.[33] There is [equally] an effect on international competition,

* École nationale d'administration; G.B.

inasmuch as the existence of different social security regimes in different countries means that international competition is distorted, and distorted to the detriment of countries with the most comprehensive social insurance cover for risks. That is to say, here again there is a source of increasing unemployment.[34] Finally, and still due to this increase in the cost of labor, there will be a speeding-up of industrial concentration, and the development of monopolies and multinationals. So, they say, the policy of social security has obvious economic consequences.

Second, not only do these consequences appear as a result of the cost of labor and produce a rise in unemployment, but on top of this, the way in which an upper limit is set for contributions, that is to say, the difference between contributions as a percentage of earnings has effects on the distribution of income.[35] Relying on a number of previous investigations, the ENA students were able to show that, [for the same wage, instead of redistribution going]* from the young to the old, from the unmarried to those with a family, from the healthy to the sick, due to the upper limit on contributions there was in fact a wide spread of real incomes which advantaged the better off to the detriment of the worse off. So, they say, the way Social Security has operated for thirty years introduces a number of specifically economic effects. Now "the objective of Social Security is not and should not be an economic objective. The ways in which it is financed should not, by distorting the law of the market, be an element of economic policy. Social Security must remain economically neutral."[36] Here you find again, almost word for word, the same things I talked about last week (or two weeks ago) with regard to the German ordoliberals' conception of social policy.[37]

Now this idea of a social policy whose effects are entirely neutralized from the economic point of view is already very clearly formulated right at the start of the period in which the neo-liberal model was being set up in France by the Finance Minister of the time, Giscard d'Estaing, that is to say, in 1972.[38] In a paper from 1972, (in a colloquium organized by Stoléru),[39] he said: What is the economic function of the state, of any modern state? It is, first, a relative redistribution of income,

* M.F.: that the redistributions, instead of going for the same wage

second, a subsidy in the form of the production of collective goods, and third, a regulation of economic processes ensuring growth and full employment.[40] These are the traditional objectives of French economic policy which could still not be challenged at that time. However, what he does challenge is the link between these three economic functions of the state: redistribution, subsidy, and regulation. He draws attention to the fact that the French budget is constructed in such a way that it is quite possible to use the same sums of money for the construction of a highway or for a specifically social type of subsidy.[41] This is intolerable, he says. In a sound policy we should "completely separate that which corresponds to the needs of economic expansion from that which corresponds to the concern for solidarity and social justice."[42] In other words, we should have two systems that as far as possible are impermeable to each other, two systems with two corresponding and completely distinct types of taxation, an economic tax and a social tax.[43] Behind this statement of principle you can see the major idea that the economy must have its own rules and the social must have its specific objectives, but that they must be decoupled so that the economic process is not disrupted or damaged by social mechanisms and so that the social mechanism has a limitation, a purity, as it were, such that it never intervenes in the economic process as a disruption.

The problem is: How can we get such a separation between the economic and the social to work? How can we carry out this decoupling? Here again, still with Giscard's text, we can see what he means. He appeals to a principle I have already spoken about which is common to German ordoliberalism and American neo-liberalism, and which is found in French neo-liberalism. This is the idea that the economy is basically a game, that it develops as a game between partners, that the whole of society must be permeated by this economic game, and that the essential role of the state is to define the economic rules of the game and to make sure that they are in fact applied. What are these rules? They must be such that the economic game is as active as possible and consequently to the advantage of the greatest possible number of people, with simply a rule—and this is the surface of contact, without real penetration, of the economic and the social—a supplementary and unconditional rule of the game, as it were, which is that it must be impossible for one of the partners of the economic game to lose everything and thus be unable to continue playing. It is, if you like, a safety clause for the player, a limiting rule that changes nothing in the course of the game itself, but which prevents someone from ever dropping totally and definitively out of the game. It is a sort of inverted social contract. That is to say, in the social contract, all those who will the social contract and virtually or actually subscribe to it form part of society until such a time as they cut themselves off from it. In the idea of an economic game we find that no one originally insisted on being part of the economic game and consequently it is up to society and to the rules of the game imposed by the state to ensure that no one is excluded from this game in which he is caught up without ever having explicitly wished to take part. The idea that the economy is a game, that there are rules of the economic game guaranteed by the state, and that the only point of contact between the economic and the social is the rule safeguarding players from being excluded from the game, is formulated by Giscard somewhat implicitly, but sufficiently clearly, I think, when he says in this 1972 text: "The characteristic feature of the market economy is the existence of rules of the game, which enable decentralized decisions to be taken, and that these rules are the same for all."[44] Between the rule of competition of production and that of the protection of the individual, a "particular game" must be established so that no player risks losing everything[45]—he says "particular game," but it would no doubt be better to say "particular rule." Now this idea that there must be a rule of non-exclusion and that the function of the social rule, of social regulation, or of social security in the broadest sense of the term, is purely and simply to ensure non-exclusion with regard to an economic game that, apart from this rule, must follow its own course, is implemented, or outlined at any rate, in a whole series of more or less clear measures.*

---

* Foucault here leaves out pages 20 and 21 of the manuscript:
"This decoupling and this economic game with a safety clause comprises two parts: 1. One purely economic: re-establishing the game of the market without taking the protection of individuals into account. And without having to pursue an economic policy which adopts the objective of maintaining employment [and] maintaining purchase power ( ... ). 2. The other part comprises two sets of measures: a. the reconstruction of 'human capital' ( ... ), b. the negative tax (Chicago)."

Because time is pressing and also because I don't want to bore you too much with this, I would just like to show you what this means, not [in terms of] the measures which were actually taken and which, due to the crisis and its intensity, could not be fully followed through or form a coherent whole, but [by taking] the example of a project which comes back several times after 1974, which is that of the negative tax. In fact, when Giscard said in 1972 that we must ensure that it never happens that someone loses everything, he already had in mind this idea of a negative tax. The negative tax is not an idea of French neo-liberalism, but of American neo-liberalism (which maybe I will talk about next week): it is an idea, anyway, which was taken up by people around Giscard, like Stoléru[46] and Stoffaës (who I will talk about shortly), and in the preparatory discussions for the 7th Plan, in 1974 or '75,[47] Stoffaës produced a report on the negative tax.[48] What is the negative tax? To summarize things very, very simply, we can say that the idea of negative tax is the following: To be socially effective without being economically disruptive, a social benefit must never, as far as this is possible, take the form of collective consumption, for, the supporters of negative tax say, experience shows that in the end it is the wealthiest who benefit most from collective forms of consumption and who contribute the least in financing them. So, if we want an effective social protection without negative economic effects, we must quite simply replace those overall forms of financing, all those more or less sectional benefits, with a cash benefit which will guarantee supplementary resources to those, and only those, who either definitively or provisionally fail to reach a sufficient threshold. In clear terms, if you like, there is no point giving the wealthy the possibility of sharing in collective consumptions of health; they are perfectly capable of taking care of their own health. On the other hand, there is a category of individuals in society who, either definitively, because they are old or have a disability, or provisionally, because they have lost their job and are unemployed, cannot reach what society considers to be the proper level of consumption. Well, it is to these and for their benefit only that we should allocate compensatory benefits, the typical benefits of cover of a social policy. Consequently, below a given level of income we will pay an additional amount, even if this means giving up the idea that society as a whole owes services like health and education to each of its members, and even if also—and this is no doubt the most important element—it means reintroducing an imbalance between the poor and others, between those receiving aid and those who are not.

Obviously, this project of a negative tax, especially in its French forms, does not have the drastic appearance that I have just given, or the simplistic appearance that you might think. In fact, negative tax as a benefit paid to people with an income which is insufficient to ensure a given level of consumption is conceived by Stoléru and Stoffaës in a relatively sophisticated way inasmuch as, in particular, one has to ensure that people do not take this supplementary benefit as a sort of means of living that will save them from looking for work and getting back into the economic game. A whole series of modulations and gradations see to it that, through the negative tax, the individual will be guaranteed a given level of consumption, but with enough motivations, or, if you like, enough frustrations, so that he still always wants to work and so that it is always preferable to work rather than receive a benefit.[49]

Let's leave aside all these details—which are important nevertheless. I would just like to note a few things. First of all, what is it that will be attenuated by the action which is explicitly sought after in the idea of a negative tax? It is the effects of poverty, and only its effects. That is to say, in no way does the negative tax seek to be an action aiming to modify this or that cause of poverty. The negative tax will never function at the level of the causes of poverty but simply at the level of its effects. This is what Stoléru says when he writes: "For some, social assistance must be motivated by the *causes* of poverty," and thus what it covers, what it is directed towards, is illness, accidents, unfitness for work, or the impossibility of finding employment. That is to say, in this traditional perspective, you cannot give someone assistance without asking why he needs it and so without seeking to change the reasons for which he needs it. "For others," those who support the negative tax, "social assistance must only be motivated by the *effects* of poverty; every human being," Stoléru says, "has basic needs, and society must help him to meet them when he cannot do so by himself."[50] So that when it comes to it, the famous distinction that Western governmentality has tried for so long to establish between the good and bad poor, between the voluntary and involuntary unemployed, is not important. After all, it does not and should not concern us to know why someone falls below the level of the social game; whether he is a drug addict or voluntarily unemployed is not important. Whatever the reasons, the only problem is whether he is above or below the threshold. The only thing that matters is that the individual has fallen below a given level and, at that point, without looking further, and so without having to make all those bureaucratic, police, or inquisitorial investigations, the problem becomes one of granting him a subsidy in such a way that the mechanism by which he is given it still encourages him to rise again to the level of the threshold and be sufficiently motivated, through receiving assistance, to have the desire, in spite of everything, to rise again above the threshold. But if he does not have the desire, this is not important and he will remain assisted. This is the first point which is, I think, very important in relation to what was developed for centuries by social policy in the West.

Second, you can see that this negative tax is a way of absolutely avoiding social policy having any kind effect in the form of a general redistribution of income, that is to say, broadly speaking, anything that could be described as a socialist policy. If we call socialist policy a policy of "relative"* poverty, that is to say, a policy which tends to alter the gaps between different incomes, if we understand socialist policy as a policy that tries to attenuate the effects of relative poverty arising from the gap between the incomes of the wealthiest and the poorest, then it is absolutely clear that the policy entailed by negative tax is the exact opposite of socialist policy. Relative poverty does not figure in any way in the objectives of such a social policy. The only problem is "absolute"† poverty, that is to say the threshold below which people are deemed not to have an adequate income for ensuring that they have a sufficient consumption.[51]

I think we should make a few remarks about absolute poverty. It should not be understood, of course, as a sort of threshold valid for the whole of humanity. Absolute poverty is relative for every society, and there are societies which will have a fairly high threshold of absolute

---

* In inverted commas in the manuscript (p. 25).
† In inverted commas in the manuscript (p. 25).

poverty and other, poor societies where it will be much lower. So, the threshold of absolute poverty is relative. Second, and this is an important consequence, you can see that this reintroduces that category of the poor and of poverty that all social policies, certainly since Liberation, but in reality all the policies of welfare, all the more or less socializing or socialized policies since the end of the nineteenth century, tried to get rid of. All these policies—the German state socialist type of policy, a welfare policy like that programmed by Pigou,[52] the New Deal policy, and social policy like that in England or France after Liberation—did not want to know the category of the poor, or, at any rate, they wanted to ensure that economic interventions were such that the population was not divided between the poor and the less poor. Policy was always situated in the spread of relative poverty, in the redistribution of incomes, in the play of the gap between richer and poorer. Here, however, we have a policy defining a given threshold which is still relative, but which is absolute for the society and which distinguishes between the poor and those who are not poor, between those who are receiving assistance and those who are not.

The third characteristic of negative tax is that, as you can see, it ensures as it were a general security, but at the lowest level, that is to say, the economic mechanisms of the game, the mechanisms of competition and enterprise, will be allowed to function in the rest of society. Above the threshold everyone will have to be an enterprise for himself or for his family. A society formalized on the model of the enterprise, of the competitive enterprise, will be possible above the threshold, and there will be simply a minimum security, that is to say, the nullification of certain risks on the basis of a low level threshold. That is to say, there will be a population which, from the point of view of the economic baseline, will be constantly moving between, on the one hand, assistance provided in certain eventualities when it falls below the threshold and, on the other, both its use and its availability for use according to economic needs and possibilities. It will therefore be a kind of infra- and supra-liminal floating population, a liminal population which, for an economy that has abandoned the objective of full employment, will be a constant reserve of manpower which can be drawn on if need be, but which can also be returned to its assisted status if necessary.

So with this system—which, again, has not been applied for a number of reasons, but whose features are clearly visible in the current economic policy of Giscard and Barre—you have the formation of an economic policy which is no longer focused on full employment, and which can only be integrated in the general market economy by abandoning the objective of full employment along with its essential instrument of centrally planned growth. Full employment and voluntarist growth are renounced in favor of integration in a market economy. But this entails a fund of a floating population, of a liminal, infra- or supra-liminal population, in which the assurance mechanism will enable each to live, after a fashion, and to live in such a way that he can always be available for possible work, if market conditions require it. This is a completely different system from that through which eighteenth and nineteenth century capitalism was formed and developed, when it had to deal with a peasant population which was a possible constant reservoir of manpower. When the economy functions as it does now, when the peasant population can no longer ensure that kind of endless fund of manpower, this fund has to be formed in a completely different way. This other way is the assisted population, which is actually assisted in a very liberal and much less bureaucratic and disciplinary way than it is by a system focused on full employment which employs mechanisms like those of social security. Ultimately, it is up to people to work if they want or not work if they don't. Above all there is the possibility of not forcing them to work if there is no interest in doing so. They are merely guaranteed the possibility of minimal existence at a given level, and in this way the neo-liberal policy can be got to work.

Now this kind of project is nothing other than the radicalization of those general themes I talked about with regard to ordoliberalism. The German ordoliberals explained that the main objective of a social policy is certainly not to take into account all the risks that may be incurred by the global mass of the population, and that a true social policy must be such that, without affecting the economic game, and consequently letting society develop as an enterprise society, mechanisms of intervention are deployed to assist those when, and only when, they need it.

---

1. See above, lecture of 10 January 1979, note 17.
2. Foucault had already expressed himself on this subject, in terms close to these, in November 1977, in his interview with R. Lefort with regard to the Croissant affair (see *Sécurité, Territoire, Population*, "Situation des cours," p. 385; *Security, Territory, Population*, "Course context," pp. 372-373), contrasting the argument of the state's tendency to fascism with the analysis of real problems raised by "security societies" ("Michel Foucault: la sécurité et l'État," *Dits et Écrits*, 3, p. 387).
3. Reference to a conversation in which F. Ewald, then Foucault's assistant at the Collège de France, contrasted denunciation with accusation, the former being made in the same name as the principles it denounces and thereby being doomed to remain abstract, while the latter, directed at someone by name, involves much greater commitment on the part of the person who formulates it (information supplied by F. Ewald).
4. W. Röpke, "Das Beveridgeplan," (see above, lecture of 7 February 1979, note 39).
5. The sentence is actually taken from *Civitas Humana*, pp 146-147: "*Still more social insurance, a still larger social bureaucracy, still more of pushing incomes about hither and thither, yet more labels and more stamps, yet further concentration of power, national income and responsibility in the hands of the state which is seeking to encompass, regulate, concentrate and control everything*, and all this with the certainty of not effecting any solution of the problem of proletarianisation but of achieving the destruction of the middle classes and thus adding still further to the centralised and state manufactured proletariat." In his notes, Foucault notes the "more detailed critique" developed in the article cited, but he does not refer to it directly. Röpke devotes pages 226-243 of his book to the critique of the Beveridge plan and specifies in a note on p. 245: "I have dwelt at greater length on this subject elsewhere [followed by a reference to the article 'Das Beveridgeplan']," adding: "But on this subject one should above all refer to the excellent work of the Catholic sociologist (formerly German and today teaching in the United States), Goetz Briefs, *The Proletariat*, New York, 1937)."
6. F. Hayek, *The Road to Serfdom*, p. 1.
7. Ibid. p. 2: "It is not to the Germany of Hitler, the Germany of the present war, that this country bears yet any resemblance. But students of the currents of ideas can hardly fail to see that there is more than a superficial similarity between the trend of thought in Germany during and after the last war and the present current of ideas in this country. There exists now in this country certainly the same determination that the organisation of the nation we have achieved for purposes of defence shall be retained for the purposes of creation."
8. Ibid. p. 3: "Few are ready to recognise that the rise of Fascism and Nazism was not a reaction against the socialist trends of the preceding period, but a necessary outcome of those tendencies."
9. See above, lecture of 7 February 1979, pp. 110-111, where he sets out the same arguments for Röpke in 1943.
10. In fact, in 1980 Foucault takes a completely different direction and, taking up again the theme of the 1978 lectures, devotes his lectures ("On the Government of the Living") to the problem of the examination of conscience and confession (*l'aveu*) in early Christianity. See the course summary, *Dits et Écrits*, 4, pp. 125-129; English translation by Robert Hurley, "The Government of the Living" in *Essential Works of Foucault*, 1, pp. 81-85.
11. This was the thesis of the leftists of the *Gauche Prolétarienne*. See *Les Temps Modernes*, 310 bis: *Nouveau Fascisme, Nouvelle Démocratie*, 1972. But Foucault's remark is especially connected to the debates taking place about Germany regarding terrorism. Police repression of the Red Army Fraction intensified after the assassination in October 1977 of the president of the employers' association, H.M. Schleyer, by members of the group. Baader and several of his fellow prisoners were found dead in their cells in the Stammheim prison in Stuttgart some days later. The official thesis of suicide was violently challenged. Foucault, while supporting the Red Army Fraction's lawyer, Klaus Croissant, against the threat of extradition from France, had broken with those who, seeing Helmut Schmidt's Germany as a state which was becoming fascist, were giving support to the terrorist struggle. See, "Va-t-on

extrader Klauss Croissant?" *Dits et Écrits*, 3, pp. 361-365, where no doubt for the first time he theorizes the "right of the governed ( ... ) more precise and more historically determinate than human rights" (p. 362). On Foucault's attitude to the "German question," see, "Situation des cours," in *Sécurité, Territoire, Population*, pp. 386-387; "Course context," in *Security, Territory, Population*, pp. 373-374.

12. Richard Nixon (1913-1994), President of the United States, 1968 to 1974.
13. James Earl ("Jimmy") Carter (born 1924), President of the United States, 1976 to 1980.
14. Raymond Barre (born 1924), professor of economic sciences, director of the office of the Minister of Industry Jean-Marcel Jeannenay, then European commissioner at Brussels from July 1967 to December 1972, was Prime Minister from August 1976 until May 1981 and also Economic and Finance Minister from August 1976 until April 1978. On 22 September 1976 he put forward a plan of austerity measures, afterwards called the "Barre plan," to combat the "stagflation" (weak growth and strong inflation) which appeared with the 1974 crisis. For the principles inspiring this policy of a struggle against inflation, see R. Barre, *Une politique pour l'Avenir* (Paris: Plon, pp. 24-27). See also in this volume (pp. 98-114) the reproduction of an interview with Jean Boissonnat, which appeared in *l'Epansion* in September 1978, "Dialogue sur le libéralisme," in which, after rejecting the diagnosis of a crisis of liberalism as well as, to his eyes, the outmoded opposition between liberalism and interventionism, Barre states: "If by economic liberalism you understand the doctrine of 'laissez faire—laissez passer,' then I am certainly not a liberal. If by economic liberalism you understand the decentralized management of a modern economy, which combines both the freedom, coupled with responsibility, of private centers of decision-making, and also the regulatory intervention of the state, then you could say I am a liberal" (pp. 105-106). Going on to state the principles which, according to him, should inspire the management of a modern economy—the free choice of economic agents and state responsibility for the overall regulation of economic activity, for maintaining competition, correcting effects of the market on employment, and for the equitable redistribution of incomes—he concludes: "That is my liberalism; it is not that different from what social democratic governments think and do" (p. 107). He then makes an explicit reference to the "social market economy," the results of which he defends against criticisms from the Chicago School: "( ... ) the exaggerated liberalism of the Chicago school cannot inspire an effective policy" (p. 108).
15. C. Stoffaës, *La Grande Menace industrielle* (Paris: Calmann-Lévy, 1978; enlarged 2nd edition, Le Livre de poche, 1979 [edition quoted here]). This book, which caused a big stir, is an extension of that by L. Stoléru, *L'Impératif industriel* (Paris: Le Seuil, 1969). "Only a *new industrial imperative*, a replica of the imperative of industrialization launched ten years ago, will enable this great danger [of the developing third world and super-industrialized countries] to be confronted" p. 48.
16. Born in 1947, a student of the École polytechnique and the École des mines, with a degree from Harvard, Christain Stoffaës was professor of industrial economics at the Institut d'études politiques in Paris and then, from 1978, director of the Centre d'études et de prévision created by André Giraud, Minister for Industry.
17. C. Stoffaës, *La Grande Menace*, 4th edition, cover: "Rejecting the temptation to hurriedly transpose the German and Japanese models, the author sets out the bases for an original industrial policy to meet the challenge confronting our country: the future of the French economy."
18. Ibid. pp. 742-743 (emphasis by C. Stoffaës).
19. Ibid. p. 743 (immediately after the previous quotation): "If we want the laws of the market to restore vigor to the economic sphere, then at the same time imagination must take back power in the collective sphere. Contrary to what is too often said, there is no incompatibility between an effective market economy open to the world and an advanced social project that would proceed faster in reducing inequalities of fortunes, incomes, and opportunities and above all in redistributing power in the enterprise and in public life."
20. Valéry Giscard d'Estaing: minister of finance and the economy from 1962 until 1966, under President de Gaul, and from 1969 until 1974, under President Georges Pompidou; President of the Republic from May 1974.
21. See above, lecture of 10 January 1979, p. 12.

22. On the 5th Plan (1965-1970), see *Rapport sur les options principales du V[e] Plan de développement économique et social* (Paris: La Documentation française, 1964). See, A. Gauron, *Histoire économique et sociale de la V[e] République*, vol. 1; *Le Temps des modernistes (1958-1969)* (Paris: La Découverte/Maspero, 1983) pp. 85-94: "The 5th Plan or the imperative of concentration." "In a market economy oriented by the plan, the report of the 5th Plan notes, the primary responsibility for industrial development falls to the heads of enterprises. The success of the policy, whose objectives and means are decided by the Plan, depends on their initiative." But, the Plan commissioner says, it would be "contrary to prudence to hand the economy over to a laisser-faire whose consequences could not be calculated or, if need be, modified." (*Rapport sur les options principales du V[e] Plan*, p. 72, quoted by A. Guaron, p. 87, who adds: "The general commissioner of the Plan does not therefore advocate a new form of the 'mixed economy': the complementarity between plan and market recognizes and organizes the preeminence of the laws of the market over the plan's objectives, and therefore of capitalist decisions over governmental policy. It suggests, in still covert terms, that this presupposes a profound transformation of the mode of state intervention ( ... ).") On the economic and social objectives of the four previous plans since the war, see, for example, P. Massé, *Le Plan, ou l'Anti-hasard* (Paris: Gallimard, 1965) pp. 146-151; P. Bauchet, *La Planification française du premier au sixième plan* (Paris: Le Seuil, 1970 [5th edition]).
23. Antoine Pinay (1891-1994), was president of the Cabinet, with the Finance portfolio, from March to December 1942. During this short period he successfully devoted himself to the stabilization of the franc and faced up to the social malaise with various measures of stabilization.
24. On 10 June 1958, Jacques Rueff sent a note to Antoine Pinay, minister of Finance and Economic affairs appointed by General de Gaulle, with the title, "Elements for a program of economic and financial renewal" in which he advocated the "restoration of a French currency," in accordance with his doctrine of the financial order, with a view to combating inflation. In spite of Pinay's reservations, this note served as the basis for the creation of a committee of experts that met from September to December 1958, under the presidency of Rueff, and presented a major austerity plan, supported by De Gaulle, which was adopted by the Cabinet at the end of December. The plan included three fundamental decisions: "a vigorous devaluation, increased taxation, the liberalization of foreign exchange" (J. Lacouture, *De Gaulle* [Paris: Le Seuil, 1985] vol. 2, p. 672).
25. Created by the provisional government of the French Republic (ruling of 4 October 1945), in conformity with the commitment of the National Council of the Resistance (CNR, *Conseil national de la Résistance*, of which A. Parodi, Minister of Labor in 1945, was a member), Social Security had the task of "ridding workers of the uncertainty of the morrow" that generates a "feeling of inferiority" and is a "real and profound basis of class distinctions." The ruling was followed by a series of laws up until May 1946. On the genesis of the French social security plan, see H.C. Galant, *Histoire politique de la Sécurité sociale: 1945-1952*, with a Preface by P. Laroque (Paris: Hachette, 1974 [reproduction of this edition, Paris: A. Colin, 1955]); N. Kerschen, "L'influence du rapport Beveridge sur le plan français de sécurité sociale de 1945." On the social program of the CNR, see above, lecture of 31 January, 1979, note 15.
26. Pierre Laroque (1907-1997): Jurist, specialist in labor law. A member of the Council of State, director general of social insurance at the Ministry of Labor, in September 1944 he was directed by A. Parodi to work out the plan of social security. He presided over the history panel of Social Security from 1973 until 1989. See, *Revue française des affaires sociales*, special issue: *Quarante ans de Sécurité sociale*, July-September 1985. He presided over the social section of the Council of State from 1964 until 1980.
27. P. Laroque, "La Sécurité sociale dans l'économie française," lecture delivered at the Club "Échos" on Saturday 6 November 1948 (Paris: Fédération nationale des organismes de sécurité sociale, [no date]), pp. 3-22.
28. Ibid. pp. 15-16: "We frequently talk of the costs, but rarely of the contribution of Social Security to the economy. This contribution is not negligible however. Every manufacturer thinks it normal and necessary to add to his receipts the sums that are indispensable for the maintenance of his material. Now to a very considerable extent, Social Security represents the maintenance of the human capital of the country. ( ... ) our economy needs and will

increasingly need manpower. ( ... ) This is one of the essential tasks of Social Security: to supply the French economy with men. Social Security is thus an essential factor in the conservation and development of the workforce and in this respect its importance for the country's economy is undeniable."

29. Ibid. p. 6: "Social Security appears to us therefore as *the guarantee that, whatever the circumstances, everyone will be able to support himself and those for whom he is responsible in reasonable conditions*." This principle was formulated by P. Laroque in 1946 ("Le plan français de sécurité sociale," *Revue française du travail*, 1, 1946, p. 9) and repeated in the same terms in 1948 ("De l'assurance sociale à la sécurité sociale: l'expérience française," *Revue internationale du travail*, 56 (6), 1948, p. 621). See N. Kerschen, "L'influence du rapport Beveridge," p. 577.
30. P. Laroque, "La Sécurité sociale dans l'économie française," p. 17: "( ... ) the increase of social security contributions has been imposed entirely on wages, and ( ... ) has not by itself put any pressure on the cost prices of the economy. In reality, Social Security is confined to the redistribution of a fraction of the mass of wage-earners' incomes. ( ... ) We are faced with a solidarity imposed on the mass of wage-earners, to the advantage of their children and the aged."
31. Ibid.: "We can even go further and claim without paradox that Social Security has made possible a reduction of the costs that weigh on the country's economy, by avoiding wage increases that without it might have been significant and difficult to avoid."
32. *Revue française des affaires sociales*, special issue: *Perspectives de la sécurité sociale*, July-September 1976. This is actually a set of reports drafted by the ENA students (promoted by GUERNICA) within the framework of their seminars, each seminar conceived of as "the multi-disciplinary study of an administrative problem with a view to finding an 'operational' solution" (G. Dupuis, ibid. p. iv). In this paragraph Foucault relies on the first report, "Le financement du régime générale de sécurité sociale," written by P. Begault, A. Bodon, B. Bonnet, J.-C. Bugeat, G. Chabost, D. Demangel, J.-M. Grabarsky, P. Masseron, B. Pommies, D. Postel-Vinnay, E. Rigal, and C. Vallet (pp. 5-66).
33. Foucault summarizes here, leaving out all the technical features of the analysis developed in the second section of the report ("The current mode of financing the general regime is not neutral with regard to economic activity"), pp. 21-27. Paragraph 2.3, "The impact of contributions on employment," concludes with these words: "The wage basis and upper limit to contributions thus seems unfavorable to employment in the short term."
34. Ibid., paragraph 2.4. pp. 24-27: "The impact of contributions on international competition." The report, however, although it emphasizes that "the distortions produced in international competition by different systems of financing social expenditure may compromise the competitiveness of French industry" (p. 26), notes that "these distortions are more than compensated for by two elements [the relative weakness of social expenditure and the level of wages in France]" and concludes: "In the final analysis, it does not seem therefore that the competitiveness of French enterprises is weakened by the size of the social costs they carry; and breaches of neutrality in international competition resulting from the present system of financing social security are sufficiently compensated for and, on their own, do not justify a reform of the system."
35. Ibid., paragraph 3, pp. 28-34: "The present way of financing the general regime aggravates income inequalities between different categories of wage-earners."
36. Ibid., p. 21: "The deduction carried out to finance the general regime exceeds 12% of the GDP and by this fact alone has economic consequences. Now, the objective of Social Security is not an economic objective, and the ways in which it is financed should not, by distorting the law of the market, be an element of economic policy. Social Security must remain neutral in this respect."
37. See above, lecture of 14 January 1979.
38. See above, this lecture, note 20.
39. *Économie et Société humaine. Rencontres internationales du ministère de l'Économie et des Finances (Paris, 20-22 juin 1972)*, Preface by V. Giscard d'Estaing, presentation by L. Stoléru (Paris: Denoël, 1972). Lionel Stoléru (born 1937) was then technical advisor to the Cabinet of Valéry Giscard d'Estaing. Foucault met him quite often.

40. Ibid., p. 445: "( ... ) for a long time economists have divided the diversity of the functions of the state into three categories:
    (1) The function of redistribution: the state transfers from the wealthiest to the poorest;
    (2) The function of subsidy: the state produces collective goods: education, health care, highways;
    (3) The function of regulation: the state regulates and supports growth and full employment through its economic policy."
41. Ibid., continuing from the previous quotation: "Now, if these three functions are really distinct on the intellectual level, they are not distinct in practice: the same tax equally finances highways and Social Security deficits, the same expenditure serves both to produce in order to expand the national rail network and to subsidize the many families who travel by train."
42. Ibid., continuing from the previous quotation: "I wonder if this mixture of kinds is in conformity with social justice and I would like to submit a personal idea for you to reflect on: Should we not separate that which corresponds to the needs of economic expansion from that which arises from the concern for solidarity and social justice?"
43. Ibid., continuing from the previous quotation: "Can we devise a system in which every citizen would pay his taxes in two distinct forms: the economic tax and the social tax?"
44. Ibid. p. 439: "That characteristic feature of the market economy is above all:
    —that there are rules of the game that enable decentralized decisions to be taken,
    —that these rules are the same for all."
45. Ibid., p. 444: "( ... ) there would remain for many years a confrontation between the mechanism of production and the mechanism of individual protection: this means that the state will have to ensure the arbitration between these two mechanisms and that it will have increasingly to intervene, not in a bureaucratic manner, but in order to fix the rules of a rather particular game, since there must be no risk of any of the players losing."
46. After being technical advisor at the Ministry of Finance from 1969 to 1974 (see above, this lecture, note 39), Lionel Stoléru was an economic advisor at the Élysée from 1974 to 1976. From 1978 he was Secretary of State for the Minister of Labor and participation (manual labor and immigration).
47. The 7th Plan corresponds to the years 1976-1980.
48. C. Stoffaës, "Rapport du groupe d'étude de l'impôt négatif. Commissariat du Plan," Paris, 1973-1974; "De l'impôt négatif sur le revenu," *Contrepoint*, 11, 1973; L. Stoléru, "Coût et efficacité de l'impôt négatif," *Revue économique*, October, 1974; *Vaincre la pauvreté dans les pays riches* (Paris: Flammarion, 1977), 2nd part, pp. 117-209: "L'impôt négatif, simple remède ou panacée?" On this subject see, H. Lepage, *Demain le capitalisme*, pp. 280-283: "The theory of the negative tax on income is simple: it involves defining *a threshold of poverty* as far as annual incomes are concerned, in terms of the size of the family (a single person or a household with children), and paying an allowance to families falling below the poverty line, enabling them to make good the gap. In other words, it is a *system of a minimum income guaranteed by the community*" (p. 280, note 1). The negative tax was again the object of debate within the Left under the government of Lionel Jospin in 2000-2001. See, for example, D. Cohen, "Impôt négatif: le mot et la chose," *Le Monde*, 6 Febrary 2001.
49. See L. Stoléru, *Vaincre la pauvreté*, pp. 138-146: "Encouragements to work: how to discourage idleness?" and p. 206: "Apart from any other administrative addition, the system of negative tax is concerned with discouraging idleness through its rate. The encouragement consists in ensuring that everyone always has an interest in working, and in working more, in order to improve his final income, which is the sum of his earnings and the benefit he receives. This encouragement is all the stronger in that the benefit diminishes more slowly than the increase in earnings, that is to say, the rate of taxation is lower."
50. L. Stoléru, ibid., p. 242; see also pp. 205-206: "Negative tax is ( ... ) totally incompatible with the social conceptions that want to know why there is poverty before providing assistance. ( ... ) Acceptance of the negative tax is therefore acceptance of a universalist conception of poverty based upon the necessity of coming to the assistance of those who are poor without seeking to know where the fault lies, that is to say based upon the situation and not on the origin."

51. See, ibid., pp. 23-24: "In the first case [i.e., that of *absolute poverty*], we will speak of a 'vital minimum,' of a level of subsistence, of a typical budget, of elementary needs ( ... ). In the second case [i.e., that of *relative poverty*], we will talk of the *gap* between the poor and the rich, of the *breadth* of the range of incomes, of the *hierarchy* of earnings, and of the *disparities* in access to collective goods, we will measure coefficients of the inequality of income distribution." See also, pp. 241-242; 292: "The border between absolute poverty and relative poverty is the border between capitalism and socialism."
52. See above, lecture of 14 February 1979, note 45.

nine

# 14 March 1979

*American neo-liberalism (I). Its context. ~ The difference between American and European neo-liberalism. ~ American neo-liberalism as a global claim, utopian focus, and method of thought. ~ Aspects of this neo-liberalism: (1) The theory of human capital. The two processes that it represents: (a) an extension of economic analysis within its own domain: criticism of the classical analysis of labor in terms of the time factor; (b) an extension of economic analysis to domains previously considered to be non-economic. ~ The epistemological transformation produced by neo-liberal analysis: from the analysis of economic processes to the analysis of the internal rationality of human behavior. ~ Work as economic conduct. ~ Its division into capital, abilities, and income. ~ The redefinition of* homo œconomicus *as entrepreneur of himself. ~ The notion of "human capital." Its constitutive elements: (a) innate elements and the question of the improvement of genetic human capital; (b) acquired elements and the problem of the formation of human capital (education, health, etcetera). ~ The interest of these analyses: resumption of the problem of social and economic innovation (Schumpeter). A new conception of the policy of growth.*

TODAY* I WOULD LIKE to start talking to you about what is becoming a pet theme in France: American neo-liberalism.[1] Obviously, I will only

---

* At the beginning of the lecture Foucault announces that he "will have to leave at eleven o'clock, because [he has] a meeting."

consider some aspects and those that may have some relevance for the kind of analysis I am suggesting.[2]

Naturally, we will start with some banalities. American neo-liberalism developed in a context not that different from the contexts in which German neo-liberalism and what we could call French neo-liberalism developed. That is to say, the three main contextual elements of the development of neo-liberalism were, first: the New Deal and criticism of the New Deal and what we can broadly call the Keynesian policy developed by Roosevelt from 1933-34. The first, fundamental text of this American neo-liberalism, written in 1934 by Simons,[3] who was the father of the Chicago School, is an article entitled "A Positive Program for Laissez-Faire."[4]

The second contextual element is of course the Beveridge plan and all the projects of economic and social interventionism developed during the war.[5] These are all important elements that we could call, if you like, pacts of war, that is to say, pacts in terms of which governments—basically the English, and to a certain extent the American government—said to people who had just been through a very serious economic and social crisis: Now we are asking you to get yourselves killed, but we promise you that when you have done this, you will keep your jobs until the end of your lives. It would be very interesting to study this set of documents, analyses, programs, and research for itself, because it seems to me that, if I am not mistaken, this is the first time that entire nations waged war on the basis of a system of pacts which were not just international alliances between powers, but social pacts of a kind that promised—to those who were asked to go to war and get themselves killed—a certain type of economic and social organization which assured security (of employment, with regard to illness and other kinds of risk, and at the level of retirement): they were pacts of security at the moment of a demand for war. The demand for war on the part of governments is accompanied—and very quickly; there are texts on the theme from 1940—by this offer of a social pact and security. It was against this set of social problems that Simons drafted a number of critical texts and articles, the most interesting of which is entitled: "The Beveridge Program: an unsympathetic interpretation," which there is no need to translate, since the title indicates its critical sense.[6]

The third contextual element was obviously all the programs on poverty, education, and segregation developed in America from the Truman[7] administration up to the Johnson[8] administration, and through these programs, of course, state interventionism and the growth of the federal administration, etcetera.

I think these three elements—Keynesian policy, social pacts of war, and the growth of the federal administration through economic and social programs—together formed the adversary and target of neo-liberal thought, that which it was constructed against or which it opposed in order to form itself and develop. You can see that this is clearly the same type of context as that which we find in France, for example, where neo-liberalism defined itself through opposition to the Popular Front,[9] post-war Keynesian policies, [and] planning.

Nevertheless, I think there are some major differences between European and American neo-liberalism. They are also very obvious, as we know. I will just recall them. In the first place, American liberalism, at the moment of its historical formation, that is to say, very early on, from the eighteenth century, did not present itself, as in France, as a moderating principle with regard to a pre-existing *raison d'État*, since liberal type claims, and essentially economic claims moreover, were precisely the historical starting point for the formation of American independence.[10] That is to say, liberalism played a role in America during the period of the War of Independence somewhat analogous to the role it played in Germany in 1948: liberalism was appealed to as the founding and legitimizing principle of the state. The demand for liberalism founds the state rather then the state limiting itself through liberalism. I think this is one of the features of American liberalism.

Second, for two centuries—whether the issue has been one of economic policy, protectionism, the problem of gold and silver, or bimetallism, the question of slavery, the problem of the status and function of the judicial system, or the relation between individuals and different states, and between different states and the federal state—liberalism has, of course, always been at the heart of all political debate in America. We can say that the question of liberalism has been the recurrent element of all the political discussions and choices of the United States. Let's say that whereas in Europe the recurrent elements of political debate in the nineteenth century were either the unity of the nation, or its independence, or the Rule of law, in the United States it was liberalism.

Finally, third, in relation to this permanent ground of liberal debate, non-liberalism—by which I mean interventionist policies, whether in the form of Keynesian style economics, planning, or economic and social programs—appeared, especially from the middle of the twentieth century, as something extraneous and threatening inasmuch as it involved both introducing objectives which could be described as socializing and also as laying the bases of an imperialist and military state. Criticism of this non-liberalism was thus able to find a double foothold: on the right, precisely in the name of a liberal tradition historically and economically hostile to anything sounding socialist, and on the left, inasmuch as it was a question not only of criticism but also of daily struggle against the development of an imperialist and military state. Hence the ambiguity, or what appears to be an ambiguity in American neo-liberalism, since it is brought into play and reactivated both by the right and the left.

Anyway, I think we can say that for all these completely banal reasons I have just mentioned, American liberalism is not—as it is in France at present, or as it was in Germany immediately after the war—just an economic and political choice formed and formulated by those who govern and within the governmental milieu. Liberalism in America is a whole way of being and thinking. It is a type of relation between the governors and the governed much more than a technique of governors with regard to the governed. Let's say, if you like, that whereas in a country like France disputes between individuals and the state turn on the problem of service, of public service, [in the United States] disputes between individuals and government look like the problem of freedoms. I think this is why American liberalism currently appears not just, or not so much as a political alternative, but let's say as a sort of many-sided, ambiguous, global claim with a foothold in both the right and the left. It is also a sort of utopian focus which is always being revived. It is also a method of thought, a grid of economic and sociological analysis. I will refer to someone who is not an American exactly, he is an Austrian whom I have spoken about several times, but who then lived in England and the United States before returning to Germany. Some years ago Hayek said: We need a liberalism that is a living thought. Liberalism has always left it to the socialists to produce utopias, and socialism owes much of its vigor and historical dynamism to this utopian or utopia-creating activity. Well, liberalism also needs utopia. It is up to us to create liberal utopias, to think in a liberal mode, rather than presenting liberalism as a technical alternative for government.[11] Liberalism must be a general style of thought, analysis, and imagination.

These then, baldly stated, are some of the general features that may enable us to make a bit of a distinction between American neo-liberalism and the neo-liberalism that we have seen implemented in Germany and France. It is precisely through this mode of thought, style of analysis, and this grid of historical and sociological decipherment that I would like to bring out some aspects of American neo-liberalism, it being understood that I have no desire and it is not possible to study it in all its dimensions. In particular, I would like to consider two elements which are at once methods of analysis and types of programming, and which seem to me to be interesting in this American neo-liberal conception: first, the theory of human capital, and second, for reasons you will be able to guess, of course, the problem of the analysis of criminality and delinquency.

First, the theory of human capital.[12] I think the interest of this theory of human capital is that it represents two processes, one that we could call the extension of economic analysis into a previously unexplored domain, and second, on the basis of this, the possibility of giving a strictly economic interpretation of a whole domain previously thought to be non-economic.

First, an extension of economic analysis within, as it were, its own domain, but precisely on a point where it had remained blocked or at any rate suspended. In effect, the American neo-liberals say this: It is strange that classical political economy has always solemnly declared that the production of goods depends on three factors—land, capital, and labor—while leaving the third unexplored. It has remained, in a way, a blank sheet on which the economists have written nothing. Of course, we can say that Adam Smith's economics does begin with a reflection on labor, inasmuch as for Smith the division of labor and its specification is the key which enabled him to construct his economic analysis.[13] But apart from this sort of first step, this first opening, and since that moment, classical political economy has never analyzed labor itself, or rather it has constantly striven to neutralize it, and to do this by reducing it exclusively to the factor of time. This is what Ricardo did when, wishing to analyze the nature of the increase of labor, the labor factor, he only ever defined this increase in a quantitative way according to the temporal variable. That is to say, he thought that the increase or change of labor, the growth of the labor factor, could be nothing other than the presence of an additional number of workers on the market, that is to say, the possibility of employing more hours of labor thus made available to capital.[14] Consequently there is a neutralization of the nature itself of labor, to the advantage of this single quantitative variable of hours of work and time, and basically classical economics never got out of this Ricardian reduction of the problem of labor to the simple analysis of the quantitative variable of time.[15] And then we find an analysis, or rather non-analysis of labor in Keynes which is not so different or any more developed than Ricardo's analysis. What is labor according to Keynes? It is a factor of production, a productive factor, but which in itself is passive and only finds employment, activity, and actuality thanks to a certain rate of investment, and on condition clearly that this is sufficiently high.[16] Starting from this criticism of classical economics and its analysis of labor, the problem for the neo-liberals is basically that of trying to introduce labor into the field of economic analysis. A number of them attempted this, the first being Theodore Schultz,[17] who published a number of articles in the years 1950-1960 the result of which was a book published in 1971 with the title *Investment in Human Capital*.[18] More or less at the same time, Gary Becker[19] published a book with the same title,[20] and then there is a third text by Mincer,[21] which is quite fundamental and more concrete and precise than the others, on the school and wages, which appeared in 1975.[22]

In truth, the charge made by neo-liberalism that classical economics forgets labor and has never subjected it to economic analysis may seem strange when we think that, even if it is true that Ricardo entirely reduced the analysis of labor to the analysis of the quantitative variable of time, on the other hand there was someone called Marx who ... and so on. Fine. The neo-liberals practically never argue with Marx for reasons that we may think are to do with economic snobbery, it's not important.

But if they took the trouble to argue with Marx I think it is quite easy to see what they could say [about] his analysis. They would say: It is quite true that Marx makes labor the linchpin, one of the essential linchpins, of his analysis. But what does he do when he analyzes labor? What is it that he shows the worker sells? Not his labor, but his labor power. He sells his labor power for a certain time against a wage established on the basis of a given situation of the market corresponding to the balance between the supply and demand of labor power. And the work performed by the worker is work that creates a value, part of which is extorted from him. Marx clearly sees in this process the very mechanics or logic of capitalism. And in what does this logic consist? Well, it consists in the fact that the labor in all this is "abstract,"* that is to say, the concrete labor transformed into labor power, measured by time, put on the market and paid by wages, is not concrete labor; it is labor that has been cut off from its human reality, from all its qualitative variables, and precisely—this is indeed, in fact, what Marx shows—the logic of capital reduces labor to labor power and time. It makes it a commodity and reduces it to the effects of value produced.

Now, say the neo-liberals—and this is precisely where their criticism departs from the criticism made by Marx—what is responsible for this "abstraction."† For Marx, capitalism itself is responsible; it is the fault of the logic of capital and of its historical reality. Whereas the neo-liberals say: The abstraction of labor, which actually only appears through the variable of time, is not the product of real capitalism, [but] of the economic theory that has been constructed of capitalist production. Abstraction is not the result of the real mechanics of economic processes; it derives from the way in which these processes have been reflected in classical economics. And it is precisely because classical economics was not able to take on this analysis of labor in its concrete specification and qualitative modulations, it is because it left this blank page, gap or vacuum in its theory, that a whole philosophy, anthropology, and politics, of which Marx is precisely the representative, rushed

* In inverted commas in the manuscript.
† In inverted commas in the manuscript.

in. Consequently, we should not continue with this, in a way, realist criticism made by Marx, accusing real capitalism of having made real labor abstract; we should undertake a theoretical criticism of the way in which labor itself became abstract in economic discourse. And, the neo-liberals say, if economists see labor in such an abstract way, if they fail to grasp its specification, its qualitative modulations, and the economic effects of these modulations, it is basically because classical economists only ever envisaged the object of economics as processes of capital, of investment, of the machine, of the product, and so on.

I think this is the general context in which we should situate the neo-liberal analyses. However, the essential epistemological transformation of these neo-liberal analyses is their claim to change what constituted in fact the object, or domain of objects, the general field of reference of economic analysis. In practice, economic analysis, from Adam Smith to the beginning of the twentieth century, broadly speaking takes as its object the study of the mechanisms of production, the mechanisms of exchange, and the data of consumption within a given social structure, along with the interconnections between these three mechanisms. Now, for the neo-liberals, economic analysis should not consist in the study of these mechanisms, but in the nature and consequences of what they call substitutable choices, that is to say, the study and analysis of the way in which scarce means are allocated to competing ends, that is to say, to alternative ends which cannot be superimposed on each other.[23] In other words, we have scarce means, and we do not have a single end or cumulative ends for which it is possible to use these means, but ends between which we must choose, and the starting point and general frame of reference for economic analysis should be the way in which individuals allocate these scarce means to alternative ends.

In this they return to, or rather put to work, a definition of the object of economics which was put forward around 1930 or 1932, I no longer remember, by Robbins,[24] who, in this respect at least, may also be taken as one of the founders of the doctrine of economic liberalism: "Economics is the science of human behavior as a relationship between ends and scarce means which have mutually exclusive uses."[25] You can see that this definition of economics does not identify its task as the analysis of a relational mechanism between things or processes, like capital, investment, and production, into which, given this, labor is in some way inserted only as a cog; it adopts the task of analyzing a form of human behavior and the internal rationality of this human behavior. Analysis must try to bring to light the calculation—which, moreover, may be unreasonable, blind, or inadequate—through which one or more individuals decided to allot given scarce resources to this end rather than another. Economics is not therefore the analysis of processes; it is the analysis of an activity. So it is no longer the analysis of the historical logic of processes; it is the analysis of the internal rationality, the strategic programming of individuals' activity.

This means undertaking the economic analysis of labor. What does bringing labor back into economic analysis mean? It does not mean knowing where labor is situated between, let's say, capital and production. The problem of bringing labor back into the field of economic analysis is not one of asking about the price of labor, or what it produces technically, or what is the value added by labor. The fundamental, essential problem, anyway the first problem which arises when one wants to analyze labor in economic terms, is how the person who works uses the means available to him. That is to say, to bring labor into the field of economic analysis, we must put ourselves in the position of the person who works; we will have to study work as economic conduct practiced, implemented, rationalized, and calculated by the person who works. What does working mean for the person who works? What system of choice and rationality does the activity of work conform to? As a result, on the basis of this grid which projects a principle of strategic rationality on the activity of work, we will be able to see in what respects and how the qualitative differences of work may have an economic type of effect. So we adopt the point of view of the worker and, for the first time, ensure that the worker is not present in the economic analysis as an object—the object of supply and demand in the form of labor power—but as an active economic subject.

Fine, how do we set about this task? People like Schultz and Becker say: Why, in the end, do people work? They work, of course, to earn a wage. What is a wage? A wage is quite simply an income. From the point of view of the worker, the wage is an income, not the price at which he sells his labor power. Here, the American neo-liberals refer to the old definition, which goes right back to the start of the twentieth century, of Irving Fisher,[26] who said: What is an income? How can we define an income? An income is quite simply the product or return on a capital. Conversely, we will call "capital" everything that in one way or another can be a source of future income.[27] Consequently, if we accept on this basis that the wage is an income, then the wage is therefore the income of a capital. Now what is the capital of which the wage is the income? Well, it is the set of all those physical and psychological factors which make someone able to earn this or that wage, so that, seen from the side of the worker, labor is not a commodity reduced by abstraction to labor power and the time [during] which it is used. Broken down in economic terms, from the worker's point of view labor comprises a capital, that is to say, it as an ability, a skill; as they say: it is a "machine."[28] And on the other side it is an income, a wage, or rather, a set of wages; as they say: an earnings stream.[29]

This breakdown of labor into capital and income obviously has some fairly important consequences. First, if capital is thus defined as that which makes a future income possible, this income being a wage, then you can see that it is a capital which in practical terms is inseparable from the person who possesses it. To that extent it is not like other capitals. Ability to work, skill, the ability to do something cannot be separated from the person who is skilled and who can do this particular thing. In other words, the worker's skill really is a machine, but a machine which cannot be separated from the worker himself, which does not exactly mean, as economic, sociological, or psychological criticism said traditionally, that capitalism transforms the worker into a machine and alienates him as a result. We should think of the skill that is united with the worker as, in a way, the side through which the worker is a machine, but a machine understood in the positive sense, since it is a machine that produces* an earnings stream. An earnings stream and not an income, precisely because the machine constituted by the worker's ability is not, as it were, sold from time to time on the labor market against a certain wage. In reality this machine has a lifespan, a

---

* Foucault adds: and which will produce something that are

length of time in which it can be used, an obsolescence, and an ageing. So that we should think of the machine constituted by the worker's ability, the machine constituted by, if you like, ability and worker individually bound together, as being remunerated over a period of time by a series of wages which, to take the simplest case, will begin by being relatively low when the machine begins to be used, then will rise, and then will fall with the machine's obsolescence or the ageing of the worker insofar as he is a machine. We should therefore view the whole as a machine/stream complex, say the neo-economists—all this is in Schultz[30] is it not—it is therefore a machine-stream ensemble, and you can see that we are at the opposite extreme of a conception of labor power sold at the market price to a capital invested in an enterprise. This is not a conception of labor power; it is a conception of capital-ability which, according to diverse variables, receives a certain income that is a wage, an income-wage, so that the worker himself appears as a sort of enterprise for himself. Here, as you can see, the element I pointed out earlier in German neo-liberalism, and to an extent in French neo-liberalism, is pushed to the limit, that is to say, the idea that the basic element to be deciphered by economic analysis is not so much the individual, or processes and mechanisms, but enterprises. An economy made up of enterprise-units, a society made up of enterprise-units, is at once the principle of decipherment linked to liberalism and its programming for the rationalization of a society and an economy.

I would say that in a sense, and this is what is usually said, neo-liberalism appears under these conditions as a return to *homo œconomicus*. This is true, but as you can see, with a considerable shift, since what is *homo œconomicus*, economic man, in the classical conception? Well, he is the man of exchange, the partner, one of the two partners in the process of exchange. And this *homo œconomicus*, partner of exchange, entails, of course, an analysis in terms of utility of what he is himself, a breakdown of his behavior and ways of doing things, which refer, of course, to a problematic of needs, since on the basis of these needs it will be possible to describe or define, or anyway found, a utility which leads to the process of exchange. The characteristic feature of the classical conception of *homo œconomicus* is the partner of exchange and the theory of utility based on a problematic of needs.

In neo-liberalism—and it does not hide this; it proclaims it—there is also a theory of *homo œconomicus*, but he is not at all a partner of exchange. *Homo œconomicus* is an entrepreneur, an entrepreneur of himself. This is true to the extent that, in practice, the stake in all neo-liberal analyses is the replacement every time of *homo œconomicus* as partner of exchange with a *homo œconomicus* as entrepreneur of himself, being for himself his own capital, being for himself his own producer, being for himself the source of [his] earnings. And I will not talk about it here, because it would take too long, but in Gary Becker there is a very interesting theory of consumption,[31] in which he says: We should not think at all that consumption simply consists in being someone in a process of exchange who buys and makes a monetary exchange in order to obtain some products. The man of consumption is not one of the terms of exchange. The man of consumption, insofar as he consumes, is a producer. What does he produce? Well, quite simply, he produces his own satisfaction.[32] And we should think of consumption as an enterprise activity by which the individual, precisely on the basis of the capital he has at his disposal, will produce something that will be his own satisfaction. Consequently, the theory, the classical analysis trotted out a hundred times of the person who is a consumer on the one hand, but who is also a producer, and who, because of this, is, as it were, divided in relation to himself, as well as all the sociological analyses—for they have never been economic analyses—of mass consumption, of consumer society, and so forth, do not hold up and have no value in relation to an analysis of consumption in the neo-liberal terms of the activity of production. So, even if there really is a return to the idea of *homo œconomicus* as the analytical grid of economic activity, there is a complete change in the conception of this *homo œconomicus*.

So, we arrive at this idea that the wage is nothing other than the remuneration, the income allocated to a certain capital, a capital that we will call human capital inasmuch as the ability-machine of which it is the income cannot be separated from the human individual who is its bearer.[33] How is this capital made up? It is at this point that the reintroduction of labor or work into the field of economic analysis will make it possible, through a sort of acceleration or extension, to move on to the economic analysis of elements which had previously totally escaped it.

In other words, the neo-liberals say that labor was in principle part of economic analysis, but the way in which classical economic analysis was conducted was incapable of dealing with this element. Good, we do deal with it. And when they make this analysis, and do so in the terms I have just described, they are led to study the way in which human capital is formed and accumulated, and this enables them to apply economic analyses to completely new fields and domains.

How is human capital made up? Well, they say, it is made up of innate elements and other, acquired elements.[34] Let's talk about the innate elements. There are those we can call hereditary, and others which are just innate; differences which are, of course, self-evident for anyone with the vaguest acquaintance with biology. I do not think that there are as yet any studies on the problem of the hereditary elements of human capital, but it is quite clear what form they could take and, above all, we can see through anxieties, concerns, problems, and so on, the birth of something which, according to your point of view, could be interesting or disturbing. In actual fact, in the—I was going to say, classical—analyses of these neo-liberals, in the analyses of Schultz or Becker, for example, it is indeed said that the formation of human capital only has interest and only becomes relevant for the economists inasmuch as this capital is formed thanks to the use of scarce means, to the alternative use of scarce means for a given end. Now obviously we do not have to pay to have the body we have, or we do not have to pay for our genetic make-up. It costs nothing. Yes, it costs nothing—and yet, we need to see ... , and we can easily imagine something like this occurring (I am just engaging in a bit of science fiction here, it is a kind of problematic which is currently becoming pervasive).

In fact, modern genetics clearly shows that many more elements than was previously thought are conditioned by the genetic make-up we receive from our ancestors. In particular, genetics makes it possible to establish for any given individual the probabilities of their contracting this or that type of disease at a given age, during a given period of life, or in any way at any moment of life. In other words, one of the current interests in the application of genetics to human populations is to make it possible to recognize individuals at risk and the type of risk individuals incur throughout their life. You will say: Here again, there's nothing we can do; our parents made us like this. Yes, of course, but when we can identify what individuals are at risk, and what the risks are of a union of individuals at risk producing an individual with a particular characteristic that makes him or her the carrier of a risk, then we can perfectly well imagine the following: good genetic make-ups—that is to say, [those] able to produce individuals with low risk or with a level of risk which will not be harmful for themselves, those around them, or society—will certainly become scarce, and insofar as they are scarce they may perfectly well [enter], and this is entirely normal, into economic circuits or calculations, that is to say, alternative choices. Putting it in clear terms, this will mean that given my own genetic make-up, if I wish to have a child whose genetic make-up will be at least as good as mine, or as far as possible better than mine, then I will have to find someone who also has a good genetic make-up. And if you want a child whose human capital, understood simply in terms of innate and hereditary elements, is high, you can see that you will have to make an investment, that is to say, you will have to have worked enough, to have sufficient income, and to have a social status such that it will enable you to take for a spouse or co-producer of this future human capital, someone who has significant human capital themselves. I am not saying this as a joke; it is simply a form of thought or a form of problematic that is currently being elaborated.[35]

What I mean is that if the problem of genetics currently provokes such anxiety, I do not think it is either useful or interesting to translate this anxiety into the traditional terms of racism. If we want to try to grasp the political pertinence of the present development of genetics, we must do so by trying to grasp its implications at the level of actuality itself, with the real problems that it raises. And as soon as a society poses itself the problem of the improvement of its human capital in general, it is inevitable that the problem of the control, screening, and improvement of the human capital of individuals, as a function of unions and consequent reproduction, will become actual, or at any rate, called for. So, the political problem of the use of genetics arises in terms of the formation, growth, accumulation, and improvement of human capital. What we might call the racist effects of genetics is certainly something to be feared, and they are far from being eradicated, but this does not seem to me to be the major political issue at the moment.

Fine, let's leave this problem of investment in and the costly choice of the formation of a genetic human capital. Obviously, the neo-liberals pose their problems and set out their new type of analysis much more from the angle of acquired human capital, that is to say, of the more or less voluntary formation of human capital in the course of individuals' lives. What does it mean to form human capital, and so to form these kinds of abilities-machines which will produce income, which will be remunerated by income? It means, of course, making what are called educational investments.[36] In truth, we have not had to wait for the neo-liberals to measure some of the effects of these educational investments, whether this involves school instruction strictly speaking, or professional training, and so on. But the neo-liberals lay stress on the fact that what should be called educational investment is much broader than simple schooling or professional training and that many more elements than these enter into the formation of human capital.[37] What constitutes this investment that forms an abilities-machine? Experimentally, on the basis of observations, we know it is constituted by, for example, the time parents devote to their children outside of simple educational activities strictly speaking. We know that the number of hours a mother spends with her child, even when it is still in the cradle, will be very important for the formation of an abilities-machine, or for the formation of a human capital, and that the child will be much more adaptive if in fact its parents or its mother spend more rather than less time with him or her. This means that it must be possible to analyze the simple time parents spend feeding their children, or giving them affection as investment which can form human capital. Time spent, care given, as well as the parents' education—because we know quite precisely that for an equal time spent with their children, more educated parents will form a higher human capital than parents with less education—in short, the set of cultural stimuli received by the child, will all contribute to the formation of those elements that can make up a human capital. This means that we thus arrive at a whole environmental analysis, as the Americans say, of the child's life which it will be possible to calculate, and to a certain extent quantify, or at any rate measure, in terms of the possibilities of investment in human capital. What in the child's family life will produce human capital? What type of stimuli, form of life, and relationship with parents, adults, and others can be crystallized into human capital? Fine, I am going quickly since we must get on. In the same way, we can analyze medical care and, generally speaking, all activities concerning the health of individuals, which will thus appear as so many elements which enable us, first, to improve human capital, and second, to preserve and employ it for as long as possible. Thus, all the problems of health care and public hygiene must, or at any rate, can be rethought as elements which may or may not improve human capital.

In the elements making up human capital we should also include mobility, that is to say, an individual's ability to move around, and migration in particular.[38] Because migration obviously represents a material cost, since the individual will not be earning while he is moving, but there will also be a psychological cost for the individual establishing himself in his new milieu. There will also be at least a loss of earnings due to the fact that the period of adaptation will certainly prevent the individual from receiving his previous remunerations, or those he will have when he is settled. All these negative elements show that migration has a cost. What is the function of this cost? It is to obtain an improvement of status, of remuneration, and so on, that is to say, it is an investment. Migration is an investment; the migrant is an investor. He is an entrepreneur of himself who incurs expenses by investing to obtain some kind of improvement. The mobility of a population and its ability to make choices of mobility as investment choices for improving income enable the phenomena of migration to be brought back into economic analysis, not as pure and simple effects of economic mechanisms which extend beyond individuals and which, as it were, bind them to an immense machine which they do not control, but as behavior in terms individual enterprise, of enterprise of oneself with investments and incomes.

What, you will ask, is the interest of all these analyses? You will be aware of the immediate political connotations and there is no need to stress them further. If there were only this lateral political product, we could no doubt brush this kind of analysis aside with a gesture, or at any rate purely and simply denounce it. But I think this would be both mistaken and dangerous. In fact, this kind of analysis makes it possible first of all to reappraise phenomena which have been identified for some time, since the end of the nineteenth century, and to which no satisfactory status has been given. This is the problem of technical progress, or what Schumpeter called "innovation."[39] Schumpeter—he was not the first, but we are just refocusing things around him—noted that, contrary to the predictions of Marx and classical economics more generally, the tendency of the rate of profit to fall actually turned out to be continuously corrected. You know that the theory of imperialism, as in Rosa Luxembourg,[40] provided an interpretation of this correction of the tendency of the rate of profit to fall. Schumpeter's analysis consists in saying that the absence of this fall, or this correction of the falling rate of profit, is not due simply to the phenomenon of imperialism. It is due, generally,* [to] innovation, that is to say, [to] the discovery of new techniques, sources, and forms of productivity, and also the discovery of new markets or new resources of manpower.[41] In any case, the explanation of this phenomenon is to be sought in the new and in innovation, which Schumpeter thinks is absolutely consubstantial with the functioning of capitalism.

[The neo-liberals take up]† this problem of innovation, and so of the tendency of the falling rate of profit, and they do not take it up as a sort of ethical-psychological characteristic of capitalism, or as an ethical-economic-psychological characteristic of capitalism, as Schumpeter did in a problematic which was not so far from Max Weber's, but they say: We cannot halt at this problem of innovation and, as it were, trust in the boldness of capitalism or the permanent stimulation of competition to explain this phenomenon of innovation. If there is innovation, that is to say, if we find new things, discover new forms of productivity, and make technological innovations, this is nothing other than the income of a certain capital, of human capital, that is to say, of the set of investments we have made at the level of man himself. Taking up the

---

* Foucault adds: and it puts *[inaudible word]* moreover as a category of this more general process.
† M.F.: the analyses of the neo-liberals are situated

problem of innovation within the more general theory of human capital, and by re-examining Western and Japanese history since 1930, they try to show that we absolutely cannot account for the considerable growth of these countries over forty or fifty years simply [on the basis of] the variables of classical analysis, that is to say, land, capital, and labor understood as time of labor, that is to say, the number of workers and hours. Only a fine analysis of the composition of the human capital, of the way this human capital has been augmented, of the sectors in which it has been augmented, and of the elements which have been introduced as investment in this human capital, can account for the real growth of these countries.[42]

On the basis of this theoretical and historical analysis we can thus pick out the principles of a policy of growth which will no longer be simply indexed to the problem of the material investment of physical capital, on the one hand, and of the number of workers, [on the other], but a policy of growth focused precisely on one of the things that the West can modify most easily, and that is the form of investment in human capital. And in fact we are seeing the economic policies of all the developed countries, but also their social policies, as well as their cultural and educational policies, being orientated in these terms. In the same way, the problems of the economy of the Third World can also be rethought on the basis of human capital. And you know that currently an attempt is being made to rethink the problem of the failure of Third World economies to get going, not in terms of the blockage of economic mechanisms, but in terms of insufficient investment in human capital. And here again a number of historical analyses are taken up again, like the famous problem of the Western economic take-off in the sixteenth and seventeenth century. To what was this due? Was it due to the accumulation of physical capital? Historians are increasingly skeptical about this hypothesis. Was it not due precisely to the existence of an accumulation, an accelerated accumulation, of human capital? So, we are invited to take up a schema of historical analysis, as well as a programming of policies of economic development, which could be orientated, and which are in actual fact orientated, towards these new paths. Of course, this does not mean eliminating the elements, the political connotations I referred to a moment ago, but rather of showing how these political connotations owe their seriousness, their density, or, if you like, their coefficient of threat to the very effectiveness of the analysis and programming of the processes I am talking about.*

---

* Foucault stops the lecture here and, due to lack of time, does not develop the final points of the last part of the lecture dealing with the relevance of this kind of analysis for (a) wages, (b) a series of problems concerning education, and (c) the possibilities of analysis of familial behavior. The manuscript ends with these lines:

"Problematizing in a different way all the domains of education, culture, and training that sociology has taken up. Not that sociology has neglected the economic aspect of this, but, confining oneself to Bourdieu,
—reproduction of relations of production
—culture as social solidification of economic differences

Whereas in the neo-liberal analysis, all these elements are directly integrated in the economy and its growth in the form of a formation of productive capital.

All the problems of [inheritance?]—transmission—education—training—inequality of level, treated from a single point of view as homogenizable elements, themselves in their [turn?] refocused no longer around an anthropology or an ethics or a politics of labor, but around an economics of capital. And the individual considered as an enterprise, i.e., as an investment/investor ( ... ).
His conditions of life are the income of a capital."

---

1. On the reception of American neo-liberal ideas in France at the end of the seventies, see in addition to the work by H. Lepage already referred to (*Demain le capitalisme*), the collective work edited by J.-J. Rosa and F. Aftalion, *L'Économique retrouvée. Vieilles critiques et nouvelles analyses* (Paris: Economica, 1977). The appearance of the former gave rise to a number of articles in the press, among which see those of J.-F. Revel, "Le Roi est habillé," *L'Express*, 27 February 1978; G. Suffert, "Économistes: la nouvelle vague," *Le Point*, 13 March 1978; R. Priouret, "Vive la jungle!" *Le Nouvel Observateur*, 11 April 1978 (which refers to the negative tax, among the social correctives remaining within the framework of the market, and refers to L. Stoléru: on both, see above, lecture of 7 March 1979); B. Cazes, "La désenchantement du monde se poursuit ... ," *La Quinzaine littéraire*, 16 May 1978; P. Drouin, "Feux croisés sur l'État," *Le Monde*, 13 May 1978, etcetera. Several of these present the spread of these ideas in France as a response to the book by J. Attali and M. Guillaume, *L'Anti-économique* (Paris: PUF, 1972), which echoed American New Left theses (see H. Lepage, *Demain le capitalisme*, pp. 9-12). See also the interview: "Que veulent les nouveaux économistes? *L'Express* va plus loin avec J.-J. Rosa," *L'Express*, 5 June 1978.
2. In addition to the books and articles cited in the following notes, Foucault had read on the subject the anthology of H.J. Silverman, ed., *American Radical Thought: The libertarian tradition* (Lexington, Mass.: D.C. Heath and Co., 1970) and H.L. Miller, "On the Chicago School of Economics," *Journal of Political Economy*, vol. 70 (1), February 1962, pp. 64-69.
3. Henry Calvert Simons (1889-1946), author of *Economic Policy for a Free Society* (Chicago: University of Chicago Press, 1948).
4. It is actually a book: *A Positive Program for Laissez-Faire: Some proposals for a liberal economic policy?* (Chicago: University of Chicago Press, 1934); republished in *Economic Policy for a Free Society*.
5. See above, lecture of 7 February 1979, note 38.
6. H.C. Simons, "The Beveridge Progam: an unsympathetic interpretation," *Journal of Political Economy*, vol. 53 (3), September 1945, pp. 212-233; republished in *Economic Policy for a Free Society*, ch. 13.
7. See above, lecture of 31 January 1979, note 7.
8. Ibid., note 9.
9. The coalition of Left parties that exercised power in France from June 1936 until April 1938. Under the presidency of Léon Blum, this government passed several measures of social reform (the 40 hour week, paid vacations, nationalization of the railways, and so on).
10. Foucault is alluding to the events that unleashed the War of Independence (1775-1783), notably the "Boston Tea Party" (16 December 1773), in the course of which some colonists, disguised as Indians, dumped in the sea a cargo of tea belonging to the East India Company to whom the English Parliament had just opened the doors of the American market. The English government responded with a series of laws—"intolerable acts"—which led to the 1st continental Congress at Philadelphia in September 1774.
11. This may be a fairly free reformulation of Hayek's reflections in his post-script to *The Constitution of Liberty*, "Why I am not a Conservative," pp. 398-399.
12. See H. Lepage, *Demain le capitalisme*, pp. 21-28; 326-372 (on G. Becker). Some chapters from this book appeared in 1977 in the columns of *Realités*. For the chapter on Becker, the author refers in addition to the lectures of Jean-Jacques Rosa, "Théorie micro-économique," IEP, 1977. See also M. Riboud and F. Hernandez Iglesias, "La théorie du capital humain: un retour aux classiques," in J.-J. Rosa and F. Aftalion, eds., *L'Économique retrouvée*, pp. 226-249; M. Riboud, *Accumulation du capital humain* (Paris: Economica, 1978). These two works were in Foucault's library.
13. See Adam Smith, *An Inquiry into the Nature and Causes of the Wealth of Nations* (Oxford: Oxford University Press, 1976), Book I, ch. 1-3. On Smith's analysis of labor, see *Les Mots et les Choses*, pp. 233-238; *The Order of Things*, pp. 221-226.
14. David Ricardo (1772-1823), *The Principles of Political Economy and Taxation* (London: Dent, Everyman's Library, 1973) ch. 1, section 2. See M. Riboud and F. Hernandez Iglesias, "La théorie du capital humain" p. 227: "[In the analysis of the classical economists], the

increase of the labor factor necessarily expressed an additional number of workers or of hours of work per man, that is to say a quantitative increase." See also the comments of J. Mincer, in his foreword to the thesis of M. Riboud, *Accumulation du capital humain*, p. iii: "The simplifying hypothesis of the homogeneity of the labor factor, made by Ricardo, created a void whose consequence was to leave the study of the structure of wages and employment to supporters of the 'institutionalist' approach (the study of the types of relations existing between workers and the management of enterprises), to the analysts of economic fluctuations, and to statisticians (descriptive statistics)."

15. On the time-labor relation in Ricardo, see *Les Mots et les Choses*, pp. 265-270; *The Order of Things*, pp. 253-259.
16. See M. Riboud and F. Hernandez Iglesias, "La théorie du capital humain" p. 231: "As for the analysis of Keynes, it is even further from the idea of investment in human capital than the Classics. For him, the labor factor is basically a passive factor of production if a sufficiently high rate of investment in physical capital exists" (this latter phrase is underlined in Foucault's copy of the book; see above, this lecture, note 12).
17. Theodore W. Schultz (1902-1998): professor of economics at the University of Chicago from 1946 to 1974. Nobel Prize for economics in 1979. His article, "The emerging economic scene and its relation to High School Education," in F.S. Chase and H.A. Anderson, eds., *The High School in a New Era* (Chicago: University of Chicago Press, 1958) opened up the field of research on human capital. See M. Beaud and G. Dostaler, *La Pensée économique depuis Keynes* (Paris: Le Seuil, 1996), pp. 387-390. See Theodore W. Schultz, translation by J. Challali, *Il n'est de richesse que d'hommes. Investissement humain et qualité de la population* (Paris: Bonnel, 1983).
18. T.W. Schultz, "Capital formation by education," *Journal of Political Economy*, vol. 68, 1960, pp. 571-583; "Investment in human capital," *American Economic Review*, vol. 51, March 1961, pp. 1-17 (reprinted in the book with the same title cited below in this note); "Reflections on investment in man," *Journal of Political Economy*, vol 70 (5), 2nd part, October 1962, pp. 1-8; *Investment in Human Capital: The role of education and research* (New York: The Free Press, 1971).
19. Gary Becker (born 1930): doctor of economics (University of Chicago, 1925); teaches at Columbia until 1968 and then returns to Chicago. Vice President of the Mont-Pèlerin Society in 1989. Nobel Prize in 1992. See H. Lepage, *Demain le capitalisme*, p. 323.
20. G. Becker, "Investment in human capital: a theoretical analysis," *Journal of Political Economy*, vol. 70 (5), 2nd part, October 1962, pp. 9-49; article republished, considerably expanded in *Human Capital: A theoretical and empirical analysis with special reference to education* (New York: National Bureau of Economic Research, 1964; 3rd edition, Chicago and London: The University of Chicago Press, 1993) pp. 29-158 ("Investment in human capital: effect on earnings," pp. 29-58, and "Investment in human capital: rates of return," pp. 59-158).
21. Jacob Mincer, born in Poland (1922); professor at the University of Columbia.
22. J. Mincer, *Schooling, Experience and Earnings* (New York: National Bureau of Economic Research, 1974); see also "Investment in human capital and personal income distribution," *Journal of Political Economy*, vol. 66, August 1958, pp. 281-302, that Theodore Schultz describes as a "pioneering paper" in his *Investment in Human Capital*, p. 46, note 33. The expression "human capital" appears for the first time in this article (see M. Beaud and G. Dostaler, *La Pensée économique*, p. 184).
23. See G. Becker, *The Economic Approach to Human Behavior* (Chicago and London: University of Chicago Press, 1976), p. 4: he rejects "the definition of economics in terms of material goods" in favor of a definition "in terms of scarce means and competing ends."
24. Lionel C. Robbins (Lord, 1898-1984): English economist, professor at the London School of Economics, and author notably of a work on the methodology of economic science, *Essay on the Nature and Significance of Economic Science* (1st edition 1932, republished, London: Macmillan, 1962). Hostile to the positions of Keynes at the time of the crisis of the thirties, he changed his position after his experience as advisor to the British government during the war.
25. Ibid., p. 16: "Economics is the science which studies human behavior as a relationship between ends and scarce means which have mutually exclusive uses" (quoted by G. Becker, *The Economic Approach*, p. 1, note 3).

26. Irving Fisher (1867-1947), a mathematician by training, professor at Yale University from 1898 until the end of his career. In particular, he is the author of *The Nature of Capital and Income* (New York and London: Macmillan, 1906). See Joseph A. Schumpeter, *History of Economic Analysis*, pp. 872-873.
27. The formulae are drawn from the article already cited by M. Riboud and F. Hernandez Iglesias, "La théorie du capital humain" p. 228: "Capital should be understood here in accordance with the conception of the market developed by Irving Fisher: we will call capital every source of future income and, reciprocally, income (all categories of income) is the product or return of the capital (of different forms of capital)." See, Joseph A. Schumpeter, *History of Economic Analysis*, pp. 898-899, and K. Pribram, *A History of Economic Reasoning*, p. 329: "According to Fisher, capital was the whole of things owned by individuals or societies at some particular moment in time, constituting claims or purchasing power and being capable of yielding interest."
28. The word "machine" seems to be Foucault's, an allusion or wink to *L'Anti-Œdipe* of Gilles Deleuze and Felix Guattari (Paris: Minuit, 1972); English translation by Robert Hurley, Mark Seem, and Helen R. Lane, *Anti-Oedipus. Capitalism and Schizophrenia* (New York: The Viking Press, 1977). On the machine/flows couple, see for example, pp. 43-44; pp. 38-39 of this book. Neither Becker nor Schultz use the term with regard to ability. The latter, however, proposes to integrate "the innate abilities of man" in "an all-inclusive concept of technology" in *Investment in Human Capital*, p. 11.
29. "Earnings stream" or "income stream." See for example, T.W. Schultz, *Investment in Human Capital*, p. 75: "Not all investment in human capital is for future earnings alone. Some of it is for future well-being in forms that are not captured in the earnings stream of the individual in whom the investments are made."
30. Ibid.
31. See G. Becker, "On the new Theory of Consumer Behavior," *Swedish Journal of Economics*, vol. 75, 1973, pp. 375-395, reprinted in *The Economic Approach*, pp. 130-149. See H. Lepage, *Demain le capitalisme*, ch. VIII: "La nouvelle théorie du consommateur (Les révolutions de G. Becker)."
32. G. Becker, *The Economic Approach*, p. 134: "( ... ) this approach views as the primary objects of consumer choice various entities, called commodities, from which utility is directly obtained. These commodities are produced by the consumer unit itself through the productive activity of combining purchased market goods and services with some of the household's own time." In his article, "A Theory of the Allocation of Time" *Economic Journal*, 75, no. 299, September 1965, pp. 493-517 (republished in *The Economic Approach*, pp. 90-114) Becker sets out for the first time this analysis of the production functions of consumption activities (see M. Riboud and F. Hernandez Iglesias, "La théorie du capital humain" pp. 241-242). See H. Lepage, *Demain le capitalisme*, p. 327: "In this perspective, the consumer is not only a being who consumes; he is an economic agent who 'produces.' Who produces what? Who produces satisfactions of which he is the consumer."
33. See T.W. Schultz, *Investment in Human Capital*, p. 148: "The distinctive mark of human capital is that it is a part of man. It is *human* because it is embodied in man, and *capital* because it is a source of future satisfactions, or of future earnings, or of both" (a phrase which is taken up again on p. 161 with regard to education as a form of human capital).
34. See M. Riboud and F. Hernandez Iglesias, "La théorie du capital humain" p. 235: "If, as the theory of human capital lays down as its hypothesis, an individual's productivity depends in part on the capabilities he has inherited at birth and in part (more importantly) on the capabilities he has acquired through investments, then his level of income at each period of his life will vary directly with the rising stock of human capital he has at his disposal at that moment."
35. On these questions, see the 6th part of Becker's *The Economic Approach*, pp. 169-250: "Marriage, fertility and the family"; T.W. Schultz, "New economic approach to fertility," *Journal of Political Economy*, vol. 81 (2) part II, March-April 1973; A. Leibowitz, "Home investments in children," *Journal of Political Economy*, vol. 82 (2), part II, March-April 1974. See M. Riboud and F. Hernandez Iglesias, "La théorie du capital humain" pp. 240-241 (on the choice between "quantity" and "quality" of children according to the human capital

that parents wish to pass on to them); H. Lepage, *Demain le capitalisme*, p. 344 ("La théorie économique de la démographie").

36. See H. Lepage, *Demain le capitalisme*, pp. 337-343: "L'investissement en 'capital humain' et les écarts de salaire."
37. See the list of forms of investment established by T.W. Schultz, *Investment in Human Capital*, p. 8: "( ... ) during the past decade, there have been important advances in economic thinking with respect to human capital. This set of investments is classified as follows: schooling and higher education, on-the-job training, migration, health, and economic information."
38. On this subject, see the list of works cited by T.W. Schultz, ibid., p. 191.
39. See above, lecture of 14 February 1979, p. 163, note 59.
40. See Rosa Luxembourg (1971-1919), *Die Akkumulation des Kapitals. Ein Beitrag zur ökonomischen Erklärung des Imperialismus* (Berlin: B. Singer, 1913); French translation by M. Ollivier, *L'Accumulation du capital. Contribution à l'explication économique de l'impérialisme* (Paris: Librairie du travail, 1935), new translation by I. Petit (Paris: F. Maspero, 1967) 2 vols.; English translation by Agnes Schwarzschild, *The Accumulation of Capital* (London: Routledge, 2003).
41. The motor of development (as opposed to the "circuit"), innovation, according to Schumpeter, is not assimilated to simple technical progress. Five categories of innovation can be distinguished: (1) the manufacture of a new good; (2) the introduction of a new method of production; (3) the opening of a new outlet; (4) the conquest of a new source of raw materials; and (5) the implementation of a new method of organization of production. See J. Schumpeter, *The Theory of Economic Development*, ch. 2, section 2. It is the concentration of capital, we recall, that tends to bureaucratize innovation, thus depriving the enterprise of its essential justification and thereby putting the very survival of capitalism in question (see above, lecture of 21 February 1979, pp. 177-178).
42. On the limits of the traditional tripartite classification—land, labor, and capital—in the analysis of economic growth and its inability to account for the "mystery of modern abundance," see T.W. Schultz, *Investment in Human Capital*, pp. 2-4.

ten

# 21 MARCH 1979

*American neo-liberalism (II). ~ The application of the economic grid to social phenomena. ~ Return to the ordoliberal problematic: the ambiguities of the* Gesellschaftspolitik. *The generalization of the "enterprise" form in the social field. Economic policy and* Vitalpolitik*: a society for the market and against the market. ~ The unlimited generalization of the economic form of the market in American neo-liberalism: principle of the intelligibility of individual behavior and critical principle of governmental interventions. ~ Aspects of American neo-liberalism: (2) Delinquency and penal policy. ~ Historical reminder: the problem of the reform of penal law at the end of the eighteenth century. Economic calculation and principle of legality. The parasitic invasion of the law by the norm in the nineteenth century and the birth of criminal anthropology. ~ The neo-liberal analysis: (1) the definition of crime; (2) the description of the criminal subject as* homo œconomicus*; (3) the status of the penalty as instrument of law "enforcement." The example of the drugs market. ~ Consequences of this analysis: (a) anthropological erasure of the criminal; (b) putting the disciplinary model out of play.*

TODAY I WOULD LIKE to talk a little about one aspect of American neo-liberalism, that is to say, the way in which [the American neo-liberals]*

---

* M.F.: they

try to use the market economy and the typical analyses of the market economy to decipher non-market relationships and phenomena which are not strictly and specifically economic but what we call social phenomena.* In other words, this means that I want to talk about the application of the economic grid to a field which since the nineteenth century, and we can no doubt say already at the end of the eighteenth century, was defined in opposition to the economy, or at any rate, as complementary to the economy, as that which in itself, in its own structure and processes, does not fall within the economy, even though the economy itself is situated within this domain. In other words again, what I think is at stake in this kind of analysis is the problem of the inversion of the relationships of the social to the economic.

Let's go back to the theme of German liberalism, or ordoliberalism. You recall that in this conception—of Eucken, Röpke, Müller-Armack, and others—the market was defined as a principle of economic regulation indispensable to the formation of prices and so to the consistent development of the economic process. What was the government's task in relation to this principle of the market as the indispensable regulating function of the economy? It was to organize a society, to establish what they call a *Gesellschaftspolitik* such that these fragile competitive mechanisms of the market can function to the full and in accordance with their specific structure.[1] Such a *Gesellschaftspolitik* was therefore orientated towards the formation of a market. It was a policy that had to take charge of social processes and take them into account in order to make room for a market mechanism within them. But what did this policy of society, this *Gesellschaftspolitik* have to consist in for it to succeed in constituting a market space in which competitive mechanisms could really function despite their intrinsic fragility? It consisted in a number of objectives which I have talked about, such as, for example, avoiding centralization, encouraging medium sized enterprises, support for what they call non-proletarian enterprises, that is to say, broadly, craft enterprises, small businesses, etcetera, increasing access to property ownership, trying to replace the social insurance of risk with individual

* In the manuscript, this lecture has the title: "The market economy and non-market relationships."

insurance, and also regulating all the multiple problems of the environment.

Obviously, this *Gesellschaftspolitik* includes a number of ambiguities and raises a number of questions. There is the question, for example, of its purely optative and "light"* character in comparison with the heavy and far more real processes of the economy. There is also the fact that it entails a weight, a field, an extraordinarily large number of interventions which raise the question of whether they do in fact correspond to the principle that they must not act directly on the economic process but only intervene in favor of the economic process. In short, there are a number of questions and ambiguities, but I would like to emphasize the following: in this idea of a *Gesellschaftspolitik* there is what I would call an economic-ethical ambiguity around the notion of enterprise itself, because what does it mean to conduct a *Gesellschaftspolitik* in the sense this is given by Röpke, Rüstow, and Müller-Armack? On one side it means generalizing the "enterprise" form within the social body or social fabric; it means taking this social fabric and arranging things so that it can be broken down, subdivided, and reduced, not according to the grain of individuals, but according to the grain of enterprises. The individual's life must be lodged, not within a framework of a big enterprise like the firm or, if it comes to it, the state, but within the framework of a multiplicity of diverse enterprises connected up to and entangled with each other, enterprises which are in some way ready to hand for the individual, sufficiently limited in their scale for the individual's actions, decisions, and choices to have meaningful and perceptible effects, and numerous enough for him not to be dependent on one alone. And finally, the individual's life itself—with his relationships to his private property, for example, with his family, household, insurance, and retirement—must make him into a sort of permanent and multiple enterprise. So this way of giving a new form to society according to the model of the enterprise, or of enterprises, and down to the fine grain of its texture, is an aspect of the German ordoliberals' *Gesellschaftspolitik*.[2]

---

* In inverted commas in the manuscript.

What is the function of this generalization of the "enterprise"* form? On the one hand, of course, it involves extending the economic model of supply and demand and of investment-costs-profit so as to make it a model of social relations and of existence itself, a form of relationship of the individual to himself, time, those around him, the group, and the family. So, it involves extending this economic model. On the other hand, the ordoliberal idea of making the enterprise the universally generalized social model functions in their analysis or program as a support to what they designate as the reconstruction of a set of what could be called "warm"† moral and cultural values which are presented precisely as antithetical to the "cold"‡ mechanism of competition. The enterprise schema involves acting so that the individual, to use the classical and fashionable terminology of their time, is not alienated from his work environment, from the time of his life, from his household, his family, and from the natural environment. It is a matter of reconstructing concrete points of anchorage around the individual which form what Rüstow called the *Vitalpolitik*.[3] The return to the enterprise is therefore at once an economic policy or a policy of the economization of the entire social field, of an extension of the economy to the entire social field, but at the same time a policy which presents itself or seeks to be a kind of *Vitalpolitik* with the function of compensating for what is cold, impassive, calculating, rational, and mechanical in the strictly economic game of competition.

The enterprise society imagined by the ordoliberals is therefore a society for the market and a society against the market, a society oriented towards the market and a society that compensates for the effects of the market in the realm of values and existence. This is what Rüstow said in the Walter Lippmann colloquium I have talked about:[4] "We have to organize the economy of the social body according to the rules of the market economy, but the fact remains that we still have to satisfy new and heightened needs for integration."[5] This is the *Vitalpolitik*. A bit later, Röpke said: "Competition is a principle of order in the domain of

* In inverted commas in the manuscript.
† In inverted commas in the manuscript.
‡ In inverted commas in the manuscript.

the market economy, but it is not a principle on which it would be possible to erect the whole of society. Morally and sociologically, competition is a principle that dissolves more than it unifies." So, while establishing a policy such that competition can function economically, it is necessary to organize "a political and moral framework," Röpke says.[6] What will this political and moral framework comprise? First, it requires a state that can maintain itself above the different competing groups and enterprises. This political and moral framework must ensure "a community which is not fragmented," and guarantee cooperation between men who are "naturally rooted and socially integrated."[7]

In comparison with the ambiguity, if you like, of German ordoliberalism, American neo-liberalism evidently appears much more radical or much more complete and exhaustive. American neo-liberalism still involves, in fact, the generalization of the economic form of the market. It involves generalizing it throughout the social body and including the whole of the social system not usually conducted through or sanctioned by monetary exchanges. This, as it were, absolute generalization, this unlimited generalization of the form of the market entails a number of consequences or includes a number of aspects and I would like to focus on two of these.

First, the generalization of the economic form of the market beyond monetary exchanges functions in American neo-liberalism as a principle of intelligibility and a principle of decipherment of social relationships and individual behavior. This means that analysis in terms of the market economy or, in other words, of supply and demand, can function as a schema which is applicable to non-economic domains. And, thanks to this analytical schema or grid of intelligibility, it will be possible to reveal in non-economic processes, relations, and behavior a number of intelligible relations which otherwise would not have appeared as such—a sort of economic analysis of the non-economic. The neo-liberals do this for a number of domains. I referred to some of these problems last week, with regard to investment in human capital. In their analysis of human capital, you recall, the neo-liberals tried to explain, for example, how the mother-child relationship, concretely characterized by the time spent by the mother with the child, the quality of the care she gives, the affection she shows, the vigilance with which she follows its development, its education, and not only its scholastic but also its physical progress, the way in which she not only gives it food but also imparts a particular style to eating patterns, and the relationship she has with its eating, all constitute for the neo-liberals an investment which can be measured in time. And what will this investment constitute? It will constitute a human capital, the child's human capital, which will produce an income.[8] What will this income be? It will be the child's salary when he or she becomes an adult. And what will the income be for the mother who made the investment? Well, the neo-liberals say, it will be a psychical income. She will have the satisfaction a mother gets from giving the child care and attention in seeing that she has in fact been successful. So, everything comprising what could be called, if you like, the formative or educational relationship, in the widest sense of the term, between mother and child, can be analyzed in terms of investment, capital costs, and profit—both economic and psychological profit—on the capital invested.

In the same way, the neo-liberals turn to the study of the problem of the birth rate and try to analyze again the fact that wealthy, or wealthier families are clearly more Malthusian than poorer families, in the sense that the higher the income the smaller the family is an old law that everyone knows. But even so, they say, this is paradoxical, since in strictly Malthusian terms more income should enable one to have more children. To which they [answer]: But is the Malthusian conduct of these wealthy people really an economic paradox? Is it due to non-economic factors of a moral, ethical, or cultural kind? Not at all, they say. Economic factors are still and always at work here inasmuch as people with high incomes are people who possess a high human capital, as is proven by their high incomes. Their problem is not so much to transmit to their children an inheritance in the classical sense of the term, as the transmission of this other element, human capital, which also links the generations to each other but in a completely different way. Their problem is the formation and transmission of human capital which, as we have seen, implies the parents having the time for educational care and so on. A wealthy family, that is to say, a high income family, that is to say, a family whose components have a high human capital, will have as its immediate and rational economic project the transmission of a human capital at least as high to its children, which implies a set of investments, both in financial terms and in terms of time, on the part of the parents.

Now these investments are not possible for a large family. So, according to the American neo-liberals, it is the necessity to transmit a human capital to the children which is at least equal to that of the parents that explains the smaller size of wealthy families.

It is still in terms of this same project, this same perspective of an economic analysis of types of relations that previously fell more in the domains of demography, sociology, psychology, and social psychology, that the neo-liberals have tried to analyze, for example, the phenomena of marriage and what takes place within a household, that is to say, the specifically economic rationalization constituted by marriage in the coexistence of individuals. There are a number of works and communications on this by a Canadian economist Jean-Luc Migué,[9] who wrote this, which is worth reading.[10] I will not go into the rest of the analysis, but he says this: "One of the great recent contributions of economic analysis [he is referring to the neo-liberal analysis; M.F.] has been to apply fully to the domestic sector the analytical framework traditionally reserved for the firm and the consumer ( ... ). This involves making the household a unit of production in the same way as the classical firm. ( ... ) What in actual fact is the household if not the contractual commitment of two parties to supply specific *inputs* and to share in given proportions the benefits of the households' *output*?" What is the meaning of the long-term contract entered into by people who live together in matrimony? What justifies it economically and on what is it based? Well, it is that this long-term contract between spouses enables them to avoid constantly renegotiating at every moment the innumerable contracts which would have to be made in order for domestic life to function.[11] Pass me the salt; I will give you the pepper. This type of negotiation is resolved, as it were, by a long-term contract, which is the marriage contract itself, which enables what the neo-liberals call—and I think they are not the only ones to call it this moreover—an economy to be made at the level of transaction costs. If you had to make a transaction for each of these actions there would be a cost of time, and therefore an economic cost, that would be absolutely insuperable for the individuals. It is resolved by the marriage contract.

This may appear amusing, but those of you who are familiar with the text left by Pierre Rivière before his death, in which he describes how his parents lived,[12] will realize that in fact the married life of a peasant couple at the beginning of the nineteenth century was endlessly forged and woven by a whole series of transactions. I will work on your field, the man says to the woman, but on condition that I can make love with you. And the woman says: You will not make love with me so long as you have not fed my chickens. In a process like this we see a sort of endless transaction emerging, in relation to which the marriage contract was supposed to constitute a form of general economy to avoid having to renegotiate at every moment. And in a way, the relationship between the father and the mother, between the man and the woman, was just the daily unfolding of this kind of contractualization of their common life, and all these conflicts were nothing other than the actualization of the contract. But at the same time the contract did not perform its role: in actual fact it did not [enable]* an economy to be made on the transaction costs that it should have assured. In short, let's say that in these economic analyses of the neo-liberals, we have an attempt to decipher traditionally non-economic social behavior in economic terms.

The second interesting use of these neo-liberal analyses is that the economic grid will or should make it possible to test governmental action, gauge its validity, and to object to activities of the public authorities on the grounds of their abuses, excesses, futility, and wasteful expenditure. In short, the economic grid is not applied in this case in order to understand social processes and make them intelligible; it involves anchoring and justifying a permanent political criticism of political and governmental action. It involves scrutinizing every action of the public authorities in terms of the game of supply and demand, in terms of efficiency with regard to the particular elements of this game, and in terms of the cost of intervention by the public authorities in the field of the market. In short, it involves criticism of the governmentality actually exercised which is not just a political or juridical criticism; it is a market criticism, the cynicism of a market criticism opposed to the action of public authorities. This is not just an empty project or a theorist's idea. In the United States a permanent exercise of this type of criticism has developed especially in an institution which was not in fact created for

* M.F.: avoid

this, since it was created before the development of the neo-liberal school, before the development of the Chicago School. This institution is the *American Enterprise Institute*[13] whose essential function, now, is to measure all public activities in cost-benefit terms, whether these activities be the famous big social programs concerning, for example, education, health, and racial segregation developed by the Kennedy and Johnson administrations in the decade 1960-1970. This type of criticism also involves measuring the activity of the numerous federal agencies established since the New Deal and especially since the end of the Second World War, such as the *Food and Health Administration*, the *Federal Trade Commission*, and so on.[14] So, it is criticism in the form of what could be called an "economic positivism"; a permanent criticism of governmental policy.

Seeing the deployment of this type of criticism one cannot help thinking of an analogy, which I will leave as such: the positivist critique of ordinary language. When you consider the way in which the Americans have employed logic, the logical positivism of the Vienna School, in order to apply it to scientific, philosophical, or everyday discourse, you see there too a kind of filtering of every statement whatsoever in terms of contradiction, lack of consistency, nonsense.[15] To some extent we can say that the economic critique the neo-liberals try to apply to governmental policy is also a filtering of every action by the public authorities in terms of contradiction, lack of consistency, and nonsense. The general form of the market becomes an instrument, a tool of discrimination in the debate with the administration. In other words, in classical liberalism the government was called upon to respect the form of the market and *laisser-faire*. Here, *laissez-faire* is turned into a *do-not-laisser-faire* government, in the name of a law of the market which will enable each of its activities to be measured and assessed. *Laissez-faire* is thus turned round, and the market is no longer a principle of government's self-limitation; it is a principle turned against it. It is a sort of permanent economic tribunal confronting government. Faced with excessive governmental action, and in opposition to it, the nineteenth century sought to establish a sort of administrative jurisdiction that would enable the action of public authorities to be assessed in terms of right, whereas here we have a sort of economic tribunal that claims to assess government action in strictly economic and market terms.

These two aspects—the analysis of non-economic behavior through a grid of economic intelligibility, and the criticism and appraisal of the action of public authorities in market terms—are found again in the analysis of criminality and the penal justice system made by some neo-liberals. I would like now to talk about the way in which the problem of criminality is taken up in a series of articles by Ehrlich,[16] Stigler,[17] and Gary Becker[18] as an example of these two uses of economic analysis. Their analysis of criminality at first appears to be the simplest possible return to the eighteenth century reformers like Beccaria[19] and especially Bentham.[20] After all, it is true that when the problem of the reform of penal law is taken up at the end of the eighteenth century the question posed by the reformers really was a question of political economy, in the sense that it involved an economic analysis or at any rate an economic style of reflection on politics or the exercise of power. It was a matter of using economic calculation, or at any rate of appealing to an economic logic and rationality to criticize the operation of penal justice as it could be observed in the eighteenth century. Hence, in some texts, more clearly in Bentham than in Beccaria, but also in people like Colquhoun,[21] there are considerations based on rough calculations of the cost of delinquency: how much does it cost a country, or at any rate a town, to have thieves running free? There is the problem of the cost of judicial practice itself and of the judicial institution in the way that it operates. And there is criticism of the ineffectiveness of the system of punishment, with reference to the fact, for example, that public torture and executions or banishment had no perceptible effect on lowering the rate of criminality, insofar as it was possible to measure this at the time. In any case, there was an economic grid underlying the critical reasoning of the eighteenth century reformer. I have already drawn attention to this[22] and will not dwell on it.

What the reformers sought by filtering the whole of penal practice through a calculation of utility was precisely a penal system with the lowest possible cost, in all the senses I have just mentioned. And I think we can say that the solution sketched by Beccaria, supported by Bentham, and ultimately chosen by the legislators and codifiers at the end of the eighteenth and beginning of the nineteenth century was a legalistic solution. This great concern of the law, the principle constantly recalled that for a penal system to function well a good law is necessary and almost sufficient, was nothing other than the desire for what could be called, in economic terms, a reduction in the transaction cost. The law is the most economical solution for punishing people adequately and for this punishment to be effective. First, the crime must be defined as an infraction of a formulated law, so that in the absence of a law there is no crime and an action cannot be incriminated. Second, penalties must be fixed once and for all by the law. Third, penalties must be fixed in law according to the degree of seriousness of the crime. Fourth, henceforth the criminal court will only have one thing to do, which is to apply to an established and proven crime a law which determines in advance what penalty the criminal must suffer according to the seriousness of his crime.[23] An absolutely simple, apparently completely obvious mechanics constitutes the most economic form, that is to say, the least costly and most effective form for obtaining punishment and the elimination of conducts deemed harmful to society. At the end of the eighteenth century, law, the mechanism of the law, was adopted as the economic principle of penal power, in both the widest and most exact sense of the word economic. *Homo penalis*, the man who can legally be punished, the man exposed to the law and who can be punished by the law is strictly speaking a *homo œconomicus*. And it is precisely the law which enables the problem of penal practice to be connected to the problem of economy.

During the nineteenth century it was discovered that this economy in fact led to a paradoxical effect. What is the source, the reason for this paradoxical effect? It is an ambiguity due to the fact that the law as law, as general form of the penal economy, was obviously indexed to the acts which breach the law. The law only sanctions acts, of course. But, in another respect, the principles of the existence of the criminal law, the need to punish in other words, as well as the grading of punishment, the actual application of the law, only have meaning inasmuch as it is not the act that is punished—since there is no sense in punishing an act—but an individual, an offender, who must be punished, corrected, and made to serve as an example to other possible offenders. So we can see how it was possible for an inner tendency of the whole system to emerge in this ambiguity between a form of the law which defines a relationship between the act and the actual application of the law which can only be directed at an individual, in this ambiguity between the crime and the criminal. A tendency towards what? Well, it is a tendency towards an increasingly individualizing modulation of the application of the law and, as a consequence of this, a reciprocally psychological, sociological, and anthropological problematization of the person on whom the law is applied. That is to say, throughout the nineteenth century, the *homo penalis* drifts towards what could be called the *homo criminalis*. And when criminology is formed at the end of the nineteenth century, exactly one century after the reform recommended by Beccaria and schematized by Bentham, when *homo criminalis* is formed a century later, we arrived in a sense at the end of the ambiguity. *Homo legalis*, *homo penalis* is now taken up within an anthropology of crime which replaces, of course, the rigorous and very economic mechanics of the law: there is an inflation of forms and bodies of knowledge, of discourse, a multiplication of authorities and decision-making elements, and the parasitic invasion of the sentence in the name of the law by individualizing measures in the name of the norm. So that the economic principle of reference to the law and of the pure mechanism of the law, this rigorous economy, lead to an inflation within which the legal system has continued to flounder since the end of the nineteenth century. Anyway, this is how I would see things were I to adopt a possible neo-liberal perspective on this evolution.

So the analysis of the neo-liberals, who are not concerned with these historical problems, Gary Becker's analysis—in an article entitled "Crime and punishment" which appeared in the *Journal of Political Economy* in 1968[24]—basically consists in taking up Beccaria's and Bentham's utilitarian filter again while as far as possible trying [to avoid]* the series of slippages which took us from *homo œconomicus* to *homo legalis*, to *homo penalis*, and finally to *homo criminalis*. It consists in keeping as far as possible, and thanks to a purely economic analysis, to *homo œconomicus* and to seeing how crime and maybe criminality can be analyzed on that basis. In other words, the analysis tries to neutralize all those effects that arise when—as in the case of Beccaria and Bentham—one seeks to reconsider the economic problems and give them a form within

* Conjecture; word omitted.

an absolutely adequate legal framework. In other words—and here again I am not saying what they say, since [history is not their problem],* but I think the neo-liberals could say this—the fault, the source of the slippage in eighteenth century criminal law, was Beccaria's and Bentham's idea that the utilitarian calculus could be given an adequate form within a legal structure. The idea of utility taking shape within law and law being constructed entirely on the basis of a calculus of utility really was one of the stakes or dreams of all political criticism and all the projects of the end of the eighteenth century. The history of criminal law has shown that the perfect fit could not be made. Therefore it is necessary to maintain the problem of *homo œconomicus* without aiming to translate it immediately into the terms and forms of a legal structure.

So, how do they go about analyzing or maintaining the analysis of the problem of crime within an economic problematic? First, the definition of crime. In his article "Crime and punishment" Becker gives this definition of crime: I call crime any action that makes the individual run the risk of being condemned to a penalty.[25] [*Some laughter.*] I am surprised you laugh, because it is after all very roughly the definition of crime given by the French penal code, and so of the codes inspired by it, since you are well aware how the code defines a criminal offence: a criminal offence is that which is punished by correctional penalties. What is a crime according to the penal code, that is to say, your penal code? It is that which is punished by physical penalties involving the loss of civil rights.[26] In other words, the penal code does not give any substantive, qualitative, or moral definition of the crime. The crime is that which is punished by the law, and that's all there is to it. So, you can see that the neo-liberals' definition is very close: crime is that which makes the individual incur the risk of being sentenced to a penalty. It is very close, with however, as you can see, a difference, which is a difference of point of view, since while avoiding giving a substantive definition of the crime, the code adopts the point of view of the act and asks what this act is, in short, how to characterize an act which we can call criminal, that is to say, which is punished precisely as a crime. It is the point of view of the act, a kind of

* A set of words which are difficult to hear.

operational characterization, as it were, which can be employed by the judge: You will have to consider as a crime any act which is punished by the law. It is an objective, operational definition made from the judge's point of view. You can see that it is the same definition when the neo-liberals say that crime is any action which makes an individual run the risk of being sentenced to a penalty, but the point of view has changed. We now adopt the point of view of the person who commits the crime, or who will commit the crime, while keeping the same content of the definition. We ask: What is the crime for him, that is to say, for the subject of an action, for the subject of a form of conduct or behavior? Well, it is whatever it is that puts him at risk of punishment.

You can see that this is basically the same kind of shift of point of view as that carried out with regard to human capital and work. Last week I tried to show you how the neo-liberals tried to address the problem of work from the point of view of the person who decides to work rather from the point of view of capital or of economic mechanisms. Here again we move over to the side of individual subject, but doing this does not involve throwing psychological knowledge or an anthropological content into the analysis, just as analyzing work from the point of view of the worker did not involve an anthropology of work. We only move over to the side of the subject himself inasmuch as—and we will come back to this, because it is very important, I am telling you this in a very rough way—we can approach it through the angle, the aspect, the kind of network of intelligibility of his behavior as economic behavior. The subject is considered only as *homo œconomicus*, which does not mean that the whole subject is considered as *homo œconomicus*. In other words, considering the subject as *homo œconomicus* does not imply an anthropological identification of any behavior whatsoever with economic behavior. It simply means that economic behavior is the grid of intelligibility one will adopt on the behavior of a new individual. It also means that the individual becomes governmentalizable,* that power gets a hold on him to the extent, and only to the extent, that he is a *homo œconomicus*. That is to say, the surface of contact between the individual and the power

---

* Foucault stumbles a bit on this word, adding: or government ... , well, yes, governmentalizable.

exercised on him, and so the principle of the regulation of power over the individual, will be only this kind of grid of *homo œconomicus*. *Homo œconomicus* is the interface of government and the individual. But this does not mean that every individual, every subject is an economic man.

So we move over to the side of the individual subject by considering him as *homo œconomicus*, with the consequence that if crime is defined in this way as the action an individual commits by taking the risk of being punished by the law, then you can see that there is no difference between an infraction of the highway code and a premeditated murder. This also means that in this perspective the criminal is not distinguished in any way by or interrogated on the basis of moral or anthropological traits. The criminal is nothing other than absolutely anyone whomsoever. The criminal, any person, is treated only as anyone whomsoever who invests in an action, expects a profit from it, and who accepts the risk of a loss. From this point of view, the criminal is and must remain nothing more than this. You can see that in view of this the penal system will no longer have to concern itself with that split reality of the crime and the criminal. It has to concern itself with a conduct or a series of conducts which produce actions from which the actors expect a profit and which carry a special risk, which is not just the risk of economic loss, but the penal risk, or that economic loss which is inflicted by a penal system. The penal system itself will not have to deal with criminals, but with those people who produce that type of action. In other words, it will have to react to the supply of crime.

What will punishment be under these conditions? Well, punishment—and here again I am referring to Becker's definition—is the means employed to limit the negative externalities[27] of certain acts.[28] Here again, you can see that we are very close to Beccaria or Bentham, to the eighteenth century problematic in which punishment is justified by the fact that the act punished was harmful and that a law was made precisely for that reason. The same principle also had to be applied to the scale of the punishment: You had to punish in such a way that the action's harmful effects are either annulled or prevented. So, we are still very close to the problematic of the eighteenth century, but, here again, with an important change. While classical theory simply tried to connect up the different, heterogeneous effects expected from punishment, that is to say, the problem of reparation, which is a civil problem, the problem of the individual's correction, and the problem of prevention with regard to other individuals, etcetera, the neo-liberals will make a connection, or rather, a different disconnection of punishment. They distinguish between two things, or rather, they basically only take up a problematic current in Anglo-Saxon legal thought and reflection. They say: On the one hand there is the law, but what is the law? The law is nothing other than a prohibition, and the formulation of the prohibition is, on the one hand, of course, an institutional reality. Referring to a different problematic, we could say, if you like, that it is a *speech act* with a number of effects.[29] This act, moreover, has a certain cost, since formulation of the law implies a parliament, discussion, and decisions taken. It is in fact a reality, but it is not only this reality. So then, on the other hand, there is the set of instruments by which this prohibition will be given a real "force."* This idea of a force of law is expressed in the frequently encountered word, *enforcement*, which is often translated in French by "reinforcement (*renforcement*)" of the law. It is not reinforcement. *Law enforcement* is more than the application of the law, since it involves a whole series of real instruments which have to be employed in order to apply the law. But this is not the reinforcement of the law, it is less than the reinforcement of the law, inasmuch as reinforcement would mean that the law is too weak and that it needs a small supplement or to be made stricter. *Law enforcement* is the set of instruments employed to give social and political reality to the act of prohibition in which the formulation of the law consists.

What will these instruments of law "enforcement" be—forgive the neologism of this transcription?† It will be the quantity of punishment provided for each crime. It will be the size, activity, zeal, and competence of the apparatus responsible for detecting crimes. It will be the size and quality of the apparatus responsible for convicting criminals and providing effective proof that they have committed a crime. It will be how quickly judges make their judgments, and how severe they are within the margins the law leaves them. It will also be the degree of effectiveness of punishment, and the degree to which the penalty

* In inverted commas in the manuscript.

† Foucault creates a French word—*enforcement*—to translate the English "enforcement"; G.B.

applied can be modified, lessened, or possibly increased by the prison administration. All of these things constitute law enforcement, everything therefore that will respond to the supply of criminal conduct with what is called a negative demand. Law enforcement is the set of instruments of action which, on the market for crime, opposes a negative demand to the supply of crime. Now this law enforcement is clearly neither neutral nor indefinitely extendable for two correlative reasons.

The first, of course, is that the supply of crime is not indefinitely or uniformly elastic. That is to say, it does not respond in the same way to all the forms and levels of the negative demand opposed to it. To put things very simply: you have certain forms of crime, or certain brackets of criminal behavior, which give way very easily before a modification or very slight intensification of negative demand. Take the most current example: consider a big store in which 20% of the turnover, a completely arbitrary figure, is misappropriated by theft. Now, it is easy to reduce this figure to 10% without making a considerable outlay on surveillance or excessive law enforcement. To reduce it to between 5% and 10% is still relatively easy. To manage to reduce it to below 5% becomes very difficult, below 2%, and so on. In the same way, it is clear that there is a whole primary bracket of crimes of passion which we could easily get rid of by making divorce easier. And then you have a core of crimes of passion which will not be changed by relaxing divorce law. So the elasticity, that is to say, the modification of supply in relation to the effects of negative demand, is not homogeneous in the different brackets or types of action considered.

Second, and this is a different aspect absolutely linked to the first, enforcement itself has a cost and negative externalities. It has a cost, that is to say, it calls for an alternative remuneration. Investment in the law enforcement apparatus cannot be employed elsewhere. It goes without saying that this calls for an alternative remuneration. It has a cost, that is to say, it involves political, social, and other drawbacks. So, the objective or target of a penal policy will not be the same as that of the eighteenth century reformers when they developed their system of universal legality, namely, the total disappearance of crime. Criminal law and the whole penal mechanism of Bentham's dreams had to be such that, at the end of the day, there would be no crime, even if this could never happen in reality. And the idea of the Panopticon—the idea of transparency, of a gaze focusing on each individual, of a scale of penalties sufficiently subtle that every individual in his calculations, in his heart of hearts, in his economic calculation, could say to himself: No, in no way, if I were to commit this crime, the penalty I would incur is too significant, and so I am not going to commit it—the idea of having this kind of general nullification of crime in its sights, was the principle of rationality, the organizing principle of penal calculation in the reforming mind of the eighteenth century. Here, instead, penal policy has absolutely renounced the objective of the complete suppression and exhaustive nullification of crime. The regulatory principle of penal policy is a simple intervention in the market for crime and in relation to the supply of crime. It is an intervention which will limit the supply of crime solely by a negative demand, the cost of which must obviously never exceed the cost of the supply of the criminality in question. This is the definition that Stigler gives of the objective of a penal policy: "The goal of law enforcement," he says, "is to achieve a degree of compliance with the rule of prescribed behavior that society believes it can procure while taking account of the fact that enforcement is costly." This is in the *Journal of Political Economy* in 1970.[30] You can see that at this point society appears as the consumer of conforming behavior, that is to say, according to the neo-liberal theory of consumption, society appears as the producer of conforming behavior with which it is satisfied in return for a certain investment. Consequently, good penal policy does not aim at the extinction of crime, but at a balance between the curves of the supply of crime and negative demand. Or again: society does not have a limitless need for compliance. Society does not need to conform to an exhaustive disciplinary system. A society finds that it has a certain level of illegality and it would find it very difficult to have this rate indefinitely reduced. This amounts to posing as the essential question of penal policy, not, how should crimes be punished, nor even, what actions should be seen as crimes, but, what crime should we tolerate? Or again: what would it be intolerable to tolerate? This is Becker's definition in "Crime and punishment." There are two questions, he says: "How many offences should be permitted? Second, how many offenders should go unpunished?"[31] This is the question of penal practice.

What does this give us in concrete terms? There are not many analyses in this style. There is an analysis of the death penalty by Ehrlich in which he concludes that, in the end, the death penalty is after all quite useful.[32] But let's leave this. This genre of analysis does not seem to me to be the most interesting or effective with regard to the object it deals with. On the other hand, it is certain that in [other] domains, and in particular where criminality more closely affects market phenomena, the results are a bit more interesting to discuss. Obviously, being itself a market phenomenon, the problem of drugs is subject to a much more accessible and immediate economic analysis, an economics of criminality.[33] Drugs, then, appear as a market and let's say that, roughly up until the seventies, the policy of law enforcement with regard to drugs was basically aimed at reducing the drug supply. What did reducing the supply of drugs, drugs crime, and drugs delinquency mean? It meant, of course, reducing the amount of drugs brought onto the market. And what did this mean? It meant controlling and dismantling the refining networks and, secondly, controlling and dismantling the distribution networks. Now we know full well what the results of this policy of the sixties were. What was achieved by dismantling the refining and distribution networks, albeit only partially and never completely, for reasons we could discuss? First, it increased the unit price of the drug. Second, it favored and strengthened the monopoly or oligopoly of some big drug sellers, traffickers, and big drug refining and distribution networks, with, as a monopoly or oligopoly effect, a rise in prices, inasmuch as the laws of the market and competition were not respected. And finally, third, another more important phenomenon at the level of criminality strictly speaking, is that drug consumption, the demand for drugs, at least for serious addicts and for particular drugs, is absolutely inelastic. That is to say, the addict will want to find his commodity and will be prepared to pay any price for it. And this inelasticity of a segment of the demand for drugs will increase criminality; in plain terms, one will bump off someone in the street for the ten dollars to buy the drug one needs. So, from this point of view, the legislation, the style of legislation, or rather, the style of law enforcement which was developed in the sixties proved to be a sensational failure.

From this came the second solution, formulated in terms of liberal economics by Eatherly and Moore in 1973.[34] They say: It is completely mad to want to limit the supply of drugs. We should free up the drug supply, that is to say, very generally and roughly, see to it that the drug is more accessible and less costly, but with the following modulations and points. What in actual fact takes place in the real drugs market? There are basically two categories of buyers and people looking for drugs: those who begin to consume drugs and whose demand is elastic because they may come up against excessively high prices and forgo consumption of the drug which certainly offers them pleasure, but which they cannot afford. And then you have the inelastic demand, that is to say, those who will buy it anyway whatever the price. What, then, is the attitude of the drug pushers? It is to offer a relatively low market price to the consumers whose demand is elastic, that is to say, to the beginners, the small consumers, and when—and only when—they have become habitual consumers, that is to say, when their demand has become inelastic, the price will be raised and the drugs provided will have the extremely high monopolistic prices which result in the phenomena of criminality. So what should the attitude be of those who direct law enforcement policy? They will have to ensure that what is called the opening price, that is to say, the price for new consumers, is as high as possible so that price itself is a weapon of dissuasion and small, potential consumers cannot take the step of becoming consumers because of the economic threshold. On the other hand, those whose demand is inelastic and who will pay any price should be given the drug at the best possible price, that is to say, at the lowest possible price, so that, since they will buy the drug anyway, they are not forced to get the money by any means to buy it—in other words, [so] that their drug consumption does not encourage crime. So we need low prices for addicts and very high prices for non-addicts. You know that this is a view which sought expression in a policy of distinguishing not so much between so-called soft drugs and hard drugs, as between drugs with an inductive value and drugs without an inductive value, and above all between elastic and inelastic types of drug consumption. From this stems a policy of law enforcement directed towards new and potential consumers, small dealers, and the small trade that takes place on street corners; a policy of law enforcement according to an economic rationality of the market differentiated in terms of the elements I have referred to.

What conclusions can be drawn from all this? First of all, there is an anthropological erasure of the criminal. It should be said that this does not mean that the level of the individual is suppressed,* but rather that an element, dimension, or level of behavior can be postulated which can be interpreted as economic behavior and controlled as such.† In his article on capital punishment, Ehrlich said: "The abhorrent, cruel, or pathological nature of the crime is of absolutely no importance. There are no reasons for thinking that people who love or hate others are less '*responsive*,'‡ less accessible, or respond less easily to changes in the gains and losses associated with their activity than persons indifferent toward the well-being of others."[35] In other words, all the distinctions that have been made between born criminals, occasional criminals, the perverse and the not perverse, and recidivists are not important. We must be prepared to accept that, in any case, however pathological the subject may be at a certain level and when seen from a certain angle, he is nevertheless "responsive" to some extent to possible gains and losses, which means that penal action must act on the interplay of gains and losses or, in other words, on the environment; we must act on the market milieu in which the individual makes his supply of crime and encounters a positive or negative demand. This raises the problem, which I will talk about next week, of the new techniques of environmental technology or environmental psychology which I think are linked to neo-liberalism in the United States.

Second, but I will come back to this too,[36] you can see that what appears on the horizon of this kind of analysis is not at all the ideal or project of an exhaustively disciplinary society in which the legal network hemming in individuals is taken over and extended internally by, let's say, normative mechanisms. Nor is it a society in which a mechanism of general normalization and the exclusion of those who cannot be normalized is needed. On the horizon of this analysis we see instead the image, idea, or theme-program of a society in which there is an optimization of systems of difference, in which the field is left open to fluctuating processes, in which minority individuals and practices are

---

* The manuscript, p. 19, adds: "not a nullification of the technologies aiming to influence individual behavior."

† Ibid.: "An economic subject is a subject who, in the strict sense, seeks in any case to maximize his profit, to optimize the gain/loss relationship; in the broad sense: the person whose conduct is influenced by the gains and losses associated with it."

‡ In English in the lecture; G.B.

tolerated, in which action is brought to bear on the rules of the game rather than on the players, and finally in which there is an environmental type of intervention instead of the internal subjugation of individuals. I will try to develop some of all this next week.[37]*

---

* The manuscript includes here six unnumbered pages, which continue the preceding argument: "These kinds of analysis pose a number of problems.

1. Concerning human technology
On the one hand, a massive withdrawal with regard to the normative-disciplinary system. The correlate of the system formed by a capitalist type of economy and political institutions indexed to the law was a technology of human behavior, an 'individualizing' governmentality comprising: disciplinary control (*quadrillage*), unlimited regulation, subordination/classification, the norm.

[2nd page] Considered overall, liberal governmentality was both legalistic and normalizing, disciplinary regulation being the switch-point between the two aspects. With, of course, a series of problems concerning
—autonomy, the [ ... ]ation [division into sectors (*sectorisation*)?] of spaces and [ ... ] regulation
—the ultimate incompatibility between legal forms and normalization.
This system no longer seems to be indispensable. Why? Because the great idea that the law was the principle of governmental frugality turns out to be inadequate:
—because '*the* law' does not exist as [principle?]. You [can have?] as many laws as you like, the overflow with regard to the law is part of the legal system.
—[3rd page] because the law can only function ballasted by something else that is its counterweight, its interstices, its supplement → prohibition (*interdiction*).

It is necessary
1 to change the conception of law, or at least elucidate its function. In other words, not confuse its form (which is always to prohibit and constrain) and its function, which must be that of rule of the game. The law is that which must favor the game, i.e., the [ ... ]ations, enterprises, initiatives, changes, and by enabling everybody to be a rational subject, i.e., to maximize the functions of utility.

2 and consider calculating its 'enforcement' instead of supplementing it with regulation, planning, and discipline
—that is to say, we must not ballast it with something else, but with that which must simply give it force;
—[4th page] but while saying clearly that this enforcement is basically the main element,
—because the law does not exist without it
—because it is elastic
—because it can be calculated

How to remain in the *Rule of law* [English in the manuscript; G.B.]? How to rationalize this enforcement, it being understood that the law itself cannot be a principle of rationalization?
—through the calculation of costs
—the utility of the law
—and the cost of its enforcement
—and by the fact that if you do not want to get out of the law and you do not want to divert its true function as rule of the game, the technology to be employed is not discipline-normalization, but action on the environment. Modifying the terms of the game, not the players' mentality.

[5th page] We have here a radicalization of what the German ordoliberals had already defined with regard to governmental action: leave the economic game as free as possible and create a *Gesellschaftspolitik*. The American liberals say: if you want to maintain this *Gesellschaftspolitik* in the order of the law, you must consider everyone as a player and only intervene on an environment in which he is able to play. An environmental technology whose main aspects are:
—the definition of a framework around the individual which is loose enough for him to be able to play;
—the possibility for the individual of regulation of the effects of the definition of his own framework;
—the regulation of environmental effects
—non damage
—non absorption
—the autonomy of these environmental spaces.

[6th page] Not a standardizing, identificatory, hierarchical individualization, but an environmentalism open to unknowns and transversal phenomena. Lateralism.
Technology of the environment, unknowns, freedoms of [interplays?] between supplies and demands.
—But does this mean that we are dealing with natural subjects?" [*end of the manuscript*]

---

1. See above, lecture of 14 February 1979, pp. 145-146.
2. See F. Bilger, *La Pensée économique libérale*, p. 186: "The sociological policy breaks down ... into several, very varied particular policies of which the main ones are, for these authors, a development of the economic space, an encouragement of small and medium sized enterprises, and above all a de-proletarianization of society through the development of private saving and the widest possible distribution of the national capital between all the citizens. By making all individuals capitalists, by establishing a popular capitalism, the social flaws of capitalism are eliminated, and this independently of the fact of an expanding 'salariat' in the economy. Someone earning a salary who is also a capitalist is no longer a proletarian."
3. See above, lecture of 14 February 1979, p. 148.
4. See above, lectures of 14 and 21 February 1979.
5. A. Rüstow, in *Colloque Walter Lippmann*, p. 83: "If, in the interests of the optimum productivity of the collectivity and the maximum independence of the individual, we organize the economy of the social body according to the rules of the market economy, there remain new and heightened needs for integration to be satisfied."
6. W. Röpke, *The Social Crisis of Our Times*, Part II, ch. 2, p. 236: "( ... ) we have no intention to demand more from competition than it can give. It is a means of establishing order and exercising control in the narrow sphere of a market economy based on the division of labor, but not a principle on which a whole society can be built. From the sociological and moral point of view it is even dangerous because it tends more to dissolve than to unite. If competition is not to have the effect of a social explosive and is at the same time not to degenerate, its premise will be a correspondingly sound political and moral framework."
7. Ibid.: "( ... ) a strong state, aloof from the hungry hordes of vested interests, a high standard of business ethics, an undegenerated community of people ready to cooperate with each other, who have a natural attachment to, and a firm place in society."
8. See the previous lecture, 14 March, pp. 229-230.
9. Jean-Luc Migué was then professor at the National School of Public Administration of Quebec.
10. "Méthodologie économique et économie non marchand," communication to the Congress of French-speaking Economists (Quebec, May 1976), partially reproduced in the *Revue d'économie politique*, July-August 1977 (see H. Lepage, *Demain le capitalisme*, p. 224).
11. J.L. Migué, cited by H. Lepage, *Demain le capitalisme*, p. 346: "One of the great recent contributions of economic analysis has been the full application to the domestic sector of the analytical framework traditionally reserved for the firm and the consumer. By making the household a unit of production in the same way as the classical firm, we discover that its analytical foundations are actually identical to those of the firm. As in the firm, the two parties living together, thanks to a contract that binds them for long periods, avoid the transaction costs and the risk of being deprived at any moment of the *inputs* of the spouse and, hence, of the common *output* of the household. What in actual fact is the household if not the contractual commitment of two parties to supply specific *inputs* and to share in given proportions the benefits of the household's *output*? In this way then, instead of engaging in a costly process of constantly renegotiating and supervising the innumerable *contracts* inherent in the exchanges of everyday life, the two parties fix in a long term contract the general terms of exchange that will govern them."
12. See, *Moi, Pierre Rivière, ayant égorgé ma mère, ma sœur et mon frère ...*, presented by Michel Foucault (Paris: Julliard, 1973); English translation by F. Jellinek, *I, Pierre Rivière ...* (New York: Pantheon, 1978, and Harmondsworth: Penguin, 1984).
13. Created in 1943, the *American Enterprise Institute for Public Policy Research (AEI)* is based in Washington. Spearhead of the deregulation struggle, through its publications (books, articles, reports) it represents one of the most important "think tanks" of American neo-conservativism.
14. Among these other agencies there are the *Consumer Safety Product Commission*, the *Occupational Safety and Health Commission*, the *Civil Aeronautics Board*, the *Federal*

*Communications Commission*, and the *Security Exchange Commission* (see H. Lepage, *Demain le capitalisme*, pp. 221-222).

15. As the later allusion to the theory of *speech acts* (p. 254) suggests, it is doubtless the works of J.R. Searle, one of the American representatives of analytical philosophy, to which Foucault is implicitly referring here. See below, this lecture, note 29. The lecture given in Tokyo the previous year, "La philosophie analytique de la politique" *Dits et Écrits*, 3, pp. 534-551, is evidence of his interest in "Anglo-American analytical philosophy" during these years: "After all, Anglo-Saxon analytical philosophy does not give itself the task of reflecting on the being of language or on the deep structures of language: it reflects on the everyday use of language in different types of discourse. Anglo-Saxon analytical philosophy involves a critical analysis of thought on the basis of the way in which one says things" (p. 541).
16. I. Ehrlich, "The deterrent effect of capital punishment: a question of life and death," *American Economic Review*, vol. 65 (3), June 1975, pp. 397-417.
17. George J. Stigler (1911-1991): professor at the University of Chicago from 1958 to 1981, researcher at the *National Bureau of Economic Research* from 1941 to 1976, he directed the *Journal of Political Economy* from 1973 until his death. He won the Nobel Prize for economics in 1982. Foucault refers here to his article "The optimum enforcement of laws," *Journal of Political Economy*, vol. 78 (3), May-June 1970, pp. 526-536.
18. G. Becker, "Crime and punishment: an economic approach," *Journal of Political Economy*, vol. 76 (2), March-April 1968, pp. 196-217; reprinted in his *The Economic Approach to Human Behavior*, pp. 39-85. On these three authors cited by Foucault, see F. Jenny, "La théorie économique du crime: une revue de la littérature" in J.-J. Rosa and F. Aftalion, eds., *L'Économique retrouvée*, pp. 296-324 (Foucault draws on information provided in this article). See also, since then, G. Radnitsky and P. Bernholz, eds., *Economic Imperialism: The Economic Approach applied outside the field of economics* (New York: Paragon House, 1987).
19. See above, lecture of 17 January 1979, note 10.
20. Jeremy Bentham (see above, lecture of 10 January 1979, p. 12); see in particular the *Traités de législation civile et pénale*, ed. E. Dumont (Paris: Boussange, Masson & Besson, 1802) and *Théorie des peines et des récompenses*, ed. E. Dumont (London: B. Dulau, 1811) 2 volumes. It was these adaptations-translations by Dumont, based on Bentham's manuscripts, which made the latter's thought known at the beginning of the nineteenth century. On the genesis of the edition of the *Traités de législation civile et pénale* based on Bentham's manuscripts, see E. Halévy, *La Formation du radicalisme philosophique* ([vol. 1, Paris: F. Alcan, 1901] Paris: PUF, 1995) Appendix 1, pp. 281-285; English translation by Mary Morris, *The Growth of Philosophical Radicalism* (London: Faber & Faber, 1972), Appendix "Traités de Législation Civile et Pénale," pp. 515-521. The first English edition of these writings dates, for the first, from 1864 (*Theory of Legislation*, translation from the French by R. Hildreth, London: Kegan Paul), and for the second, from 1825 (*The Rationale of Reward*, translation from the French by R. Smith, London: J. & A. Hunt) and 1830 (*The Rationale of Punishment*, translation from the French by R. Smith, London: R. Heward).
21. See Patrick Colquhoun, *A Treatise on the Police of the Metropolis* (London: C. Dilly, 5th ed., 1797).
22. See *Surveiller et Punir*; *Discipline and Punish.*
23. On these different points, see "La vérité et les formes juridiques" (1974), *Dits et Écrits*, 2, pp. 589-590; English translation by Robert Hurley, "Truth and Juridical Forms" in *Essential Works of Foucault*, 3, pp. 70-71.
24. See above, this lecture, note 18.
25. This phrase is not found in Becker's article. Foucault relies on the synthesis of Becker's and Stigler's works provided by Jenny, "La théorie économique du crime ... " p. 298: "Rejecting, here as in the other domains of economic theory, any moral judgment, the economist distinguishes criminal activities from lawful activities solely on the basis of the type of risk incurred. Criminal activities are those that make the individual engaged in them incur a particular type of risk: that of being caught and condemned to a penalty (amends, imprisonment, execution)."
26. The first article of the 1810 Penal Code, which remained in force in its essential provisions until 1994, based the division of infractions—contraventions, misdemeanors, and

crimes—on the nature of the penalty decreed. It reserved the qualification of "crime" for "the infraction that the laws punish by a physical penalty involving loss of civil rights."

27. On this concept, first introduced in 1920 by Pigou in his *Economics of Welfare*, see P. Rosanvallon, *La Crise de l'État-providence*, pp. 59-60. See also, Y. Simon, "Le marché et l'allocation des ressources," in J.-J. Rosa and F. Aftalion, *L'Économique retrouvée*, p. 268: "Externalities are monetary or non-monetary costs and benefits arising from phenomena of social interdependence. ( ... ) For the theorists of welfare economics ( ... ), externalities reflect the failure of the market in the process of the allocation of resources and require public intervention to reduce the divergence between social and private costs."
28. See F. Jenny, "La théorie économique du crime ... " p. 298: "If crime enables the individual who commits it to maximize his own utility, it nevertheless generates negative externalities at the level of the community. The overall level of this activity or of this industry must therefore be limited. One way of limiting the negative externalities resulting from crimes is to arrest the criminals and inflict penalties on them ( ... )."
29. Foucault is referring here to the theory of speech acts developed in the framework of Wittgenstein's pragmatic linguistics by J.L. Austin in *How To Do Things with Words* (London: Oxford University Press, 1962), P.F. Strawson, "Intention and convention in speech-acts" in *Logico-Linguistic Papers* (London: Methuen, 1971), and J.R. Searle, *Speech Acts: An essay in the philosophy of language* (London: Cambridge University Press, 1969). The French translation of the latter, *Les Actes de langage. Essai de philosophie du langage* (Paris: Hermann, 1972) contains an important preface by O. Ducrot, "De Saussure à la philosophie du langage." These four authors are briefly referred to by Foucault in a round table discussion in Rio de Janeiro in 1973 concerning "the analysis of discourse as strategy" following the lectures "La vérité et les formes juridiques" *Dits et Écrits*, 2, p. 631. [The discussion is omitted from the English translation of these lectures; G.B.] See also, on the notion of speech acts, *L'Archéologie du savoir* (Paris: Gallimard, 1969) pp. 110-111; English translation by A. Sheridan, *The Archeology of Knowledge* (London: Tavistock, and New York: Pantheon, 1972) pp. 83-84, and Foucault's answer to Searle, with whom he was in correspondence some weeks after these lectures: "As to the analysis of speech acts, I am in complete agreement with your remarks. I was wrong in saying that statements were not speech acts, but in doing so I wanted to underline the fact that I see them under a different angle than yours" (letter to Searle of 15 May 1979) quoted by H. Dreyfus and P. Rabinow, *Michel Foucault: Beyond Structuralism and Hermeneutics* (Chicago: University of Chicago Press, 1982) p. 46, note 1.
30. G.J. Stigler, "The optimum enforcement of laws," p. 40: "The goal of enforcement, let us assume, is to achieve that degree of compliance with the rule of prescribed (or proscribed) behavior that the society believes it can afford. There is one decisive reason why the society must forego 'complete' enforcement of the rule: enforcement is costly."
31. G. Becker, "Crime and punishment," p. 40: "( ... ) how many offenses should be permitted, and how many offenders should go unpunished?"
32. I. Ehrlich, "The deterrent effect of capital punishment" p. 40: "In view of the new evidence presented here, one cannot reject the hypothesis that law enforcement activities in general and executions in particular do exert a deterrent effect on acts of murder. Strong inferences to the contrary drawn from earlier investigations appear to have been premature." Ehrlich is aiming especially at the arguments developed by T. Sellin against the death penalty in his book *The Death Penalty: A report for the model penal code project of the American Law Institute* (Philadelphia: Executive Office, American Law Institute, 1959).
33. On the drugs question, see F. Jenny, "La théorie économique du crime" pp. 315-316.
34. B.J. Eatherly, "Drug-law enforcement: should we arrest pushers or users?" *Journal of Political Economy*, vol. 82 (1), 1974, pp. 210-214; M. Moore, "Policies to achieve discrimination on the effective price of heroin," *American Economic Review*, vol. 63 (2), May 1973, pp. 270-278. Foucault relies here on the synthesis of these articles given by F. Jenny, p. 316.
35. I. Ehrlich, "The deterrent effect of capital punishment" p. 399: "The abhorrent, cruel and occasionally pathological nature of murder notwithstanding, available evidence is at least not inconsistent with these basic propositions [1) that [murder and other crimes against the person] are committed largely as a result of hate, jealousy, and other interpersonal conflicts involving pecuniary and non pecuniary motives or as a by-product of crimes against

property; and 2) that the propensity to perpetrate such crimes is influenced by the prospective gains and losses associated with their commissions] ( ... ) There is no reason a priori to expect that persons who hate or love others are less responsive to changes in costs and gains associated with activities they may wish to pursue than persons indifferent toward the well-being of others."

36. Foucault does not return to this point in the subsequent lectures.
37. Here again, the following lecture will not keep this promise.

# eleven

## 28 March 1979

*The model of* homo œconomicus. ~ *Its generalization to every form of behavior in American neo-liberalism.* ~ *Economic analysis and behavioral techniques.* ~ Homo œconomicus *as the basic element of the new governmental reason appeared in the eighteenth century.* ~ *Elements for a history of the notion of* homo œconomicus *before Walras and Pareto.* ~ *The subject of interest in English empiricist philosophy (Hume).* ~ *The heterogeneity of the subject of interest and the legal subject: (1) The irreducible nature of interest in comparison with juridical will. (2) The contrasting logics of the market and the contract.* ~ *Second innovation with regard to the juridical model: the economic subject's relationship with political power. Condorcet. Adam Smith's "invisible hand": invisibility of the link between the individual's pursuit of profit and the growth of collective wealth. The non-totalizable nature of the economic world. The sovereign's necessary ignorance.* ~ *Political economy as critique of governmental reason: rejection of the possibility of an economic sovereign in its two, mercantilist and physiocratic, forms.* ~ *Political economy as a science lateral to the art of government.*

TODAY I WOULD LIKE to start from the things I have been explaining over the last weeks and go back a bit toward what I took as my starting point at the beginning of the year. Last week I tried to show how American neo-liberals apply, or at any rate try to apply economic analysis to a series of objects, to domains of behavior or conduct which were not market forms of behavior or conduct: they attempt to apply economic analysis to marriage, the education of children, and criminality, for example. This of course poses a problem of both theory and method, the problem of the legitimacy of applying such an economic model, the practical problem of the heuristic value of this model, etcetera. These problems all revolve around a theme or a notion: *homo œconomicus*, economic man. To what extent is it legitimate, and to what extent is it fruitful, to apply the grid, the schema, and the model of *homo œconomicus* to not only every economic actor, but to every social actor in general inasmuch as he or she gets married, for example, or commits a crime, or raises children, gives affection and spends time with the kids? So there is a problem of the validity of the applicability of this grid of *homo œconomicus*. Actually, this problem of the application of *homo œconomicus* has become one of the classics of neo-liberal discussion in the United States. The background* of this analysis, well, the first text, is the book by von Mises, *Human Action*,[1] and you will also find in the years 1960-1970, and especially in 1962,[2] a series of articles in the *Journal of Political Economy*: articles by Becker,[3] Kirzner,[4] and others.

This problem of *homo œconomicus* and its applicability seems to me to be interesting because I think there are important stakes in the generalization of the grid of *homo œconomicus* to domains that are not immediately and directly economic. The most important stake is no doubt the problem of the identification of the object of economic analysis with any conduct whatsoever entailing an optimal allocation of scarce resources to alternative ends, which is the most general definition of the object of economic analysis as defined, roughly, by the neo-classical school.[5] But behind this identification of the object of economic analysis with conducts involving an optimal allocation of scarce resources to alternative ends we find the possibility of a generalization of the economic object to any conduct which employs limited means to one end among others. And we reach the point at which maybe the object of economic analysis should be identified with any purposeful conduct which involves,

* In English in the lecture; G.B.

broadly speaking, a strategic choice of means, ways, and instruments: in short, the identification of the object of economic analysis with any rational conduct. In the end, is not economics the analysis of forms of rational conduct and does not all rational conduct, whatever it may be, fall under something like economic analysis? Is not a rational conduct, like that which consists in formal reasoning, an economic conduct in the sense we have just defined, that is to say, the optimal allocation of scarce resources to alternative ends, since formal reasoning consists in deploying certain scarce resources—a symbolic system, a set of axioms, rules of construction, and not just any symbolic system or any rules of construction, but just some—to be used to optimal effect for a determinate and alternative end, in this case a true rather than a false conclusion which we try to reach by the best possible allocation of scarce resources? So, if it comes to it, we do not see why we would not define any rational conduct or behavior whatsoever as the possible object of economic analysis.

In truth, this already extremely extensive definition is not even the only one, and Becker, for example—the most radical of the American neo-liberals, if you like—says that it is still not sufficient, that the object of economic analysis can be extended even beyond rational conduct as defined and understood in the way I have just described, and that economic laws and economic analysis can perfectly well be applied to non-rational conduct, that is to say, to conduct which does not seek at all, or, at any rate, not only to optimize the allocation of scarce resources to a determinate end.[6] Becker says: Basically, economic analysis can perfectly well find its points of anchorage and effectiveness if an individual's conduct answers to the single clause that the conduct in question reacts to reality in a non-random way. That is to say, any conduct which responds systematically to modifications in the variables of the environment, in other words, any conduct, as Becker says, which "accepts reality," must be susceptible to economic analysis.[7] *Homo œconomicus* is someone who accepts reality. Rational conduct is any conduct which is sensitive to modifications in the variables of the environment and which responds to this in a non-random way, in a systematic way, and economics can therefore be defined as the science of the systematic nature of responses to environmental variables.

This is a colossal definition, which obviously economists are far from endorsing, but it has a certain interest. It has a practical interest, if you like, inasmuch as if you define the object of economic analysis as the set of systematic responses to the variables of the environment, then you can see the possibility of integrating within economics a set of techniques, those called behavioral techniques, which are currently in fashion in the United States. You find these methods in their purest, most rigorous, strictest or aberrant forms, as you wish, in Skinner,[8] and precisely they do not consist in analyzing the meaning of different kinds of conduct, but simply in seeing how, through mechanisms of reinforcement, a given play of stimuli entail responses whose systematic nature can be observed and on the basis of which other variables of behavior can be introduced. In fact, all these behavioral techniques show how psychology understood in these terms can enter the definition of economics given by Becker. There is little literature on these behavioral techniques in France. In Castel's last book, *The Psychiatric Society*, there is a chapter on behavioral techniques and you will see how this is precisely the implementation, within a given situation—in this case, a hospital, a psychiatric clinic—of methods which are both experimental and involve a specifically economic analysis of behavior.[9]

Today though, I would like to emphasize a different aspect. This is that Becker's definition, which, again, although it is not recognized by the average economist, or even by the majority of them, nonetheless, despite its isolated character, enables us to highlight a paradox, because *homo œconomicus* as he appears in the eighteenth century—I will come back to this shortly—basically functions as what could be called an intangible element with regard to the exercise of power. *Homo œconomicus* is someone who pursues his own interest, and whose interest is such that it converges spontaneously with the interest of others. From the point of view of a theory of government, *homo œconomicus* is the person who must be let alone. With regard to *homo œconomicus*, one must *laisser-faire*; he is the subject or object of *laissez-faire*. And now, in Becker's definition which I have just given, *homo œconomicus*, that is to say, the person who accepts reality or who responds systematically to modifications in the variables of the environment, appears precisely as someone manageable, someone who responds systematically to systematic modifications artificially introduced into the environment. *Homo œconomicus* is someone who is eminently governable. From being the intangible partner of *laissez-faire*, *homo œconomicus* now becomes the correlate of a governmentality which will act on the environment and systematically modify its variables.

I think this paradox enables us to pinpoint the problem I would like to say something about, which is precisely this: since the eighteenth century, has *homo œconomicus* involved setting up an essentially and unconditionally irreducible element against any possible government? Does the definition of *homo œconomicus* involve marking out the zone that is definitively inaccessible to any government action? Is *homo œconomicus* an atom of freedom in the face of all the conditions, undertakings, legislation, and prohibitions of a possible government, or was he not already a certain type of subject who precisely enabled an art of government to be determined according to the principle of economy, both in the sense of political economy and in the sense of the restriction, self-limitation, and frugality of government? Obviously, the way in which I have formulated this question gives the answer straightaway, but this is what I would like to talk about, that is to say, *homo œconomicus* as the partner, the vis-à-vis, and the basic element of the new governmental reason formulated in the eighteenth century.

In actual fact, to tell the truth there is no theory of *homo œconomicus*, or even a history of his notion.[10] You practically have to wait for what are called the neo-classical economists, Walras[11] and Pareto,[12] to see the more or less clear emergence of what is understood by *homo œconomicus*. But this notion was in fact employed even before Walras and Pareto, although it was not conceptualized very rigorously. How can we consider this problem of *homo œconomicus* and its appearance? To simplify things, and somewhat arbitrarily, I will start, as from a given, with English empiricism and the theory of the subject which is in fact put to work in English empiricist philosophy, with the view that—once again, I am making a somewhat arbitrary division—the theory of the subject in English empiricism probably represents one of the most important mutations, one of the most important theoretical transformations in Western thought since the Middle Ages.

What English empiricism introduces—let's say, roughly, with Locke[13]—and doubtless for the first time in Western philosophy, is a subject who is not so much defined by his freedom, or by the opposition of soul and body, or by the presence of a source or core of concupiscence marked to a greater or lesser degree by the Fall or sin, but who appears in the form of a subject of individual choices which are both irreducible and non-transferable. What do I mean by irreducible? I will take Hume's very simple and frequently cited passage,[14] which says: What type of question is it, and what irreducible element can you arrive at when you analyze an individual's choices and ask why he did one thing rather than another? Well, he says: "You ask someone, 'Why do you exercise?' He will reply, 'I exercise because I desire health.' You go on to ask him, 'Why do you desire health?' He will reply, 'Because I prefer health to illness.' Then you go on to ask him, 'Why do you prefer health to illness?' He will reply, 'Because illness is painful and so I don't want to fall ill.' And if you ask him why is illness painful, then at that point he will have the right not to answer, because the question has no meaning." The painful or non-painful nature of the thing is in itself a reason for the choice beyond which you cannot go. The choice between painful and non-painful is a sort of irreducible that does not refer to any judgment, reasoning, or calculation. It is a sort of regressive end point in the analysis.

Second, this type of choice is non-transferable. I do not mean that it is non-transferable in the sense that one choice could not be replaced by another. You could perfectly well say that if you prefer health to illness, you may also prefer illness to health, and then choose illness. It is also clear that you may perfectly well say: I prefer to be ill and that someone else is not. But, in any case, on what basis will this substitution of one choice for another be made? It will be made on the basis of my own preference and on the basis of the fact that I would find someone else being ill more painful, for example, than being ill myself. In the end the principle of my choice really will be my own feeling of painful or not-painful, of pain and pleasure. There is Hume's famous aphorism which says: If I am given the choice between cutting my little finger and the death of someone else, even if I am forced to cut my little finger, nothing can force me to think that cutting my little finger is preferable to the death of someone else.[15]

So, these are irreducible choices which are non-transferable in relation to the subject. This principle of an irreducible, non-transferable, atomistic individual choice which is unconditionally referred to the subject himself is what is called interest.

What I think is fundamental in English empiricist philosophy—which I am treating completely superficially—is that it reveals something which absolutely did not exist before. This is the idea of a subject of interest, by which I mean a subject as the source of interest, the starting point of an interest, or the site of a mechanism of interests. For sure, there is a series of discussions on the mechanism of interest itself and what may activate it: is it self-preservation, is it the body or the soul, or is it sympathy? But this is not what is important. What is important is the appearance of interest for the first time as a form of both immediately and absolutely subjective will.

I think the problem and that which gets the problematic of *homo œconomicus* underway is whether this subject of interest or form of will called interest can be considered as the same type of will as the juridical will or as capable of being connected to the juridical will. At first sight, we can say although interest and the juridical will cannot be completely assimilated to each other, they may perfectly well be reconciled. And in fact this is what we see from the end of the seventeenth century up to the middle of the eighteenth century and a jurist like Blackstone:[16] a kind of mixture of juridical analysis and analysis in terms of interest. For example, when Blackstone addresses the problem of the original contract, of the social contract, he says: Why have individuals entered into the contract? Well, they have entered the contract because they have an interest. Every individual has his interests, but in the state of nature and before the contract, these interests are threatened. So, to protect at least some of their interests they are forced to sacrifice others. The immediate will be sacrificed for what is more important and possibly deferred.[17] In short, interest appears here as an empirical source of the contract. And the juridical will which is then formed, the legal subject who is constituted through the contract, is basically the subject of interest, but a purified subject of interest who has become calculating, rationalized, and so on. Now in relation to this, if you like, somewhat loose analysis, in which juridical will and interest are mixed together and intertwined, generating each other, Hume notes that it's not like this and that things are not so simple. Why, Hume says, do you enter the contract? Out of interest. You enter the contract out of interest, because you realize that if you were alone and had no ties with others your interests would be harmed. But once you have entered the contract, why do you respect it? The jurists say, and Blackstone in particular said around this time: You respect the contract because once individual subjects of interest have recognized the interest in entering the contract, the obligation of the contract constitutes a sort of transcendence in relation to which the subject finds himself, in a way, subjected and constrained, so that, having become a subject of right, he will obey the contract. Hume replies to this: But this won't do at all, because in fact, if you obey a contract this is not because it is a contract, because you are held by the obligation of the contract, or, in other words, because you have suddenly become a subject of right and ceased being a subject of interest. If you continue to respect the contract it is simply because you hold to the following reasoning: "The commerce with our fellows from which we draw such great advantages would have no security if we did not respect our engagements."[18] This means that it is not because we have contracted that we respect the contract, but because it is in our interest that there is a contract. That is to say, the appearance and the emergence of the contract have not replaced a subject of interest with a subject of right. In a calculation of interest, the subject of interest has constituted a form, an element in which he will continue to have a certain interest right to the end. And if, moreover, the contract no longer offers an interest, nothing can oblige me to continue to comply with it.[19] So, juridical will does not take over from interest. The subject of right does not find a place for itself in the subject of interest. The subject of interest remains, subsists, and continues up to the time a juridical structure, a contract exists. For as long as the law exists, the subject of interest also continues to exist. The subject of interest constantly overflows the subject of right. He is therefore irreducible to the subject of right. He is not absorbed by him. He overflows him, surrounds him, and is the permanent condition of him functioning. So, interest constitutes something irreducible in relation to the juridical will. This is the first point.

Second, the subject of right and the subject of interest are not governed by the same logic. What characterizes the subject of right? Of course, at the outset he has natural rights. But he becomes a subject of right in a positive system only when he has agreed at least to the principle of ceding these rights, of relinquishing them, when he has subscribed to their limitation and has accepted the principle of the transfer. That is to say, the subject of right is, by definition, a subject who accepts negativity, who agrees to a self-renunciation and splits himself, as it were, to be, at one level, the possessor of a number of natural and immediate rights, and, at another level, someone who agrees to the principle of relinquishing them and who is thereby constituted as a different subject of right superimposed on the first. The dialectic or mechanism of the subject of right is characterized by the division of the subject, the existence of a transcendence of the second subject in relation to the first, and a relationship of negativity, renunciation, and limitation between them, and it is in this movement that law and the prohibition emerge.

On the other hand—and this is where the economists' analysis links up with this theme of the subject of interest and gives it a sort of empirical content—the subject of interest is not at all governed by the same mechanism. What the analysis of the market shows, for example, what the physiocrats in France, the English economists, and even theorists like Mandeville[20] reveal, is that fundamentally the subject of interest is never called upon to relinquish his interest. Consider, for example, what takes place with the grain market—you recall, we talked about this last time[21]—when there is an abundant harvest in one country and dearth in another. The legislation in most countries prohibited unlimited export of wheat from the rich country to the country suffering from dearth so as not to cause shortages in the country which had reserves. The economists' [response] to this is: Absurdity! Let the mechanism of interests operate, let the sellers rush their grain to the countries where there is dearth, where grain is dear and sells easily, and you will see that the more they pursue their own interests the better things will be and you will have a general advantage which will be formed on the basis of the maximization of the interest of each. Not only may each pursue their own interest, they must pursue their own interest, and they must pursue it through and through by pushing it to the utmost, and then, at that point, you will find the elements on the basis of which not only will the interest of others be preserved, but will thereby be increased. So, with the subject of interest, as the economists make him function, there is a mechanism which is completely different from the dialectic of the subject of right, since it is an egoistic mechanism, a directly multiplying mechanism without any transcendence in which the will of each harmonizes spontaneously and as it were involuntarily with the will and interest of others. We could not be more distant from the dialectic of renunciation, transcendence, and the voluntary bond of the juridical theory of the contract. The market and the contract function in exactly opposite ways and we have in fact two heterogeneous structures.

To summarize this, we could say that at first sight it seems that the analysis of interest in the eighteenth century can be linked to the theory of the contract without too much difficulty, but when it is examined more closely it in fact gives rise to what I think is a completely new, heterogeneous problematic in relation to the typical elements of the doctrine of the contract and the subject of right.* At the point of intersection, as it were, of the empirical conception of the subject of interest and the analyses of the economists, a subject can be defined who is a subject of interest and whose action has a multiplying and beneficial value through the intensification of interest, and it is this that characterizes *homo œconomicus*. In the eighteenth century the figure of *homo œconomicus* and the figure of what we could call *homo juridicus* or *homo legalis* are absolutely heterogeneous and cannot be superimposed on each other.

Given this heterogeneity, I think we need to go further and say first of all that not only are the economic subject and the subject of right formally heterogeneous for the reasons I have just given, but it seems to me that, partly as a consequence of this, the economic subject and the subject of right have an essentially different relationship with political power. Or, if you like, with regard to the question of the foundation and exercise of power, the question posed by the problematic of economic man is completely different from that which could be posed by the figure and element of juridical man, the legal subject. To understand what is radically new in economic man from the point of view of the problem of power and of the legitimate exercise of power, I would like to start by quoting a text from Condorcet, which seems to me to be rather illuminating on this.

---

* The manuscript, p. 9, adds: "a) First by an empirical radicalism in the manner of Hume, b) then by an analysis of the mechanisms of the market."

It comes from *Les Progrès de l'esprit humain*, in the Ninth era. Condorcet says: If we consider the interest of an individual apart from the general system of a society—he does not mean an individual isolated from society (that is to say, he does not consider an individual alone), he means: take an individual in society, and consider his own, peculiar interest—then this specifically individual interest of someone who finds himself within the general system of not only one society, but of societies, has two characteristics. The first is that it is an interest which is dependent upon on an infinite number of things. The interest of the individual will depend on accidents of nature about which he can do nothing and which he cannot foresee. It depends on more or less distant political events. In short, the individual's enjoyment is linked to a course of the world that outstrips him and eludes him in every respect. The second characteristic is that, on the other hand, despite everything "in this apparent chaos," Condorcet says, "we see nonetheless, through a general law of the moral world, the efforts each makes for himself serving the good of all."[22] This means, on the one hand, that each is dependent on an uncontrollable, unspecified whole of the flow of things and the world. In a way, the most distant event taking place on the other side of the world may affect my interest, and there is nothing I can do about it. The will of each, the interest of each, and the way in which this interest is or is not realized are bound up with a mass of elements which elude individuals. At the same time, this individual's interest, without him knowing it, wishing it, or being able to control it, is linked to a series of positive effects which mean that everything which is to his advantage will turn out to be to the advantage of others. So that economic man is situated in what we could call an indefinite field of immanence which, on the one hand, links him, in the form of dependence, to a series of accidents, and, on the other, links him, in the form of production, to the advantage of others, or which links his advantage to the production of the advantage of others. The convergence of interests thus doubles and covers the indefinite diversity of accidents.

The situation of *homo œconomicus* could therefore be described as doubly involuntary, with regard to the accidents which happen to him and with regard to the benefit he unintentionally produces for others. It is also doubly indefinite since, on the one hand, the accidents upon which his interest depends belong to a domain which cannot be covered or totalized and, on the other, the benefit he produces for others by producing his own benefit is also indefinite and cannot be totalized. His situation is therefore doubly involuntary, indefinite, and non-totalizable, but all these involuntary, indefinite, uncontrollable, and non-totalizable features of his situation do not disqualify his interest or the calculation he may make to maximize it. On the contrary, all these indefinite features of his situation found, as it were, the specifically individual calculation that he makes; they give it consistency, effect, insert it in reality, and connect it in the best possible way to the rest of the world. So, we have a system in which *homo œconomicus* owes the positive nature of his calculation precisely to everything which eludes his calculation. We arrive here, of course, at the unavoidable text, Adam Smith's famous words in the second chapter of Book IV, the only place, as you know, in *The Wealth of Nations*, where he speaks of this famous thing, and where he says: "By preferring the support of domestick to that of foreign industry, he intends only his own security; and by directing that industry in such a manner as its produce may be of the greatest value, he intends only his own gain, and he is in this, as in many other cases, led by an invisible hand to promote an end which was no part of his intention."[23] So we are at the heart of the problematic of the invisible hand, which is the correlate of *homo œconomicus* if you like, or rather is that kind of bizarre mechanism which makes *homo œconomicus* function as an individual subject of interest within a totality which eludes him and which nevertheless founds the rationality of his egoistic choices.

What is this invisible hand? Well, of course, it is usually said that the invisible hand refers to a more or less well thought-out economic optimism in Smith's thought. It is also usually said that we should see the invisible hand as the remains of a theological conception of the natural order. Through the notion of the invisible hand, Smith would be someone who more or less implicitly fixed the empty, but nonetheless secretly occupied place of a providential god who would occupy the economic process a bit like Malebranche's God occupies the entire world down to the least gesture of every individual through the relay of an intelligible extension of which He is the absolute master.[24] Smith's invisible hand would be something like Malebranche's God, whose intelligible extension would not be occupied by lines, surfaces, and bodies, but by merchants, markets, ships, carriages, and roads. A consequence of this would be the idea that there is an essential transparency in this economic world and that if the totality of the process eludes each economic man, there is however a point where the whole is completely transparent to a sort of gaze of someone whose invisible hand, following the logic of this gaze and what it sees, draws together the threads of all these dispersed interests. Therefore, there is the requirement, if not a postulate, of the total transparency of the economic world. Now if we read the text a bit further on, what does Adam Smith say? He is speaking of those people who, without really knowing why or how, pursue their own interest and this ends up benefiting everyone. Each only thinks of his own gain and, in the end, the whole of industry benefits. People, he says, only think of their own gain and do not think about the benefit of everyone. And he adds that it is not always the worse for society that the end of benefiting all does not enter into merchants' concerns.[25] "I have never known much good done by those who affected to trade for the publick good. It is an affectation, indeed, not very common among merchants."[26] We can say, roughly: Thank heaven people are only concerned about their interests, thank heaven merchants are perfect egoists and rarely concern themselves with the public good, because that's when things start to go wrong.

So, in other words, there are two, absolutely coupled elements. For there to be certainty of collective benefit, for it to be certain that the greatest good is attained for the greatest number of people, not only is it possible, but it is absolutely necessary that each actor be blind with regard to this totality. Everyone must be uncertain with regard to the collective outcome if this positive collective outcome is really to be expected. Being in the dark and the blindness of all the economic agents are absolutely necessary.[27] The collective good must not be an objective. It must not be an objective because it cannot be calculated, at least, not within an economic strategy. Here we are at the heart of a principle of invisibility. In other words, what is usually stressed in Smith's famous theory of the invisible hand is, if you like, the "hand," that is to say, the existence of something like providence which would tie together all the dispersed threads. But I think the other element, invisibility, is at least as important. Invisibility is not just a fact arising from the imperfect nature of human intelligence which prevents people from realizing that there is a hand behind them which arranges or connects everything that each individual does on their own account. Invisibility is absolutely indispensable. It is an invisibility which means that no economic agent should or can pursue the collective good.

But we must no doubt go further than economic agents; not only no economic agent, but also no political agent. In other words, the world of the economy must be and can only be obscure to the sovereign, and it is so in two ways. We are already familiar with one of these and there's no point in stressing it too much, which is that since the economic mechanism involves each pursuing his own interest, then each must be left alone to do so. Political power is not to interfere with this dynamic naturally inscribed in the heart of man. The government is thus prohibited from obstructing individual interests. This is what Adam Smith says when he writes: the common interest requires that each knows how to interpret his own interest and is able to pursue it without obstruction.[28] In other words, power, government, must not obstruct the interplay of individual interests. But it is necessary to go further. Not only must government not obstruct the interests of each, but it is impossible for the sovereign to have a point of view on the economic mechanism which totalizes every element and enables them to be combined artificially or voluntarily. The invisible hand which spontaneously combines interests also prohibits any form of intervention and, even better, any form of overarching gaze which would enable the economic process to be totalized. A text from Ferguson is very clear on this point. In his *Essay on the History of Civil Society*,[29] he says: "the more [the individual] gains for himself, the more he augments the wealth of his country ... When the refined politician would lend an active hand, he only multiplies interruptions and grounds of complaint; when the merchant forgets his own interest to lay plans for his country, the period of vision and chimera is near."[30] Ferguson takes the example of French and English settlements in America, and analyzing the French and English mode of colonization, he says: The French arrived with projects, administration, and their definition of what would be best for their American colonies. They constructed "great projects" that were only ever "in idea" and the French colonies in America collapsed. What did the English bring to colonize America? Did they bring grand projects? Not at all. They arrived with "limited views." They had no other project than the immediate advantage of each, or rather, each had in mind only the limited view of their own project. As a result, industry was active and settlements flourished.[31] Consequently, the economy, understood as a practice but also as a type of government intervention, as a form of action of the state or sovereign, can only be short-sighted, and if there were a sovereign who claimed to be long-sighted, to have a global and totalizing gaze, he would only ever see chimeras. In the middle of the eighteenth century, political economy denounces the paralogism of political totalization of the economic process.

That the sovereign is, can, and must be ignorant is what Adam Smith says in chapter 9 of Book IV of *The Wealth of Nations*, clarifying perfectly what he means by the invisible hand and what is important in the adjective "invisible." Smith says: "Every man, as long as he does not violate the laws of justice, must be able to pursue his interest and bring his capital where he pleases."[32] So, the principle of *laissez-faire*: in any case, every man must follow his own interest. And as a result, he says somewhat hypocritically—I am the one saying it is hypocritical—the sovereign can only find this to his advantage, since he "is completely discharged of a duty, in the attempting to perform which he must always be exposed to innumerable delusions ... the duty of superintending the industry of private people, and of directing it towards the employments most suitable to the interest of the society."[33] I say this sentence is "hypocritical" because it could also be taken to mean that if the sovereign, one person surrounded by more or less loyal advisors, were to undertake the infinite task of superintending the totality of the economic process, there is no doubt that he would be deceived by disloyal administrators and ministers. But Smith also means that it is not just due to his ministers' disloyalty or the complexity of an inevitably uncontrollable administration that he would make mistakes. He would make mistakes for an, as it were, essential and fundamental reason. He could not fail to be mistaken, and what is more this is what the sentence says when speaking of this task, this duty, of which the sovereign must be relieved, that of superintending the totality of the economic process, "for the proper performance of which no human wisdom or knowledge could ever by sufficient."[34]

Economic rationality is not only surrounded by, but founded on the unknowability of the totality of the process. *Homo œconomicus* is the one island of rationality possible within an economic process whose uncontrollable nature does not challenge, but instead founds the rationality of the atomistic behavior of *homo œconomicus*. Thus the economic world is naturally opaque and naturally non-totalizable. It is originally and definitively constituted from a multiplicity of points of view which is all the more irreducible as this same multiplicity assures their ultimate and spontaneous convergence. Economics is an atheistic discipline; economics is a discipline without God; economics is a discipline without totality; economics is a discipline that begins to demonstrate not only the pointlessness, but also the impossibility of a sovereign point of view over the totality of the state that he has to govern. Economics steals away from the juridical form of the sovereign exercising sovereignty within a state precisely that which is emerging as the essential element of a society's life, namely economic processes. Liberalism acquired its modern shape precisely with the formulation of this essential incompatibility between the non-totalizable multiplicity of economic subjects of interest and the totalizing unity of the juridical sovereign.

The problematic of the economy is by no means the logical completion of the great problematic of sovereignty through which eighteenth century juridical-political thought strove to show how, by starting from individual subjects of natural right, one could arrive at the constitution of a political unity defined by the existence of an individual or collective sovereign who is the holder of part of the totality of these individual rights and at the same time the principle of their limitation. The economic problematic, the problematic of economic interest, is governed by a completely different configuration, by a completely different logic, type of reasoning, and rationality. In fact, from the eighteenth century the political-juridical world and the economic world appear as heterogeneous and incompatible worlds. The idea of an economic-juridical science is strictly impossible and what is more it has never in fact been constituted. *Homo œconomicus* is someone who can say to the juridical sovereign, to the sovereign possessor of rights and founder of positive law on the basis of the natural right of individuals: You must not. But he does not say: You must not, because I have rights and you must not touch them. This is what the man of right, *homo juridicus*, says to the sovereign: I have rights, I have entrusted some of them to you, the others you must not touch, or: I have entrusted you with my rights for a particular end. *Homo œconomicus* does not say this. He also tells the sovereign: You must not. But why must he not? You must not because you cannot. And you cannot in the sense that "you are powerless." And why are you powerless, why can't you? You cannot because you do not know, and you do not know because you cannot know.

I think this is an important moment when political economy is able to present itself as a critique of governmental reason. I am using "critique" here in the specific, philosophical sense of the term.[35] Kant too, a little later moreover, had to tell man that he cannot know the totality of the world. Well, some decades earlier, political economy had told the sovereign: Not even you can know the totality of the economic process. There is no sovereign in economics. There is no economic sovereign. This is a very important point in the history of economic thought, certainly, but also and above all in the history of governmental reason. The absence or impossibility of an economic sovereign is a problem which will ultimately be raised throughout Europe, and throughout the modern world, by governmental practices, economic problems, socialism, planning, and welfare economics. All the returns and revivals of nineteenth and twentieth century liberal and neo-liberal thought are still a way of posing the problem of the impossibility of the existence of an economic sovereign. And with the appearance of planning, the state-controlled economy, socialism, and state socialism the problem will be whether we may not overcome in some way this curse against the economic sovereign which was formulated by political economy at its foundation and which is also the very condition of existence of political economy: In spite of everything, may there not be a point through which we can define an economic sovereignty?

On a more limited scale, it seems to me that the basic function or role of the theory of the invisible hand is to disqualify the political sovereign. If we situate it in its immediate context, and not in the history of liberalism over the last two centuries, it is very clear that this theory, understood as the disqualification of the very possibility of an economic sovereign, amounts to a challenge to the police state I talked about last year.[36] The police state, or the state governed by *raison d'État*, with its mercantilist policies, was, from the seventeenth century, the perfectly explicit effort to constitute a sovereign who would no longer be a sovereign of right and in terms of right, but who could also be an administrative sovereign, that is to say, a sovereign who would, of course, be able to administer the subjects over whom he exercises sovereignty, but also the possible economic processes taking place between individuals, groups, and states. The police state, the state which implements the both voluntarist and mercantilist policy of sovereigns, or at any rate, of some seventeenth and eighteenth century sovereigns, like the French sovereign, rests in fact on the postulate that there must be an economic sovereign. Political economy is not just a refutation of mercantilist doctrines or practices. Adam Smith's political economy, economic liberalism, amounts to a disqualification of this entire project and, even more radically, a disqualification of a political reason indexed to the state and its sovereignty.

It is interesting to see even more precisely what the theory of the invisible hand is opposed to. It is opposed, very precisely, to what the physiocrats said almost at the same time or, at any rate, to what they were saying some years earlier, because from this point of view the position of the physiocrats is very interesting and very paradoxical. In France, the physiocrats analyzed the market and market mechanisms in precisely the terms I have talked about several times[37] and proved that the government, the state, or the sovereign must absolutely not interfere with the mechanism of interest which ensures that commodities go where they most easily find buyers and the best price. Physiocracy was therefore a strict critique of all the administrative rules and regulations through which the sovereign's power was exercised on the economy. But the physiocrats straightaway added this: Economic agents must be left free, but, first, we must take account of the fact that the entire territory of a country is basically the sovereign's property, or at any rate that the sovereign is co-owner of all the land of the country and so is therefore co-producer. This enabled them to justify taxation. So, in the physiocrat's conception, the sovereign, as co-owner of a country's lands and co-producer of its products, will correspond perfectly, as it were, in principle and right as well as in fact, to all the production and all the economic activity of a country.

Second, the physiocrats say that the existence of an Economic Table, which enables the circuit of production and the formation of rent to be followed very exactly, gives the sovereign the possibility of exact knowledge of everything taking place within his country, thus giving him the power to control economic processes. That is to say, the Economic Table will offer the sovereign a principle of analysis and a sort of principle of transparency in relation to the whole of the economic process. So that if the sovereign leaves economic agents free, it is because, thanks to the Economic Table, he knows both what is taking place and how it should be taking place. Thus, in the name of this total knowledge, he will be able to accept freely and rationally, or rather, he will be forced by reason, knowledge, and truth to accept the principle of the freedom of economic agents. So that there will be a second perfect correspondence between the sovereign's knowledge and the freedom of individuals.

Finally, third, a good government—that is to say, the government of a sovereign who, thanks to the Economic Table, knows exactly what is taking place with regard to economic processes—will have to explain to the different economic agents, to the different subjects, how and why things are as they are and what they have to do to maximize their profit. There will have to be an economic knowledge spread as widely and uniformly as possible among all these subjects, and this economic knowledge, whose principle is found in the Economic Table drawn up by the physiocrats, will be common to economically well-educated subjects and to the sovereign who will be able to recognize the fundamental laws of the economy. So at the level of knowledge, at the level of the consciousness of truth, there will be a third perfect correspondence between the sovereign and the economic processes, or at least the economic agents. You can see therefore that the principle of *laissez-faire* in the physiocrats, the principle of the necessary freedom of economic agents can coincide with the existence of a sovereign who is all the more despotic and unrestrained by traditions, customs, rules, and fundamental laws as his only law is that of *évidence*, of a well-formed, well-constructed knowledge which he will share with the economic agents. It is here, and only here, that we have in fact the idea of a mutual transparency of the economic and the political. It is here, and only here, that we can find the idea that economic agents must be allowed their freedom and that a political sovereignty will cover the totality of the economic process with a gaze in the uniform light, as it were, of evidence.

Adam Smith's invisible hand is the exact opposite of this. It is the critique of this paradoxical idea of total economic freedom and absolute despotism which the physiocrats tried to maintain in the theory of economic evidence. The invisible hand posits instead, as a rule, that this is not possible, that there cannot be a sovereign in the physiocratic sense, and that there cannot be despotism in the physiocratic sense, because there cannot be economic evidence. So you can see, from the start—if we call Adam Smith's theory and liberal theory the start of political economy—economic science never claimed that it had to be the line of conduct, the complete programming of what could be called governmental rationality. Political economy is indeed a science, a type of knowledge (*savoir*), a mode of knowledge (*connaissance*) which those who govern must take into account. But economic science cannot be the science of government and economics cannot be the internal principle, law, rule of conduct, or rationality of government. Economics is a science lateral to the art of governing. One must govern with economics, one must govern alongside economists, one must govern by listening to the economists, but economics must not be and there is no question that it can be the governmental rationality itself.

It seems to me that this is how we can comment on the theory of the invisible hand in relation to the problem of governmental rationality or of the art of governing. So, a problem arises: what will government be concerned with if the economic process, and the whole of the economic process, is not in principle its object? I think it is the theory of civil society, which I will try to talk about next week.

1. Ludwig von Mises, *Human Action: A treatise on economics.*
2. See in particular *Journal of Political Economy*, vol. 70 (5), October 1962, 2nd part, coordinated by T. Schultz, entirely devoted to the problem of the "investment in human beings."
3. G. Becker, "Investment in human capital: a theoretical analysis."
4. I.M. Kirzner, "Rational action and economic theory," *Journal of Political Economy*, vol. 70 (4), August 1962, pp. 380-385.
5. See above, lecture of 14 March 1979, notes 23 and 25.
6. See G. Becker, "Irrational action and economic theory," *Journal of Political Economy*, vol. 70 (1), August 1962, pp. 153-168.
7. Ibid., p. 167: "Even irrational decision units must accept reality and could not, for example, maintain a choice that was no longer within their opportunity set. And these sets are not fixed or dominated by erratic variation, but are systematically changed by different economic variables ( ... )."
8. Burrhus Frederic Skinner (1904-1990), American psychologist and psycho-linguist, is one of the main representatives of the behaviorist school. Harvard professor from 1947, he published many books, amongst which, *Science and Human Behavior* (London: Collier-Macmillan, 1953); *Verbal Behavior* (Englewood Cliffs, NJ: Prentice Hall, 1957); and *Beyond Freedom and Dignity* (New York: A.A. Knopf, 1971). Hostile to the use of statistics, he thought individual behavior should be studied, "which presupposes control of the environment in which the subject is placed and the definition of informative measures of response. ( ... ) When a subject moves in his environment, some of his behavior produces detectable modifications in the latter (contingencies of reinforcement). The effective response is a class of responses defined by the consequences it has for the subject and emitted in a given situation without being causally dependent on a stimulus of the situation. A rigorous control of the contingencies thus enables repeatable behavior to be selected" *Encyclopaedia Universalis*, Thesaurus, 1975, vol. 20, p. 1797. The end sought is therefore "selection of the relevant behavior by manipulation of programs of reinforcement" ibid.
9. F. Castel, R. Castel and A. Lovell, *La Société psychiatrique avancée: le modèle américain* (Paris: Grasset, 1979) ch. 4, pp. 138-139; English translation by Arthur Goldhammer, *The Psychiatric Society* (New York: Columbia University Press) pp. 113-115, on behavior modification, inspired by the principles of conditioning (Pavlov) and behaviorism (Thorndike, Skinner) in the psychiatric milieu (see also ch. 8, pp. 299-302; English, pp. 265-266).
10. See now P. Demeulenaere's book, *Homo œconomicus. Enquête sur la constitution d'un paradigme* (Paris: PUF, 1996).
11. See above, lecture of 21 February 1979, note 12.
12. Vilfredo Pareto (1848-1923), Italian sociologist and economist, Walras' successor at the University of Lausanne. *Manuel d'économie politique* (1906), in *Œuvres complètes*, vol. VII (Geneva: Droz, 1981) pp. 7-18; English translation by Ann S. Schwier, *Manual of Political Economy* (London: Macmillan, 1972) pp. 12-14. See J. Freund, *Pareto, la théorie de l'equilibre* (Paris: Seghers, 1974) pp. 26-27 (*homo œconomicus* according to Pareto), which Foucault had read.
13. John Locke (1632-1704), the author of *Essay concerning Human Understanding* (London: printed by E. Holt for T. Basset, 1690).
14. David Hume (1711-1776), *An Enquiry Concerning the Principles of Morals* (1751) in *Enquiries Concerning Human Understanding and Concerning the Principles of Morals*, ed. L.A. Selby-Bigge (Oxford: The Clarendon Press, 1975, 3rd edition), Appendix 1, "Concerning Moral Sentiment" p. 293: "Ask a man *why he uses exercise*; he will answer, *because he desires to keep his health.* If you then enquire, *why he desires health*, he will readily reply, *because sickness is painful.* If you push your enquiries farther, and desire a reason *why he hates pain*, it is impossible he can ever give any. This is an ultimate end, and is never referred to any other object."
15. See D. Hume, *A Treatise of Human Nature* (1739-40), ed. L.A. Selby-Bigge (Oxford: Clarendon Press, 1978) Book III, Part III, section III, p. 416: "Where a passion is neither founded on false supposition, nor chuses means insufficient for the end, the understanding

can neither justify nor condemn it. 'Tis not contrary to reason to prefer the destruction of the whole world to the scratching of my finger."

16. William Blackstone (1723-1780): conservative jurist and professor of Law at Oxford, where Bentham was his student 1763-64 (who later appears, on the basis of his *Fragment on Goverment* (1776) as the "anti-Blackstone" (Halévy)). The author of *Commentaries on the Laws of England* (Oxford: Clarendon Press, 1765-1769) in 4 volumes. See E. Halévy, *La Formation du radicalisme philosophique*, vol. 1, 1995 ed., pp. 55-56; *The Growth of Philosophic Radicalism*, pp. 35-36; Mohammed El Shakankiri, *La Philosophie juridique de Jeremy Bentham* (Paris: LJDJ, 1970) pp. 223-237.
17. See *Commentaries*, vol. 1 (there is a good summary in M. El Shakankiri, pp. 236-238). On the mixture of juridical and utilitarian principles in Blackstone's justification of the penalty, see E. Halévy, *La Formation du radicalisme philosophique* p. 101; *The Growth of Philosophic Radicalism*, p. 58, who detects here a lack of coherence.
18. D. Hume, "Of the Original Contract" in *Essays Moral, Political, and Literary*, ed. Eugene F. Miller (Indianapolis: Liberty*Classics*, 1987) p. 481: "We are bound to obey our sovereign, it is said; because we have given a tacit promise to that purpose. But why are we bound to observe our promise? It must here be asserted, that the commerce and intercourse of mankind, which are of such mighty advantage, can have no security where men pay no regard to their engagements." See also *A Treatise of Human Nature*, Book III, Part II, section VIII, "Of the source of allegiance."
19. *A Treatise of Human Nature*, Book III, Part II, section IX, p. 553: "( ... ) if interest first produces obedience to government, the obligation to obedience must cease, whenever the interest ceases, in any great degree, and in a considerable number of instances."
20. Bernard Mandeville (1670-1733), author of the famous *Fable of the Bees, or Private Vices, Publick Benefits* (1714) (Oxford: Clarendon Press, 1924; reprinted Indianapolis: Liberty*Classics*, 1988).
21. Foucault means "last year." See *Sécurité, Territoire, Population*; *Security, Territory, Population*, lectures of 18 January and 5 April 1978.
22. Condorcet (Jean-Antoine-Nicolas Caritat, marquis de, 1743-1794), *Esquisse d'un tableau historique des progrès de l'espirit humain* (1793), Ninth era (Paris: Garnier-Flammarion, 1988) p. 219: "How, in this astonishing variety of works and products, of needs and resources, in this frightening complication of interests, which links the isolated individual's subsistence and well-being to the general system of societies, which makes him dependent on all the accidents of nature and every political event, which, as it were, extends his capacity to experience enjoyment or privation to the entire globe, how, in this apparent chaos, do we see nonetheless, through a general law of the moral world, the efforts each makes for himself serving the well-being of all, and, despite the external clash of opposed interests, the common interest requires that each knows how to interpret his own interest and is able pursue it without obstruction?" [See below, note 28; G.B.]
23. Adam Smith, *An Inquiry into the Nature and Causes of the Wealth of Nations*, eds. R.H. Campbell and A.S. Skinner (Oxford: Oxford University Press, 1976), Vol. I, Book IV, ch. 2, p. 456.
24. Nicolas Malebranche (1638-1715), philosopher and theologian, member of the Oratorians. Foucault is referring here to the "occasionalist" thesis, or theory of "occasional causes," defended by Malebranche in several of his works—*De la Recherche de la vérité* (1674), XV$^{e}$ Éclaircissment, *Œuvres,* t. I (Paris: Gallimard, 1979) pp. 969-1014; *Entretiens sur la métaphysique et la religion* (1688), VII, *Œuvres*, t. II (1992) pp. 777-800, etcetera—according to which "only God is a real cause. What we call a natural cause is not at all a real and genuine cause, but simply, if we insist on keeping the name, an occasional cause, which, as a consequence of general laws, determines that God manifests his action, which alone is effective, in this way" (V. Delbos, "Malebrance et Maine de Biran," *Revue de métaphysique*, 1916, pp. 147-148). This omnipresent, but hidden God is the source of every movement and active inclination: "God, who alone can act in us, is now hidden from our eyes; his operations are not perceptible, and although he produces and conserves every being, the mind that so ardently seeks the cause of every thing has difficulty recognizing it, although it encounters it at every moment" (*De la Recherche de la vérité*, XV$^{e}$ Éclaircissement, p. 969). On the theological sources of Smith's conception of the "invisible hand," see J. Viner, *The*

*Role of Providence in Social Order* (Philadelphia: Independence Square, 1972) ch. 3: "The invisible hand and the economic order."

25. A. Smith, *An Inquiry into the Nature and Causes of the Wealth of Nations*, p. 456: "Nor is it always the worse for the society that it [the end, promotion of the publick interest] was no part of it [the individual's intention]."
26. Ibid. Smith adds: "and very few words need be employed in dissuading them from it."
27. On this necessary "blindness," see above, lecture of 21 February 1979, the analysis of the Rule of law and the criticism of planning according to Hayek.
28. Adam Smith, *An Inquiry into the Nature and Causes of the Wealth of Nations*, p. 456: "By pursuing his own interest he frequently promotes that of the society more effectually than when he really intends to promote it." [The words Foucault attributes to Adam Smith here are in fact from Condorcet's *Esquisse d'un tableau historique des progrès de l'espirit humain*, quoted above in note 22. But see too, Smith, p. 531: "But the law ought always to trust people with the care of their own interest, as in their local situations they must generally be able to judge better of it than their legislator can do" and p. 540: "The natural effort of every individual to better his own condition ... is so powerful a principle, that it is alone, and without any assistance, not only capable of carrying on the society to wealth and prosperity, but of surmounting a hundred impertinent obstructions with which the folly of human laws too often incumbers its operations"; G.B.]
29. Adam Ferguson, *An Essay on the History of Civil Society*, ed. Duncan Forbes (Edinburgh: Edinburgh University Press, 1966). Ferguson's *Essay* was first published in Edinburgh in 1767. The French translation by M. Bergier, *Essai sur l'histoire de la société civile*, appeared in the Librairie Mme Yves Desaint in 1783, although the text was printed five years previously. This translation, revised and corrected, was republished with an important introduction by C. Gautier (Paris: PUF, 1992).
30. Adam Ferguson, *An Essay on the History of Civil Society*, p. 144. The sentence ends with these words "and the solid basis of commerce withdrawn."
31. Ibid. p. 144: "the event has shewn, that private interest is a better patron of commerce and plenty, than the refinements of state. One nation lays the refined plan of a settlement on the continent of North America, and trusts little to the conduct of traders and short-sighted men; another leaves men to find their own position in a state of freedom, and to think of themselves. The active industry and limited views of the one, made a thriving settlement; the great projects of the other were still in idea."
32. A. Smith, *An Inquiry into the Nature and Causes of the Wealth of Nations*, p. 687: "Every man, as long as he does not violate the laws of justice, is left perfectly free to pursue his own interest in his own way, and to bring both his industry and capital into competition with those of any other man, or order of men."
33. Ibid.
34. Ibid.
35. On the way in which Foucault interprets the Kantian critique at this time, see his lecture the previous year, "Qu'est-ce que la critique?" delivered on 27 May 1978 at the Société française de philosophie, *Bulletin de la société française de philosophie*, no. 2, April-June 1990, pp. 38-39 (not included in *Dits et Écrits*).
36. See *Sécurité, Territoire, Population*; *Security, Territory, Population*, lectures of 29 March and 5 April 1978.
37. See above, lecture of 17 January 1979 and *Sécurité, Territoire, Population*; *Security, Territory, Population*, lectures of 18 January and 5 April 1978.

twelve

# 4 APRIL 1979

*Elements for a history of the notion of* homo œconomicus *(II).* ~ *Return to the problem of the limitation of sovereign power by economic activity.* ~ *The emergence of a new field, the correlate of the liberal art of government: civil society.* ~ Homo œconomicus *and civil society: inseparable elements of liberal governmental technology.* ~ *Analysis of the notion of "civil society": its evolution from Locke to Ferguson. Ferguson's* An Essay on the History of Civil Society *(1787). The four essential characteristics of civil society according to Ferguson: (1) it is an historical-natural constant; (2) it assures the spontaneous synthesis of individuals. Paradox of the economic bond; (3) it is a permanent matrix of political power; (4) it is the motor of history.* ~ *Appearance of a new system of political thought.* ~ *Theoretical consequences: (a) the question of the relations between state and society. The German, English, and French problematics; (b) the regulation of political power: from the wisdom of the prince to the rational calculations of the governed.* ~ *General conclusion.*

LAST WEEK I TOUCHED on the theme of *homo œconomicus* which has permeated economic thought, and especially liberal thought, since around the middle of the eighteenth century. I tried to show how *homo œconomicus* was a sort of non-substitutable and irreducible atom of interest. I tried to show that this atom of interest could not be superimposed on, was not identifiable with, and was not reducible to the essential characteristics of the subject of right in juridical thought; that *homo œconomicus* and the subject of right were therefore not superposable, and finally that *homo œconomicus* and the subject of right are not integrated into their respective domains according to the same dialectic, that is to say, that the subject of right is integrated into the system of other subjects of right by a dialectic of the renunciation of his own rights or their transfer to someone else, while *homo œconomicus* is integrated into the system of which he is a part, into the economic domain, not by a transfer, subtraction, or dialectic of renunciation, but by a dialectic of spontaneous multiplication.

I also tried to show that this difference, this irreducibility of *homo œconomicus* to the subject of right entails an important modification with regard to the sovereign and the exercise of sovereign power. In fact, the sovereign is not in the same position vis-à-vis *homo œconomicus* as he is vis-à-vis the subject of right. The subject of right may well, at least in some conceptions and analyses, appear as that which limits the exercise of sovereign power. But *homo œconomicus* is not satisfied with limiting the sovereign's power; to a certain extent, he strips the sovereign of power. Is power removed in the name of a right that the sovereign must not touch? No, that's not what's involved. *Homo œconomicus* strips the sovereign of power inasmuch as he reveals an essential, fundamental, and major incapacity of the sovereign, that is to say, an inability to master the totality of the economic field. The sovereign cannot fail to be blind vis-à-vis the economic domain or field as a whole. The whole set of economic process cannot fail to elude a would-be central, totalizing bird's-eye view. Let's say that in the classical conception of the sovereign in the Middle Ages, and still in the seventeenth century, there was something above the sovereign which was impenetrable, and this was God's intentions. A sovereign could be absolute and marked out as God's representative on Earth, but the designs of Providence still eluded him and encompassed him in their destiny. Now, beneath the sovereign, there is something which equally eludes him, and this is not the designs of Providence or God's laws but the labyrinths and complexities of the economic field. To that extent I think the emergence of the notion of *homo œconomicus* represents a sort of political challenge to the traditional, juridical conception, whether absolutist or not, of the sovereign.

So, in relation to this, and considering things very abstractly and schematically, I think there were two possible solutions. We can say that if economic practice or economic activity, if the set of processes of production and exchange elude the sovereign, then, very well, we will limit the sovereign's sovereignty geographically, so to speak, and fix a sort of frontier to the exercise of his power: the sovereign will be able to intervene everywhere except in the market. The market will be, if you like, a sort of free port or free space in the general space of sovereignty. This is the first possibility. The second possibility is the concrete proposal supported by the physiocrats. It consists in saying that the sovereign really must respect the market, but this does not mean that there will be a sort of zone within his sovereignty in which he will not be able to intervene or from which he is excluded. Rather, it means that vis-à-vis the market the sovereign will have to exercise a completely different power than the political power he has exercised hitherto. Vis-à-vis the market and the economic process, the sovereign will not be someone who, by some right, possesses an absolute decision-making power. His relationship to the market will have to be like that of a geometer to geometrical realities, that is to say, he will have to recognize it: he will have to recognize it through an *évidence* which will put him in a position of both passivity with regard to the intrinsic necessity of the economic process and, at the same time, of supervision and, as it were, checking, or rather of total and constant verification of this process. In other words, in the physiocrats' perspective the sovereign will have to pass from political activity to theoretical passivity in relation to the economic process. He will become a sort of geometer of the economic domain forming part of his field of sovereignty. The first solution, that of limiting the activity of the sovereign to everything not pertaining to the market, consists in maintaining the same form of governmental reason, the same form of *raison d'État*, by simply carrying out a subtraction of the market object, or of the market or economic domain. The second solution, that of the physiocrats, consists in maintaining the full extent of the activity of governmentality, but fundamentally altering the very nature of this activity, since it changes its coefficient, its index, and from governmental activity it becomes theoretical passivity, or alternatively it becomes *évidence*.

In actual fact, neither of these solutions was able to be any more than a theoretical and programmatic virtuality which was never really applied in history. A complete [readjustment (*rééquilibrage*)],* a complete reorganization of government reason was carried out on the basis of this problem of the specificity of *homo œconomicus* and his irreducibility to the sphere of right. More precisely, let's say that the problem which is posed by the simultaneous and correlative appearance of the problematic of the market, of the price mechanism, and of *homo œconomicus* is this: the art of government must be exercised in a space of sovereignty—and it is the law of the state which says this—but the trouble, misfortune, or problem is that this space turns out to be inhabited by economic subjects. Now, if we take things literally and grasp the irreducibility of the economic subject to the subject of right, then these economic subjects require either the sovereign's abstention, or the subordination of his rationality, his art of governing, to a scientific and speculative rationality. What can be done to ensure that the sovereign does not surrender any of his domains of action and that he is not converted into a geometer of the economy? Juridical theory is unable to take on and resolve the question of how to govern in a space of sovereignty inhabited by economic subjects, since precisely (as I tried to show last week) the juridical theory of the subject of right, of natural rights, and of the granting and delegation of rights does not fit together and cannot be fitted together with the mechanical idea, the very designation and characterization of *homo œconomicus*. Consequently, neither the market in itself, in its specific mechanism, nor Quesnay's scientific Table, nor the juridical notion of the contract can define and delimit in what respects and how the economic men inhabiting the field of sovereignty are governable.† The governability or governmentability—forgive these barbaric terms—of these individuals, who inhabit the space of sovereignty

---

* M.F.: *une rééquilibration*

† Foucault adds: I was going to say government ... , yes governable
Manuscript: "governmentable (*gouvernementables*)."

as subjects of right and, at the same time, as economic men, can only be assured, and in reality it was only possible for it to be assured, by the emergence of a new object, a new domain or field which is, as it were, the correlate of the art of government being constructed at this time in terms of this problem of the relation between the subject of right and the economic subject. A new plane of reference is needed, and clearly this new plane of reference will not be the set of subjects of right, or the set of merchants, or economic subjects or actors. These individuals who are still subjects of rights as well as being economic actors, but who are not "governmentable"* as one or the other, are only governable insofar as a new ensemble can be defined which will envelop them both as subjects of right and as economic actors, but which will bring to light not just the connection or combination of these two elements, but a series of other elements in relation to which the subject of right and the economic subject will be aspects, partial aspects, which can be integrated insofar as they belong to a complex whole. And I think it is this new ensemble that is characteristic of the liberal art of governing.

Let's say again, that for governmentality to preserve its global character over the whole space of sovereignty, for it not to be subject to a scientific and economic reason which would entail the sovereign having to be either a geometer of the economy or a functionary of economic science, for the art of governing not to have to split into two branches of an art of governing economically and an art of governing juridically, in short, to preserve the unity and generality of the art of governing over the whole sphere of sovereignty, and to keep the specificity and autonomy of the art of governing with respect to economic science, to answer these three questions, the art of governing must be given a reference, a domain or field of reference, a new reality on which it will be exercised, and I think this new field of reference is civil society.

What is civil society? Well, all in all, I think the notion and analysis of civil society, the set of objects or elements that are brought to light in the framework of this notion of civil society, amount to an attempt to answer the question I have just mentioned: how to govern, according to

* In inverted commas in the manuscript.

the rules of right, a space of sovereignty which for good or ill is inhabited by economic subjects? How can a reason, a rational principle be found for limiting, other than by right or by the domination of economic science, a governmental practice which must take responsibility for the heterogeneity of the economic and the juridical? Civil society is not a philosophical idea therefore. Civil society is, I believe, a concept of governmental technology, or rather, it is the correlate of a technology of government the rational measure of which must be juridically pegged to an economy understood as process of production and exchange. The problem of civil society is the juridical structure (*économie juridique*) of a governmentality pegged to the economic structure (*économie économique*). And I think that civil society—which is very quickly called society, and which at the end of the eighteenth century is called the nation—makes a self-limitation possible for governmental practice and an art of government, for reflection on this art of government and so for a governmental technology; it makes possible a self-limitation which infringes neither economic laws nor the principles of right, and which infringes neither the requirement of governmental generality nor the need for an omnipresence of government. An omnipresent government, a government which nothing escapes, a government which conforms to the rules of right, and a government which nevertheless respects the specificity of the economy, will be a government that manages civil society, the nation, society, the social.

*Homo œconomicus* and civil society are therefore two inseparable* elements. *Homo œconomicus* is, if you like, the abstract, ideal, purely economic point that inhabits the dense, full, and complex reality of civil society. Or alternatively, civil society is the concrete ensemble within which these ideal points, economic men, must be placed so that they can be appropriately managed. So, *homo œconomicus* and civil society belong to the same ensemble of the technology of liberal governmentality.

You know how often civil society has been invoked, and not just in recent years. Since the nineteenth century, civil society has always been referred to in philosophical discourse, and also in political discourse, as

---

* M.F.: indispensable

a reality which asserts itself, struggles, and rises up, which revolts against and is outside government or the state, or the state apparatuses or institutions. I think we should be very prudent regarding the degree of reality we accord to this civil society. It is not an historical-natural given which functions in some way as both the foundation of and source of opposition to the state or political institutions. Civil society is not a primary and immediate reality; it is something which forms part of modern governmental technology. To say that it belongs to governmental technology does not mean that it is purely and simply its product or that it has no reality. Civil society is like madness and sexuality, what I call transactional realities (*réalités de transaction*). That is to say, those transactional and transitional figures that we call civil society, madness, and so on, which, although they have not always existed are nonetheless real, are born precisely from the interplay of relations of power and everything which constantly eludes them, at the interface, so to speak, of governors and governed. Civil society, therefore, is an element of transactional reality in the history of governmental technologies, a transactional reality which seems to me to be absolutely correlative to the form of governmental technology we call liberalism, that is to say, a technology of government whose objective is its own self-limitation insofar as it is pegged to the specificity of economic processes.

A few words, now, on this civil society and what characterizes it. I would like to try to show, at least in principle, because we are now coming to the end of the lectures, how this notion of civil society may indeed resolve the problems I have just tried to indicate. So, to start with, I will make a deplorably banal remark about civil society, namely, that the notion of civil society completely changed during the eighteenth century. Practically until the start of the second half of the eighteenth century, civil society designated something very different from what it will subsequently designate. In Locke, for example, civil society is precisely a society characterized by a juridical-political structure. It is society, the set of individuals who are linked to each other through a juridical and political bond. In this sense, the notion of civil society is absolutely indistinguishable from political society. In Locke's *Second Treatise of Government*, chapter 7 is entitled: "Of Political or Civil Society."[1] So, until then, civil society is always a society characterized by the existence of a juridical and political bond. It is from the second half of the eighteenth century, precisely at the time when the questions of political economy and of the governmentality of economic processes and subjects are being addressed, that the notion of civil society will change, if not totally, then at least in a significant way, and it will be thoroughly reorganized.

Of course, the notion of civil society is presented from different angles and in various forms throughout the second half of the eighteenth century. To simplify matters, I will take the most fundamental, almost statutory text regarding the characterization of civil society. This is Ferguson's famous text, translated into French in 1783 with the title *Essais sur l'histoire de la société civile*,[2] and which is very close to Adam Smith's *Wealth of Nations*, the word "nation" in Smith, moreover, having more or less the same meaning as civil society in Ferguson.[3] We have here the political correlate, the correlate in terms of civil society, of what Adam Smith studied in purely economic terms. Ferguson's civil society is actually the concrete, encompassing element within which the economic men Smith tried to study operate. I would like to pick out three or four essential characteristics of this civil society in Ferguson: first, civil society understood as an historical-natural constant; second, civil society as principle of spontaneous synthesis; third, civil society as permanent matrix of political power; and fourth, civil society as the motor element of history.

First, civil society as an historical-natural constant. For Ferguson, in fact, civil society is a given beyond which there is nothing to be found. Nothing exists before civil society, says Ferguson, or if something exists, it is absolutely inaccessible to us, so withdrawn in the depths of time, so anterior, so to speak, to what gives man his humanity, that it is impossible to know what really could have taken place before the existence of civil society. Whether this non-society is described in terms of solitude and isolation, as if there could have been men scattered in nature without any union or means of communication, or whether it is described, as in Hobbes, in the form of an endless war or of a war of all against all, in any case, all this—solitude or war of all against all—should be located in a sort of mythical background which is of no use in the analysis of the phenomena which concern us. Human history has always existed "taken in groups," Ferguson says on page four of the first volume of his *Essay on the History of Civil Society*.[4] On page six he says society is "as old as the individual," and it would be as idle to imagine men not speaking to each other as it would be to imagine them without feet or hands.[5] Language, communication, and so a certain constant relationship between men is absolutely typical of the individual and society, because the individual and society cannot exist without each other. In short, there was never a moment, or anyway it is pointless trying to imagine a moment when we passed from nature to history, or from non-society to society. The nature of human nature is to be historical, because the nature of human nature is to be social. There is no human nature which is separable from the very fact of society. Ferguson evokes the kind of myth or methodological utopia which was often taken up in the eighteenth century: Take a group of children, he says, who have been left to bring themselves up outside any other form of society. Imagine some children put in a desert and left to fend for themselves from the youngest age, and to develop all alone, without instruction or guidance. Well, what will we see if we return five, ten, or fifteen years later, provided, of course, that they are not dead? "We would see the members of this little society eating and sleeping, herding together and playing, developing a language, dividing and quarreling," striking up friendships and forsaking their own self-preservation for the sake of others.[6] So, the social bond develops spontaneously. There is no specific operation to establish or found it. There is no need of the institution or self-institution of society. We are in society anyway. The social bond has no pre-history. Saying that the social bond has no pre-history means that it is both permanent and indispensable. Permanent means that however far back we go in the history of humanity, we will find not only society, of course, but nature. That is to say, there is no need to look somewhere else for the state of nature sought by philosophers in the reality or myth of the savage, we can find it right here. We will find the state of nature in France as well as at the Cape of Good Hope, since the state of nature requires man to live in the social state.[7] Society studied even in its most complex and developed forms, society with the greatest state of consistency will always tell us what the state of nature is, since the state of nature requires us to live in society. So, the state of nature is permanent in the state of society, and the state of society is also indispensable for the state of nature, that is to say, the state of nature can never appear in the naked and simple state. Ferguson says: "In the condition of the savage, as well as in that of the citizen, are many proofs of human invention."[8] And he adds this phrase which is characteristic, not because it is a sort of point of origin, but because it points towards the theoretical possibility of an anthropology: "If the palace be unnatural, the cottage is so no less."[9] That is to say, the primitive cottage is not the natural and pre-social expression of something. We are not closer to nature with a primitive cottage than with a palace. It is simply a different distribution, a different form of the necessary intertwining of the social and the natural, since the social is part of the natural and the natural is always conveyed by the social. So, we have the principle that civil society is an historical-natural constant for humanity.

Second, civil society assures the spontaneous synthesis of individuals. This returns us to what I have just said: spontaneous synthesis means there is no explicit contract, no voluntary union, no renunciation of rights, and no delegation of natural rights to someone else; in short, there is no constitution of sovereignty by a sort of pact of subjection. In fact, if civil society actually carries out a synthesis, it will quite simply be through a summation of individual satisfactions within the social bond itself. "How," Ferguson says, "can we conceive a happy public if its members, considered apart, be unhappy?"[10] In other words, there is reciprocity between the whole and its components. Basically, we cannot say, we cannot imagine or conceive an individual to be happy if the whole to which he belongs is not happy. Better, we cannot even assess exactly an individual's quality, value, and virtue, we cannot attribute a coefficient of good or evil to the individual unless we think of it [the coefficient] in the reciprocity, or at any rate unless we think of it on the basis of the place he occupies, the role he performs, and the effects he produces within the whole. Every element of civil society is assessed by the good it will produce or bring about for the whole. We can say that a man is good, that he is fine only insofar as he is right for the place he occupies and, Ferguson says, "produces the effect it must produce."[11] But conversely, the value of the whole is not an absolute and is not to be attributed to the whole and only the whole, but to each member of this whole: "it is likewise true, that the happiness of individuals is the great end of civil society."[12]

So you can see that we are not dealing with a mechanism or system of the exchange of rights. We are dealing with a mechanism of immediate multiplication that has in fact the same form as the immediate multiplication of profit in the purely economic mechanism of interests. The form is the same, but not the elements and contents. And this is why civil society can be both the support of the economic process and economic bonds, while overflowing them and being irreducible to them. For in civil society, that which joins men together is indeed a mechanism analogous to that of interests, but they are not interests in the strict sense, they are not economic interests. Civil society is much more than the association of different economic subjects, although the form in which this bond is established is such that economic subjects will be able to find a place and economic egoism will be able to play its role within it. In fact, what links individuals in civil society is not maximum profit from exchange, it is a series of what could be called "disinterested interests." What will this be? Well, Ferguson says, what links individuals to each other in civil society is instinct, sentiment, and sympathy, it is the impulses of benevolence individuals feel for each other, but is also the loathing of others, repugnance for the misfortune of individuals, but possibly the pleasure taken in the misfortune of others with whom one will break.[13] This, then, is the first difference between the bonds that bring economic subjects together and those that bring together individuals belonging to civil society: there is a distinct set of non-egoist interests, a distinct interplay of non-egoist, disinterested interests which is much wider than egoism itself.

The second, equally important difference that we see emerging by bringing in these elements I have just been talking about is that the bond between economic subjects is, if you like, non-local. The analysis of the market proves that the multiplication of profits will ultimately be brought about through the spontaneous synthesis of egoisms over the whole surface of the globe. There is no localization, no territoriality, no particular grouping in the total space of the market. On the other hand, in civil society the bonds of sympathy and benevolence between some individuals are, as I was saying, the correlates of contrary bonds of repugnance and the absence of support for or benevolence towards others. This means that civil society always appears as a limited ensemble, as one particular ensemble among others. Civil society does not coincide with humanity in general; it exists in the form of ensembles at the same or different levels which bring individuals together in a number of units. Civil society, Ferguson says, leads the individual to enlist "on the side of one tribe or community."[14] Civil society is not humanitarian but communitarian. And in fact we see civil society appear in the family, village, and corporation, and, of course, at higher levels, reaching that of the nation in Adam Smith's sense, [in the sense given to it]* at more or less the same time in France. The nation is precisely one of the major forms, [but] only one of the possible forms, of civil society.

Having said this, you can see that the bond of economic interest occupies an ambiguous position in relation to these bonds of disinterested interests which take the form of local units and different levels.† On the one hand, you can see that the economic bond, the economic process which brings economic subjects together, will be able to lodge itself in this form of immediate multiplication which does not involve the renunciation of rights. Formally, therefore, civil society serves as the medium of the economic bond. But the economic bond plays a very strange role within civil society, where it finds a place, since while it brings individuals together through the spontaneous convergence of interests, it is also a principle of dissociation at the same time. The economic bond is a principle of dissociation with regard to the active bonds of compassion, benevolence, love for one's fellows, and sense of community, inasmuch as it constantly tends to undo what the spontaneous bond of civil society has joined together by picking out the egoist interest of individuals, emphasizing it, and making it more incisive. In other words, the economic bond arises within civil society, is only possible through [civil society], and in a way strengthens it, but in another way it undoes it. Thus, on page nineteen of the *Essay on the History of Civil*

---

* M.F.: as it is employed

† Foucault adds: which (have the look?) of communitarian bonds [*words difficult to hear*]

*Society*, Ferguson says: The bond between individuals is never stronger than when the individual has no direct interest; it is never stronger than when it is a question of sacrificing oneself for a friend, for example, or of staying with one's tribe rather than seeking abundance and security elsewhere.[15] It is very interesting that this corresponds exactly to how economic rationality is defined. When the economic subject sees that he can make a profit by buying wheat in Canada, for example, and selling it in England, he will do so. He does it because it is to his advantage, and furthermore it will benefit everyone. However, the bonds of civil society mean that one prefers to stay in one's community, even if one finds abundance and security elsewhere. So, it is "in a commercial state where men may be supposed to have experienced, in its full extent, the interest which individuals have in the preservation of their country* ... that man is sometimes found a detached and solitary being: he has found an object which sets him in competition with his fellow-creatures."[16] Consequently, the more we move towards an economic state, the more, paradoxically, the constitutive bond of civil society is weakened and the more the individual is isolated by the economic bond he has with everyone and anyone. This is the second characteristic of civil society: a spontaneous synthesis within which the economic bond finds its place, but which this same economic bond continually threatens.

The third characteristic of civil society is that it is a permanent matrix of political power. How does power come to a civil society which in a way plays the spontaneous role of the social contract, of the *pactum unionis*? What is the equivalent of the jurists' *pactum subjectionis*, the pact of subjection, which obliges obedience to certain individuals? Well, just as there is no need of a *pactum unionis* to join individuals together in civil society, so for political power to emerge and function within civil society there is no need of a *pactum subjectionis*, of the surrender of certain rights and the acceptance of someone else's sovereignty. There is a spontaneous formation of power. How does this come about? It is brought about

* Foucault stops here, not managing to read what he has written ("... fine, listen, the text roughly says this, as in Medieval manuscripts, the manuscript is a bit spoiled"), but the quotation [from the French translation; G.B.] he gives is accurate, apart from a minor variation.

quite simply by a de facto bond which links different concrete individuals to each other. In fact, these differences between individuals are expressed, of course, in the different roles they play in society and in the different tasks they perform. These spontaneous differences immediately give rise to divisions of labor in the collective decision-making processes of the group: some give their views, others give orders; some reflect, others obey. "Prior to any political institution whatever," says Ferguson, "men are qualified by a great diversity of talents, by a different tone of the soul, and ardour of the passions, to act a variety of parts. Bring them together, each will find his place. They censure or applaud in a body; they consult and deliberate in more select parties; they take or give an ascendant as individuals."[17] That is to say, in civil society the group's decision appears to be the decision of the whole group, but when we look more closely at how this takes place we see that the decisions were taken, he says, in "more select parties." As individuals, some have assumed authority and others have allowed these to acquire authority over them. Consequently, the fact of power precedes the right that establishes, justifies, limits, or intensifies it; power already exists before it is regulated, delegated, or legally established. "We follow a leader, before we have settled the ground of his pretensions, or adjusted the form of his election: and it is not till after mankind have committed many errors in the capacities of magistrate and subject, that they think of making government itself a subject of rules."[18] The juridical structure of power always comes after the event or fact of power itself.* So it cannot be said that men were isolated, that they decided to constitute a power, and then here they are living in a state of society. This was, roughly, the analysis made in the seventeenth and at the start of the eighteenth century. But neither can we say that men join together in society and then [think]: Wouldn't it be good, or convenient, or useful to establish a power and regulate its modalities. In actual fact, civil society permanently, and from the very start, secretes a power that is neither

---

* Foucault adds: In short, civil society secretes its own power that is neither its first condition nor its supplement.
The sentence is repeated a bit below.

its condition nor supplement. "It is obvious," Ferguson says, "that some mode of subordination is as necessary to men as society itself."[19] You recall that Ferguson said that we cannot conceive of a man without society. We cannot conceive of a man without language and communication, no more than we can conceive of a man without hands and feet. Thus man, his nature, his feet, his hands, his language, others, communication, society, and power all constitute an interdependent whole characteristic of civil society.

The fourth characteristic of civil society is that it constitutes what could be called—using a word from much later which to some extent is now discredited but which it seems to me may find a first point of application here—the motor of history. It is the motor of history precisely because, if we take up the two elements I have been talking about—on the one hand, civil society as spontaneous synthesis and spontaneous subordination, and, [on the other], the existence of an element which finds its place quite naturally within this spontaneous synthesis and subordination but which is also the principle of dissociation, namely interest, the egoism of *homo œconomicus*, the economic processes—then [first of all], with the idea of civil society as spontaneous synthesis and subordination we have the principle, or theme, or idea, or hypothesis that we are dealing with a stable equilibrium. After all, since men are spontaneously brought together by bonds of benevolence, and since they form communities in which subordination is established by immediate consent, then it should not change and consequently everything should remain in place. And, in actual fact, there are a number of communities which appear with this first aspect of, I would say, if you like, a functional equilibrium of the whole. On page 86, describing North American savages, or reporting observations of North American savages, Ferguson says: "Thus, without any settled form of government, or any explicit bond of union, and by an effect in which instinct seems to have a greater part than reason [the families of these North American savages] conducted themselves with the intelligence, the concert, and the force of a nation. Foreigners, without being able to discover who is the magistrate ( ... ) always find a council with whom they may treat ( ... ). Without police or compulsory laws, their domestic society is conducted with order."[20] So, there is a spontaneous bond and spontaneous equilibrium.

However, precisely inasmuch as within this spontaneous bond there is another, equally spontaneous, but dissociative bond, then disequilibrium is introduced as a result, either spontaneously or by virtue of the economic mechanism. Sometimes Ferguson refers to pure and simple egoism: "He who first ranged himself under a leader," he says, "did not perceive, that he was setting the example of a permanent subordination, under the pretence of which, the rapacious were to seize his possessions, and the arrogant to lay claim to his service."[21] So, there is a mechanism of dissociation which is due simply to the egoism of power. But more frequently and regularly Ferguson invokes actual economic interest and the way in which economic egoism takes shape as the principle of dissociation of the spontaneous equilibrium of civil society. This is how—and here I refer you to those famous texts—Ferguson explains how civil societies regularly pass through three stages: savagery, barbarism, and civilization.[22] How is savagery characterized? The characteristic feature of savagery is precisely and above all a certain way of fulfilling or effectuating the interests of economic egoisms. What is savage society? It is a society of hunting, fishing, and natural production, without agriculture or cattle-rearing. It is therefore a society without property in which some elements, the beginnings of subordination and government are found.[23] And then, with economic interests and egoisms coming into play, with everyone wanting their own share, we move on to barbaric society. As a result we have—I was going to say a new mode of production—we have new economic-political institutions: herds belonging to individuals, pastures belonging either to communities or to individuals. Private society begins to be established, but a private society which is not yet guaranteed by laws, and at this point civil society takes on the form of relations between patron and client, master and servant, family and slave, and so on.[24] You can see that in this we have a specifically economic mechanism which shows how, starting from civil society and from the economic game which it harbors within itself, so to speak, we move on to a whole series of historical transformations. The principle of dissociative association is also a principle of historical transformation. That which produces the unity of the social fabric is at the same time that which produces the principle of historical transformation and the constant rending of the social fabric.

In the theory of *homo œconomicus* which I talked about last week, you [recall] how the collective interest arose from a necessarily blind interplay between different egoistical interests. Now you find the same kind of schema of an effect of totality, of a global reality arising through the blindness of each individual, but with regard to history. The history of humanity in its overall effects, its continuity, and in its general and recurrent forms—savage, barbarous, civilized, and so on—is nothing other than the perfectly logical, decipherable, and identifiable form or series of forms arising from blind initiatives, egoistic interests, and calculations which individuals only ever see in terms of themselves. If you multiply these calculations over time and get them to work, the economists say, the entire community will enjoy ever increasing benefits; Ferguson, however, in the name of civil society, says there will be an endless transformation of civil society. I do not mean that this is the entry of civil society into history, since it is always in history, but that this is the motor of history in civil society. It is egoistic interest, and consequently the economic game which introduces the dimension through which history is permanently present in civil society, the process through which civil society is inevitably and necessarily involved in history. "Mankind," he says on page 122, "in following the present sense of their minds, in striving to remove inconveniencies, or to gain apparent and contiguous advantages, arrive at ends which even their imagination could not anticipate, and pass on, like other animals, in the track of their nature, without perceiving its end. ( ... ) Like the winds, that come we know not whence, and blow withersoever they list, the forms of civil society* are derived from an obscure and distant origin."[25] In short, the mechanisms which permanently constitute civil society are therefore the same as those which permanently generate history in its general forms.

With this kind of analysis—which, once again, is only one example of the many analyses of civil society in the second half of the eighteenth century, or anyway, at the end of the eighteenth and the beginning of the nineteenth century—we are, I think, at an important crossroads, since, [first], we see a domain opening up of collective and political units

* The word "civil" is added by Foucault here; Ferguson has just "society."

constituted by social relations and bonds between individuals which go beyond the purely economic bond, yet without being purely juridical: civil society is characterized by bonds which are neither purely economic nor purely juridical, which cannot be superimposed on the structures of the contract and the game of rights conceded, delegated, and alienated, and which, in their nature if not their form, are also different from the economic game. Second, civil society is the articulation of history on the social bond. History is not the extension, like a pure and simple logical development, of a juridical structure given at the start. Nor is it a principle of degeneration producing negative phenomena which obscure the original transparency of a state of nature or original situation. There is a never-ending generation of history without degeneration, a generation which is not a juridical-logical sequence but the endless formation of new social fabric, new social relations, new economic structures, and consequently new types of government. Finally, third, civil society makes it possible to designate and show an internal and complex relationship between the social bond and relationships of authority in the form of government. These three elements—the opening up of a domain of non-juridical social relations, the articulation of history on the social bond, in a form which is not one of degeneration, and government as an organic component of the social bond and the social bond as an organic feature of the form of authority—are what distinguish the notion of civil society from (1) Hobbes, (2) Rousseau, and (3) Montesquieu. It seems to me that we enter into a completely different system of political thought and I think it is the thought or political reflection internal to a new technology of government, or to a new problem which the emergence of the economic problem raises for techniques and technologies of government.

I would like to move on now very quickly to conclude—or rather to open up a series of problems. On the one hand, you can see that with this notion of civil society we have a set of questions, problems, concepts, and possible analyses which enable us to avoid the theoretical and juridical problem of the original constitution of society. Certainly, this does not mean that the juridical problem of the exercise of power within civil society does not arise, but the way in which it is posed is reversed. In the seventeenth and eighteenth centuries the problem was how to find a juridical form at the origin of society, at the very root of society, which would limit the exercise of power in advance. Here, rather, we are dealing with an existing society with phenomena of subordination, and so of power, and the problem is simply how to regulate and limit power within a society in which subordination is already at work. It is in this way that the question which has obsessed practically all political thought from the end of the eighteenth century to the present arises, that is to say, the question of the relations between civil society and the state. Obviously, the problem could not be formulated in this way before the second half of the eighteenth century and it appears in the following way: With its juridical structure and institutional apparatus, what can the state do and how can it function in relation to something, society, which is already given?

I will just mention a series of possible solutions to this.[26] First the state will appear as one of the dimensions and forms of civil society. This is the theme developed by Jung-Stilling at the end of the eighteenth century, saying that society has three axes, the family, the household or estate, and then the state.[27] Then there will be the, let's say, genetic and historical analysis of Bensen, for example, which says that we should conceive of civil society as having passed through three stages: family society, civil society itself, and state society or society of state control.[28] And then there is the typological analysis you find in Schlözer, who says that several types of society can be found. There is an absolutely universal type which is valid for all time and especially for all space and in every part of the world, that is to say, there can be no society without this familial society. And then, he says, presently there is a type of society, civil society, which appears in all the forms of human gatherings presently known to us. As for the state, it characterizes some forms of civil society, those with which we are familiar today.[29] And, of course, there is Hegel—about whom I will not speak—and the state as the self-consciousness and ethical realization of civil society.[30]

Fine, I don't have time to dwell on all this. Let's say, if you like, for a whole range of easily imaginable reasons, civil society is analyzed in Germany in terms of the opposition and relation between civil society and the state. Civil society is only ever questioned in terms of its capacity to support a state, or inasmuch as the state is either the contradictory element in relation to civil society, or instead the element which reveals and finally realizes its truth. In England, and again for easily imaginable reasons, the analysis of civil society is developed in terms of government rather than in terms of the state, since the state has never been a problem for England. That is to say, the problem is whether there is need for a supplementary government if it is true that civil society is already there, that it ensures its own synthesis, and that it has a sort of internal governmentality. Does civil society really need a government? This is the famous question posed by Paine at the end of the eighteenth century and which will haunt English politics at least until the twentieth century: Could not society exist without government, or at any rate, without a government other than the government it has created spontaneously and without need of institutions which take charge of civil society, as it were, and impose constraints which it does not accept? Paine's question: We should not, he says, confuse society and government. "Society is produced by our wants, and government by our wickedness ... The one encourages intercourse, the other creates distinctions. The first is a patron [in the English sense of the word, a protector; M.F.], the last a punisher."[31] In France the problem is not posed in either the English or German terms.* The problem addressed in France is not that of "government in relation to civil society" or of "the state in relation to civil society." Here again, for well-known political and historical reasons, the problem is posed differently. The problem is that of the Third Estate as a political, theoretical, and historical problem up until the middle of the nineteenth century: the idea of the bourgeoisie as the element which was the vector and bearer of French history from the Middle Ages until the

---

* Foucault here diverges from the manuscript, pp. 20-21:

"In France, the problem was retranscribed in the debate on the need for a Declaration of the Rights of Man.

Rights of Man: a complex notion that conveys both the juridical idea of a natural right that it is the function of the political pact to guarantee [p. 21] and the idea of conditions that society imposes on the state so as to enable it to exist and to recognize its legitimacy.

This practice of Rights of Man is referred to a conception of democracy. To which rather, according to the English schema, liberals will oppose the idea that freedoms are what remain after one has delimited government action, that they are not to be fixed as right 'before the entrance into politics,' but to be obtained, preserved, and expanded by transactions, guarantees, an electoral system, opinion, and so on."

nineteenth century[32] is basically a way of posing the problem of civil society, of government and power in relation to civil society. Whether it is German philosophers, English political analysts, or French historians, I think you always find the same problem of civil society as the major problem of politics and political theory.

The other aspect, on which I will end this year's lectures, is, of course, that with this idea of civil society there is a redistribution, or a sort of re-centering/de-centering of the governmental reason I tried to talk about last year. Let's look again at the general problem. It seems to me that from the sixteenth century, and already in the Middle Ages moreover, we see the appearance of the [following] question: How can the exercise of power, that very singular practice which men cannot escape, except in part and at times in particular processes and individual or collective acts which pose a number of problems to jurists and historians, be regulated and measured in the person who governs? Well, let's say in a very general, overall way that for a long time the idea of regulating, measuring, and so limiting the indefinite exercise of power was sought in the wisdom of the person who would govern. Wisdom was the old answer. Wisdom means governing in accordance with the order of things. It means governing according to the knowledge of human and divine laws. It means governing according to God's prescriptions. It means governing according to what the general human and divine order may prescribe. In other words, when one sought to identify how the sovereign had to be wise and in what his wisdom consisted, one basically tried to regulate and model government in terms of the truth. It was the truth of religious texts, of revelation, and of the order of the world that had to be the principle of the regulation, or adjustment rather, of the exercise of power.

What I tried to show last year is that from the sixteenth and seventeenth century it does not seem that the exercise of power was adjusted in accordance with wisdom, but according to calculation, that is to say, the calculation of force, relations, wealth, and factors of strength. That is to say, one no longer tries to peg government to the truth; one tries to peg government to rationality. It seems to me that we could describe the modern forms of governmental technology as control of government by pegging it to rationality. Now, this adjustment to rationality—and again

I am being very schematic—has taken two successive forms. The rationality according to which power is regulated may take the form of the rationality of the state understood as sovereign individuality. In this case—this is the period of *raison d'État*—governmental rationality is the rationality of the sovereign himself, of whomever it is who can say "me, the state." This obviously raises a number of problems. First of all, what is this "me," or alternatively, what is this "I" that identifies the rationality of government with the rationality of a sovereign maximizing his own power? And thus the juridical question of the contract arises. There is also the factual question: How can this rationality of the sovereign who claims to say "I" be exercised with regard to problems like those of the market or, more generally, economic processes in which rationality not only completely dispenses with a unitary form but absolutely excludes both the unitary form and the bird's-eye view? Hence there is a new problem, the transition to a new form of rationality to which the regulation of government is pegged. It is now a matter not of modeling government on the rationality of the individual sovereign who can say "me, the state," [but] on the rationality of those who are governed as economic subjects and, more generally, as subjects of interest in the most general sense of the term. It is a matter of modeling government [on] the rationality of individuals insofar as they employ a certain number of means, and employ them as they wish, in order to satisfy these interests in the general sense of the term: the rationality of the governed must serve as the regulating principle for the rationality of government. This, it seems to me, is what characterizes liberal rationality: how to model government, the art of government, how to [found]* the principle of rationalization of the art of government on the rational behavior of those who are governed.

It seems to me that this is the important dividing point, the important transformation which I have tried to localize, but which is far from meaning that the rationality of state-individual or of the individual sovereign who can say "me, the state" is abandoned. We can even say, in a general, overall way, that the principle of rationality of all the nationalist

* M.F.: find

and statist politics will be pegged to the rationality or, if you prefer, in other terms, to the interest and to the strategy of interests of the individual sovereign, or of the state insofar as it constitutes a sovereign individuality. Similarly, we can say that government regulated according to the truth also has not disappeared. For after all, what in the end is something like Marxism if not the pursuit of a type of governmentality which will certainly be pegged to a rationality, but to a rationality which is not the rationality of individual interests, but the rationality of history progressively manifesting itself as truth? You can see that in the modern world, in the world we have known since the nineteenth century, a series of governmental rationalities overlap, lean on each other, challenge each other, and struggle with each other: art of government according to truth, art of government according to the rationality of the sovereign state, and art of government according to the rationality of economic agents, and more generally, according to the rationality of the governed themselves. And it is all these different arts of government, all these different types of ways of calculating, rationalizing, and regulating the art of government which, overlapping each other, broadly speaking constitute the object of political debate from the nineteenth century. What is politics, in the end, if not both the interplay of these different arts of government with their different reference points and the debate to which these different arts of government give rise? It seems to me that it is here that politics is born. Good, well that's it. Thank you.*

* (*A bit of a hubbub follows.*) Foucault responds briefly to a number of isolated questions and asks someone at some point if he has "any transcriptions of the lectures delivered last year and in previous years," "because," he says, "I don't have any."

---

1. John Locke, *The Second Treatise of Government*, ch. 7, "Of Political or Civil Society" in *Two Treatises of Government*, ed. Peter Laslett (Cambridge: Cambridge University Press, 1960) p. 361.
2. Adam Ferguson, *An Essay on the History of Civil Society*; French translation by C. Gautier, *Essai sur l'histoire de la société civile*. As C. Gautier notes, the *Essay* is actually a considerably expanded version of text written in 1755-56, but not published, with the title, *Treatise on Refinement*.
3. On this point, see P. Rosanvallon, *Le Capitalisme utopique* (Paris: Le Seuil, 1979) pp. 68-69 (republished with the title *Le Libéralisme économique. Histoire de l'idée de marché*, Paris: Le Seuil, 1989). Foucault acknowledged this "important book" in Spring 1979, in the Course Summary (see below, p. 320), and perhaps he was familiar with its content when he was giving these lectures.
4. A. Ferguson, *An Essay on the History of Civil Society*, p. 4: "Mankind are to be taken in groupes, as they have always subsisted."
5. Ibid. p. 6: "With [man] the society appears to be as old as the individual, and the use of the tongue as universal as that of the hand or the foot."
6. Ibid., p. 4: "The history of the individual is but a detail of the sentiments and thoughts he has entertained in the view of this species: and every experiment relative to this subject should be made with entire societies, not with single men. We have every reason, however, to believe, that in the case of such an experiment made, we shall suppose, with a colony of children transplanted from the nursery, and left to form a society apart, untaught, and undisciplined, we should only have the same things repeated, which, in so many different parts of the earth, have been transacted already. The members of our little society would feed and sleep, would herd together and play, would have a language of their own, would quarrel and divide, would be to one another the most important objects of the scene, and, in the ardour of their friendships and competitions, would overlook their personal danger, and suspend the care of their self-preservation."
7. Ibid., p. 8: "If we are asked, therefore, Where the state of nature is to be found? we may answer, It is here; and it matters not whether we are understood to speak in the island of Great Britain, at the Cape of Good Hope, or the Straits of Magellan. While this active being is in the train of employing his talents, and of operating on the subjects around him, all situations are equally natural."
8. Ibid.
9. Ibid.
10. Ibid., pp. 58: "if the public good be the principal object with individuals, it is likewise true, that the happiness of individuals is the great end of civil society: for in what sense can a public enjoy any good, if its members, considered apart, be unhappy?"
11. Ibid., pp. 57-58: "[Man] must forgo his happiness and his freedom, where these interfere with the good of society. He is only part of the whole; and the praise we think due to his virtue, is but a branch of that more general commendation we bestow on the member of a body, on the part of a fabric or engine, for being well fitted to occupy its place, and to produce its effect."
12. Ibid., p. 58. See above, note 10.
13. See Part One, section 3, "Of the principles of Union among Mankind" and section 4, "Of the principles of War and Dissension."
14. Ibid., p. 11: "[Man] has one set of dispositions which refer to his animal preservation, and to the continuance of his race; another which lead to society, and by inlisting him on the side of one tribe or community, frequently engage him in war and contention with the rest of mankind."
15. Ibid., p. 19: "Men are so far from valuing society on account of its mere external conveniences, that they are commonly most attached where those conveniences are least frequent; and are there most faithful, where the tribute of their allegiance is paid in blood."
16. Ibid., p. 19. The sentence continues: "and he deals with them as he does with his cattle and his soil, for the sake of the profits they bring."
17. Ibid., p. 63: "Prior to any political institution whatever, men are qualified by a great diversity of talents, by a different tone of the soul, and ardour of the passions, to act a variety of

parts. Bring them together, each will find his place. They censure or applaud in a body; they consult and deliberate in more select parties; they take or give an ascendant as individuals."

18. Ibid., p. 63.
19. Ibid.
20. Ibid., p. 86: "Thus, without any settled form of government, or any bond of union, but what resembled more the suggestion of instinct, than the invention of reason, they conducted themselves with the concert, and the force of nations. Foreigners, without being able to discover who is the magistrate, or in what manner the senate is composed, always find a council with whom they may treat, or a band of warriors with whom they may fight. Without police or compulsory laws, their domestic society is conducted with order, and the absence of vicious dispositions, is a better security than any public establishment for the suppression of crimes."
21. Ibid., p. 122.
22. See Parts Two and Three. On these stages of social development, Foucault had read, in particular, R.L. Meek, *Economics and Ideology and other essays* (London: Chapman & Hall, 1967) pp. 34-40.
23. *An Essay*, p. 81: "Of the nations who dwell in those, or any other of the less cultivated parts of the earth, some intrust their subsistence chiefly to hunting, fishing, or the natural produce of the soil. They have little attention to property, and scarcely any beginnings of subordination or government."
24. Ibid., p. 81: "Others having possessed themselves of herds, and depending for their provision on pasture, know what it is to be poor and rich. They know the relations of patron and client, of servant and master, and suffer themselves to be classed according to their measures of wealth."
25. Ibid., p. 122. The final sentence concludes: "they arise long before the date of philosophy, from the instincts, not from the speculations, of men."
26. See the article by M. Riedel, "Gesellschaft bürgerliche" in O. Brunner, W. Conze, R. Koselleck, eds., *Geschichtliche Grundbegriffe* (Stuttgart: E. Klett, 1975) t. 2, pp. 719-800, which was used by Foucault.
27. Johann Heinrich Jung-Stilling (1740-1817), *Die Grundlehre der Staatswirthschaft* (Marbourg: 1792 [modern edition, Königstein/Ts: Scriptor-Verlag, 1978]) p. 680: "Das gesellschaftliche Leben ist dreifach: 1) bezieht es sich auf die Famille oder auf das häusliche Verhältnis, 2) auf das Zusammenwohnen der Hausväter oder auf die bürgerliche Gesellschaft, und 3) auf das Verhältnis gegen die regierende Gewalt und ihre Gesetze, das ist: auf die Staatsgesellschaft"; quoted by M. Riedel, "Gesellschaft bürgerliche" p. 753.
28. Carl Daniel Heinrich Bensen (1761-1805), *System der reinen und angewandten Staatslehre für Juristen und Kameralisten* (Eerlangen: Palm, 1804) t. I: "Unsere Staaten und ihre Bewohner haben nur allmählich ihre jetzige Form erhalten. Von der häuslichen Gesellschaft rückte nämlich das Menschengeschlecht zur bürgerlichen und von dieser zur Staatsgesellshaft fort"; quoted by M. Riedel, "Gesellschaft bürgerliche" p. 754.
29. August Ludwig von Schlözer (1735-1809), *Stats-Anzeigen* (Göttingen: 1792) t. 17, p. 354: "Alle bisher bekannt gewordene Menschenhaufen alter, mittler und neuer Zeiten, leben in den 3 Arten häuslicher Gesellschaft. Alle ohne Ausnahme alle, leben in bürgerlicher Gesellschaft. Und bei weitem die allermeisten, wenngleich nicht alle, leben in Staats-Gesellschaft, oder unter Obrigkeit"; quoted by M. Riedel, "Gesellschaft bürgerliche" p. 754. See also, G. Gurvitch, *Traité de sociologie* (Paris: PUF, 1958) pp. 31-32, consulted by Foucault: "The followers of Leibniz—Nettelbladt in particular—in simplifying his ideas, will distinguish *regimen societatis*, or bloc of varied groups of activity, preferably economic, from *regimen civitatis* or bloc of local groups culminating in the state. This was the source of the opposition between civil and economic society (*bürgerliche Gesellschaft*) and the state. Formulated for the first time by the German historian and statistician, A.L. Schlötzer, this opposition was the object of meditation for a number of German, French, and British thinkers in the second half of the eighteenth and the first half of the nineteenth century."
30. G.W.F. Hegel, *Grundlinien der Philosophie des Rechts*, 3rd Part, 2nd section, §182-256 (Berlin: Librairie Nicolaï, 1821); French translation by R. Derathé, *Principes de la philosophie du droit*

(Paris: Vrin, 1975) pp. 215-217; English translation by T.M. Knox, *Hegel's Philosophy of Right* (Oxford: Oxford University Press, 1967) pp. 122-155. See M. Riedel, "Gesellschaft bürgerliche" pp. 779-783, as well as J. Hyppolite, "La conception hégélienne de l'État," *Cahiers internationaux de sociologie*, 1947, t. II, p. 146, and B. Quelquejeu, *La Volonté dans la philosophie de Hegel* (Paris: Le Seuil, 1973), which are referred to in Foucault's notes.

31. T. Paine, *Common Sense Addressed to the Inhabitants of America* (Philadelphia: W. & T. Bradford, 1776; Peterborough, Ontario/Plymouth: Broadview Editions, 2004) p. 47. See H.K. Girvetz, *From Wealth to Welfare* (Stanford, California: Stanford University Press, 1950) p. 44, that Foucault read in preparation for this lecture, and P. Rosanvallon, *Le Capitalisme utopique*, p. 144. Although Thomas Paine (1737-1809) was in fact of British origin, we should make it clear that *Common Sense* was published fourteen months after his settlement in America and that the book, written at the request of Benjamin Franklin, expressed the aspirations of the American people at the beginning of the War of Independence.
32. See *"Il faut défendre la société"* lecture of 10 March 1976, pp. 193-212; *"Society Must Be Defended"* pp. 215-238.

# Course Summary*

THIS YEAR'S COURSE ENDED up being devoted entirely to what should have been only its introduction. The theme was to have been "biopolitics," by which I meant the attempt, starting from the eighteenth century, to rationalize the problems posed to governmental practice by phenomena characteristic of a set of living beings forming a population: health, hygiene, birthrate, life expectancy, race ... We know the increasing importance of these problems since the nineteenth century, and the political and economic issues they have raised up to the present.

It seemed to me that these problems were inseparable from the framework of political rationality within which they appeared and took on their intensity. This means "liberalism," since it was in relation to liberalism that they assumed the form of a challenge. How can the phenomena of "population," with its specific effects and problems, be taken into account in a system concerned about respect for legal subjects and individual free enterprise? In the name of what and according to what rules can it be managed? The debate that took place in England in the middle of the nineteenth century concerning public health legislation is an example of this.

⚜

What should we understand by "liberalism"? I relied on Paul Veyne's reflections concerning historical universals and the need to test a

---

* Published in the *Annuaire du Collège de France, 78ᵉ année. Histoire des systèmes de pensée, année 1977-1978, (1978)*, pp. 445-449, and in *Dits et écrits, 1954-1988*, eds. D. Defert and F. Ewald, with the collaboration of J. Lagrange (Paris: Gallimard, 1994), vol. 3, pp. 719-723. An alternative translation of this summary by Robert Hurley appears in M. Foucault, *The Essential*

nominalist method in history. And continuing with previous methodological decisions, I tried to analyze "liberalism," not as a theory or an ideology, and even less, obviously, as a way in which "society" "represents itself," but as a practice, that is to say, a "way of doing things" directed towards objectives and regulating itself by continuous reflection. Liberalism, then, is to be analyzed as a principle and method of the rationalization of the exercise of government, a rationalization which obeys—and this is what is specific about it—the internal rule of maximum economy. While any rationalization of the exercise of government aims to maximize its effects whilst reducing its costs as much as possible (in the political as well as economic sense of costs), liberal rationalization starts from the premise that government (not "government" as an institution, obviously, but as the activity that consists in governing people's conduct within the framework of, and using the instruments of, a state) cannot be its own end. Its *raison d'être* is not found in itself, and even under the best possible conditions the maximization of government should not be its regulative principle. In this respect, liberalism breaks with the "*raison d'État*" that, from the end of the sixteenth century, sought in the existence and strengthening of the state the end which could justify an expanding governmentality and regulate its development. The *Polizeiwissenschaft* developed by the Germans in the eighteenth century—either because they lacked a large state form, or also because the limited scale of their territorial divisions gave them access to units that were much more easy to examine with the technical and conceptual instruments of the time—always followed the principle: Not enough attention is being given to things, too much escapes control, too many domains lack rules and regulation, order and administration are lacking. In short, there is too little government. *Polizeiwissenschaft* is the form taken by a governmental technology dominated by the principle of *raison d'État*, and in a way it is "quite natural" that it take into account problems of population, which, from the point of view of the state's strength, must be as large and as active as possible: health, birth rate, and hygiene find an important place here without any problem.

---

*Works of Michel Foucault, 1954-1984, Vol. 1: Ethics: subjectivity and truth*, ed. Paul Rabinow, trans. Robert Hurley and others (New York: New Press, 1997) pp. 73-79.

Liberalism, on the other hand, is imbued with the principle: "One always governs too much"—or at least, one should always suspect that one governs too much. Governmentality should not be exercised without a "critique" far more radical than a test of optimization. It should not only question itself about the best (or least costly) means for achieving its effects, but also about the possibility and even legitimacy of its project for achieving effects. The question behind the suspicion that there is always the risk of governing too much is: Why, after all, is it necessary to govern? Hence the fact that the liberal critique is not really separate from a problematic, new at the time, of "society": it is by reference to the latter that one will try to ascertain why government is necessary, in what respects it can be dispensed with, and in what areas its interventions are pointless or harmful. The rationalization of governmental practice in terms of *raison d'État* implied its optimization under optimal conditions insofar as the state's existence immediately presupposes the exercise of government. Liberal thought does not start from the existence of the state, finding in government the means for achieving that end that the state would be for itself; it starts instead from society, which exists in a complex relation of exteriority and interiority vis-à-vis the state. It is society—as both condition and final end—that makes it possible to no longer ask: How can one govern as much as possible at the least possible cost? Instead, the question becomes: Why must one govern? That is to say: What makes government necessary, and what ends must it pursue with regard to society in order to justify its own existence? It is the idea of society which permits the development of a technology of government based on the principle that it is already in itself "too much," "excessive"—or at least that it is added as a supplement whose necessity and usefulness can and must always be questioned.

Instead of turning the distinction between the state and civil society into an historical universal enabling us to examine every concrete system, we may try to see in it a form of schematization peculiar to a particular technology of government.

✣

So, we cannot say that liberalism is an always unrealized utopia—unless one takes the kernel of liberalism to be the projections it has been led to formulate by its analyses and criticisms. It is not a dream that comes up against a reality and fails to insert itself within it. It constitutes—and this is the reason for both its polymorphism and its recurrences—a tool for the criticism of reality: criticism of a previous governmentality from which one is trying to get free; of a present governmentality that one is trying to reform and rationalize by scaling it down; or of a governmentality to which one is opposed and whose abuses one wants to limit. So, in different but simultaneous forms, it will be possible to find liberalism both as a regulative schema of governmental practice and as a sometimes radical oppositional theme. This multiple use of liberalism is a highly characteristic feature of English political thought at the end of the eighteenth and in the first half of the nineteenth century. And this is especially so in the case of the developments or ambiguities of Bentham and the Benthamites.

The market as reality and political economy as theory both certainly played an important role in the liberal critique. However, as Pierre Rosanvallon's important book has confirmed, liberalism is neither their consequence nor their development.[1] Rather, the market's role in the liberal critique has been that of a "test," of a privileged site of experiment in which one can pinpoint the effects of excessive governmentality and take their measure: the aim of the analysis of the mechanisms of "dearth," or of the mid-eighteenth century grain trade more generally, was to show the point at which governing was always governing too much. Whether it is a matter of the physiocrats' Table or of Smith's "invisible hand," that is to say, of an analysis aiming to make the formation of value and the circulation of wealth visible—in the form of "evidence"—or, on the contrary, of an analysis which presupposes that the connection between the individual pursuit of profit and the growth of collective wealth is intrinsically invisible, in any case economics shows a fundamental incompatibility between the optimal development of the economic process and a maximization of governmental procedures. This, more than through the interplay of notions, was how eighteenth century French or English economists broke with mercantilism and cameralism; they freed reflection on economic practice from the hegemony of *raison d'État* and from saturation by governmental intervention. By using it as the measure of "too much government" they placed it "at the limit" of governmental action.

Undoubtedly liberalism does not derive from juridical thought any more than it does from an economic analysis. It is not born from the idea of a political society founded on a contractual bond. Rather, in the search for a liberal technology of government, it emerged that the juridical form was a far more effective instrument of regulation than the wisdom or moderation of governors. (Due to their mistrust of law and the juridical institution, the physiocrats were more inclined to seek this regulation in the recognition, by a despot with institutionally unlimited powers, of the "natural" laws of the economy which are imposed on him as evident truth.) Regulation has not been sought in the "law" because of the supposedly natural legalism of liberalism, but because the law defines forms of general intervention excluding particular, individual, and exceptional measures, and because participation of the governed in drawing up the law in a parliamentary system is the most effective system of governmental economy. The *État de droit*, the *Rechtsstaat*, the *Rule of law*, and the organization of a "truly representative" parliamentary system were therefore closely bound up with liberalism throughout the early nineteenth century, but just as political economy, employed first of all as a criterion of excessive governmentality, was not liberal either by virtue or nature, and even quickly led to anti-liberal attitudes (such as nineteenth century *Nationalökonomie* or twentieth century economic planning), so too democracy and the Rule of law have not necessarily been liberal, and nor has liberalism been necessarily democratic or bound to the forms of law.

So, rather than a more or less coherent doctrine or a politics pursuing some more or less precise aims, I would be inclined to see in liberalism a form of critical reflection on governmental practice. This criticism may come from within or outside governmental practice, and it may be based on this or that economic theory or refer to this or that legal system without any necessary and one-to-one connection. The question of liberalism, understood as a question of "too much government," has been one of the constant dimensions of that recent European phenomenon which seems to have emerged first of all in England, namely: "political life." It is even one of its constituent elements, if it is true that political life exists when the possible excess of governmental practice is limited by the fact that it is the object of public debate regarding its "good or bad," its "too much or too little."

Of course, this is not an "interpretation" of liberalism that would claim to be exhaustive, but a possible level of analysis, that of "governmental reason," of those types of rationality that are implemented in the methods by which human conduct is directed through a state administration. I have tried to carry out this kind of analysis on two contemporary examples: German liberalism of the years 1948-1962, and the American liberalism of the Chicago School. In both cases, liberalism arose in a very precise context as a critique of the irrationality peculiar to excessive government, and as a return to a technology of frugal government, as Franklin would have said.

This excess was represented in Germany by the war regime, by Nazism, but, beyond that, it was a type of directed and planned economy that was the outcome of the 1914-1918 period and the general mobilization of resources and men; it was also "state socialism." In fact, the German liberalism of the years after the Second World War was defined, programmed, and even to some extent applied by men who, from the years 1928-1930, belonged to the Freiburg School (or who were at least inspired by it) and who later expressed their point of view in the journal *Ordo*. At the point of intersection of neo-Kantian philosophy, Husserl's phenomenology, and Max Weber's sociology, close on some points to the Viennese economists, and mindful of the correlation between economic processes and legal structures apparent in history, men like Eucken, W. Röpke, Franz Böhm, and von Rüstow advanced their criticisms on three different political fronts: Soviet socialism, National Socialism, and Keynesian interventionist policies. But they addressed themselves to what they considered to be a single adversary: a type of economic government that systematically ignores the market mechanisms that alone can ensure regulation of the formation of prices. Working on the fundamental themes of the liberal technology of government, ordoliberalism tried to define what a market economy could be, organized (but not planned or directed) within an institutional and legal framework, which, on the one hand, would offer the guarantees and limitations of the law, and, on the other, would ensure that the freedom of economic processes did not produce any social distortion. The first part of the course was devoted to the study of this ordoliberalism which inspired the economic choice of the general policy of the German Federal Republic at the time of Adeneuer and Ludwig Erhard.

The second part was devoted to a few aspects of what is called American neo-liberalism. This is generally grouped under the Chicago School which also developed in reaction to the "too much government" which, since Simons, was represented in its eyes by the New Deal, wartime planning, and the big economic and social programs mostly supported by post-war Democratic administrations. As with the German ordoliberals, criticism made in the name of economic liberalism is justified by the danger represented by the inevitable sequence: economic interventionism, inflation of governmental apparatuses, over-administration, bureaucracy, rigidification of all the power mechanisms, and, at the same time, the production of new economic distortions, which would lead to new interventions. However, what aroused the attention of this American neo-liberalism is a movement which is the complete opposite of that found in the German social market economy: while the latter considers regulation of prices by the market—the only basis for a rational economy—to be so fragile in itself that it must be supported, managed, and "ordered" by an internal and vigilant policy of social interventions (involving assistance to the unemployed, health care cover, a housing policy, etcetera), American neo-liberalism seeks instead to extend the rationality of the market, the schemas of analysis it offers and the decision-making criteria it suggests, to domains which are not exclusively or not primarily economic: the family and the birth rate, for example, or delinquency and penal policy.

What should now be studied, therefore, is the way in which the specific problems of life and population have been posed within a technology of government which, although far from always having been liberal, since the end of the eighteenth century has been constantly haunted by the question of liberalism.

⚜

This year the seminar was devoted to the crisis of juridical thought in the last years of the nineteenth century. Papers were given by François Ewald (on civil law), Catherine Mevel (on public and administrative law), Éliane Allo (on the right to life in legislation concerning children), Nathalie Coppinger and Pasquale Pasquino (on penal law), Alessandro Fontana (on security measures), François Delaporte and Anne-Marie Moulin (on police and health policy).

---

1. P. Rosanvallon, *Le Capitalisme utopique. Critique de l'idéologie économique* (Paris: Le Seuil, 1979).

# Course Context

Michel Senellart*

FROM THE FIRST WEEK, these lectures appear as the direct continuation of the previous year's lectures. Stating his intention to continue what he had started to say the previous year, Foucault first of all clarifies the choice of method that will govern his analysis[1] and then summarizes the final lectures devoted to the government of *raison d'État* and criticism of this in terms of the problem of grain. In the eighteenth century, the principle of the external limitation of *raison d'État* by right is replaced by a principle of internal limitation in the form of the economy.[2] Political economy, in fact, contains within itself the requirement of a self-limitation of governmental reason founded on knowledge of the natural course of things. It therefore marks the irruption of a new rationality in the art of government: governing less, out of concern for maximum effectiveness, in accordance with the naturalness of the phenomena one is dealing with. Foucault calls this government, which is linked to the question of truth in its permanent effort of self-limitation, "liberalism." The object of the lectures is to show how this liberalism constitutes the condition of intelligibility of biopolitics:

> With the emergence of political economy, with the introduction of the restrictive principle into governmental practice itself, an

* Michel Senellart is professor of political philosophy at the Lyon École normale supérieure des lettres et sciences humaines. He is the author of *Machiavélisme et Raison d'État* (Paris: PUF, 1989) and *Les Arts de gouverner* (Paris: Le Seuil, 1995). He is also the translator of M. Stolleis, *Histoire du droit public en Allemagne, 1600-1800. Théorie du droit public et science de la police* (Paris: PUF, 1998).

important substitution, or doubling rather, is carried out, since the subjects of right on which political sovereignty is exercised appear as a *population* that a government must manage.

This is the point of departure for the organizational line of a "biopolitics." But who does not see that this is only part of something much larger, which [is] this new governmental reason?

Studying liberalism as the general framework of biopolitics.[3]

The following plan is announced: to study liberalism first of all in its original formulation and its contemporary, German and American, versions, and then come to the problem of the politics of life.[4] In actual fact, only the first part of this program is realized, Foucault being led to develop his analysis of German neo-liberalism at greater length than he envisaged.[5] This interest in the social market economy is due not only to the paradigmatic character of the German experience. It is also explained by reasons of "critical morality," faced with "that kind of laxity" that, in his eyes, constitutes an "inflationist critique of the state" that is quick to denounce fascism in the functioning of Western democratic states.[6] The "German question" is thus placed at the heart of the methodological, historical, and political questions that form the framework of the course.

The second and third lectures (17 and 24 January) are devoted to the specific features of the liberal art of government as outlined in the eighteenth century. In the first place, in these lectures Foucault explains the link between truth and liberal governmentality through an analysis of the market as a site of veridiction, and he specifies the modalities of internal limitation that derive from this. Thus he reveals two ways of limiting public power corresponding to two heterogeneous conceptions of liberty: the revolutionary, axiological way, which founds sovereign power on the rights of man, and the radical, utilitarian way, which starts from governmental practice in order to define the limit of governmental competence and the sphere of individual autonomy in terms of utility. These two ways are distinct, but they are not mutually exclusive; the history of European liberalism since the nineteenth century should be studied in the light of their strategic interaction. It is also this interaction that clarifies, or puts in perspective, the way in which, from 1977, Foucault problematizes the "rights of the governed," in comparison with the more vague and abstract invocation of "human rights."[7]

After having examined the question of Europe and of its relations with the rest of the world according to the new governmental reason, in the third lecture Foucault returns to his choice of calling "liberalism" what in the eighteenth century appears rather as a naturalism. The word liberalism is justified by the role liberty plays in the liberal art of government: a liberty no doubt guaranteed, but also produced by this art of government, which, in order to achieve its ends, needs continually to create, maintain, and frame it. Liberalism can thus be defined as the calculation of risk—the free play of individual interests—compatible with the interest of each and all. That is why the incitement to "live dangerously" entails the establishment of multiple mechanisms of security. Liberty and security: it is the procedures of control and forms of state intervention required by this double exigency that constitute the paradox of liberalism and are at the origin of the "crises of governmentality"[8] that it has experienced for two centuries.

The question now then is whether that crisis of governmentality characterizes the present world and to what revisions of the liberal art of government it has given rise. Starting from the fourth lecture (31 January 1979), the study of the two great neo-liberal schools, German ordoliberalism[9] and American anarcho-liberalism,[10] correspond to this diagnostic task and is Foucault's sole incursion into the field of contemporary history throughout his teaching at the Collège de France. These two schools do not just participate in an identical project of the radical reform of liberalism. They also represent two distinct forms of the "critique of the irrationality peculiar to excessive government,"[11] one stressing the logic of pure competition on the economic terrain, while framing the market through a set of state interventions (theory of the "policy of society"), and the other seeking to extend the rationality of the market to domains hitherto considered to be non-economic (theory of "human capital").

The final two lectures deal with the birth in eighteenth century thought of the idea of *homo œconomicus* as a subject of interest distinct from the subject of right, and of the notion of "civil society" as correlative of the liberal technology of government. Whereas in its most classical version liberal thought opposed society to the state, as nature to artifice or spontaneity to constraint, Foucault highlights the paradox that constitutes their relation. Society, in fact, represents the principle in the name of which liberal government tends to limit itself. It obliges it to ask itself constantly whether it is not governing too much and, in this respect, plays a critical role with regard to all excessive government. But it also forms the target of a permanent governmental intervention, not in order to restrict formal liberties on the level of practical reality, but in order to produce, multiply, and guarantee those liberties that the liberal system needs.[12] Society thus represents at once "the set of conditions of least liberal government" and the "surface of transfer of governmental activity."[13]

---

1. In the manuscript of the course Foucault clarifies the political effects of his methodological choices. See *Sécurité, Territoire, Population*, lecture of 8 February 1978, pp. 123-124 fn; *Security, Territory, Population*, pp. 119-120 fn.
2. In the manuscript on "government," which served as the introduction to the 1979 seminar, Foucault describes this transition as "the great shift from juridical veridiction to epistemic veridiction."
3. Manuscript for the first lecture. See above, lecture of 10 January 1979, p. 22 fn.
4. See above, lecture of 10 January, p. 21 *sq*. The plan outlined here is made more specific (and, thereby, retrospectively clarified) later on. See the lecture of 31 January 1979, p. 80 *sq*.
5. See, ibid. beginning of the lecture of 7 March 1979, p. 185: "( ... ) I really did intend to talk about biopolitics, and then, things being what they are, I have ended up talking at length, and maybe for too long, about neo-liberalism, and neo-liberalism in its German form." See also above, "Course summary," p. 317: "This year's course ended up being devoted entirely to what should have been only its introduction."
6. Ibid. lecture of 7 March 1979, pp. 188-190.
7. Obviously, this is not a matter of reducing the problematic of the "rights of the governed," inseparable from the phenomenon of dissidence (see "Va-t-on extrader Klaus Croissant?" p. 364), to that of the independence of the governed according to the utilitarian calculus, but of stressing a proximity, which is no doubt not foreign to Foucault's interest in liberalism at this time.
8. See above, lecture of 24 January 1979, pp. 68-69.
9. The French bibliography on the subject being extremely limited, apart from the thesis of F. Bilger, *La Pensée économique libérale de l'Allemagne contemporaine* (Paris: Librairie générale de Droit, 1964) that Foucault made use of, we note the recent appearance of the colloquium, P. Commun, ed., *L'Ordolibéralism allemand. Aux sources de l'économie sociale de marché* (Université de Cergy-Pontoise, CIRAC/CICC, 2003).
10. See above, "Course summary," pp. 322-324.
11. Ibid. p. 321.
12. See the final lecture of *Security, Territory, Population* (5 April 1978) pp. 352-354 (fr pp. 360-362) to which Foucault explicitly refers to above, p. 296, when he speaks of "an omnipresent government" which, while respecting "the specificity of the economy" must "manage society ( ... ) manage the social."
13. 1981 manuscript on "Liberalism as art of government" in which Foucault, referring to the seminar of the previous year, recapitulates his analysis of liberalism. This analysis notably connects up with the analysis put forward by P. Rosanvallon, *Le Capitalisme utopique. Critique de l'idéologie économique* (Paris: Le Seuil, "Sociologie politique," 1979) pp. 68-69 (republished with the title *Le Libéralisme économique. Histoire de l'idée de marché* [Paris: Le Seuil, "Points Essais," 1989]) with which it sometimes seems to enter into dialogue (see Foucault's reference to this book above, "Course summary," p. 320).

# Index of Names

*Compiled by Sue Carlton*

*Note*: Page numbers followed by n refer to notes

# Index of Concepts and Notions

*Compiled by Sue Carlton*

*Note:* Page numbers followed by n refer to notes